WINES

WINES

THEIR SENSORY EVALUATION

Revised and Enlarged

Maynard A. Amerine

Edward B. Roessler

UNIVERSITY OF CALIFORNIA, DAVIS

Carlos Mackie j

W. H. Freeman and Company

New York   San Francisco

Cartoon on page 18: Courtesy of William Hamilton

Cartoon on page 172: Drawing by Levin; © 1980 *The New Yorker* Magazine, Inc.

Library of Congress Cataloging in Publication Data

Amerine, M. A. (Maynard Andrew), 1911–
    Wines, their sensory evaluation.

    Bibliography: p.
    Includes index.
    1. Wine tasting.   I. Roessler, Edward Biffer,
1902–   . II. Title.
TP548.5.A5A4   1983   641.2′22   83-1539
ISBN 0-7167-1479-5

Printed in the United States of America

1 2 3 4 5 6 7 8 9 MP 1 0 8 9 8 7 6 5 4 3

Contents

Preface

This book is primarily about the sensory evaluation of wines, more than about the sensory enjoyment of wines. In the real world, they are interrelated and we drink wine to enjoy it. Evaluation, however, has its own pleasures. We hope that those who are interested in enjoyment will profit by the information on sensory evaluation. No one can quantify enjoyment. That is subjective and personal. But knowing the difference between low and high volatile acidity may help us distinguish vinegar from wine.

The phrase "sensory evaluation of wines" is more cumbersome than "wine tasting" but it is more accurate. Taste is only one facet of the evaluation of wine quality and not even the most important one. Sensory evaluation is also a better term because it emphasizes that our senses are the means by which we react to external stimuli. We hasten to admit that our sensory responses, and especially our perceptions of sensory quality, are usually modified by a variety of physiological and psychological factors and by subtle, and not so subtle, cultural influences. The amateur wine enthusiast and the professional wine judge are susceptible to a greater or lesser degree to such effects. The professional learns to avoid them as best he can and to refine his sensory skills so as not to be "fooled" by extraneous external influences. The amateur can do this too; all it takes is a sensible approach and practice.

We agree with Don (1977) that "it is essential to approach the subject of wine with an open mind and to develop one's own opinions, for the opinions of others are of limited value before they have been put to the test of one's own palate. Do not be discouraged by people who make dogmatic pronouncements on wine, because the chances are that they know very little themselves or they would not be so overbearing. The man who really knows his wine will have to revise his ideas so often in the light of ever widening knowledge, that he will probably have become quite modest."

Lastly, beware of the Wine Snob, defined by Raymond Postgate, as a person "who uses a knowledge of wine, often imperfect, to impress others with a sense of his superiority," and make sure you don't become one yourself. As Alexander Pope said, "A little learning is a dangerous thing."

In this book we describe what we believe is a sound approach to wine evaluation. We are sure that it will be useful to wine professionals and students. We are equally hopeful that it will be useful to serious amateurs—those who drink wine regularly and wish to make more meaningful judgments about wine quality, a most elusive quality to define. In fact, wine quality is easier to recognize than to define. Professional judges, of course, must make such decisions routinely, and the commercial consequences of their decisions are often far reaching.

The text is divided into two parts. Part I (Chapters 2 through 6) deals with wines and their sensory examination and Part II (Chapters 7 through 13) with the statistical procedures used to evaluate the data obtained. These procedures are not merely useful in deriving meaningful judgments from the results of panel evaluations (whether professional or amateur)—they are essential. As you read the book, you will see why. You do not *need* to read Part II to profit from this book, but you will profit much more if you do, especially if you are (or want to be) in the wine industry in a professional capacity. Some of the material may look difficult to those whose exposure to mathematics ended with their high school days, but it really isn't. To understand it, all you need is a little high school algebra and some common sense—mainly the latter. Furthermore, calculators have made the computations easier and much faster.

Wine is a very complex liquid that is much more than just a dilute alcoholic solution. What makes wine so interesting is its infinite variety: its subtle nuances of color, odor, tastes, flavor, and texture—all of which are determined by the chemical composition of the wine. In the proper balance, these sensory characteristics combine to stimulate the one thing that provides the most enduring pleasure and appreciation—the aesthetics of the wine. It is, therefore, natural to try to relate chemical composition to aesthetic quality. Such an approach need not diminish one's appreciation of wine quality. On the contrary, we believe that it will enhance appreciation, even though the ultimate aesthetic quality can never be "explained."

We hope, therefore, that this book will lead to a better understanding of the sensory and aesthetic qualities of wine, by the consumer as well as by the student and the professional. We also trust that, by more careful sensory evaluation of their wines, winemakers will make better wines. We make no apology for appealing to such varied audiences. We hope that each will find the sections most useful to themselves.

We also urge our readers (amateur or professional) to indulge themselves in sensory laboratory work with wines. One cannot really learn to swim without getting into the water. Just so with wine appreciation. It helps if you have a sympathetic and skilled teacher to help you. No book can do this for you as well as someone who knows participating with you. Becoming a good judge of wines is different from becoming a good skier or a competent judge in dog shows, but one progresses faster with a good teacher. Experience is the secret—*years* of it.

We are aware of our unfinished and incomplete treatment of the sensory evaluation of wine. Considering time, this is probably the last we shall have to say on the subject. We rejoice, however, for our younger colleagues. They will have more complete and better things to say as research reveals new aspects of the subject.

We conclude with a mention of an elegant but little used word that describes what this book is about: *degustation* (from the verb *degust*—to taste or savor appreciatively, as a connoisseur). Although its Latin derivation suggests tasting alone, it is commonly used in French, Italian, and Russian wine terminology to include all aspects of sensory evaluation. We recommend its increasing use in English in this broad sense—the sense that Robert Louis Stevenson surely had in mind when he wrote, "Wine . . . a deity to be invoked by two or three, all fervent, hushing their talk, degusting tenderly."

St. Helena and Davis   Maynard A. Amerine
May, 1982   Edward B. Roessler

Acknowledgments

During the past forty-five years we have discussed the problems of sensory evaluation with a great many people. We thank them all. Professor Rose Marie Pangborn, with whom we collaborated on a more general book on sensory evaluation, has been particularly helpful. Our colleagues, Professors George A. Baker, Harold W. Berg, James Gallander, the late James F. Guymon, Ann C. Noble, Cornelius S. Ough, Vernon L. Singleton, and A. Dinsmoor Webb, have been constructively critical in this field over a long period. Professors Gallander and Noble have read the text and made many helpful criticisms. We thank Mr. Robert Gorman of San Francisco for his perceptive comments on the aesthetics of wine appreciation.

Concerning this edition we thank not only the foregoing advisors, but also Dr. Bryce Rankine of Roseworthy, South Australia and Mr. Philip Wagner of Baltimore. Their criticisms and suggested changes have been most appreciated. The errors that remain are ours, not theirs.

We are indebted to Mr. Alfred A. Blaker for making the photographs of the wine glasses (Plates 7–10) and the "tears" of wine (Plates 13 and 14).

ACKNOWLEDGMENTS

We are grateful to the literary executor of the late Sir Ronald A. Fisher, F.R.S., to Dr. Frank Yates, F.R.S., and to Longman Group Ltd., London, for permission to reprint portions of Tables III, IV, V, and VII from *Statistical Tables for Biological, Agricultural, and Medical Research*, 6th ed., 1974. We are also grateful to Professors D. B. Duncan and A. Kramer, J. W. Tukey and D. L. Wallace, and to Dr. H. L. Harter for permission to use parts of various tables that they compiled.

For many illustrations we are indebted to the original publisher. The source of each is given with the illustration.

M.A.A.

E.B.R.

A Note to Our Readers

As we have noted in our preface, this book is intended for various audiences, from rank amateurs to experienced enophiles and professionals who earn their living making decisions based on sensory evaluation. We are aware that the professional may also be an enophile and the amateur may later aspire to become one. We suggest here chapters and pages that may be of interest to these three basic groups.

For the beginning amateur, we suggest the Preface; Chapter 1, pages 3–24; Chapter 2, pages 25–56; Chapter 3, pages 57–66; Chapter 5, pages 87–138; Chapter 13, pages 289–304; and the Glossary.

For the experienced enophile we suggest the above plus Chapter 6, pages 139–170; Chapter 7, pages 173–188; Chapter 9, pages 211–224; and Chapter 12, pages 275–288.

Finally, for the professional who must be sure that his decisions are correct, we respectfully suggest that he may need parts of all the chapters.

I
WINES
AND THEIR
SENSORY EXAMINATION

This wine is full of gases
which are to me offensive.
It pleases all you asses
because it is expensive.

A. P. HERBERT

Pour être utile, le dégustateur doit dépasser son goût personnel et être capable
de motiver son choix.

E. PEYNAUD

CHAPTER 1

Wine Quality

 Quality in wines is much easier to recognize than to define. This is, of course, of little help to the amateur. Most amateurs readily recognize that there are important qualitative and quantitative differences among wines. What the amateur cannot know intuitively, but can learn by assiduous practice, is how to recognize the relative value of each of the factors that contribute to wine quality. It is from such knowledge, gained only by experience, that the aesthetics and ultimate pleasure of wine are derived. As Boileau wrote in the nineteenth century, "Drinking well makes one sage, but he who knows not what to drink knows nothing."

There are two basic approaches to the sensory evaluation of wines: the subjective, emotional, intuitive, or romantic, and the objective, reasoned, analytic, or classic. There is nothing "wrong" with either point of view, but they do not necessarily lead to the same conclusions. The romantic approach is more superficial, with years, labels, regions, producers, and other extraneous factors unduly influencing aesthetic judgment. Bad wines are made in "bad" years, good in "good" years. By contrast, the classic approach pays little attention to such external matters and seeks to discover the underlying reasons for a wine's good or bad qualities—that is, for the aesthetic pleasure that its consumption brings. It is our thesis that the classic approach leads to more consistent, defensible results. Unfortunately the popular wine literature is filled mainly with the special pleadings of the romantic approach. The wine is good because it is from a certain vineyard. But no vineyard always produces fine wines. In any event, the romanticists often do not understand what the classicists are talking about. We hope that this book will contribute to a better understanding of the classicists' motivations, methods, and terminology.

For a discussion of the meaning of quality, see Pirsig (1974). We do not agree with Pirsig that the analytic approach to quality destroys appreciation. If anything, it should enhance appreciation. For us and for many whom we know, it certainly does.

Gale (1975) argues that wine quality judgments are based entirely on "factual" or observable—that is, perceptual—data.* He admits, however, that these data acquire part of their meaning and all of their organization from some theory or theories that link simple perceptual judgments (beginning with sensory observations) to ever more theoretical judgments (culminating in conclusions about quality). Indeed, he says, the observations themselves must imply the theory, and it is for this reason that judgments based on such observations must be empirically either true or false. He uses the Davis wine score card (page 214) to show how a theoretical model (the score card) can be used to measure quality. Nevertheless, as we will see below, aesthetic judgments cannot be easily formalized.

---

*Harries (1973) has emphasized that food scientists now accept sensory data as objective, though perhaps not quite equivalent to instrumental data.

Aesthetics

Aesthetics has to do with the subjective and objective appraisal of works of art: music, art, architecture, literature—and wine. The properties that we associate with aesthetic appreciation are symmetry, balance, harmony, complexity, and so on. We believe that the full appreciation of an aesthetic object requires some degree of formal training, or at least conscious study. There is, of course, no perfect predictive equation for evaluating the relative importance of all the factors that contribute to the aesthetic quality of a work of art. Nor *can* there be any such perfect equation, certainly not for all types of wine. (This is the fundamental error of *all* score cards for wine.) The very inexplicability of the parameters of aesthetic quality is surely an integral part of the attraction of a great work of art. Nevertheless, one can obtain predictive equations, however imperfect, that may be not only useful but commercially valuable for specific types of wine.

We agree with Leavis (1948) that "the term 'aesthetic,' with its trail of confusion . . . is a term the literary critic would do well to abjure." Perhaps the wine critic also should use the term warily, though it does open up the world of appreciation (even if this is still a somewhat confused world).

Wine offers a splendid field for the study of aesthetic quality. First, it has an ancient, generally recognized, and continuing tradition of quality evaluation. Second, wine has an immense range of types and of quality variations within each type. Third, new types of wines are continually being created, requiring that existing standards of aesthetic quality be constantly refined and that new ones be established when necessary.

The wide variety of old and new production methods available to the winemaker may—and often does—modify the quality of the wine, making it essential that consumers continuously reevaluate their aesthetic standards for wine. Some wine judges believe that excessive use of modern filters or fining (clarifying) agents diminishes the quality of wine in subtle (and sometimes not so subtle) ways. Unfortunately the greater the intrinsic quality of the wine, the greater the effect is likely to be. On the other hand, proper use of filters and fining agents can prevent clouding and microbial spoilage and thus enhance quality. Also, we are skeptical that avoiding clarification always results in higher quality, even when clouding or spoilage does not occur. At least we have not found any convincing evidence in the literature or in our own experience that completely "natural" wines are better than wines that have been properly processed. Peynaud (1980) especially notes that sensory evaluation should control technology and legal standards.

Everyone acknowledges that different wines give varying degrees of transitory or lasting pleasure to different individuals. The greater our understanding of the factors that affect our reactions to wines, the greater our confidence to judge them and the keener our capacity to enjoy them. Naturally there will always be wide differences in individual preferences, and, if these preferences are based on experience and considered judgment, we must accept them at face value.

Our first reaction to an aesthetic object, such as wine, is apt to be purely subjective: we like it or dislike it. For a more lasting judgment however, we apply certain objective criteria, consciously or unconsciously. These criteria may enhance our enjoyment of the wine, confirm our aversion to it, or otherwise change our initial reaction. As we gain experience with a certain type of wine, we may reverse our original judgment. Sometimes we come to enjoy a wine we originally found undesirable. Or, more likely, we may find with experience that the wine we once praised no longer pleases us. This is a part of the learning process that everyone undergoes in arriving at personal standards for evaluating the quality of any aesthetic object.

Our enjoyment of wine is thus essentially a learned response and is a complex mixture of intellectual and sensory pleasures. In addition, it has overtones of sensual pleasure and is obviously related to and supported by social customs. Our appreciation of wine is to a major extent subject to sensory skills and aesthetic principles that depend on experience. Individual preferences are, of course, important; to the individual they are all-important. All we can do is postulate that they have some rational basis and hope that some general aesthetic principles may eventually emerge. To secure universal agreement on aesthetic principles for even one type of wine appears almost impossible.

Jounela-Eriksson (1981) compared the ability of three panels to distinguish the "quality" of fine red wines. The panels were "expert" professionals, laboratory judges, and a control group. The wines were a "good year *château*" Bordeaux claret, a "regional" Bordeaux red, a Spanish red, a Hungarian red, and a *vin ordinaire*. The experts found the more significant differences between the aroma, taste, and ranking of the wines. The ability of the experts was attributed to their knowledge of the quality and value of the different wines. The other panels preferred freshness and mellowness. Color was not a significant factor. See also pages 25–30.

Pitfalls   Appreciation of the quality of a wine does *not* depend on its reputation, tradition, or price. This is all the more important to remember in a world in which the Madison Avenue huckster has made a fine art of touting just about anything as a superlative "quality" product. Unwary consumers may easily be fooled as to the actual quality of a wine if they rely on Old or New World romance, price, region, producer, vintage, and so on. Each of these, to be sure, may have some relation to what is generally accepted as quality. It is the sensory quality of the wine in the glass that is important, however, not the words on the bottle label, or the price, or the excellence and extent of the advertising.

The intelligent wine connoisseur must therefore have the sensory skill and aesthetic appreciation to be able to ignore with confidence both the ad agencies and the wine snobs. The latter would often have us believe that the expensive and the imported are automatically better, and that wines from certain vineyards, producers, or vintages are always, ipso facto, superior. The expensive may be poor because it is too old; the imported can be inferior, especially when it is shipped by a careless merchant; and *every* vineyard, producer, and vintage has its failures. Even in the most disastrous year, some lucky producer may obtain a good or even great wine. We know of at least one 1967 California Cabernet Sauvignon of superlative quality, although generally the wines of this variety and year in this state were not memorable. Similar examples could be cited for many vintages of Bordeaux, Burgundy, Rhine, Moselle, and other wines.

Pleasure

What is the difference between an ordinary wine and a great wine? The first principle is pleasure. But suppose the wine that greatly pleases us displeases our neighbor? Such marked variations in appreciation do occur, but usually among judges of very different degrees of vinous experience. Differences in experience or prejudices arising from cultural, familial, or religious customs may explain many of these individual preferences or aversions. Some, of course, may be inherent in our own philosophical attitudes. Obviously each one of us is the final authority on what is poor, fair, good, or superlative for ourselves. It is also true, however, that the well-trained, experienced wine judges of France, Australia, Germany, South Africa, and the United States agree rather consistently in their overall appraisals of the quality of the standard types of table wines. We base this conclusion on the results of close observation of a number of judgings, both national and international, and on our discussions with qualified, experienced enologists who have participated in such judgings.

Disagreement almost always occurs when the panel includes a less experienced judge or judges who are less familiar with the type of wine in question. Scores or rankings of the judges also differ significantly when (1) too many wines are judged at a single session;

(2) the wines are either very similar or very different in quality; or (3) some or all of the wines are not typical of the type, variety, year, or region. The maximum number of wines that can be ranked accurately at one session may be as few as 5 and is certainly no more than 10 to 15 (pages 152–155).

Finding an appreciative audience for a new wine type or for wines from a new producer or region is often difficult. The need in the wine industry is always for more consumers who will sympathetically *try* the new product and see whether it gives them pleasure. Only wine snobs arbitrarily condemn new wine types, wines from new producers or regions, or wines made by new processes. There is no substitute for a personal sensory evaluation of the product in reaching a fair conclusion. Wines are made to be drunk with pleasure, but "drinking without thinking is like hearing without listening" (Robinson 1979).

Can we agree that an adequate judgment of an aesthetic object, such as a truly fine wine, can be made only when it represents the accumulated experience of many prior judgments? Our initial judgment of a fine wine is apt to be superficial and untrustworthy unless we have had considerable experience with wines of similar character and quality. If the wine is of very limited aesthetic appeal, on the other hand, no complicated evaluation is needed or even possible.

We feel justified in rejecting a reliance on tradition or on someone else's questionable authority to form our aesthetic judgments of the quality of wines. Nevertheless, we can learn from those with more experience. Of course, wine critics, however experienced, at best have blind spots and, at worst, conflicts of interest. Since aesthetic judgments are partially subjective, we must ultimately make our own decisions. We either find pleasure in a given wine or we do not.

Variation in judgment, even among experts, is why we reject single-judge evaluations and some journalistic evaluations. An adequate panel should have five or more qualified judges (see page 143). We confess, however, to a certain admiration for artists who insist on the aesthetic value of their work even when the world does not. Just consider the history of painting in the past 100 years. Clearly, today's philistine may be tomorrow's most appreciated "artist," and sometimes vice versa. Or consider wines. By and large, nineteenth-century standards for wine appreciation did not condemn high volatile acidity (acescence), cloudiness, darkening of the color of white wines, brownish-red colors in red wines, or relatively low ethanol content (Sudraud 1977). Need we add that none of these is tolerated, much less appreciated, by wine connoisseurs today? Modern enology has created the wines we now appreciate (Peynaud 1980).

But we emphasize again that, in order to arrive at meaningful judgments, a panel must have wide experience with the types of wine under study. Otherwise there is just a hodgepodge of personal preferences, not a vote on quality (see also page 145). Wu et al. (1977) make the useful point that "sampling of wines analytically possibly produce[s] a different result than might have been attained had the wines been drunk in their normal setting. The characteristics that make them complement other foods perhaps do not serve them well when they are sampled alone and under the stress of analytical though[t] instead of emotional appeal."

Complexity

Like fine art, fine wines are made by impeccable workmanship plus a clear concept of the aesthetic standards by which they will be judged. All truly fine wines produce feelings other than mere pleasure. There is a sense of awe in appreciating a fine wine—a feeling that here is a complex and superior or ideal juxtaposition of appearance, color, odor, taste, and texture. We say the wine is balanced, but in a truly great wine there is more than just balance. The components must complement one another synergistically and excite our aesthetic appreciation. A great wine should have so many facets of quality that as we sample it we are continually finding new ones. It is this complexity that enables us to savor such a wine without losing our interest in it. For a great wine, we cannot find enough words to describe the complexity of sensory qualities. For a simple, ordinary wine, the few words that come to mind seem to suffice.

Having spoken earlier of pleasure, we should add that all truly fine wines are *memorably* pleasurable. True, we also remember the characteristics of a bad wine—but not with pleasure. Wines falling between these extremes easily drop out of mind. The wine that does not excite us enough to be remembered pleasurably cannot be a great wine. This does not mean that the wine in the middle range may not be saleable and drinkable. Many less-than-great products of the industry sell very well indeed. Somewhere between "sales volume measures quality" and "price measures quality" there must be a middle ground. Obviously neither sales nor price alone is an appropriate measure of quality.

Peterson (1981) has recommended that one should divide wine score by price to get a "relative value." Thus a wine scoring 12 and selling at $3 would have a "relative value" of 4, whereas one scoring 18 and selling at $10 would have a "relative value" of 1.8. Perhaps so, but is that relative *value*? It is cost per drink, a quite different thing. If one wants a very fine wine, one will have to pay the $10. The below-commercial or just acceptable wine is not for the connoisseur at prices of $3 or $2 or even if free!

To summarize, fine wines have a complexity of sensory qualities that defy analysis. When pleasure and complexity combine to create a memorable experience for the enophile, we have a great wine.

Types of Consumers

Nelson (1980) distinguishes between novices, amateurs, and experts. At the "novice" level, the subject is primarily interested in pleasure. Novices are often "gulpers and swallowers" (Robinson 1979). There is no objection to being a novice, though; we all were once! Don't worry if you don't progress further.

Peynaud (1980) quotes a classification that he attributes to Pierre Coste: gulpers, label drinkers, those with appreciation of well-structured simple white and red wines (usually relatively young), and connoisseurs of the complexities of great wines as works of art. At the third or "amateur" level, reasoned enjoyment is important, and it is to these "amateurs" who wish to quantify and enhance their enjoyment that much of our text is directed. At the fourth or expert level, one tries to evaluate quality, whatever that may mean to experienced palates. The difference between pleasure and enjoyment is not clear.

Mesnier (1981) identifies four kinds of degustation: by the consumer (the most subjective); for choosing (as by a merchant purchasing wine for his taste and that of his clients); in a formal judging (subjectivity is believed tempered by the professionalism of the panel); and for research (classifying, defining types, operation control, and so on, which should be done only by experts).

In terms of the sensory evaluation of wines, there are obviously many different types of consumers. The great majority of consumers evaluate wine in terms of their past experience, however slight, and their personal likes and dislikes. For our purposes, we have categorized consumers into three groups: ordinary consumers, appreciative drinkers, and professional wine judges.

Ordinary consumers are not interested in the wine as an aesthetic object. It is just another part of the meal, and ordinary consumers do not think about its quality any more than they "think" about the quality of the salad or beans. They consume the wine mainly because it is the culturally acceptable table beverage, and they enjoy it for perhaps the same reason, in addition to its pleasant sensory (and physiological) effects. But they do not attempt to analyze the reasons why they find it pleasant.

Even at this level, however, some aesthetic judgments are being made. Almost all consumers will reject (or at least resist) foods or wines they find unpleasant, no matter how common that class of food or wine is in their diet. But it is not primarily the aesthetic quality of the wine that is important to such consumers, who usually choose low-priced wines with nondistinctive flavors. The sales generated by such consumers are important to the wine industry, but we do not yet know how important are the various sensory factors that affect their wine purchases (color, sugar content, and so on). It is true, of course, that many people (perhaps most) can afford or choose to buy only the relatively low priced wines. Much potential aesthetic appreciation of wines is undoubtedly stifled by economic limitations.

The production of *distinctively flavored, high-quality wines* requires expensive grapes (often specific varieties grown in special regions and fermented by special techniques) and usually requires (in red wines) longer aging than for ordinary wines. These factors partially account for their higher price. In general, inexpensive wines have innocuous sensory characteristics, and more expensive wines have a greater complexity of odors and flavors. The most difficult problem for enologists is to find the right balance of complexity and distinctiveness without grotesqueness.

Fortunately not all consumers drink wine without regard to quality—otherwise all wines might as well be the same. We do not know when a consumer changes from the mere drinking of wines to a degree of personal evaluation of the quality of each wine consumed, but cultural patterns and economic status are doubtless factors. In wine-drinking countries, the typical wine consumer may normally be only a wine drinker. But on special occasions (feast days and so on as determined by social custom) or with special friends, the wine drinker may become an appreciative and critical consumer.

Our second group of consumers falls into the category of appreciative drinkers. For such consumers, wine is more than just a table beverage, and wine drinking has aspects of an aesthetic experience. Later (page 14) we will try to analyze this group's reactions to wine and the specific standards they develop. We agree with Peynaud (1980): "Avec du travail, presque tout le monde peut devenir un bon dégustateur. *Il suffit de quelques années de pratique assidue*" (italics added). [With some work nearly everyone is able to become a good dégustateur. *All that is needed is some years of assiduous practice.*]

The third group of consumers includes the professional wine judges. Their task is to evaluate the sensory quality of wines *according to some agreed-on standards*. Generally their personal preferences in wines do not come into play or are consciously ignored. It is vital for professional judges to have common, fixed standards for each type of wine. To achieve such standards, a great deal of experience with the types of wines they are called upon to judge is absolutely essential. Some professional judges may not like sweet table wines but can still be good, dispassionate judges of their quality if they have had sufficient experience with them: *years* of experience!

Several different situations may arise in a professional wine evaluation. At competitions, the standard used by the judges is often relative: the best wine of a given type—for example, the best Pinot noir. Or the judges may be required to score the wines on some absolute scale, such as 1 to 20, in which a score of 20 would be given to a "perfect" Pinot noir and a score of 1 to a hopelessly spoiled wine. Either way it is of crucial importance that all the judges have a clear, fixed, and preestablished concept of a fine-quality and a poor-quality Pinot noir wine. This is why judges in quality wine competitions *must* have wide and critical experience with the types they are asked to judge. Such experience is also essential when the judges are required simply to rank the wines in order of merit, regardless of how good the wine ranked first may be. In this case the "meaning" of each rank is difficult to assess.

Another reason that experience is vital is that inexperienced judges, lacking a standard or a frame of reference, tend to drift in their sensory evaluations as a series of wines of the same type is presented. Apparently inexperienced judges "learn" as they proceed through the series. If all the samples are poor, they may rate the best of the lot too high. Conversely, if all the samples are very good, they are likely to rate some of them too low. Even experienced judges, when asked their opinion of a single wine without any other wines for comparison, may find it difficult to rate it correctly. They are almost certain, however, to be more nearly correct in their judgments than are inexperienced judges. Statistical measures of the reliability of the judges and of their results are therefore necessary (see pages 174 and 245). These measures will also reveal drifts in scoring.

Experienced, professional judges are essential in winery operations. Although chemical analyses are clearly of importance to the enologist, there are times when a detailed and critical sensory analysis is indispensable—for example, in blending, in determining how much fining agent to use, in deciding whether further barrel or cask aging is necessary, and so on. Statistical measures of the significance of the differences between treatments are essential (see page 195).

One difference between experienced and inexperienced judges is revealed when descriptive comments are required (page 34). Inexperienced judges lack the full range of vocabulary to describe their impressions, and they do not use whatever vocabulary they do have consistently and meaningfully. Thus they may say the taste is "tart" one time and "green" another, or that it is "sour" when they mean "bitter." Communication between judges is difficult or impossible in such cases.

Probably what is most needed now in California, and in all the areas that are developing new types of wine or are trying to improve their present types, are judges specializing in a specific subregion or a certain variety. Bordeaux has experts on St. Emilion wines who would never attempt to evaluate St. Julien wines, much less a wine of Burgundy. Yet we have "experts" in California who almost daily publish lists of wines with ex cathedra statements about their quality (or lack thereof). This may have been justified when California had only a few wineries producing regional and/or varietal wines. Who can have the experience to become familiar with the California Cabernet Sauvignons produced by 150 wineries each year? One of a judge's most difficult problems is to comprehend not only the different types of wines but also the different criteria of quality appropriate to each. The same problem exists concerning the ex cathedra statements by some "experts" on the value, or lack of it, of California geographical appellations for different varieties of grapes. Again, who can control all the variables of climate and production and be familiar with all the varieties from all of the microclimates and producers of the state?

Some Shibboleths That Need to Be Questioned

We list here some popular axioms about wine. Their real meanings have often been perverted by wine snobs who glibly use them without understanding. In fact, the wine industry suffers enormously from wine snobs who praise the wrong wines, usually for reasons that have little to do with quality. For a short, fictional play on what quality is, and is not, see Amerine (1969).

1. Grape vines that "struggle" produce better wines.

What is the vine "struggling" about? Plants don't struggle physically as animals do. Does it mean they produce better grapes when lacking moisture or nutrients? If so where is the experimental evidence from field studies? Perhaps the reverse statement is better. When vines are overcropped, there is insufficient photosynthetic ability to supply sufficient sugar to the grapes to ripen properly and to develop normal flavor.

If the fruit ripens to about 20 percent sugar content and the vine then suffers moisture deficiency, there is the possibility of berry shriveling. The sugar and acid contents of the berries will increase only marginally, and unbalanced vines are produced. Woe to the overcropped vine that suffers moisture deficiency before the fruit reaches about 15 percent sugar. About all one can expect in such cases is an unbalanced must that will produce a poor, and sometimes undrinkable, wine.

Vines in poor soils seldom overcrop. If the growth they have is sufficient to ripen their relatively low crop, the wines may be of good quality. Vines subjected to serious moisture or nutrient deficiencies for a period of time die, languish, or become marginal; they do not per se produce better wines.

2. Wine judges are *born* wine judges.

There is just enough truth in this to fool many people. Persons born into a wine-drinking family, especially one that consumed wine critically, have a big advantage in experience. Once in a blue moon, some unfortunate individual has a low sensitivity to odor and/or taste sensations. The rest of us, the overwhelming majority, have all the physical equipment we need to become excellent judges of wine quality, even if our parents drank nothing but beer. Of course, we may not *want* to become sensitive judges of wine quality or even be interested in quality. We may be lazy or disinclined to train our senses to detect subtle differences in quality among wines. So be it.

On the other hand, if we apply ourselves, we can acquire the requisite experience. With any luck at all, we should be able to provide ourselves with a frame of reference that will enable us to evaluate the quality of the usual types of wines. We should not, however, underestimate the amount of experience that is necessary to become a truly reliable judge of the entire range of quality of wines of a given district or type. None can aspire to become a qualified judge of all the different types of wines in the world.

3. There are wine "experts" who can identify any wine presented to them.

One must agree with Brady (1978) that this is "poppycock, balderdash and twaddle." No one can identify a wine with which he or she has had no experience. And there are, as we have just said, far too many wines in the world for anyone to experience them all.

4. Only experts can enjoy the quality of a wine.

This too is nonsense. It is a rare individual who, with even a little experience, may not enjoy drinking wine. Experts may know *why* they enjoy certain wines, but they would be presumptuous to claim that they enjoy them more than amateurs. The latter may, in fact, enjoy a certain wine more fully than an expert precisely because

"They were relatively nice men, Caroline. What do you suppose turned them into enophiles?"

they do *not* have the knowledge and experience to make all the possible comparisons among wines. However, it is also demonstrable that amateurs are generally not able to maintain their preferences as consistently as experts. We should not, however, question the pleasure of amateurs or their value judgments for themselves.

We concede that experts do gain a different type of pleasure from their intellectual appreciation of the complex sensory perceptions yielded by a truly fine wine.

5. Heaven keeps some sort of order of merit for the relative quality of certain vineyards, producers, or vintages.

This is sacrilegious. Even a lowly vineyard may occasionally produce a glorious wine. Need we add that some of the most prestigious vineyards and producers have given us some notoriously poor wines? Consider the wines of certain Bordeaux *châteaux* of 1963! Some years ago in the restaurant of a "luxury" hotel, frequented by what was then called the "jet set," the wine list looked marvelous, with listings of famous *châteaux* and vineyards of France, Germany, and Italy. The prices matched the luxury of the hotel and the reputation of the vineyards. But, alas, all the wines were of the years no self-respecting restaurateur would stock: 1933, 1937, 1942, 1944, 1963, and so on.

There is, however, a germ of truth here in the opposite sense. Famous vineyards, renowned vintages, and producers of great reputation did not usually acquire their prestige unearned. [This may not be true currently when Madison Avenue is so often involved.] The point, however, is that you should not use such prestige as your standard for judging the quality of a wine. The wine may be good or bad, but *you* are the one who should determine this—for yourself.

What fools so many people is that the name and year on the label are no guarantee of quality. The practice of the Bordeaux *châteaux* in recent years in bottling the wines of bad years as *châteaux*-bottled vintage wine is well known and deplorable, if not scandalous. Hanson (1982) documents similar practices in Burgundy.

6. Small wineries produce better wines than large wineries.

Some of the worst wines we have ever suffered came from small, picturesque wineries. We abhor the term *boutique wineries* and hope that it soon disappears. We hasten to add that some of the best wine also came from small wineries. It is the aesthetic and technological standards of the producer, and a fair amount of luck, that determine the quality of the wines produced, not the size of the winery. The myth that the small winery, ipso facto, produces the finest wines is a myth. Naturally the small winery plays up this myth because, since the winery has only a limited amount of wine, the myth appeals to the snob who wants something no one else has— and can pay any foolish amount for it.

In theory, a large winery should be able to make a more careful selection of varieties and lots for aging and thus produce finer wines. This has happened in some cases, of course, but economics, marketing objectives, and other factors may dictate the goals of the large winery.

7. Wines of one area are, ipso facto, better than those of another area.

This presupposes that all wines are to be judged by the same standard. One cannot compare wines meaningfully if they differ from each other in a fundamental way; for example, white wines of one area have their own character and cannot be compared with white wines of another area, which have a different character. The same is true of red wines, of fortified versus nonfortified wines, of still versus sparkling wines, and so on. Comparisons of quality among different types of wines are therefore usually unprofitable and often misleading.

Furthermore, people do have their own preferences. There is no law that says we must prefer one kind of wine over another. One may cultivate a taste for the wines of one producer or vineyard over those of others, even among the wines of a given area. We like the things that we know best more than those that we know less well. To prefer a wine over others simply because we are more familiar with it is provincial and short-sighted.

8. All bottled wines improve indefinitely with age.

This is untrue for many white table wines and eventually is untrue for red table wines. *Some* white table wines improve in quality when kept under proper conditions for a few years. Many red table wines improve with aging in the bottle for several or many years. But we recall red wines that were at their best within a few months or years of bottling. In addition, we find many wines that were bottled after too long a period in the barrel or cask or that had been kept in the bottle for too long.

It is true that, with aging, *some* red wines acquire nuances of bouquet that young wines lack. With still longer aging, however, they may also become oxidized in flavor and brown in color. To praise the old wine for its age and ignore its overaged characteristics is an error of judgment—unless, of course, one is foolish enough to prefer age rather than quality.

Owners of old wines almost always overrate their quality. Preferences for overaged and oxidized wines can develop—for example, the preference of English university undergraduates for "flat" Champagne. We need not imitate their taste (or lack of it!).

9. Wines always improve if opened (1 to ? hours) before serving.

It is true that some wines do improve if decanted before serv-ing. We can postulate several reasons for this fact: Overly gassy still wines lose their excess carbon dioxide. Wines with small amounts of undesirable fermentation odors are improved, particularly when such odors are present at or near the threshold level (see footnote on page 69). Wines that have off-odors owing to microbial changes during aging may also improve. Wines with too much sulfur dioxide may lose some of the free sulfur dioxide and make a better odor impres-sion. Loss of carbon dioxide facilitates these losses.

However, the claim that leaving a wine open or decanting it results in an *increase* in the desirable odors is hard to substantiate. What chemical reactions could take place within a few minutes or a few hours that would produce enough additional desirable odors to be recognizable? There is also the possibility, even the probability, that wines may *lose* desirable odors, especially after decanting. One admits that subtle losses in one odor constituent compared with others may, and probably does, change the overall odor character of the wine, sometimes favorably.

Nevertheless, it is risky to predict what will happen. For each example of an apparent improvement in the sensory impression with early opening of the bottle or decanting of the wine, we can cite examples of wines, particularly old red wines, in which the quality deteriorated rapidly. Decanting is more likely to prove beneficial for young wines than for older wines. There are times when decanting is necessary to separate the clear wine from the sediment. Then we prefer to open the bottle and decant it *just* before serving.

10. Expensive wines are better than inexpensive wines.

Some are, many are not. Price depends on many factors that are not necessarily related to quality. Those who buy wines on a price basis deserve what they get. The law of compound interest means that old wines will always have to be sold at a higher price than corresponding young wines. But, as we have said earlier, this does not mean that they are better wines.

Advertising, snobbism, scarcity, local and state taxes, and the markup of the wine shop or restaurant also determine price. It is regrettable, but the markup on different wines is not uniform. Greed and snobbism know no limits!

As usual, however, there is some truth in this shibboleth. The finest wines are more expensive to produce. Producers must charge higher prices for their higher costs. But it is the quality of the wine, not the price, that is important. Some famous vineyards, secure in the knowledge that they have an established market, often charge whatever the market will bear, even for wines of inferior quality. A well-known St. Émilion *château* got away with this deception for years! This means that some famed wines are not worth the higher price if quality is the criterion for selection.

11. Certain types of wines should be consumed only with certain foods.

The truth in this statement may be that we like food combinations with which we are familiar better than those with which we are not familiar. This does not explain the origins of the social custom of drinking certain wines with one food in preference to another. One can justify serving tart white wines with fish on the same basis that we serve a tart sauce with fish: the tartness represses the fishiness of the fish. But other recommendations—such as Cabernet Sauvignon or a particular vineyard or *château* wine with lamb, and Pinot noir only with beef—appear to us to be tenuous at best. The reductio ad absurdum would appear to be the recommendation that a particular wine be served only with lamb chops and another wine with lamb stew.

A corollary is the prejudice *against* serving certain types of wines with certain foods; for example, red wines are not usually served with fish. Except for the advantage of the higher acidity of most white wines, as mentioned above, and prejudice, we can see no good reason for this practice, except custom. It is probably not the best idea to serve a salad with a vinegary dressing with a fine wine of exceptional bouquet. Even then, however, it is our observation that most people clearly distinguish the vinegary odor of the salad from the bouquet of the wine. We certainly doubt that this odor would spoil our enjoyment of a lesser wine.

Nevertheless, some wines do seem to give greater pleasure with one dish than another. Why, we do not know.

12. One can rely on various vintage charts to determine when a particular type of wine is ready to drink and what its quality will be.

Nonsense! At best, such charts are very approximate guides. At worst, they may lead one to pay an excessive price for a poor wine of a so-called great vintage year. Some good (and occasionally great) wine is produced by some lucky producer even in a year of poor climatic conditions, and some bad wine may be made from even the finest grapes by a careless winemaker. The quality of the wines of a given vineyard vary with the vineyardist's care of the vines, the timing of the harvest, and the skill of the winemaker in making and aging the wines. The vineyardist who overcrops his vineyard, as some do in Burgundy (*and* elsewhere), cannot produce as good a wine as those who don't overcrop. Picking too soon can be as disastrous as picking too late. The conditions of storage and transportation can be critical. The moral is that whatever quality a wine has is found in the wine in the glass, not in newspapers, magazines, books, vintage charts, or anything else.

Et ne sommes-nous pas environnés de gourmets qui peuvent indiquer la latitude sous laquelle un vin a mûri tout aussi sûrement q'un élève de Biot ou d'Arago sait prédire une éclipse.

Are there not epicures among us who can discern in which latitude the grapes of a given wine have ripened as confidently as a meteorologist can predict an eclipse? [Not an exact translation—the answer is probably no.]

BRILLAT-SAVARIN

Pour bien déguster, il n'est que d'avoir de bons sens et du bon sens.

P. POUPON

De gustibus non est disputandum.

The eyes, ears, nose, taste and touch are the only parts of our equipment that we can't rely on for complete and accurate information.

HENRY STANLEY HASKINS

24

CHAPTER 2

The Senses

 Everything we know about the world around us we learn through our senses. This is, of course, true for wines and our value judgments of them. Our appreciation of a wine depends, at least initially, on our sensory impressions. The senses that are important in wine appreciation are sight (vision), smell (olfaction), taste (gustation), touch (tactile sensitivity or feel), pain, and temperature. With experience, some synthesis of sensory impressions enters into our judgment; for example, the ratio of sugar to acid seems to be important, and experienced judges perceive this sugar/acid ratio separately from the sugar or acid content alone. The central nervous system can and does mediate complex interactions of sensory impressions from the various receptors.

Vision

Tint and depth of color and clarity are the primary visual attributes of wine that must be considered, for two reasons: the pleasure that the appearance and color give us and the information about the prospective odors and tastes that these visual attributes reveal.

Color   Appreciation of color is a learned response and is highly subjective. One must admit that some wines have a more appealing color than others—red versus brown, for example. Yet we do enjoy brown sherries. What we apparently appreciate most is a color that we have learned to regard as *appropriate* to the type of wine in question.

White wines are not really white; they range in color from straw yellow to dark amber. White table wines are either straw yellow or yellow. As the wine ages, it usually darkens in color. When the wine has been treated excessively with sulfur dioxide, darkening is slower. Wines made from very ripe white grapes contain more pigment than those made from grapes that have not ripened fully. Hence wines made from grapes grown in cool regions where the grapes barely ripen are usually lighter in color. In fact, underripe grapes sometimes produce wines with a greenish tint. The ripe-grape types of wines (Chardonnay, white Burgundy, Tokaj, the *Auslese* types from Germany, and so on) have more a gold than yellow color.

When white table wines are kept in the cask or bottle for a long time (several years), they eventually turn amber or brown. Whether one appreciates brownish-colored "white" table wines is a personal matter. We consider such a preference to be an affectation of wine snobs who glory in old wines simply because they are old and expensive. If one wants a brown, sherrylike wine, why not buy brown-colored sherry—at a much lower price? Oloroso sherries, Madeiras, Marsalas, and many other dessert wines are amber in color even when young, because of the effects of processing. Their somewhat oxidized flavor also reflects this processing and aging. Curiously, most very amber wines (Marsalas, for example) *lighten* in color during long aging in the bottle, owing to precipitation of some of the dark-colored pigments.

Rosé wines should be pink, normally without any brown, purple, orange, or tawny tint. With rare exceptions, brown or tawny hues in rosé wines mean that the wine has been aged too long or processed with too much oxidation. Rosé wines made from Grenache grapes grown in a warm climate often have an orange tint. Purple tints indicate high-pH (low-acidity) wines, which sometimes result from excessive malo-lactic fermentation.

Most of the wines of the world are red, and for them there is a wide range of acceptable colors, depending on the variety of grape used and the duration of aging. The anthocyanin pigments are responsible for much of the red color in the early years, but, after aging for 5 to 10 years, they represent only a few percent of their original color level. The polymeric red pigments are then responsible for most of the red color. Very young red wines, particularly of red-juice varieties (such as Alicante Bouschet, Rubired, and Royalty), may have a distinct purple-red color. Also, wines of high-pH grapes have a purple tint. Fortunately time reduces the purple tint, but, alas, it seldom improves the flavor of these wines.

What is desired in commercial red table wines up to about 5 years of age is a ruby color. Red wines that are further aged in the bottle eventually develop an amber (or tawny) tint and, one hopes, the typical and desirable "bottle bouquet." A similar tint may be induced by heating the wine, but excessive heat causes a browning of the color. Furthermore, heating the wine may produce a "heated" or off-odor, and the entrancing bottle bouquet of a bottle-aged, high-quality red wine does not develop.

If the brown color is not induced by heating and is not accompanied by an oxidized flavor, it may be acceptable and even desirable. Taxes, growing consumer interest, and diminishing stocks of old red table wines have resulted in few tawny-colored (from long bottle aging) red table wines reaching the market. We wish to emphasize that the amber color in a red wine is tolerable only if it is not accompanied by undesirable odors.

The tint (hue) and depth of color (lightness or luminance) thus tell us a great deal about what may be wrong or right with the wine. Thus alerted, we look for certain desirable and undesirable odors and flavors in the wine. However, it is well known that spurious conclusions about wine quality are likely to be reached if color is considered independently of odor and flavor factors. Even experienced judges may be led astray when confronted with false clues in the form of nonnormal colors (e.g., when the normal color of a wine is deliberately changed in the laboratory). Nevertheless, the perceptive judge will gain considerable information about the prospective odors and flavors of the wine from its color.

The tint and depth of color are not all that the judge sees. The third parameter of color perception is *purity* or saturation (an attribute that determines its degree of difference from the achromatic (gray) color of the same luminance). Inexperienced (and sometimes even experienced but color-blind) judges find it difficult to think of color as being determined by three, not two, parameters. For the color-sensitive judge, experience surely helps. About 8% of the male population are color-blind, but only 4% of the female population are. In practice, the two parameters tint and depth of color suffice for most comparisons of the colors of wines. Lyle (1977) noted that the eye had definite advantages over instrumental procedures in assessing red meat color, but judging red meat color is not known to be comparable to judging red wine color, though it may be.

The human eye is most sensitive to differences in the tint of color in the green region of the spectrum. Of course, the apparent color is greatly modified by the background color and the illumination. It is thus important, even critical, to examine wines under a constant and adequate source of illumination. If one has always examined wines by candlelight, one may have learned to compensate for the low level of illumination compared with direct or reflected "northern" daylight. But, as the level of illumination decreases, the ability to recognize and discriminate between degrees of color difference decreases. Modern illumination systems do not always help; for example, fluorescent lamps and mercury-arc lamps produce false or misleading tints in wines. Under low light intensity at a dinner table, wines of quite different color characteristics may appear to be of approximately the same color.

There is no easy guide for judging the appropriateness of the color in a given type of wine. With experience, however, one comes to recognize whether the color is appropriate for the type and age of the wine and, if it is not, whether this is due to the use of poor varieties of high-pH grapes, oxidation, excess metal content, or other disorder. White wines that are high in iron may have a greenish-yellow tint. Red wines of high iron content may have an iridescent film on the surface. Both conditions are rare; they are nonexistent in wines from well-run wineries.

Serving white wines in colored glasses in Germany apparently originated as a means of concealing the brown color of the wine. An amber tint was known to be a sign of overaging or of other poor winemaking practices. Serving the wine in green, blue, or brown glasses prevented the consumer from perceiving the brown color of the wine. Modern German wine technology rarely allows brown-colored wines. We should note that consumers in some countries (Argentina, Chile, and Italy, for example) have been more tolerant of brown color in white table wines, but recently they too have produced less of such wines.

Contradictory results on the effects of added color on taste thresholds have been reported by Maga (1974), who found that green increased sensitivity to sweetness, whereas yellow decreased sensitivity and red had no effect. For sourness, both yellow and green decreased sensitivity and again red had no effect. Red did decrease sensitivity to bitterness but yellow and green had no effect. Apparently psychological color associations do modify our responses to certain tastes. This is a compelling reason for always observing the color of wines under identical, neutral light conditions, especially in sensory threshold studies.

Somers and Evans (1974) reported a correlation between color and the ionized anthocyanin content of red wines and their overall reported quality. Was this due to the color preference of the panel or to some (unknown) relationship between color, odor, and taste? Tromp and Van Wyk (1977) found that 92% of the variation in wine quality could be mathematically explained on the basis of the color of the wine. Overall wine quality was correlated with total color and anthocyanin pigments. However, odor and taste were jointly responsible for 74% of the variation in quality. Simple color measurement of an acidified red wine provided useful information on the quality of young Beaujolais wines. Timberlake (1981) found better correlation between flavor and content of total pigments and total anthocyanins (sum of colored and noncolored anthocyanins). How much of this is coincidence and how much real, we do not know.

Clarity   The other important visual aspect of wines is their clarity, or freedom from suspended material. Wines may be cloudy because of faulty treatment or microbial spoilage, of because aging has left a deposit.

The consumer finds by experience that wines that are cloudy because of faulty treatment or microbial spoilage are also usually defective in odor or flavor, or both. Even when there is only a slight haziness, the critical judge will concentrate his attention on its possible causes. A floating white film may indicate the growth of aerobic microorganisms; these lead to oxidation if they are from yeasts, or vinegariness (acescence) if they are from bacteria. A flocculent deposit in a semisweet white table wine is usually a result of yeast growth. A milky cloudiness may be due to excess iron or a copper–protein reaction. Excess copper–protein cloudiness may be accompanied by a reddish-brown precipitate. In some instances, a haze may signal the early stages of yeast growth. A cloudiness with a crystalline deposit can be caused by excess potassium acid tartrate or calcium tartrate.

Sometimes the texture of the wine is affected by suspended material. The growth of certain bacteria results not only in haziness but also in increased viscosity. Fortunately this condition is rare in modern commercial wines, but we have noted it too often in homemade wines.

On the other hand, the cloudiness or deposit may be associated with normal aging. Sound white table wines may develop a deposit after many years. Dark amber dessert wines also deposit some colored material with time. In red wines, the problem is more acute. The deposition of colored material often begins with a fine, colloidal haze. Eventually this is deposited on the sides or bottom of the bottle. The amount of deposit depends on the amount of color in the original wine. The nature of the deposit varies greatly from one wine to another. Sometimes it adheres tightly to the bottle; at other times it does not adhere at all and causes problems in decanting the wine (page 21). Sometimes the deposit is heavy and granular, sometimes light and easily disturbed. With the deposition of colored material there is a gradual reduction in the amount of red color and, eventually, the appearance of more and more of an amber tint.

Odor

Our sensory appreciation of wines is due mainly to their odor. The olfactory sense is incredibly sensitive to odorous substances. The olfactory (odor-sensitive) region is very small and is located in the upper part of the nose. During normal breathing little air passes over this region. For us to detect an odor, the inhaled air stream must be diverted to the olfactory region. Sniffing is the way to do this. All good judges of wine quality learn to sniff. A quick, forceful sniff is considered best. It should not be repeated right away, however, because the olfactory sense is subject to rapid adaptation (fatigue). The best practice is to sniff the wine quickly, then remove the glass. After 15 to 30 seconds one may again sniff the wine. As olfactory fatigue progresses, the nature of the perceived odor may also change.

Not only is the olfactory region small and located in a remote part of the nose, but the amount of air that reaches it, even with sniffing, is only a small fraction of that inhaled. Many of the odorous molecules are absorbed by the mucous membranes en route to the olfactory region. Furthermore, the olfactory slit (channel) to this region closes when the nasal passages are swollen. Moral: do not attempt to make critical decisions on the odor of wines when you have a cold. In fact, people who are prone to colds or allergies should not be selected for objective sensory evaluation panels.

Not all the odor comes to the olfactory region during inhalation. When wine is taken in the mouth, its temperature rapidly rises to body temperature. This releases more odorous substances, which reach the olfactory region by diffusion and through exhalation. These in-mouth odors are an important part of what is called flavor (see page 44). When we have a cold, our food seems essentially flavorless—but not tasteless, which is something else (page 44 et seq.).

Normal individuals can identify a large number of different odors, and several levels of each. The number that can be identified at any one time depends on the individual's inherent ability and experience, the concentrations of the odorous constituents present, and the relative amounts of other odorous constituents. With experience, one can identify 1,000 or more different odors at different times, and one can detect differences between various levels of a given odor. There is no shortcut for acquiring this ability. For evaluating wines, one should practice as much as possible with experts who can identify the various odors. Otherwise one's training is likely to bog down on missed odors or semantic confusion in identifying the odors. To give an idea of the complexity of the problem, typical wines contain more than 400 organic compounds, of which probably 200 are more or less odorous (page 67). Of course, in a given wine many compounds are present in subthreshold amounts or are masked or react synergistically to the presence of other compounds. Even so, the number of distinguishable odors in wines is very large.

Various classifications of odors have been made—from 7 to 10 or more groups. Unfortunately none of these have been completely satisfactory in sensory–psychological studies. The reasons for this failure are threefold: the same odor sensation appears different to different people, different odors are seldom "pure," and odor perception is mixed up with degree of pleasantness and unpleasantness. Superimposed on these factors is the imagination of the individual (see stimulus error, page 62).

It is rare to find anosmic individuals (those who, from accident, disease, or congenital defect, cannot smell). Of the more than one thousand individuals tested, only two or three were partially anosmic to ordinary odors and only one was a complete anosmic. If one is a poor judge of odor quality, it is unlikely to be due to an inability to smell.

Odors at high concentrations often smell quite differently than at low concentrations. Mixtures of odors may result in masking (not additive), may have relatively little effect, or may act synergistically (the sum of the odors is more than the summation of the individual odors).

Although we may have difficulty in discriminating between odors, we have a remarkable ability to remember a specific odor (Engen 1980). In fact, our ability to remember odors is better than retention of visual sensations. The proverbial ability of wine judges to identify a wine's origin by its odor may thus have a sensory basis. The task of the judge is to evaluate the wine aroma that contains a large number of compounds. Identified in wine aromas are at least 181 esters, 52 alcohols, 75 aldehydes and ketones, 22 acetals, 18 lactones, 6 secondary acetamides, 11 phenols, 29 nitrogen-containing compounds, 18 sulfur-containing compounds, 2 ethers, 11 furans, and 18 epoxides, as well as 30 miscellaneous compounds (see Chapter 4 for individual components). Many of these are modified in various ways by aging and cellar treatment, and they can and do react with each other or have additive, masking, or synergistic properties.

Aroma Wine odors derived from the grape itself are called aroma. The finest wines are produced from grape varieties that give the wine a characteristic, recognizable aroma. The unfermented grape itself may or may not have the characteristic aroma, or the specific aroma may be present in too small an amount to be detected. When fermented in contact with the skins, however, the wine acquires its varietal aroma or the already existing aroma is enhanced. For a detailed discussion of varietal aromas, see Chapters 4 and 5.

Bouquet Whereas odors derived from the grapes themselves are called the aroma, those derived from fermentation, processing, or aging are called the bouquet. All young wines have a yeasty, reduced fermentation bouquet. If not too pronounced, such bouquet can add to the olfactory tone of white table wines of low varietal character. Many young white wines of Switzerland, Austria, Italy, and elsewhere are pleasant for this reason. But, alas, the period during which the wines have an attractive, fresh, young odor is short—usually less than a year. (For a discussion of excess fermentation bouquet see page 41.) Normally, white and red table wines and dessert wines lose most of their fermentation bouquet before or within a few months of bottling. Wines prepared by the *macération carbonique* process (as in some Beaujolais) may retain a "reduced," special fermentation bouquet. In this process, whole grapes are held under anaerobic conditions for about a week, during which time they undergo an intracellular fermentation. We do not find the odor pleasant, but it has its fans.

Processing odors are often important, even essential. Bottle-fermented sparkling wines held on the yeast for 1 to 4 years acquire a special bouquet. Film-yeast (or submerged-culture) flor sherries have a very distinctive and desirable aldehyde bouquet plus other nuances of aged bouquet. Wines to which reduced musts are added (e.g., Marsala) have a production bouquet. Wines that have been baked (Madeira, California nonflor sherry) have a very distinctive caramel-like processing bouquet (including hydroxymethylfurfural). Wines with added grape concentrate of ordinary quality may have a similar odor, depending on the amount of concentrate used.

Aging wines in wood can add a desirable bouquet if it is not too pronounced. (For a discussion of excessive woodiness see page 36). Aging wines in the bottle often leads eventually to a special bouquet, particularly in dry red table wines and ports. The nature of this bottle bouquet has not been established. It is not due to any specific ester, although esterification is probably a part of the process (see page 80). It is much easier to recognize than to define. Certainly it is more subtle than most aromas. Occasionally it blends with, or may even develop from, the aroma. Apparently wines do not age in the bottle because of oxygen but rather, at least partially, because of the absence of oxygen. The bottle bouquet is produced, at least in part, by reduction (Peynaud 1980).

Not only are there table wines (still and sparkling, flavored or not) and dessert wines (flavored or not), but within each type there are many and subtle variations. These arise from the varieties used, their composition at maturity (which depends on climate), and the method of processing and aging used. From the same grapes, harvested on the same date from the same vineyard, two winemakers may produce two quite different wines, differing markedly in aroma (by earlier or later pressing) and bouquet (by storage at different temperatures, or for different lengths of time, or in different sizes of cooperage of varying origin). Who knows?

Even after the wines are finished, one may be stored at 27°C (80°F) and another at 10°C (50°F). After a few months the wines will be noticeably different in odor. Wines that have been shaken up in transportation may have an oxidized odor. Airplane companies, commuters, and importers should note this. Usually the wines will recover if not too old or too shaken up. The desirable odors may be further modified by foreign or undesirable odors that are due to spoilage or mishandling. Thus no wine connoisseur can hope to explain completely the origins of all the odorous components of a wine.

Some enologists attach significance to the length of time the more intense odor persists after sniffing. Vedel et al. (1972) have incorporated this factor into their system of wine evaluation: persistence of <3, 4 to 6, 7 to 9, 10 to 12, and >12 seconds. The problem is in securing consistent results. Olfactory fatigue and variations in degree of sniffing lead to variable results here. Nevertheless we know of no adequate test of Vedel's proposal or, indeed, whether persistence is a quality factor. It may be, but how to measure? The persistence of the aftertaste is another matter.

Foreign and Undesirable Odors   A major problem with wines is foreign odors. How much woody odor, for example, can be tolerated in a white table wine? Almost all enologists would agree that a *conspicuously* woody odor in a white table wine is undesirable, even intolerable. Most enologists would also agree that at very low concentrations (at least in white table wines of higher ethanol content) a nonrecognizable woody odor may contribute to the complexity of the wine and thus be a positive quality factor. In between, enologists disagree, some criticizing the least trace of woody odor and others tolerating substantial amounts. We believe that a recognizably woody odor is a negative quality factor since it is a foreign odor. The desirable odor (or undesirable, depending on the concentration) may be 3-methyl-4-hydroxyoctanoic acid-4-lactone (Kepner et al. 1972). A threshold of 0.05 milligrams per liter (mg/l) (in 9.4% w/w ethanol) is reported (Salo et al. 1972). For the *cis-* and *trans-* forms, 0.8 and 0.07 mg/l were reported with new oak containers (Otsuka et al. 1974), but wines in used containers also acquired a woody odor. A number of phenols of the oak extract contribute to the "woody" odor (Singleton and Noble, 1976).

When one is accustomed to smelling a defective wine, eventually the defect will not be noted or may even come to be preferred. We feel that some enologists and enophilists have become so accustomed to the woody odor (in, say, their Chardonnay) that they have come to prefer it. We agree wholeheartedly with Peynaud (1980): *"Le vin vieux ne doit pas être une décoction de bois."* Furthermore, wines aged too long in wood acquire off-odors other than woodiness. Moldiness and mushroomlike odors have been reported.

An undesirable and not uncommon odor in white table wines is that of sulfur dioxide. People vary greatly in sensitivity to this compound. Furthermore, olfactory adaptation to high sulfur dioxide concentrations in wines is very rapid. The smell of free sulfur dioxide is easily identified and is, ipso facto, a negative quality factor in any wine. Fortunately sulfur dioxide is only occasionally found in wines in recognizable amounts, and normally only in white wines, especially those of low pH (as in German wines). Aside from its intrinsic undesirability, sulfur dioxide is unwanted because it masks or interferes with the desirable odors. More important, it can affect the trigeminal nerve, causing sneezing and transitory pain. Noticeable sulfur dioxide odor in a wine is a sign of poor winemaking practice. With poor-quality grapes, as in rainy seasons, it is at best a necessary evil.

The sulfur dioxide odor in wine is due to the free (unbound) sulfur dioxide—that is, that which is not bound to aldehydic groups. The ratio of free to total sulfur dioxide is a function of pH—the lower the pH, the greater the proportion of free sulfur dioxide. However, this ratio is also a function of the total sulfur dioxide concentration itself: in a given wine, the higher the total concentration, the greater the proportion of the free compound (see Amerine and Joslyn 1970, for a description of the chemical reactions). Free sulfur dioxide can be detected by some judges at concentrations of 5 to 10 mg/l, although most individuals do not recognize the odor until somewhere between 15 and 40 mg/l. With aging of the wine, the free sulfur dioxide content decreases as it is oxidized or fixed.

At bottling, the maximum free sulfur dioxide of red table wines should not be more than 10 to 20 mg/l. In any white table wine, 20 to 30 mg/l should suffice, while, in sweet white table wines, as much as 50 mg/l is tolerable in young wines, less in finished wines.

There is an international movement to reduce the legal limits for total sulfur dioxide in wines from 350 mg/l to about 200 mg/l. From the quality point of view we applaud, but from the health side we do not find this reduction persuasive—the toxicity limit is much higher than that normally found in wines. There are reports of allergeniclike reactions from sulfur dioxide, but few indict wine.

The other undesirable odors can be classified as those derived from the fruit, from the fermentation and processing, and from microbial spoilage. Among those probably derived from the fruit are earthy, green, raisin, stemmy, and, sometimes, moldy odors. Earthiness is apparently associated with the raw product because it occurs in wines made from grapes from specific localities. However, it is probably not associated with soil on the grapes because wines made from grapes that have been washed may still be earthy. Nor has the odor been identified with compounds in the fruit. Since it is not apparent until the wine warms up in the mouth, higher-boiling substances are probably responsible. It is seldom noted in many areas. Some German wines have it; occasionally it is present in Rhône wines of France; some Rioja wines of Spain have it; and it appears in a few California wines. Our own guess is that it is associated with the microbiological flora on the grapes and perhaps also the microflora on the equipment and cooperage.

The green odor is the same as or similar to a leafy odor. The six-carbon-atom alcohols and aldehydes are among the compounds responsible (page 76). Grapes grown in cool climates or seasons and grapes harvested before full maturity have this odor. It often appears in the Muscadet wines of the Loire, also in some Chablis wines and lesser-quality Alsatian Sylvaners, and in some German Sylvaners and White Rieslings. Southern Austrian wines have it. It is rare in California wines. It appears to be associated more with unripe grapes than with the presence of leaves.

Vineyards located next to eucalyptus trees may have a eucalyptus odor from leaves that drop onto the vines and get into the containers as the grapes are harvested.

The raisin odor is found by design in the wines of Málaga and in some sweet sherries from Spain, since in these regions the fruit is partially sun-dried before crushing. (Only rarely does the fruit hang on the vine long enough to dry to the raisin or semi-raisin stage.) The resulting caramel odor is easy to recognize. It somewhat resembles the odor of grape concentrate (see page 316) but is probably not due to exactly the same compound or compounds. We have noted it in hot years in wines of several varieties: Gewürztraminer, Muscat of Alexandria, Petite Sirah, Pinot noir, Ruby Cabernet, and especially in Zinfandel.

Stemminess as an odor has largely disappeared with the almost universal use of crusher-stemmers. However, the green stems of some varieties are brittle, and, if too many get into the crushed fruit, they may cause a stemmy odor. Stemminess is mainly a problem with red wines. The nature of the compounds responsible is not known.

Occasionally the harvested fruit is so moldy as to impart an odor to the wine. A *Penicillium* odor was found in some red wines made from grapes picked very late in a wet season in the Napa Valley. If the fruit is harvested early enough or if the infected clusters are rejected by the pickers in the field, this odor should be rare. (See more on moldiness, page 42.)

Then there are a number of off-odors associated with fermentation and processing. Among these are acetic, baked, bitter almond, cooked, corked, fusel, hydrogen sulfide, mercaptan, moldy, mousy, oxidized, rubbery, sauerkraut, sophisticated, woody, and yeasty. No doubt there are many more. See Chapter 5 and Glossary, page 305.

A century ago, due to lack of care and ignorance of the danger of aerobic conditions, the vinegary odor of ethyl acetate and acetic acid was a common odor of wines. Post-Pasteur wines (i.e., wines produced since Pasteur's studies of the causes of microbial spoilage) have had progressively less of these compounds (Sudraud 1977). The odor may still be noted from time to time in wines that are distributed in bulk (occasionally in Italy, Portugal, and Spain).

Legal limits have been set for acetic acid in most countries. However, it is the ethyl acetate (page 80) that contributes much of the vinegary odor. The vinegary odor is more pronounced at a pH of <3.4. One should note that acetic acid has a sour taste as well as an odor. This is apparently why United States regulations have permitted adding up to 0.4 gallon of acetic acid per 1,000 gallons of wine (about 0.04%). Sudraud (1977) notes that the legal limit for acetic acid in wines in France in this century has been reduced from 0.25% to 0.11% and 0.12% for white and red wines, respectively. These are the same as the present California limits.

Madeiras and some California sherries are baked at 49° to 60°C (120° to 140°F) during processing to achieve a caramel (page 316) odor, which is considered desirable. Hydroxymethylfurfural (page

75) and other compounds are formed. On the other hand, some sweet table wines are baked for stability. If a distinct caramel odor is produced in such wines, it is considered a negative quality factor. The same is also true of ports and other dessert wines that are baked to hasten maturation.

A cooked odor is not the same as a baked odor. High fermentation temperatures may give some red wines such an odor. It was formerly noted in some California table wines made in the warmer regions, but now that adequate cooling equipment and processes are used we seldom find it.

In a few European countries, potassium ferrocyanide is used to remove excess amounts of iron and copper. The practice is called "blue fining" and is not used as such in the United States. A blue precipitate forms, which is usually completely removed by filtration. If the filtration is poorly done, however, some of the blue precipitate (a ferrocyanide complex) may get into the bottle. With time, traces of hydrogen cyanide will develop from the decomposition of the complex and the wine will acquire a characteristic bitter almond odor. We have rarely observed this odor, and then only in imported wines. The problem is now very rare, as stainless steel has displaced iron, copper, and bronze equipment almost everywhere, so there is no need for blue fining.

Corked is an odor that can develop in wines stored in cork-finished bottles. The moldy odor associated with corks is different from the odor due to moldy grapes. Bureau et al. (1974) attributed an off-odor in Champagne to *Candida* sp. and *Rhodotorula* sp. present in the corks used. On the basis of their own and earlier studies Davis et al. (1981) consider the four genera *Penicillium, Trichoderma, Cladosporium,* and *Monilia* to be the natural inhabitants of cork. Another mold found in other studies was *Aspergillus*. Of the bacteria present, *Bacillus* sp. was most frequent. On purely subjective grounds, we believe most true corkiness is due to *Penicillium* sp. Dubois and Rigaud (1981) attributed it to methyl tetrahydronaphthalene. To reduce development of corkiness in wines, Charpentier

(1977) recommended only short and dry storage of the corks before use. Davis et al. (1982) suggested treating the corks with sulfur dioxide.

Once recognized, this unpleasant odor is never forgotten. Fortunately it is not common, although we have seen most of an entire bottling with poor corks contaminated by it. In buying wines, never select a bottle that shows evidence of leakage (ullage) since it is more likely to have a corked odor. If too much air space develops, the wine may also be vinegary or oxidized.

Another type of corkiness, we believe, is described by Tanner and Zanier (1982), who reported 2,4,6-trichloroanisole responsible for a corky odor. Sound wines contain only 2 to 8 ppt (parts per trillion or ng/l). The threshold is about 10 ppt, and corked wines had 20–370 ppt. This and other chlorinated compounds apparently originate from the chlorination of lignin-related substances. The chlorine is from that used for bleaching the cork during processing. The message seems clear: don't use corks that have been chlorine-treated (see pages 317–318).

The higher-boiling alcohols (commonly called fusel oils, from the German *Fusel,* bad liquor) produce a distinctive off-odor called the fusel odor, particularly in some dessert wines. A wine having this foreign odor would surely be penalized in any judging. At lower concentrations, the odor undoubtedly contributes to the complexity of the wine and may then be a positive quality factor. One exception to the undesirability of this odor is found in ports from Portugal. There, by long usage, a recognizable odor of fusel oils is tolerated and even expected. But this odor is not condoned elsewhere for sweet red wines or any other type of wine. The odor threshold for mixed fusel oils in wines appears to be about 300 mg/l. Isoamyl is most often noticed (Rankine 1967).

Between the frankly yeasty and the obviously mercaptan odor there is a range of odors that resemble each other. All very young wines have a yeasty, beerlike odor that usually disappears after the first racking. It is probably due mainly to hydrogen sulfide in concentrations near the absolute threshold of detection: about 1 to 5 ppb (parts per billion). If the odor remains after the first racking, it is usually hydrogen sulfide and is certainly a negative quality factor. It can be removed, however. Sometimes mercaptans (garlicky or onion-like) are formed. This is even more serious because they are difficult to remove, owing to their relatively high boiling points.

Charpentier and Maujean (1981) considered that the sunlight off-odor of sparkling wines exposed to light was due to methyl mercaptan (MeSH), dimethyl sulfide (Me_2S), and dimethyl disulfide (Me_2S_2). Reactions between riboflavin and sulfur-containing amino acids were said to be responsible. Addition of copper (Cu^{2+}) and tannins inhibited formation of the off-odor.

Moldiness from the fruit has already been noted. Mold growth can also develop in poorly cleaned or poorly drained wooden cooperage, especially under warm storage conditions. Unless the mold is removed before the containers are filled with wine, a moldy odor may be picked up by the wine. One of the reasons some European wineries favor new barrels annually, despite the cost, is the desire to avoid such foreign odors from used cooperage. If the wood containers are filled with water, bacterial and fungal growth may occur in the water and may transmit a moldy odor to the wine unless the container is thoroughly cleaned. This is sometimes called the water-logged odor; fortunately it is rare. Perhaps it is extinct in modern well-organized wineries.

The musty (*Muffton*) odor of wines is associated with 2,3,4,6-tetrachloranisole and pentachloranisole at 4 to 12 ppt. They are formed by fungi from impurities in pentachlorphenol, which is used as a preservative of wood staves. Such preservatives should obviously be avoided, according to Tanner et al. (1981). They also attribute a corked odor to this mechanism, though it is not clear how the precursor gets into corks. Tanner and Zanier (1982) suggest it may be present in the glue used for labels. Wines with musty (*Muffton*) odor contained less than 1 ppt of trichloranisole (see page 41).

Another bacterial off-odor found in wines is the sauerkraut odor (lactic acid and some other compounds), which results from the excessive growth of lactic acid bacteria. It is found in some table wines produced by pressure fermentation, warm storage, or late racking, especially when high-pH musts are used. In pressure fermentations, the long, slow fermentation in the presence of sugar sometimes promotes bacterial growth and accumulation of this particularly odious odor. Control is not difficult if sulfur dioxide is used (*Lactobacillus* is very sensitive to sulfur dioxide), along with low storage temperatures, early racking, and so on. The sauerkraut odor is uncommon in California wines. Some *macération carbonique* wines have traces of this odor.

In dessert wines, especially baked types of relatively low ethanol content (17%) and high pH, a mousy odor may develop. When this odor is suspected, a simple method of identifying it is to place a few drops of the wine in the palm of one hand, rub the hands together, and then sniff them. Appropriate amounts of sulfur dioxide and careful technological control should prevent the problem. We have also noted mousiness in a few high-pH table wines.

The oxidized odor is not difficult to recognize; in fact, experienced enologists can identify it even when the acetaldehyde level is relatively low. The so-called bottle-sickness odor following bottling is really an oxidized odor. When low-sulfur-dioxide white table wines are bottled, they often acquire this odor, which may persist for several weeks; it then disappears.

As wines age from several years to many years, the acetaldehyde odor develops, whether in the bottle or the cask. This is undesirable in table wines. In dessert wines, it may be desirable (as in dry sherries), tolerable (as in sweet sherries), or undesirable (as in sweet red wines, such as ports).*

The rubbery odor is of unknown composition. However, Brown (1950) definitely associated it with wines made from the fer-

---

*A curious exception to the latter example is the old tawny-red dessert wines of Priorato in northeastern Spain, where these high-aldehyde, rancio-flavored, tawny-colored wines are appreciated, possibly because many are nearly dry and make an admirable aperitif.

mentation of high-pH grapes in the San Joaquin Valley and hence called it the Fresno odor. (It is also known in the industry as the rubber boot odor; see page 328.) We feel that it probably results from bacterial growth in high-pH musts; its origins may thus be similar to those of the mousy odor. Is it due to higher sulfides?

The term *sophisticated* refers to all foreign odors, other than those discussed above, that are intentionally or unintentionally added to wines. In France, herbs are sometimes used to give wines a muscat-like character. Before World War II, a sparkling red wine with some blackberry essence added was produced in California. We have seen no intentionally sophisticated wines since World War II in this country. Unintentional odors occur when a tank containing vermouth is not thoroughly cleaned before being filled with a nonvermouth wine, or when grape and fruit wines become mixed.

Flavor

According to Acree (1980), "flavor is generally defined in terms of three components: odor, taste, and texture." Many French enologists use *goût* for all in-mouth sensations. We take flavor to mean primarily in-mouth odors. They are not the same as in-glass odors, which are those volatile at room temperature. In-mouth odors are those released at body temperature and are greater than and different from the in-glass odors. Furthermore, they may be mixed with food odors if taken during a meal. Many French commentators consider wine flavor to be more important than in-glass odors. Amerine (1966) used *flavor* in a wide sense for all the in-mouth tastes and odors. Flavor was considered an important quality attribute of wines. According to psychologists, flavor should be expressed on an increasing intensity or ordinal scale (1, 2, 3, etc.).

Taste

The sense of taste is almost entirely localized on the tongue. Tastes are those nontactile sensations that are perceived when a food—for example, wine—is taken in the mouth. As we have just noted, many of the so-called flavors of wine are really odor. They are usually identified as flavors perceived in the mouth. If the nose is closed very tightly, the sensations are from taste receptors on the tongue or in the mouth.

In judging wines, taste is considered to be less important than odor. However, if the taste characteristics are poorly balanced—too bitter, too sweet, too acid, too sweet for the acidity, and so on—then taste may be the sensory characteristic that leads to rejection of the wine. Low titratable acidity and high pH may be accompanied by undesirable odor characteristics. This often simplifies the judge's task. A balance of tastes that is appropriate to the type of wine is certainly essential. Taste must not be neglected in judging wines. Indeed, it may need more emphasis than it is commonly given.

We have seen that the olfactory sense detects minute quantities of many compounds and undergoes rapid adaptation. Physical loss of the odorous substances by evaporation to a level below the olfactory threshold is a major problem. With taste we are dealing with compounds at much higher molecular concentrations. Adaptation is still a problem, but loss of taste due to evaporation does not occur unless the evaporation unduly concentrates one taste characteristic— for example, the sourness (acidity). It is generally agreed that the sour and bitter tastes and the astringent tactile sensation fatigue their sensory receptors more rapidly than other tastes or tactile sensations. When a wine is tasted, the sweet sensation, if present, appears first. Later the sour and bitter tastes appear.

McBurney (1974) has summarized 11 lines of evidence that there are indeed four primary tastes. He indicates that there may be four separate physiological systems for coding taste information. The problems of the taste of water and the influence of one taste on another are beyond the scope of this text (see Bartoshuk 1975).

There are basically only three tastes that are important in wines: sweetness, sourness, and bitterness. The sweetness/sourness balance seems to be a separate factor from sweetness and sourness considered individually. The fourth taste that we are capable of perceiving, saltiness (see Glossary, page 328), is seldom noted in wines, although it may be a factor in some very dry sherries and wines from grapes grown near an ocean. Wines that are high in potassium sulfate as a result of treatment of the musts with calcium sulfate (i.e., wines that are "plastered") may have a slightly salty taste. Wines overtreated in sodium-ion-exchangers may also have a salty taste but this practice has been abandoned by intelligent winemakers and is not legal in some countries.

Sweetness People not only differ in their ability to detect sweetness (or lack of it) but also as to the meaning of words describing it. Peynaud (1980) reported considerable confusion of 16 French *dégustateurs* (Table 2–1). While 74% of the judges marked a 0.15% sugar solution "dry," 3% marked a 1.6% wine "dry."

People also, to an enormous degree, differ in their preference for or aversion to sweetness. Even for such a typically dry wine as Zinfandel, samples on the sweet side are occasionally found. We confess that we see no great harm in this, although it does confuse and annoy the consumer who prefers a dry Zinfandel and unexpectedly

Table 2–1 Comparative sweetness of wine. The percentage of judges identifying the wines' dryness by the words at the left can be compared to the actual sugar content of the wines.

	Actual Sugar in Wine (%)							
	0.15	0.4	0.8	1.2	1.6	2.4	3.2	4.8
Dry (*sec*)	74	56	7	4	3	0	0	0
Nearly dry (*demi-sec*)	26	41	74	64	49	11	11	8
Slightly sweet (*moelleux*)	0	3	19	32	48	62	61	60
Sweet (*liquoreux*)	0	0	0	0	0	27	28	32

Note: Obviously some of these individuals did not have a very clear idea of the meaning of *sec* or *demi-sec*.

gets a sweet one. Possibly some labeling requirement for sugar content would be useful, especially for rosés, Chenin blanc, White Reisling, dry sherry, and sparkling wines labeled *brut*. Both sweet and dry types of *bruts* are common. Some winemakers might wish to state the sugar content on a voluntary basis.

Table wines with an inappropriate degree of sweetness, particularly in relation to the acidity, have an undesirable *sweetish* taste. We find this a useful term, but others don't. On the positive side, the *sweet* taste appears to round out and blend with some flavor components. In addition, there is a definite, pleasant mouth-feel effect at high (but not too high) sugar concentrations.

For fruit juices at higher sucrose levels, the bitter, sour, astringent (puckery), and vinegary sensory responses are reduced, causing the odor notes of such juices to seem more pleasant. Von Sydow et al. (1974) concluded that increased sweetness "appears to enhance desirable aroma by reducing the harsh taste of some beverages, on a psychological level, rather than acting upon any chemical constituents and thus modifying the vapor composition." Thus the milder, more acceptable taste impression enables the judge not to be distracted "by harsh taste impressions and to focus on the interplay of aroma attributes. In this respect, oversweetening the juice would be as disastrous as undersweetening." How the sensory responses of knowledgable wine judges to dry types of wine would be affected by oversweetening is not clear. Also, with vinegariness, oversweetening appears to be as objectionable in sweet dessert wines as in dry table wines. Nevertheless, many of the standard table wines on the United States market are now 1% to 3% in sugar.

Sourness   Sourness is the tart taste of wines. Unfortunately, in the wine industry vernacular, sourness means wines of high ethyl acetate and acetic acid content—that is, wines that are vinegary. This is *not* sourness in the psychological–physiological sense that we will be using here. By sourness we mean the taste in the mouth due primarily to the nonvolatile acids (see page 83 for individual acids).

Boulton (1980) proposed a relationship between total acidity, titratable acidity, and pH. He was able to predict juice pH from simultaneous solution of the ionization equations for malic and tartaric acids. The perceived acid taste is apparently a function of both associated and dissociated acids.

The difference threshold for the total (titratable) acidity in table wines varies from 0.02% to 0.05% (Amerine et al. 1965b). A difference of only 0.05 pH unit could be distinguished.

The order of decreasing sourness of the principal organic acids of wine (based on their pK_a values—a measure of acid strength) should be tartaric, citric, malic, and lactic. In fact, the order in wines is probably malic, tartaric, citric, and lactic if the titratable acidity is the same for all the acids, according to Amerine et al. (1965b). The published results vary as to the relative sourness of the acids. Recently Philbrick et al. (1982) have shown that the decreasing sourness order is more likely to be lactic = succinic, tartaric = malic, fumaric, and citric, *if* pH, titratable acidity, *and* anion concentration are controlled.

The actual sour taste of a wine is thus a complex function of numerous factors. Certainly almost all wines with a pH less than 3.1 or a titratable acidity of more than 0.9% will taste sour, whereas those with a pH greater than 3.75 or a titratable acidity of less than 0.5% will taste flat. Excessive deacidification of musts may lead to wines of high pH (3.6–3.8), a flat taste, and undesirable flavor and keeping quality (Schlotter 1982).

The sourness of various acids appears to be additive. Moskowitz (1974) says, "It may well turn out that like-tasting compounds add together according to a simple arithmetic manner, with synergism or suppression (masking) simply phenomena that reveal a failure to account in an adequate way for the law of summation." Compounds with different tastes appear to suppress each other. Tannin, ethanol, and higher sugar levels all interfere with perception of sourness, increasing the sourness difference threshold. The interfering effect of tannins on perceived sourness is less in sweet wines than in dry wines. However, sweetness minimizes the tannic effect. Furthermore, the buffering capacity of the wine and of the person's saliva, the sweetness of the wine, the particular balance of different acids, and other factors all appear to have some effect on the degree of sourness.

Because sourness has a special meaning (acetic acid) in the wine industry and to much of the public, we propose that the terms *low, normal,* and *high total acidity* be used in judging wines, even though we would prefer to use the terms *low, normal,* and *high sourness.* The terms *green* and *unripe* for high-acid wines (particularly white wines) seem useful to us, although green also refers to a specific odor (page 38). *Tart* appears unequivocal as a term for normal to high sourness. *Fruity,* however, probably has odor implications. Although it seems to be associated with above moderate acidity, it should probably be avoided unless a true fruitlike odor is present. If it is associated with a moderately high sour taste it is a true fruity flavor. *Acidulous* is a term that denotes excessive (high) total acidity (particularly in wines of low ethanol content). *Flat* is the term used for wines of insufficient (low) total acidity.

Bitterness and Astringency   A surprising number of inexperienced people confuse sourness, bitterness, and astringency. O'Mahoney et al. (1979) and Robinson (1970) confirmed the sour–bitter confusion, especially in untrained consumers. Robinson attributes this confusion to differences in skill in naming the sensation rather than to differences in sensitivity. He adds, "Since few or no food substances are predominantly bitter it must not be difficult to go through life never clearly identifying the bitter taste. This may be the reason for the sour/bitter confusion." He also notes that people who do not have the ability to use correctly the word *bitter* may still use the term, most likely with an unpleasant taste experience, usually for very sour foods. The phenomenon is not analogous to color-blindness.

Bitterness is a taste that the inexperienced judge finds most difficult to evaluate uniformly, either positively or negatively. Most inexperienced judges find a noticeably bitter taste unpleasant. Experienced connoisseurs, however, find some bitterness in red wines to be pleasant. It is a true taste because it is experienced by the taste buds in the mouth. However, it is often confused with the tactile sensation of astringency, even by some experienced wine judges. Bitterness and astringency are two separate sensations, and, with adequate training, they can be distinguished. The discussion in Amerine et al. (1959, pp. 505, 507) is misleading on this subject. For both bitterness and astringency, people show wide variation in sensitivity and in their understanding of the terms. For bitterness, we now prefer descriptive terms such as *not bitter, slightly bitter, moderately bitter,* and *highly bitter.* We no longer favor the terms *smooth, slightly rough,* and so on because it is not clear whether they refer to the bitter taste or to the tactile sensation of astringency.

Excessive bitterness or astringency may overstimulate the free nerve endings and result in mild pain sensations (as with bitter coffee). Experts question whether it is a true pain sensation (see below).

Neither bitterness nor astringency is normally a problem with white wines because the polyphenolic content of white wines is low. However, white table wines of over 0.02% tannin may be bitter (Berg et al. 1955a). This may be due to bitter products of bacterial activity. French enologists consider acrolein the primary bitter compound produced by bacteria in wines. Very dry white wines with high acidity may *appear* to have a bitter taste. This is sensory confusion, a problem that even afflicts experienced judges.

Red wines of higher polyphenolic content age better than those of lower polyphenolic content. In this sense, a degree of bitterness or astringency in young red table wines may be associated with eventual wine quality. The tannin content decreases as wines are aged; hence old red wines are less bitter and less astringent. Nevertheless, excessively bitter or astringent wines of any age are (and should be) criticized. We should recognize, however, that people differ profoundly in their sensory response to bitterness. Vedel et al. (1972) and Ribéreau-Gayon (1973) emphasize that the actual bitterness is due not only to bitter-tasting compounds but also to the interaction of bitter, sour, and sweet tastes and to the ethanol content. More information on this interrelationship would be welcome.

Finally, probably because of less semantic confusion about bitterness and astringency, *experienced* judges are able to distinguish lower levels of polyphenolic compounds than inexperienced judges (Berg et al. 1955a). Surprisingly, sweetness in a wine does not interfere appreciably with difference thresholds to bitterness, though more data would be welcome. High sulfate wines are slightly bitter. White wines fermented on the skins are often bitter. There are undoubtedly other examples.

We have seen that astringency (the puckery feel) is different from bitterness (true taste). Singleton et al. (1975) indicate that the only astringent substances normally found in wines are the polyphenolic compounds, especially the tannins. Their panel was able to differentiate astringency from bitterness. They noted, however, that high astringency tended to mask bitterness. Arnold et al. (1980) came to a similar conclusion. On a constant weight basis, the condensed tannin fraction was the most astringent and bitter, and the catechins were the least astringent and bitter.

For increasing astringency the terms *not astringent, slightly astringent, moderately astringent,* and *highly astringent* are appropriate. We know of no definitive experiment that includes threshold-level responses, but astringency appears almost always to be a negative quality factor in white table wines and probably in other types of wines as well. The astringency of young red table wines decreases during aging.

Touch

Foods and beverages give a variety of tactile (feel) sensations in the mouth: astringent, thin, full, and so on. It is important that taste sensations be distinguished from the tactile sensations—those of touch.

The viscosity of dry wines is due primarily to ethanol, although other compounds have an effect. Wines of very low ethanol content ($<10\%$) are thin, low in body, and of low viscosity, whereas table wines of high ethanol content ($>12\%$) are full in body. The sugar content also affects the feel of the wine. For example, a wine of 10% sugar and 10% ethanol is noticeably viscous, despite the low ethanol content. One thing is certain: the body of the wine is not due to the glycerol content. Glycerol, like sugar, has a high viscosity, but its maximum concentration in most wines is only about 1.5% by weight, at which concentration it will only contribute to sweetness; the tactile sensation due to this amount of glycerol is barely perceptible. Since glycerol is a normal by-product of alcoholic fermentation, high-ethanol wines are also high in glycerol. Even at a concentration of 2%, glycerol primarily contributes to sweetness. The addition of glycerol to wines has been practiced in some areas, but we do not believe it is justified. Furthermore, at least in this country, it is illegal.

It is not known whether several other compounds stimulate tactile or pain receptors. The burning sensation associated with high ethanol content may be the result of stimulation of both types of receptors. Iron and copper have an astringent character when present in unusually high concentrations (above 20 and 2 mg/l, respectively). Modern wines contain much lower amounts. The prickly, in-mouth sensation of wines containing excess carbon dioxide (more than about 0.3–0.5 g/100 ml) is no doubt tactile in origin. Overly sweet wines (more than about 15% sugar), such as cream sherries, white port, and so on, have an unctuous texture.

The third important touch sensation is astringency—the puckery sensation of tannins and related compounds. Apparently the astringence increases as the size of the molecules increase, up to very large molecules that are less astringent. *p*-Coumaroyl tartaric acid and caffeoyl tartaric acid are reported to be present in Koshu Japanese wines at over-threshold amounts for astringency and bitterness.

Pain

Pain sensations result from overstimulation of sensory receptors, as anyone who eats chili peppers can attest. It is rare for a wine to be so acid as to give genuine pain, although some cold-year German and southern Austrian wines and Portuguese *vinho verde* wines approach it. A *little* pain may not be objectionable. Some people tolerate, even prefer, more than others—for example, in their chilis or hot curries.

The effect of excessive sulfur dioxide in overstimulating the trigeminal nerve endings in the nose (resulting in sneezing) is a pain reaction. High ethanol concentrations (particularly in the absence of sugar) can result in pain. It is usually the high ethanol content that is responsible, but ethanol per se cannot account for the burning sensation in some dessert wines and brandies. We have little evidence regarding the pain-inducing syndrome in alcoholic beverages.

The following factors may be associated at times with mild pain reactions from wines or brandies: excessive amounts of butanol or propanol; high ethanol in brandy or in wine; high ethanol in the absence of sugar (particularly at high acidity); high ethanol/high aldehyde (as in some sherries); very high total acidity and very low pH; high acidity/low ethanol; high acidity/low sugar/low ethanol (as in some German wines); high acidity/low sugar/low ethanol/high carbon dioxide (as in some sparkling wines); high polyphenolic content (as in young red wines); high polyphenolic content/low sugar; and sulfur dioxide (particularly in low-pH white table wines). There are undoubtedly others.

Temperature

Temperature is important in wine evaluation—first because of the warm and cold sensations themselves, and second because of the effects of temperature on the compounds affecting the senses of smell, taste, touch, and pain.

The cold sensation is intrinsically pleasant in white and sparkling wines. It is also valuable because at low temperatures wines retain their carbon dioxide better. With dry white table wines there are relatively few points of sensory interest to begin with, so the cold sensation adds to our interest in such wines. Furthermore, white wines are more often high in sulfur dioxide, and the low temperature reduces the volatility of this compound. Custom is probably the most important factor. The greater retention of carbon dioxide at lower temperatures is certainly a factor with sparkling wines.

With respect to taste, the effect of temperature is not clearly established. Some experiments (see Amerine et al. 1965a) indicate that the palate is more sensitive to sweetness and sourness at higher temperatures (about 35°C, 95°F) and more sensitive to bitterness at lower temperatures (about 10°C, 50°F). However, these results may be artifacts of practice or experience, and one should be cautious in viewing them as significant.

It is surely true that odorous compounds are more volatile at higher temperatures. For example, ethyl acetate has about twice as much odor at 23°C (74°F) as at 18°C (64°F). But at 28°C (82°F) it has twice the odor as at 23°C (74°F). Just how high the temperature should be for optimum taste and odor is not clearly established.

On the other hand, perhaps we prefer a warmer temperature for red wines because that results in greater volatility of desirable odors. But that preference might be a conditioned response also. The question is, why did we become accustomed to serving wines at certain temperatures?

Interrelation of the Senses

There is undoubtedly some interaction between the senses. For example, consider a cloudy wine. The odor is almost always perceived as less pleasant and less distinctive than if the wine is brilliantly clear.

This is a stimulus error (see page 62). Similarly, if a wine has a very distinctive varietal aroma, most judges are less apt to recognize taste deficiencies after smelling the wine. In fact, Ribéreau-Gayon (1973) noted that odors do interfere with judgments on taste. Doubtless other interactions also exist. Puisais et al. (1969, 1974), listed several other possible interactions: the effect of music on color and pleasantness of the wine, the effect of light on pleasantness and odor, the effect of color on taste and odor, and so on. Unfortunately no data are given to substantiate the observations.

The art of appreciative tasting depends on the union of sight, scent, and palate.

P. M. SHAND

Smell is the essential sense for degustation.

Nothing is more indisputable than the existence of our senses.

J. D'ALEMBERT

Un goût imaginé et prévu est déjà à moitié perçu.

E. PEYNAUD

CHAPTER 3

Factors Affecting
Sensory Response

 We all have different inherent sensitivities to sensory stimuli. Not only are there differences in sensitivity, but there are major differences in ability to describe sensations. We also differ from each other in our judgment on how to compare the sensations of one wine with another. These inherent differences are modified by the effects of experience. For example, an individual who has been regularly exposed to varying levels of a certain odor is more likely to recognize it, and at a lower threshold, than one who has not been so exposed. Unfortunately not all people respond equally to training. Some learn rapidly and others slowly, but everyone *can* learn to refine their sensory abilities.

Physiological Factors

For each of the senses, human sensitivity varies over a wide range in very complex ways. Thus, some people are more sensitive to color differences than others (about 8% of males are color-blind in varying degrees). Some are more sensitive or less sensitive to sweetness, sourness, bitterness, various odors, pain, temperature, and so on. A given individual may differ markedly in sensory responses to various types of compounds. For example, a person may be ultrasensitive to sourness and relatively insensitive to sweetness, or vice versa.

Physiologically, we change in sensitivity with age (with experience as a complicating factor). We are apparently more sensitive, especially to sweet, bitter, and salty tastes, at 20 to 40 years of age than at 40 to 60. It appears that age has less effect on sensitivity to sourness. Again, individuals vary markedly. An inexperienced judge 20 years old may be less able to identify odors or tastes than an experienced judge of 50 or 60 years.

No final evidence of any effect of tobacco on the ability to judge wines appears in the literature. Generally little or no difference is found between smokers and nonsmokers. For example, McBurney and Moskat (1975) found no significant difference between college-age smokers and nonsmokers in taste thresholds for the detection or recognition of sweetness and saltiness. However, some nonsmokers judging wines are disturbed by the odor of tobacco smoke. We recommend that smokers abstain from smoking for an hour before attempting to judge wines. Of course, smoking should never be permitted in the room where the wines are judged.

Disease or accident may result in altered, diminished, or lost sensory response. Fortunately these aberrations are relatively rare. Much more common are cases of specific taste blindness. For example, about one-third of the American population is insensitive to the bitter taste of phenylthiourea (a compound that is not known to occur in wines). Other types of taste blindness are also known. None of them are believed to affect the ability to judge the quality of wine or any other food, but the possibility does exist.

Sensitivity to odors and tastes varies during the day—differently for different individuals, it seems. Most enologists believe that their sensitivity is greatest just before a meal—that is, when they are hungry. If wines are to be tasted after a meal, it is recommended that the meal be light and not spicy.

Adaptation is a problem with all the senses. With odor, the sensation after a few minutes' exposure is only two-thirds that of the original.

Psychological Factors

There are also many factors affecting sensory response that can be classified as psychological in origin. They include motivation; concentration; memory; and errors in time–order, contrast, stimulus, logic, leniency, proximity, association, and central tendency. We will discuss each of these in turn.

Motivation   Proper motivation improves sensory performance. This is called the payoff function because some form of reward helps to maintain interest. The reward may take the form of personal achievement, time off from work, money, prizes, public recognition of one's ability, and so on. Interest in making the correct judgment increases the chance of doing just that. Knowledge of the results is thus an essential motivating factor. It shows judges their mistakes and thus alerts them not to make them again. It also shows them how they performed within the group. Everyone wants to do well in making difference or aesthetic judgments. Knowing that one's ratings or ranking of the various wines will be openly compared with those of other individuals and with the group averages is thus a powerful stimulus to encourage careful evaluation. This presupposes that the subjects have had similar experience and training.

Concentration   Good powers of concentration (or attention) are obviously an advantage for any judge of wine quality. First, it is believed that by concentrating on a specific sense the threshold for that sense will be lowered; that is, sensitivity will be increased. Second, by concentrating on each sense separately, the judge is less likely to overlook any important negative or positive factors affecting quality. People differ markedly in their ability to concentrate. By conscious practice, one can improve one's concentration ability. Lack of distractions (extraneous noise, etc.) probably aids concentration more than anything else.

Memory   Memory is aided by concentration. The ability to recognize sensory characteristics quickly is obviously important: it saves time. This ability should result in less sensory adaptation, better results, and more time for judging more samples. Experience is the obvious prerequisite for memory. One cannot remember, much less identify, an odor that one has not experienced previously. Theoretically a retentive memory should help us distinguish more levels of quality or at least repeat our quality judgments more consistently. This has not been demonstrated with wines, but we believe it is a fact. We certainly can improve our memory span, not only by concentration, but also by associating odors and so on with specific clues.

The psychological errors are no less real for being psychological. They can and do introduce biases in sensory judgments—biases that are often difficult to detect. Possibly personality differences also influence different subjective judgments.

Time-Order and Contrast   Perhaps the most common error is that of *time-order*—that is, the prejudicial selection of one sample over others on the basis of its place in the order of presentation. In practice, the first sample presented tends to be preferred, although preference for a latter sample does occur. Kim and Setser (1980) found the second sample to be preferred over the first with a consumer panel judging sponge cakes. A probable reason for preference for the first sample is that, in making the quality judgment on the first sample, one has no immediate frame of reference for purposes of comparison. The second sample, however, has the first sample for comparison. Another reason for preference for the first sample is simply that one is apt to be less critical with the first sample. The time–order error is made for any series of wines, whether of the same type or not. It is impossible to avoid this error when two or three different types of wines are being served sequentially with a meal. In judging and in laboratory tests in which several wines of the same type are served simultaneously, it is possible to minimize the effects of the error by having each judge start with a different wine. The time–order error is still being studied. When the same stimulus is presented sequentially, the second stimulus must be larger than the previous stimulus in order to get the same reaction (Walk 1966).

The *contrast* error appears simple but is by no means simple to interpret. It has some aspects of the time–order error and may take different forms. For example, a wine of exceptional quality is served first, followed immediately by a wine of much lower quality. Is the second wine rated lower than it should be because of the effective contrast with the high quality of the first wine? Often, yes. Conversely, a very poor wine may be served first, followed by a fine wine. Is the appraisal of the second wine more favorable than it should be because of the effective contrast with the low quality of the first wine? Probably. In other words, effective contrast leads to more favorable sensory impressions when a pleasant, although perhaps merely ordinary, sample follows an unpleasant one. The opposite effect should occur when an unpleasant sample follows a pleasant one; that is, the latter seems more unpleasant than it really is.

In tests with foods, the first contrast error (i.e., better after poorer appears better) seems to prevail. The opposite error has not been substantiated. Tests have also shown that, if a series of *equally* poor samples is presented, the quality of successive samples appears to deteriorate. This is not true, however, if a good sample is presented somewhere in the series. Due attention to these errors should be given in tests with amateurs. The means of avoiding them is clear: present the samples in a random order so that, statistically, good samples follow poor samples as often as they precede them. Obviously in the usual dinner situation this is not practical.

Stimulus and Related Errors The *stimulus* error is also common. It occurs when the judge uses irrelevant criteria in making a judgment. For example, knowing that one wine is from a bottle with a screw-cap closure and another is from a bottle with a cork stopper may prejudice the judge in favor of the latter wine. It is true that the less-than-fine wines are generally sold in bottles with screw-cap closures, but this is no guarantee that a good wine may not be found in such a bottle, or that a poor wine may not be found in a cork-stoppered bottle. To give a wine a low or high rating automatically because of the type of closure or other irrelevant factor is a stimulus error. To eliminate this error, the wines should be served in identical glasses without any identification except a number and, if appropriate, an idea as to the type. It is surprising how many so-called wine experts are "label drinkers." Their sensory judgment is based on the source or reputation of the wine, or its producer, or the year of production. But none of these are guarantees of the quality of the wine *in the bottle*. Perhaps the wine was opened or decanted too early, or was inadvertently shaken, or heated, or frozen. Thus, although other bottles of the wine of that vineyard, producer, and year may be splendid, this one may be inferior—or vice versa, superlative.

We admit, however, that at home or in a restaurant we like to see the bottle, preferably before the cork is drawn! Aside from normal curiosity about what we are about to drink, knowing that a certain wine is to be served alerts us about what to expect. We recall the last time we had the wine. We know what level of color or acidity or sweetness to expect. We apparently put ourselves in a mood to enjoy this particular wine. And our chances of really enjoying it are greater, perhaps partly because of the stimulus error. Can this be wrong, since we are drinking the wine for pleasure? Obviously, no.

The *logical* error occurs when a judge associates two characteristics of a wine or food because they are logically related. Of course, for the specific wine in question they may *not* be related, and a form of stimulus error occurs. For example, it is usually true that a slightly amber white table wine is too old or has been exposed to air and will have an oxidized odor. But it is possible for a slightly amber white wine to be young and fresh. A white wine made from red grapes is an example. Just because amber color and oxidized odor are "logically" related does not mean that they *must* occur simultaneously.

Leniency is another form of the stimulus error. One is apt to make overly lenient judgments on wine quality in the presence of the winemaker or in the home of one's best friend. Although we have not observed it, the opposite error may also occur: downgrading a wine precisely because we do not know the winemaker or the host. The insidious thing about this and other types of psychological errors is that they occur without our knowing it.

The *proximity* error is also a form of the stimulus error, and is associated with the use of scoring scales. For example, a wine rates high in one characteristic—say, color. This favorable appraisal then influences the judge to have more favorable impressions of related (proximate) characteristics—taste, odor, etc. It is difficult to avoid this error.

Yet another form of the stimulus error is the *association* error, the tendency to repeat previous impressions. This is somewhat of a contradiction of the example given earlier for a succession of equally poor samples apparently getting worse under the contrast error. However, inexperienced judges do tend to repeat previous impressions. Possibly the association error is a combination of the central tendency error and lack of concentration.

Central Tendency   The error of *central tendency* is committed by timid or inexperienced judges who are fearful of making the wrong judgment. Suppose the judges have four commercial Cabernet Sauvignons to score (see page 214) on a 20-point scale, with 13 being the break-even point for commercial acceptability. The judges know that their scores probably must be at least 13 and cannot be more than 20. They are thus likely to make the least error by giving scores in the middle of the acceptable scale—that is, from about 15 to 17. If they are timid or lack experience with Cabernet Sauvignons, they may subconsciously take the safest course by giving such scores. This is again a form of stimulus error, in that their judgments are the result of factors not necessarily related to the quality of the wine.

Inexperienced judges also sometimes give wildly erratic quality judgments, in both directions. As judges become more experienced, their confidence in their abilities increases, and errors of central tendency occur less frequently. We should add that some people do not seem to be subject to the error of central tendency. They simply don't care what others think of their quality judgments. Hurrah for them, we say.

Bias is also introduced when the panelist remembers or knows the result of a previous test. We have yet to find a judge who does not wish to be consistent and who will use this information.

The dearest wine is not always the best.

C'est toujours un aveu difficile pour le dégustateur de dire qu'il ne trouve aucune différence et peu sont capables de cette franchise.

E. PEYNAUD

Wine is the mirror of the heart.

G. ASHER

On the tongue the wine speaks.

P. POUPON

CHAPTER 4

Composition of Wines

 The lay reader may wonder why in a book on the sensory evaluation of wines we have devoted a whole chapter to the chemical constituents of grapes and wines. First is to help identify the revealing compounds for specific sensory responses. One hopes also to be able to identify how various constituents interact to influence sensory quality, probably differently for individuals and certainly differently from one wine type to another. Finally, some compounds or mixtures of compounds may be found for use as odor, taste, or flavor standards, in place of the cumbersome "like bramble berries," "like leeks," and so on (see pages 292–293). Until better descriptions are found, these will continue to be used. We have also included data on odor and taste thresholds. These should be used with caution when applied to something as complicated as wine. Masking and synergism are unavoidable problems.

Webb and Muller (1972) and Schreier (1979) list a large number of volatile compounds present in wines and for some indicate the biosynthetic pathway of their formation. Williams (1982) notes the rapid increase in the number of wine constituents that have been identified since 1955 (Figure 4–1).

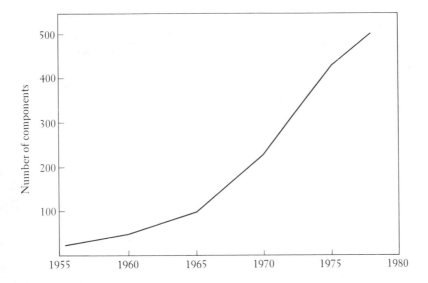

Figure 4-1 Number of volatile wine components identified since 1955 (Williams 1982).

Water

The amount of water in wines varies from 75% to 90% by volume. This aqueous ethanol solution is the solvent for all the other constituents of the wine. Aside from a possible water "taste" and its tactile sensation, this is water's primary function in wine.

Alcohols

Methanol   This alcohol is not a direct product of alcoholic fermentation. Its primary source in wines appears to be from hydrolysis of pectins. Therefore, fruit wines and especially spirits carelessly distilled from fruit wines are high in methanol. In grape wines, a methanol content of 0 to 269 mg/l, average 100 mg/l, is reported (Amerine and Ough 1980).* Red wines are higher in methanol than whites. While the methanol itself in wines has little sensory impact, methyl esters may contribute to the odor of wines.

Ethanol   The second most important component of wines is ethanol. A few types of wine ("light," "soft") have only 5% to 10% ethanol by volume. Most commercial table wines have 9% to 14%, and dessert wines range from 14% to 21%. The question of what is a table wine is normally determined by government regulations—in the United States, less than 14% ethanol. However, the specific regulations of various countries differ. In terms of wine production, many (but by no means all) wines with more than 14% ethanol have had wine spirits added—that is, have been fortified. Some of the very low alcohol wines may have had some ethanol removed.

Ethanol (ethyl alcohol or often just "alcohol") has a distinctive odor, taste, and feel. For solutions of ethanol in water, Parker (1922) reported absolute thresholds[†] of 0.55% (by volume) for odor, 17.5% for taste, and 32.3% for pain. Meilgaard and Reid (1979) found odor thresholds of 0.28 to 9.0 g/100 g. These thresholds, especially that for taste, need to be reinvestigated. In addition, the wide variations

---

*Where concentrations are given without a source, see this reference or Amerine (1954) or, usually, Schreier (1979). See also Webb and Muller (1972) and Zeeman et al. (1982).

[†]The word *threshold* need not disturb the nontechnical reader. The *absolute threshold* for a given compound (e.g., salt) is the minimum concentration in an aqueous solution that a person can correctly identify (e.g., as "salty"). At concentrations below the absolute threshold, the compound is not identified, although the presence of odor may sometimes be perceived. Since different people have different thresholds (and the same person has different thresholds at different times), some statistical measure of absolute threshold must be defined. Usually we define it as the minimum concentration that 50% of the population can correctly identify. We are aware of recent research based on a signal-detection model that questions the concept of an absolute sensory threshold.

among individuals, the effects of their experience, and the known effects of the method of testing should be taken into account. Wilson (1972), for example, reported a taste threshold of 4.2% ±0.2% for ethanol in water and a pain threshold of 21.2% ±1.2%.

The difference threshold* for ethanol in water varies with the ethanol concentration (Berg et al. 1955b). At low ethanol concentrations (about 5% by volume), this threshold is about 1%. In other words, 50% of the population can distinguish between 4% and 5% ethanol or between 5% and 6%. At 10% ethanol, the difference threshold is about 2.0%; at 14% ethanol, it is about 3.0%; and at 19% ethanol, it is about 3.5%. In red and white table wines of 12% and 11% ethanol, the difference threshold for ethanol was 4% in the studies of Hinreiner et al. (1955a); that is, it was almost twice as great as the difference threshold for ethanol in water.

It is also of some interest to know that adding sugar to an ethanol–water solution increases the absolute threshold for ethanol. The more sugar is added, the greater the absolute threshold becomes. Surprisingly, sweetening wines does not increase the difference threshold for ethanol. It can also be shown that the increase in the absolute threshold for ethanol at higher sugar levels is somewhat suppressed by acids.

Ethanol has some effects on the acid taste of wines. If a wine is carefully dealcoholized and then brought back to the original volume

---

*The *difference threshold* for a given compound at a given concentration (above the absolute threshold) is the minimum difference that can be detected between that concentration and another. The higher the concentration of the compound in the solution, the greater the difference threshold. In other words, at low concentrations one can detect smaller differences in concentration between two samples than at high concentrations. This is hardly surprising, because a difference in concentration of, say, 1% at a 5% concentration level is proportionally greater than a difference of 1% at a 20% concentration level. A given difference between two small numbers is always more significant than the same difference between two large numbers. Like the absolute threshold, the difference threshold is usually defined on a statistical basis, namely, as the minimum difference in concentration that 50% of the population can detect.

with water, it will taste more acidulous and unbalanced than the original wine. This is because ethanol has a slightly sweet taste. But the ethanol also undoubtedly affects the activity of the acids. Furthermore, it determines the viscosity (body) of the wine, which may affect the degree of acid taste. Ethanol also acts as a fixer for odors, but as applied to wines this has not been, to our knowledge, investigated. In fermented ciders, 0.5% to 0.75% ethanol enhances the fruity aroma (Williams and Rosser 1981). This is probably due to the effect of ethanol on the vapor pressure of other compounds.

Finally, ethanol has its well-known physiological effects on the central nervous system. At above-normal blood ethanol levels, there are increasing effects on memory and judgment. The conclusion is clear: when making critical decisions about wine quality, *avoid* consumption. In Grosser's (1965) tests, six or seven wine judges had low blood alcohols after 50 wines (0.01% to 0.03%). The seventh judge had 0.08%, but he also consumed the most wine. Most, but unfortunately not all, wine judges that we have observed do not swallow wines during their examination of wines. However, Engen et al. (1975) observed an increase in odor sensitivity per se at a blood level of 0.07%. Even if this is true, since the legal limit on blood ethanol level is about 0.10%, one cannot ethically recommend that wine judges tipple during their deliberations.

Other Alcohols A number of aliphatic alcohols with more than two carbon atoms exist in musts, or are produced by various mechanisms during alcoholic fermentation, and are found in wines. If the wines are fortified with wine spirits, these may be a supplemental source of higher alcohols.

The most important aliphatic alcohols in wines and wine spirits are 3-methyl-1-butanol (isoamyl, 83–400 mg/l), 2-methyl-1-butanol (active amyl, 19–96 mg/l), and 2-methyl-1-propanol (isobutyl, 6–174 mg/l). Lesser amounts of many others have been reported, including 1-propanol (11–68 mg/l), 1-butanol (t), 2-butanol (t), 1-pentanol (<0.4 mg/l), 1-hexanol (0.5– 12 mg/l), 1-octanol (0.2–1.5 mg/l), and traces (t) of others. Many of these alcohols have more or less of the "fusel oil" odor. It is believed that n-octanol is important in Cabernet aroma. At high concentrations ($>$300 mg/l), fusel oils are certainly a negative quality factor, but at lower levels they may add to the desirable odor complexity of the wine. More higher alcohols are formed with crushing, aeration, and high fermentation temperatures and less with sulfur dioxide, settling, and low fermentation temperatures. The threshold for 2-methyl-1-propanol was reported as 228 mg/l by Van der Merwe and Van Wyk (1981). For 3-methyl-1-butanol, it was only 14.5 mg/l. The most desirable level varies with the type of wine and with the sensitivity and personal preference of the consumer.

Grapes and wines contain 1-phenethanol, 2-phenethanol (25–105 mg/l, roselike), benzyl alcohol, 3-(methylthio)-1-propanol (0.05–2 mg/l), and other alcohols. Sufficient amounts of *meso-, levo-,* and *dextro-*2,3-butandiol may be present (165–1250 mg/l) to be detected or at least to contribute to odor (and taste) complexity. Smaller amounts of 2,3-pentandiol are reported.

A number of terpene alcohols (and linalool oxides) are also present in grapes: linalool (t–0.4 mg/l), geraniol (particularly in the skins), nerol (t); α-terpineol (t–0.4 mg/l), hotrienol (t–0.25 mg/l), *trans*-linalool oxide, crystallized linalool oxide (in the solid portions), *cis-* and *trans*-roseoxides, and nerol oxide (Di Stefano 1981). More recently, Williams et al. (1981) classified the monoterpenoids of muscat grapes into free and conjugated precursors. They identified *cis-* and *trans*-furan linalool oxide, nerol oxide, linalool, hotrienol, myrcenol, *cis-* and *trans*-ocimenol, α-terpineol, *cis-* and *trans*-pyran linalool oxide, nerol, geraniol, *cis-* and *trans*-1,8-terpin, and five others. Two monoterpene hydrocarbons were found in grapes. In wines, limonene and myrcene are reported (Schreier 1979), but Boidron (1981) did not find limonene or *p*-cymen in musts or wines. Monoterpene glycoside and nor-isoprenoid precursors have also been identified (Williams et al. 1982).

The recognition threshold of α-terpineol is about 5 mg/l. It is believed to increase during aging of the wine, while linalool decreases. The recognition threshold for linalool is much lower than that for α-terpeneol. The aromatic odor due to linalool decreases during aging, especially if the wine is exposed to light. Di Stefano (1981) found that much of the linalool was often present in the combined form. If it could be released, there should be more muscat aroma. Linalool was the most abundant of the terpene alcohols present in Muscat blanc grapes. It and geraniol are abundant in the skins, which suggests that muscat aroma could be increased by better extraction from the skins. Also present in grapes and wines of *V. vinifera,* and to a lesser extent in *V. labrusca,* was 3,7-dimethyl-1,5-octa-dien-3,7-diol (Rapp and Knipser 1979). Rapp et al. (1980a) also found, 3,7-dimethyl-octa-1,7-dien-3,6-diol in muscat grapes.

Hotrienol (ho-trienol) has a tea aroma (Schreier 1979). Linalool and α-terpineol have muscatlike odors. Dilute geraniol is more or less geraniumlike. Fagan et al. (1981) found small amounts of linalool, *cis-* and *trans*-nerolidol, and *trans*-farnesol in wines produced by film yeast growth. Williams et al. (1980) also found 3,7-dimethyl-octa-1,5-dien-3,7-diol, 3,7-dimethyl-octa-1,7-dien-3,6-diol, 3,7-dimethyl-octa-1-ene-3,6,7-triol, and 3,7-dimethylocta-1-ene-3,7-diol in muscat grapes and wines. In the Muscat blanc grown in the Piedmont region of Italy, Usseglio-Tomasset (1981) found terpene alcohols and oxides, hotrienol, and di- and tri-terpentenoids.

Since these compounds are little changed by fermentation, they have been used to differentiate various varieties of muscat-flavored grapes: Pinot gris (Ruländer), Morio-Muskat, Gewürztraminer, Scheurebe, Müller-Thurgau, and White Riesling (Schreier et al. 1976, 1977, and Rapp and Hastrick 1976, 1978). Methods of differentiating varieties of grapes based on fermentation by-products is of questionable validity (Schreier et al. 1976) because of complicated interconnected aerobic and anaerobic pathways during fermentation, plus the varying effects of various strains of yeasts and bacteria.

The amounts of the terpene alcohols and oxides may also be used roughly to classify grapes as to the degree of muscat aroma. If the sum of linalool, nerol, and geraniol was less than 800 mg/l, the muscat aroma was too low to be classified as a muscat; if over 1,200 mg/l, it was too pronounced (Boidron 1981). See Boidron and Torres (1979) for slightly different figures. Nonmuscat but aromatic varieties (White Riesling, Gewürztraminer, Müller-Thurgau, Sylvaner, Sauvignon vert [the Bordeaux Muscadelle], and Sémillon) contain more terpenes than less aromatic varieties (Sauvignon blanc, Ugni blanc [St. Émilion, Trebbiano], Merlot, Grenache, and Chasselas doré).

The glycerol content of wines varies, from about 0.2% to 2.0%. It has a slightly sweet taste at 0.5% and up. Compared to glucose and fructose, its sweetness is thus important in only a limited number of wines. The glycerol threshold is higher with increased acidity or ethanol. At the upper limits in dry wines, it might influence the tactile (viscosity) sensation, but this is unlikely to be significant. See also pages 50 and 51.

Sorbitol and mannitol are sugar alcohols. Ranges of 5–394 and 84–1,510 mg/l have been reported (Amerine and Ough, 1980). Apples may have ten times as much. Erythritol (33–272 mg/l) and arabitol (13–329 mg/l) are also sugar alcohols found in wines, particularly when made from moldy fruit.

Hydrocarbons

At least 20 hydrocarbons have been reported in wines. Of these, 3,8,8-trimethyl dihydronaphthalene and vitispirane develop during storage of the wine. They are present in relatively large amounts in the headspace of matured wines. Their significance, if any, to wine quality needs to be established.

Aldehydes and Ketones

Traces of a number of aldehydes are found in grapes. Few of these are found in wines since they are reduced to alcohols during fermentation. Most of the ketones reported in grapes are also found in wine, though in small amounts.

Acetaldehyde (10–<100 mg/l, more in flor sherries) is a primary product of alcoholic fermentation and directly or indirectly is an important odor constituent of many wines. Directly its odor is responsible for the oxidized odor of table wines (50–<100 mg/l). Sherries produced by aging often contain more than 100 mg/l and flor and submerged-culture sherries larger amounts (200–500 mg/l). In these cases, it is a desirable odor note (though by no means the only odor). Sweet Hungarian Tokajs are nowadays produced by oxidative processes and are normally high in acetaldehyde. In pre-Pasteurian wineries, casks and so on were not kept full, and aerobic surface yeasts formed films and produced high amounts of acetaldehyde. Since most wines contained similar amounts, this was tolerated then but would not be now.

Propanal and 2-methylpropanal are present in grapes and also in wines. Cinnamaldehyde, vanillin, furfural, and 5-hydroxymethylfurfural are found in many wines, particularly if they have been heated. Furfural is usually thought to be a product of distillation, but Schreier (1979) considers it a product of storage. Its odor is believed important in brandy and possible in old Tokajs. Vanillin originates from the lignin of the oak. It has a mild vanillalike odor. Syringaldehyde has a similar origin and odor. Cinnamaldehyde has the artificial grape-drink odor. Nerolidol is reported to decrease during aging of Champagnes, while benzaldehyde and vitispirane increase (Loyaux et al. 1981).

During the aging of sweet wines, 5-hydroxymethylfurfural (hmf) is formed from the dehydration of fructose. It is said to have the odor of camomille. It has been found (to 87 mg/l) in old Tokaj (>10 years). Much larger amounts are found in sweet wines that have been heated (to 600 mg/l)—for example, in California sweet sherries and tawny ports produced by baking. In Australian ports, Simpson (1980) reported furfural, 2-acetylfuran, 5-methylfurfural, ethyl levulinate, and ethyl furoate, as well as 5-hydroxymethylfurfural.

Hexanal and hexenals are found in grapes, grape juices, and wines. Drawert (1974) attributes the grassy odor of grape juices to them, especially if made from unripe grapes. The fruity aroma of some wines may be due to cis- and trans-2,6,6-trimethyl-2-vinyl-4-acetoxytetrahydropane (Williams 1982).

The ketones, α-diketones, and α-hydroxyketones include acetone (<0.4 mg/l) and 3-hydroxy-2-butanone (acetoin) (to 44 mg/l in table wines and 350 mg/l in submerged culture sherries). Old Tokajs are also reported to be high in acetoin. Also found are 2,3-butanediol (380–680 mg/l), 2,3-pentanedione (t–2.8 mg/l), 3-hydroxy-2-pentanone (0.5–2.8 mg/l), and 2,3-pentanediol (7–18 mg/l). These seem to have little sensory impact. Pinot noir constituents identified by Schreier (1980) included 11 ethoxy and acetyloxy derivatives of hydroxy ketones and hydroxy esters, none by themselves very distinctive.

Diacetyl (2,3-butanedione) is important in oxidized red table wines (up to 7.5 mg/l) and in some bacterially spoiled wines. The detection threshold in wine is about 3 mg/l; however, Meilgaard and Reid (1979) reported thresholds of 0.018–0.28 mg/l. A buttery odor appears at high concentrations. Whether it adds a desirable complexity to the odor of red wines at concentrations of 3–5 mg/l is not known, but it may.

β-Ionone and damascenone are present, but the amounts present are not now known.

A number of acetals were found in old Tokajs and sherry wines (Schreier 1979) and ports (Simpson 1980): 1-1-diethyloxyethane, 1-1-diethoxypropan-2-one, 1-ethoxy-1-(3-methylbutoxy)ethane, 1-ethoxy-1-(2-methylbutoxy)ethane, cis-5-hydroxy-2-methyl-1,3-dioxane, and cis-4-hydroxymethyl-2-methyl-1,3-dioxolane. Their specific odor and their contribution to the consumer's perception of quality are unknown. Schreier believes that some of the higher aldehydes reported in wines are really acetals.

Lactones are reported to be important to the odor of sherries (and perhaps to that of other types as well). γ-Butyrolactone, pentolactone, and several isomeric 4,5-dihydroxyhexanoic acid γ-lactones seem to be an integral part of the sherry odor (Webb and Noble 1976). 4-Hydroxy-3-methyloctanoic acid γ-lactones are constituents of oak. The *trans*-isomer has about ten times the odor of the *cis*-isomer. The *trans*-isomer plus isopentyl and isobutyl alcohols has a strong whiskey odor. The thresholds of the γ-lactones are relatively low.

Yeast metabolism may play a role in the synthesis of some lactones. Because of the influence of various metabolic pathways on lactone formation, Schreier (1979) believes they play only a subordinate role in the specific varietal character of wines. They appear to be more important physiologically in film sherries.

Phenols

The volatile nonflavonoid phenols include phenol (<0.01 mg/l), *o*-cresol (<0.01 mg/l), *m*-cresol (0.01 mg/l), *p*-cresol (0.01 mg/l), 2-ethyl phenol (0.05 mg/l), 4-ethyl phenol (0.35 mg/l), 4-vinyl phenol (0.02 mg/l), 2-hydroxybenzaldehyde (0.15 mg/l), 4-hydroxybenzaldehyde (0.03 mg/l), 2-hydroxyacetophenone (0.12 mg/l), 4-hydroxyacetophenone (0.4 mg/l), 4-methyl guaiacol (<0.01 mg/l), 4-ethyl guaiacol (0.08 mg/l), 4-vinyl guaiacol (0.05 mg/l), vanillin (0.04 mg/l), eugenol (0.01 mg/l), eugenol, methyl ester (<0.01 mg/l), ethyl syringinol (0.04 mg/l), tyrosol (4.9 mg/l), tyrosol acetate (0.37 mg/l), acetovanillin (0.15 mg/l), syringaldehyde (0.035 mg/l), and isopropyl syringinol (<0.01 mg/l). The nonvolatile nonflavonoid phenols (all acids) include: salicylic (16 mg/l), vanillic (6 mg/l), gentisic (4.5 mg/l), syringic (5.5 mg/l), *p*-coumaric (4 mg/l), gallic (red wine) (35 mg/l), gallic (white wine) (2 mg/l), ferulic (3.5 mg/l), and caffeic (5 mg/l). Some of these have distinctive odors. Except for acetovanillin, all the volatile phenol compounds exist only in wines. They are the result of bacterial and yeast metabolism or as products of the hydrolysis of higher phenols from grapes.

Singleton (1981) found more vanillin and related compounds, especially "oak lactone" (*trans*-β-methyl-γ-octalactone) in American oak (*Quercus alba*) than in European oak (*Q. sessilis* or *Q. pedunculata*). However, European oak has 150% more total extractables and twice the extractable phenols, including tannins. It also has more extractable colored compounds. See also esters of hydroxycinnamic acids (page 81).

Polyphenolic Compounds

Polyphenolic compounds (especially the tannins) have two sensory characteristics: true taste bitterness and tactile astringency. Fractions of grape seed phenolics (one catechin) were both bitter and astringent, according to Arnold et al. (1980), and all fractions were more bitter than astringent. The low molecular weight phenols are more bitter than astringent. The intermediate-molecular-weight trimeric and tetrameric anthocyanogens were significantly more bitter.

The tannins of wine react with proteins. Saliva contains mucoproteins that react with tannins. As more wine is consumed, it is believed that the wine will appear more astringent because of lack of mucoproteins (Glories 1981).

Sulfur-Containing Compounds

The most important representative of the sulfur-containing compounds present in wines is hydrogen sulfide. Its recognition threshold is very low ($<$0.001 mg/l). Wine made from grapes containing free elemental sulfur (sprayed on the grapes for control of mildew) may form high amounts during fermentation. Dimethyl sulfide is formed by yeast metabolism from cysteine, cystine, and glutathione.

Meilgaard and Reid (1979) reported recognition thresholds of 7.1 to 160 μg/l. 3-Methylthio-1-propanol is formed from methionine (t to 2). Other evil-smelling compounds reported include ethanethiol, ethylmethyl sulfide, diethyl sulfide, dimethyl sulfide, diisopropyl sulfide, and so on. At low concentrations (below the identification threshold), some of these may contribute to the desirable odor of young wines and others to old wines.

Amines, N-Acetylamines, and Amino Acids

The differences and similarities in amino acid content were used by Ooghe et al. (1981) to distinguish Beaujolais, Bordeaux, and Burgundy red wines. But the number of samples was limited, and the influence of differences in vineyard location and winery technology were not evaluated.

A number of simple amines have been identified: methyl- (0.07 mg/l), dimethyl- (t), ethyl- (0.52 mg/l), ethanol- (t), propyl- (t), isopropyl- ($\simeq$0.05 mg/l), α-amyl- (t–0.001 mg/l), butyl- (t), isobutyl- ($\simeq$0.05 mg/l), isoamyl- (1–28 mg/l), pentyl- (t), isopentyl- (t), hexyl- (0.4–0.7 mg/l), 2-phenethanol- (0–9 mg/l), and 3-(methylthio)-propylamine (t). Also reported are pyrrolidine (0.06 mg/l) and morpholine (>0.7 mg/l). See Schreier (1979) and Ough et al. (1981). These compounds are found in grapes and wines. Their importance to the odor of wines is doubtful, as is that of N-acetylamines, which are also present. Ough and Daudt (1981), extrapolating from beer data, believe that there may be sufficient ethyl and isoamyl amines in White Riesling wine to have a specific sensory effect.

Tyramine, puttescine, histamine, and pyrrolidine are more likely to have physiological effects rather than detectable olfactory properties.

Numerous amino acids have been identified in wines. They have bitter, sweet, or sour tastes, but the amounts present are small.

Esters

Esterification is slow and generally incomplete in wines. Esters are found in grapes and are also formed during the fermentation and aging of wine. Many esters have no discernible odor, others are present in subliminal amounts, and only a few are present in recognizable quantities. However, additive and synergistic effects of ethyl esters may occur. Ethyl acetate ($<$50 mg/l) has a pleasant odor at low concentrations and a vinegary, unpleasant odor at higher levels ($>$150 mg/l). A recognition threshold of 12 mg/l was reported by Van der Merwe and Van Wyk (1981) in wines; in grape musts, Corison et al. (1979) reported spoiled thresholds at 60–115 mg/l.

The relatively high amounts of ethanol, isobutanol, and isopentanol result in relatively high amounts of the ethyl, isobutyl, and isopentyl esters. Ethyl esters of hydroxycarboxylic acids are also found. Isoamyl acetate has a threshold of 0.18–2.82 mg/l (Meilgaard and Reid 1979).

Other esters listed by Schreier (1970) with quantitative data, are 3-(methylthio)-propyl lactate (t), isobutyl acetate ($<$0.2 mg/l), isopentyl acetate ($<$8 mg/l), n-hexyl acetate ($<$2 mg/l), 2-phenethyl acetate ($<$4.6 mg/l), ethyl butyrate ($<$0.4 mg/l), ethyl propanoate ($<$1.2 mg/l), ethyl 2-hydroxypropanoate ($<$400 mg/l), ethyl caproate ($<$2 mg/l), ethyl caprylate ($<$2 mg/l), isopentyl 2-hydroxypropanoate ($<$2 mg/l), ethyl 2-methylbutanoate (t), ethyl 3-methylbutanoate (t), ethyl caprate ($<$1 mg/l), ethyl n-hexenoate ($<$2 mg/l), ethyl trans-2-hexenoate (t), ethyl trans-2-decenoate (t), ethyl 2,4-decadienoates (isomers) (t), 2,5-dimethyl-4-methoxy-3(2H)-furanone ($>$0.15 mg/l), ethyl butanoate ($<$0.03 mg/l), methyl-3-hydroxybutanoate ($>$10 mg/l), ethyl-3-hydroxybutanoate (0.01–1.0 mg/l), ethyl-2-butenoate (0.02–0.33 mg/l), ethyl n-octanoate ($<$2 mg/l), isopentyl octanoate (t), ethyl n-decanoate ($<$3 mg/l), ethyl laurate ($<$0.4 mg/l), diethyl malonate (t), diethyl succinate ($<$20 mg/l), diethyl glutarate (t), ethyl phenylacetate ($<$3 mg/l), and methyl anthranilate ($<$3 mg/l). A mixture of isoamyl ($<$9 mg/l), *n*-hexyl (<1.7 mg/l), and 2-phenethanol acetates and a mixture of ethyl *n*-hexanoate (<1.1 mg/l), ethyl *n*-octanoate (<1.5 mg/l), and ethyl *n*-decanoate (<0.51 mg/l) improved the odor quality and intensity of a white table wine (Van der Merwe and Van Wyk 1981), and a mixture of all six esters improved it even more. This emphasizes the importance of more complex mixtures of odors in the quality of the wine. In apples, the ratio of hexyl acetate to 2- and 3-methylbutyl acetate was roughly related to fruitiness. Isoamyl butyrate and hexyl acetate are reported to decrease during Champagne aging (Loyaux et al. 1981).

Ethyl acid malate, ethyl acid tartrate, and ethyl acid succinate (0.1–>5 mg/l) may contribute some odor. *Cis*- and *trans*-caffeoyl tartrate (55 mg/l), *cis*- and *trans*-coumaroyl tartrate, and *trans*-feruloyl tartrate are present in White Riesling wine. They are believed important as potential browning and oxidation substrates and contribute to bitterness; thus, they should be related to sensory values (Baranowski and Nagel 1981). Similar conclusions were reached by Okamura and Watanabe (1981) with Japanese white wines.

Total esters in new table wines amount to 2–3 millequivalents, whereas in 2 or 3 years they amount to 6 or 7, and in 20 years to 9 or 10 (Peynaud 1981). The basic odor of wines is attributed to four esters (ethyl acetate, isoamyl acetate, ethyl caproate, and ethyl caprylate); two alcohols (isobutyl and isoamyl); and one aldehyde (acetaldehyde) (Avakyants et al. 1981). Other compounds obviously modify this basic odor.

Sugars

Sweetness in wines is due primarily to the reducing sugars glucose and fructose and, to a lesser extent, glycerol and ethanol. The average threshold for detecting sweetness from sugars in wines is about 1.0% by weight (as reducing sugar), although individuals differ widely in their sensitivity to sweetness. We have found individuals who can regularly detect about 0.5% sugar in wines and some who fail to detect as much 2.5%.

We are more sensitive to fructose than to glucose, but by a factor that depends on the fructose concentration itself: we are about 50% more sensitive up to about 5% fructose, and about 35% more sensitive between 5% and 15% fructose. Variation in the fructose/glucose ratio may thus account for some of the differences in the reported sugar thresholds in wines. Wines from grapes of different maturity and wines fermented with various strains of yeasts do have different fructose/glucose ratios. Most sweet wines, however, contain about equal percentages of these sugars. For a detailed discussion of this subject, see Amerine et al. (1965a). Ethanol increases the apparent sweetness of sweet wines; that is, it decreases the absolute thresholds of the sugars. Tannins, however, increase the absolute and difference thresholds of sugars, according to Berg et al. (1955b).

Small amounts of other sugars have been reported: galactose, mannose, cellobiose, melibiose, raffinose, arabinose, rhamnose, xylose, ribose, fucose, a mannoheptulose, a sedoheptulose, four other heptuloses, and an altroheptulose (Amerine and Ough 1980).

Small amounts of 2,3-butanediol are also present in wines and may add to the sweetness; pentoses and some amino acids may also contribute. It can also be shown that ethanol has a "sweet" parameter. One important characteristic of sweet compounds is that, for many people, they reduce the sourness due to the acidity. This is not universally true, however, especially among experienced judges.

Acids

Lactic acid has a distinctive odor. It is D-(+)-lactic acid when formed by yeasts under anaerobic conditions and L-(+)-lactic acid when produced by bacteria. The amount produced by yeast activity is usually below threshold except with special yeasts. Lactic acid is produced remarkably rapidly in table wines under warm conditions by bacteria. Generally the wine loses its fruitiness and becomes gassy. Relatively few of the organic acids found in wines are volatile enough to contribute to their odor. The nonvolatile acids include tartaric ($<$1000–$>$2000 mg/l), malic ($<$50–$>$5000 mg/l), citric (130–400 mg/l), isocitric (t–60 mg/l), succinic (50–750 mg/l), oxalic ($<$90 mg/l), gluconic (t–$<$30.90 mg/l), glucuronic (1–140 mg/l), galactaronic (10–$>$2000 mg/l), tetrahydroxyadipic (t–$>$650 mg/l), adipic ($<$30 mg/l), pimelic ($<$20 mg/l), azelaic ($<$30 mg/l), sebacic ($<$10 mg/l), fumaric ($<$52 mg/l), furan-3,4-carboxylic ($<$10 mg/l), cis-aconitic ($<$50 mg/l), tricarballyhic ($<$10 mg/l), benzoic (t), 4-methybenzoic (t), 2-phenylacetic (t), glycolic ($<$40 mg/l), 2-hydroxypropanoic (0.01–3000 mg/l), 2-hydroxy-3-phenyl-2-hydroxypropanoic (t), 2-methyl-2,3-dihydroxybutanoic (threo) (40–200 mg/l), ditto (erythrol) (t–95 mg/l), glyoxylic (t–6 mg/l), pyruvic (8–50 mg/l), oxalacetic (t–30 mg/l), 2-ketoglutaric (30–60 mg/l), levulinic (t–40 mg/l), 3-hydroxybutanoic (t), lauric (0.18 mg/l), myristic (t), and trans-geranoic (0.06 mg/l).

Of the aliphatic acids one finds formic ($<$60 mg/l), acetic (t–$<$600 mg/l), capronic ($<$1 mg/l), 2-methylpropionic ($<$1 mg/l), 2- and 3-methybutyric ($<$1 mg/l), 3-(methylthio)-propanoic (t), propanoic (t), 2-methylpropanoic (t), n-butanoic (butyric) ($<$0.5 mg/l), 2-methylbutanoic ($<$0.5 mg/l), 3-methylbutanoic ($<$0.5 mg/l), pentanoic (t), hexanoic (1–$>$3 mg/l), ethylhexanoic (t), 2-ethylhexanoic (t), cis-3-hexanoic (t), heptanoic (t), octanoic (2–$>$17 mg/l), nonanoic (t), decanoic (0.5–7 mg/l), 9-decenoic (0.1–0.5 mg/l), undecanoic (t), and dodecanoic ($>$1 mg/l) have been identified. All of these are nearly odorless except acetic (vinegary), butanoic (spoiled butter), and propanoic (goaty). A butanoic limit of 5 mg/l was suggested for New Zealand wines (Robertson et al. 1976). In musts, Corison et al. (1979) reported spoiled thresholds of 0.09%–0.119%. There are 132 acids in wine in Schreier's (1979) list. See also Kepner et al. (1969).

Small amounts (0.03–0.06%) of acetic acid are produced in alcoholic fermentation of sound must with pure yeast cultures. With high-sugar musts (such as from *Botrytis cinerea*) >0.1% may be formed. More is also formed from the juice of the last pressing compared to the first or the free-run. Formic acid is present in the must, but in small amounts.

Sugar acids, such as gluconic, glucuronic, galacturonic, and tetrahydroxyadipic are present in small amounts in wines from normal grapes. Wines from botrytised grapes contain much higher amounts. These acids have little odor, but odorous compounds may be formed from them.

Some other compounds appear to be of little olfactory importance but may have taste and tactile properties: 2-furoic ($<$30 mg/l), 4-hydroxybenzoic ($<$1 mg/l), 3,4-dihydroxybenzoic ($<$5 mg/l), 4-hydroxy-3-methoxybenzoic (vanillic) ($<$5 mg/l), gentisic ($<$5 mg/l), syringic ($<$5 mg/l), shikimic ($<$5 mg/l), quinic ($<$20 mg/l), *o*- and *p*-coumaric ($<$1 and $<$20 mg/l), caffeic ($<$20 mg/l), ferulic ($<$5 mg/l), sinapic ($<$5 mg/l), chlorogenic ($<$20 mg/l), isochlorogenic ($<$1 mg/l), neochlorogenic (t), nicotinic (t), 2-carboxy-5-methoxyindol ($<$10 mg/l), 3-indoylacetic ($<$10 mg/l), and indolylacrylic ($<$10 mg/l).

Gases

Carbon dioxide is present in all wines. Above about 0.5 g/l it may have a tactile sensation. In low-acid white wines, this may have a positive sensory quality. But in red wines above 0.5 g/l, it may give an undesirable prickly sensation. Haushofer and Meier (1981) recommend reducing the carbon dioxide content by vacuum treatment or by stripping with nitrogen.

Wine is the intellectual part of a meal; meats are merely the material part.

A. DUMAS

Music and wine are one.

R. W. EMERSON

CHAPTER 5

Types of Wines

Wines differ from each other because of the composition of the grapes used (color, maturity, region where grown, climatic factors, diseases, etc.), fermentation processes used (time of pressing, settling, centrifugation, yeast flora, temperature, cap management, etc.), and aging (blending, size and time of cooperage, temperature, length of storage, etc.).

In California, climatic zones have been identified as regions I to V, with I being the coolest and V the warmest. The cooler the region, the higher the acidity and color and the slower the accumulation of sugar, and vice versa for the warmest region.

In this chapter, we attempt to distinguish the many basic types of wines, in outline style. For each type, we list the most important (but by no means all) quality factors that must be considered in the sensory evaluation. Because the outline is rather detailed and extends through the entire chapter, it is helpful to get an overview of the material by seeing a condensed form (no text) of the outline, given on the following pages.

The types of wines named are primarily those produced in or imported to the United States. The name of a wine is capitalized when it is that of a specific grape variety or the geographic region in which the wine was actually made, or when it is a proprietary (trademarked) product. The words used to define the flavor and styles of the wines are our own. Obviously it is still too early in California wine history to describe precisely the sensory quality of every type of wine. For a very general discussion of California wine types, see Wine Institute (1978) and Glossary, page 305.

Wines with No Added Flavors

I. Wines having excess carbon dioxide (sparkling and carbonated wines).
   A. Champagne* (*Sekt, spumante, espumante, champagne* and *igristoe vino*).
   B. Pink (or rosé) champagne.
   C. Sparkling burgundy, crackling, and cold duck.
   D. Sparkling muscat: Italy, California.
   E. Low-pressure fermented.
   F. Carbonated.

II. Wines having no excess carbon dioxide (still wines).
   A. Wines having 14% ethanol or less (table wines).
      1. White—having distinguishable varietal character.
         a. *District named: France, Germany, Greece, Spain, Portugal, Italy, United States, Australia, South Africa,* and so on.
         b. *Non-Vitis vinifera.*
         c. *Muscats.*
         d. *V. vinifera.*
      2. White—having no distinguishable varietal aroma (many generic-named California wines, some prestigious Euro-

---

*The problem of nomenclature is evident here. We reserve Champagne for wines produced from the area of that name in France. Otherwise, we use champagne for a generic wine produced outside the delimited region of France.

pean types of off-years. Also areas where no distinctive wine grape varieties are planted, such as much of Argentina, Italy, Spain, Soviet Union, and areas in California.

3. Pink (or rosé).
4. Red—having distinguishable varietal character.
   a. *District named:* See II.A.1.a.
   b. *Non-V. vinifera.*
   c. *Muscats.*
   d. *Varietal named:* The Cabernet family and others.
5. Red—having no distinguishable varietal character. See II.A.1a, 2.

B. Wines having more than 14% ethanol (dessert wines).

1. Sherry—dry
   a. *Baked process:* California.
   b. *Yeast process on surface:* Spain, Australia, South Africa, Soviet Union.
   c. *Yeast process in submerged culture:* California, Canada, Soviet Union.
2. Sherry—sweet.
   a. *Baked process:* California.
   b. *Aging process:* Spain, Australia, South Africa.
3. Madeira.
4. Málaga: Spain.
5. Marsala: Sicily.
6. Muscatel: many countries.
7. Port: red and white; various countries.
8. Tokaj: Hungary (most often less than 14%).

Wines with Added Flavors

I. Herb-based.

A. Vermouth—dry: many countries.

B. Vermouth—sweet: many countries.

C. Byrrh: France.

D. Dubonnet: France.

II. Fruit-based and fruit-flavor-based.

Wines with No Added Flavors

Wine was originally just fermented grape juice; that is, no flavors were added. The most numerous and important types of commercial wines still fall in this category. Our discussion of them constitutes the bulk of this chapter.

I. Wines having excess carbon dioxide (sparkling and carbonated wines).

At least four different types of sparkling wine are produced: fermented in the bottle; fermented in the bottle, transferred to a tank, and filtered into the bottles; fermented in tanks of over 2 gallons; and carbonated.

A. Champagne (*Sekt* [Germany], *spumante* [Italy], *espumante* [Portugal and Spain], *igristoe vino* [Soviet Union], champagne or sparkling wine [United States].

Sparkling wines produced by bottle fermentation should be light yellow, the exact tint of which will vary depending on whether the base wine was made from white grapes or from a blend of musts from white and red grapes. (Wines made from the blend will be slightly darker.) The varietal character will be subdued. There must be an appreciable bouquet due to bottle aging in contact with the yeast. Enologists consider 1–2 years before disgorging to be necessary. The wine must have enough acid that the secondary fermentation in the bottle is free of bacterial growth. These wines should not be too acidulous.

From the standpoint of marketing, the finer the quality (aroma, bouquet, taste, and flavor) of the sparkling wine, the drier it should be. Since the base cuvée is always a blend, the winemaker has the opportunity to introduce complexity and individuality by selecting wines of varying composition and character. The more common problems of bottle-fermented champagnes are a yeasty odor when they are disgorged too soon after fermentation, excess acidity due to the use of unripe grapes, and too obvious a varietal flavor.

In France, Chardonnay and Pinot noir grapes are preferred for Champagne (the Pinot noir being crushed by pressing). Because of the very cool climatic conditions of the Champagne region, the earlyripening Pinot noir is needed to ensure adequate sugar. The new wines have only about 9% to 10% ethanol. Even in Champagne in warm seasons, Chardonnay ripens sufficiently to produce a balanced wine by itself. Often the wine is sold at a high price as blanc de blancs.

In other years, wines of both varieties and even some older wine are blended to give the necessary minimum ethanol content and flavor. In other parts of France, sparkling wines are produced from Chenin blanc, Clairette blanche, and other varieties. In Germany, imported white wines or wines made from less-ripe White Riesling grapes from the cooler years are often used for blending. The aromatic character of ripe-grape White Riesling wines is a disadvantage. In other European countries, various varieties of neutral-flavored grapes are used for blending.

In California, a large number of varieties have been and are employed. For the best sparkling wines, Chardonnay and Pinot noir are used by several companies. Because of the warm climatic conditions of California, these varieties are harvested very early (often in August). Individual wineries have varying preferences—some prefer only 10% ethanol, others 11%. Other wineries use Chenin blanc or Sylvaner. Traditionally, Burger, Folle blanche, and Green Hungarian were popularly, but these varieties are now (thankfully) seldom available. If quality is not a consideration, Thompson Seedless wine has been used (but the grapes should be harvested very early). French Colombard has been used for its acidity, but winemakers should blend down or out its distinctive flavor. Complexity, not strength of character, and a fruity flavor with no off-odor should be looked for.

Sparkling wines made by the bulk or tank process or by the transfer process can and do differ in character from those produced by the bottle process. There are at least two reasons for this: the former wines are not normally aged on the yeast, and there is some oxidation associated with transfer of the wine or with filtration. Such wines have appreciably more acetaldehyde. To prevent the early development of an oxidized odor, some sulfur dioxide is often added to fix the acetaldehyde. Again, the best sparkling wines are usually the driest, but sweeter types are available for those who prefer them. Although brut is the driest type, the brut of some producers is sweeter than it should be. Sparkling wines labeled brut should have less than 1.5% sugar, and 1% is better. Extra dry wines should not have more than 3% sugar. The distinction between extra dry and sec is not clearly defined or maintained in practice. One or the other of these designations would suffice. Few doux or sweet sparkling nonmuscat wines are produced in California. Tastes differ. Most Soviet sparkling wines are sweet.

Important quality problems with sparkling wines are lack of pressure, rapid loss of gassiness (the bubbles are then large), oxidation (accompanied by early darkening of the color), lack of acidity, and a yeasty or sulfide odor (due to the use of too much yeast and/or too high a fermentation temperature).

Though everyone admits that the bouquet of the finest bottle-fermented sparkling wines is due to the autolysis of yeast during 2 or more years' aging on the yeast, the biochemical mechanism is unknown. Feuillat (1980) reported 2-methyl-2-ethoxyfurane, 4,5-dimethyltetrahydroxyfurane-2,3-dione, 5-ethoxybutyrolactone, 4-ethylphenol, and 4-ethylguaiacol to be components of this bouquet. In Champagne wines, Loyaux et al. (1981) reported increases in total volatile content the first year. Thereafter, hexyl acetate, isoamyl butyrate, nerolidol, and the monoterpene alcohols decreased. Benzaldehyde and vitispirane increased up to 16 years.

Enologists also agree that bottle-fermented wines should be aged at a relatively low (10°C, 50°F) temperature. With sparkling muscat wines, Castino and Di Stefano (1981) reported color and quality deterioration when the wines were stored 470 days at 20°C (68°F) compared with storage at 10°C (50°F). The terpene alcohols and fatty acid esters were much lower in the wines stored at 10°C (50°F).

B. Pink (or rosé) champagne.

A pink color without amber, orange, or purple is desired. Of course, the finished product should be brilliantly clear. The best pink champagnes, in our opinion, are those that have a tart, fruity flavor and that have been finished with less than about 2% sugar. Nevertheless, some commercial products are low in acid, flat-tasting, and contain 3% sugar or more.*

C. Sparkling burgundy and cold duck.

A sparkling red wine called sparkling burgundy has been marketed for many years. In recent years, some sparkling red wines have been labeled cold duck. We have been unable to find any consistent chemical or flavor differences between the two types. Cold duck seems more often to have some Con-

---

*For these and other wines, we wish that the producers would use appropriate and uniform labeling to enable the purchaser to distinguish the dry wines from the moderately sweet, as in some Canadian provincial goverment stores.

cord flavor, but sparkling burgundy with a Concord flavor has been made in New York and Ohio since before Prohibition.

Most sparkling red wines contain about 5% sugar. With less sugar, such wines have a bitter and astringent character due to the interaction of the tannins and the carbon dioxide ($>$400–600 mg/l). This sensation is objectionable to the consumer. Adding sugar helps to cover the bitterness and astringency. If there were a demand for higher-quality sparkling red wines, we believe more attention would be paid to making the blend and reducing the sweetness. So far the demand appears to be small, in Europe or the United States or elsewhere.

D. Sparkling muscat.

Only a few wines of this type are produced; most of those on the United States market are from Italy. The reason there are so few is possibly because a muscat flavor may be too strong and distinctive and the palate soon tires of it. Such wines usually contain 8% to 11% ethanol. They are always made very sweet because the muscat-flavored wines without sugar are almost always flat- and bitter-tasting. A high sugar content overcomes these defects but also tires the palate.

Because the muscat grapes are harvested when fully ripe (to secure good flavor and sugar), the color tends to be yellow-gold. With aging, of course, it darkens. One accepts this unless the flavor is frankly oxidized (sherrylike).

E. Low-pressure fermented wines.

A wide variety of wines of this type is now produced. The "pearl" wines, which originated in Germany, are tank-fermented wines. They have only 1 to 2 atmospheres of pressure and are more often than not on the sweet side. Some are higher in sulfur dioxide than others. They have not yet achieved a large market in the United States or, so far as we know, elsewhere.

F. Carbonated wines.

Because fully carbonated wines are heavily taxed in the United States, they are almost as expensive as regular sparkling wines. Although United States regulations now permit a relatively high degree of carbonation without the excessive tax of a fully carbonated wine, these lightly carbonated wines so far have attracted only a small market. Carbonated wines are seldom produced in the United States. Some have a fruit-grape wine base. Unfortunately, some are too sweet, in our opinion. We suspect that they are often served over ice as an inexpensive substitute for a cocktail (with or without the addition of bitters).

One variant is the low-ethanol, low-carbon dioxide moscato amabile of the L. M. Martini winery in California. The muscat must is fermented at very low temperature—about 0°C (32°F)—for a year or more. When the fermentation slows down or "sticks," the wine is filtered and bottled. Enough carbon dioxide remains to give the wine perceptible gassiness. The ethanol content may be only 8% and the sugar content up to 10%. The wine is not only strong in muscat flavor but also retains some of its fermentation (yeasty) odor. As with all strong-flavored wines, the first glass is very pleasant, but the muscat odor and high sweetness may limit the appeal of subsequent glasses. One disadvantage of the wine is that it is not fermentation-stable and the bottled wine must be kept refrigerated.

II. Wines having no excess carbon dioxide (still wines).

A. Wines having 14% ethanol or less (table wines).

This group of wines is distinguished from all the rest not only by definition but also with respect to legal and tax considerations. Generally, the lowest taxes are paid on these unflavored still wines having 14% ethanol or less.

1. White—having distinguishable varietal character.

The most important requirement of this large group of wines is that they have a recognizable varietal character. Not all wines carrying varietal names meet this requirement, owing to their neutral character under too warm or cool a climate for the grapes, overcropping, harvesting too soon, or excessive blending with neutral-flavored wines.

It is possible to distinguish Chardonnay, French Colombard, and White Riesling by headspace analysis (Noble et al. 1980). As many as 19 peaks were necessary by principal component anlaysis. Using stepwise discriminate analysis, 24 wines were correctly separated into the three varieties using discrimination functions with five components. This, of course, holds true only for the varieties indicated under the conditions in which the grapes were grown and the fermentation, treatment, and aging processes employed. See also pages 289–303.

The most common infirmities of this group of wines (besides lack of varietal character) are excessive sulfur dioxide, too dark or light a color, an oxidized odor, and cloudiness (from bacteria, yeast, or excess metal). Some white table wines are too noticeably high in wood (oak) flavor, from being aged in new or old barrels for too long. Our rule is that if you can identify the odor as woody, it is excessive. The woody odor should be a subtle, indistinguishable aspect of the complexity of the wine.

Excessive ethanol content (over 14%) is not illegal if one pays the higher tax. However, experience shows that dry white table wines with more than 14% ethanol are usually too low in acidity, alcoholic, and often have off-odors from overripe or moldy grapes. Sweet table wines made from botrytised grapes can have slightly more than

14% ethanol without deterioration. Even among the sweet types, some of the best are not high in ethanol: many German *Auslese* types have only 8% to 10%, for example.

a. *District named. France:* Chablis (Chardonnay), Graves (Sauvignon blanc and Sémillon), Mâcon, Meursault, Montrachet, Pouilly-Fuissé (all Chardonnay), Sancerre (Sauvignon blanc), and so on. Alsace has varietal wines from White Riesling, Sylvaner, Gewürztraminer, and other varieties.

Germany: Franken, Mosel (Piesport*), Rheingau (Hattenheim*), Rheinhessen, and so on. White Riesling, Sylvaner, Müller-Thurgau and a number of new hybrids are used.

A few varietally distinct white wines are produced in Italy, Greece and Spain. Pinot gris (Pinot griglio), Traminer, and Walschriesling (Italian Riesling) may be noted in Italy. In Austria, Hungary, Yugoslavia, and Romania, one finds several white table wines with distinctive varietal odors, likewise in Australia, South Africa and the United States.

Some of the district-labeled wines may also have varietal labels. Many have both the district and the vineyard given on the label. District labels are meaningful only when the varieties and methods of production used in the district in question are standardized and, of course, when the district is capable of producing distinctive wines. Not all districts are.

The distinctiveness of varietal character varies markedly depending on the region and the season, the time of harvest, the amount of overcropping, and the amount of blending with neutral-flavored wines.

---

*Name of village within district. The label may also have the vineyard name.

b. *Non-Vitis vinifera.* The varieties of apparent *V. la-brusca* parentage (Catawba, Concord, Delaware, Ives Seedling, Niagara, and some of the old *V. vinifera* × *V. labrusca* direct-producer hybrids) are characterized by an odor—the so-called foxy or American grape juice odor. The odor may be so distinctive, to be unpleasant to some consumers. According to Reynolds et al. (1982), this odor has been called "foxy" since at least 1908. It may be so obvious that one tires of it easily. Hybrids that do not contain *V. labrusca* (*V. vinifera* × *V. rupestris*, × *V. lincecumnii*, × etc.) often do not have this odor or have it only mildly. Stevens et al. (1965) suggested methyl-3-buten-2-ol to be of significance, as well as ethyl acetate. The latter had been reported earlier. Stern et al. (1967) considered crotonate esters, an alkylthio ester, as well as ethyl acetate and methyl anthranilate to be important in *V. labrusca* cultivars or hybrids.

Fuleki (1975) used the sum of the methyl anthranilate and total volatile esters (the Vineland Grape Flavor Index) as an index to "labrusca" flavor. Inheritance of this flavor appears to be a dominant character (Reynolds et al. 1982), making it difficult to eliminate the foxiness by breeding.

Acree (1981) showed that compounds other than methyl anthranilate contribute to the characteristic odor of Catawba grapes. He reported *trans*-2-hexen-1-ol, damascenone, and furaneol, but not methyl anthranilate, to be important. However, Schreier and Paroschy (1981) found methyl anthranilate in large amounts in Concord (*V. labrusca*) and Niagara grapes. They also found methyl- and ethyl-3-hydroxybutano-ate, ethyl-2-butenoate, and 2,5-dimethyl-4-methoxy 3(2H)-furanone (caramellike). Elvira (*V. riparia*) contained only trace amounts of these. They consider the question of whether the "labrusca" aroma is due to one or a number of compounds to be undecided. Surely more than one compound is involved.

We have had too little experience with native and direct-producer wines to comment on their flavor characteristics. We find Catawba, Delaware, Niagara, and other native varieties to be of such a strong foxy flavor that it is difficult to cultivate a taste for them. Amerine and Singleton (1976) give the following description: Beta (grassy); Cascade (prunish, bituminous); Chambourein (fruity, tarry); Chelois (fruity, spicy); Colobel (bitter, "hybrid"); Rosette (bitter); Seyval blanc (fruity, pommade—i.e., perfumed); Verdelet (fruity, spicy); Vidal blanc (hybrid, coarse); and Vignoles (fruity, crisp).

In hybrids with *V. labrusca,* Rapp et al. (1980b) have identified 2,5-dimethyl-4-hydroxy-2,3-dihydro-3-furanone and 2,5-dimethyl-4-methoxy-2,3-dihydro-3-furanone. Both had a strawberrylike aroma (others say raspberrylike). Cobb et al. (1978) identified 26 compounds in Aurore, a popular hybrid.

V. rotundifolia is a native of the southeastern United States. A number of cultivars have been developed: Summit, Magnolia, and Carlos for the whites. Their aroma is distinctive and quite different from *V. labrusca* or *V. vinifera* or hybrids of the two. Phenethanol, benzyl acetate, and other compounds are responsible for the odor. Wines of *V. rotundifolia* grapes are said to be nonfoxy. All or most of them are sold sweet.

c. *Muscats.* The muscat family—Flora, Gewürztraminer, Gold, Malvasia bianca, Muscat of Alexandria, Muscat blanc, Orange Muscat, Muscat Ottonel, and many other muscats—have a pronounced odor of linalool oxide, nerol, *cis*-linalool oxide, and geraniol (see page 72). The possibility of a legal control on minimum levels of these compounds is interesting. No one should find it difficult to identify this floral odor, or even the nuances of odor among different varieties. Some wines made from ripe White Riesling grapes have a slight, but distinct, muscatlike odor. Research has revealed that the ripe fruit of this variety also contains linalool (Van Wyk et al. 1967).

A number of table and dessert wines have been produced from Muscat blanc (Muscat Canelli, Muscat Frontignan) and Muscat of Alexandria grapes in California. The table wine types have usually been high in muscat aroma and sweet (5%–15% sugar). If they have a fault, it is their generally low acidity, but the high sugar helps to offset this. The Muscat blanc has a fruitier muscat aroma than Muscat of Alexandria. Its wines are sometimes labeled Muscat de Frontignan. Similar types are produced in Australia, France, Portugal, and the Soviet Union. Some have retained their muscat character for many years but they eventually darken in color.

We have had mixed experiences with Flora (a cross between Sémillon and Gewürztraminer). Commercial samples have rarely been distinctive. However, the grapes were usually from young, and probably overcropped, vines. Some experimental samples have been fruity and spicy but not as distinctive as the wines of Gewürztraminer. Flora has only been produced by a few California wineries, and the standards for the type are not yet clearly established. Possibly its future is as a sweet table wine. Whether it is spicy enough to develop consumer recognition is not known. A sparkling wine from this variety has been more successful.

Gewürztraminer has a delicate to intense and unmistakably floral and spicy muscatlike aroma. It is a small producer and matures its fruit early in the season. This presents a critical problem for the grape grower as the grapes can become overripe in a few hot days. A range of types have been produced—from low-acid, rather heavy alcoholic ($>12\%$) wines that are flat and often oxidize easily, to some delightfully spicy, relatively low alcohol (11%), slightly sweet (1%– 2% sugar) wines. Generally, Gewürztraminer wines should be consumed when relatively young (1 to 5 years).

Sauvignon vert (believed to be the Muscadelle of Bordeaux) is also a muscat-flavored variety. In California, it is subject to attack by bees and acetification. The wines have often been flat and bitter; the variety is not recommended for California, and its acreage in Bordeaux has been decreasing. At its best, it should have a spicy, low-muscat odor.

Emerald Riesling is another muscat-flavored variety. It was released in California because of its distinctive flavor and high acidity. It has not been planted by many growers because winemakers object to its pulpy musts, the tendency of its musts and wines to darken in color, and the slightly bitter taste in its dry wines. Nevertheless, it is an excellent producer and its high acidity is an asset for a muscat-flavored variety. Perhaps it should be tried for a slightly sweet instead of a dry type. It should not be unduly blended.

d. *V. vinifera*. Aligoté is a secondary variety of the Burgundy region of France, where it has the reputation of producing rather neutral tart wines. It produces probably twice as much as the Chardonnay, but its wines there are not worth much. It has found a happier home in the Soviet Union. There it produces rather neutral white wines, used both for still and for sparkling wines. It is not, however, entirely neutral in flavor and deserves its place as a varietal type. Perhaps someone will find a place for it elsewhere.

Chardonnay (not Pinot Chardonnay) wine has an entrancing, applelike, ripe-grape aroma. It has also been characterized as hazelnut-, fig- or melon-like. At its best, it is one of the most intriguing of all wine aromas. During aging in the cask and/or bottle, its character changes from simple and fruity to complex. Nevertheless, the varietal character should not be overpowered by an obviously woody odor as it sometimes is in Australia, California, and France. However, this is a command decision of the winemaker. In California, Chardonnays vary from low-ethanol (10%– 11%), no-oak, and low-varietal aroma to high ethanol ($>$13%), frankly oaky (some with vanillinlike), and very distinct varietal aroma, and gradations between these extremes. Some wineries (in California and France) have had problems with stuck fermentations, and slightly sweet (1%–2% residual sugar) Chardonnays have appeared on the market. We consider these aberrant types.

Wines made from the same clone of Chardonnay growing under three different soil conditions in California did not differ significantly in aroma or composition (Noble 1979) when the skins were left in contact with the juice for up to 16 hours. During contact, total flavonoids and nonflavonoids, phenolics, and "total" and "fruity" aromas as determined by sensory evaluation increased. Bitterness and astringency did not significantly increase (Arnold and Noble 1979).

There are differences between Chardonnays produced in different climatic regions. This is partially due to differences in degree of maturity when harvested. Noticeable free sulfur dioxide is to be deplored. The vines are small producers, and high-quality Chardonnays will always be expensive. The wines age well in the bottle. They darken very slowly. We have seen some 15-year old Chardonnays with a fine full yellow color and an excellent bouquet. The ripe-grape and faintly applelike aroma should be looked for.

Chenin blanc (Pineau blanc de la Loire; Steen or White Pinot by error) is a native of the Loire in France but it is now found in Australia, South Africa, and particularly in California. It bears well, sometimes too well, and its fruit has a tendency to bunch rot in rainy periods. In California, it is grown in regions I to V. In recent years, it has been widely planted in regions IV and V as a general-purpose grape for a sparkling-wine base or California chablis. The wines should be fruity and very mildly aromatic. They are not great wines but they are pleasant: those made from less-ripe grapes are grassy or flowery in aroma; those made from riper grapes have a guavalike odor (possibly 2,4-decandienal isomers, Augostyn and Rapp 1982)—of recognizable character at their best, especially when grown in cooler regions. As in France, some have from 1% to 5% sugar.

Folle blanche is believed to be a native of France, where it was once used for distilling material. Whether it is the same as the variety of this name in France has been questioned. In Australia and California, it produces small crops and is subject to mildew and irregular crops. But its wines are pleasantly fruity, tart, and slightly, but not overly, distinctive. They have been used for sparkling-wine cuvées because of their low-ethanol and high-acid content. Perhaps the burden of irregular small crops is too much for the variety to stand in California or elsewhere. It is also grown to a limited extent in Argentina.

French Colombard (either Colombard or Colombar is correct) is very widely planted in regions II to V in California. Small acreages are found in France (where it originated), South Africa, Australia, and elsewhere. It is a fine producer, and the musts have a good acidity (and relatively low pH). The problem of the vineyardist is to harvest when the varietal aroma is not too obvious nor the acidity too low. The fermentations are exemplary, and, in many respects, it is a winemaker's dream. The musts, especially late in the season, may require clarification by centrifuging. The wines clarify well.

The wines are not neutral-flavored as once thought. In fact, a number of dry table wines under this name are on the market deservedly, in our opinion. We do not know how to characterize the distinctive aroma of the wines—perhaps spicy and not aromatic. Enologists usually say the wines have a strong, coarse (strawlike?) flavor, but we do not quite know what they mean. It is sufficiently pronounced as not to be favored as an ingredient in sparkling-wine cuvées. We do not say it is a great wine, but it is different in aroma from other varieties.

Grey Riesling (probably really Trousseau gris) is apparently from France (in spite of the name). It is a vigorous vine and produces well. The fruit is usually very clean, and it ferments well. With a few exceptions, California Grey Riesling wines have been sold as dry table wines. Unfortunately the variety ripens very early and, if not picked promptly, will make flat-tasting wines. If picked too soon, it lacks the spicy-fruity aroma. At best, its wines are pleasant drinking wines with no great pretensions: certainly not Rieslinglike.

Helena is found, so far as we know, only in California. Only a few wines labeled Helena have been marketed. Amerine and Singleton (1976) could only call its wines fruity. Others have not been so kind. Further trials to find the best conditions for producing a quality wine from this variety are obviously needed.

The Müller-Thurgau grape ripens early and is hence particularly well adapted to cool climates (Germany, New Zealand, etc.). In the best years, its wines have a distinct, but modest, muscat (i.e., floral) odor. Others—that is, those from unripe grapes—are nearly neutral.

Pinot blanc (Melon on the lower Loire is the same or a very similar variety and is the preferred name) is grown in California, but only in limited areas. It bears moderate crops of good-quality grapes. The musts are often murky, and the new wines darken in color easily. The musts should be clarified as the skins are high in flavonols. Otherwise the wines may be bitter-tasting. Moderately distinctive flavors (weedy?) are reported. At their best, they are fruity and well balanced.

Pinot gris (Pinot griglio, Ruländer) is an early ripening grape from France. It has been widely grown in Bulgaria, Great Britain, Italy, Romania, and the Soviet Union. There it is used for producing dry and sweet table wines. The vines are not productive, but can be overcropped, and the fruit ripens early. Its aroma is described as fruity–aromatic but we are not sure we could recognize it. It is not recommended for planting in warm regions, such as regions III to V in California. How many sweet white table wines do we need?

Rkatsiteli is very widely grown in the Soviet Union, where it produces wines somewhat like French Colombard—tart and fruity. It is a good producer. The wines are not very distinctive, either in the Soviet Union or California, and are certainly not recommended for a varietal type here.

In California, Sauvignon blanc (Fumé blanc) wines range from very fruity low ethanol (11%) to richer moderate ethanol (12%–13%), with various intermediate types. Some of its wines have had a noticeable oaky odor, but most do not and they should not. As with Chardonnay, the odor of free sulfur dioxide should be unobtrusive. From the growers', winemakers', and consumers' point of view, Sauvignon blanc is a fine variety—good production, clean fermentations, and, at the moderate ethanol levels, the wines age well in the bottle. Some Livermore Sauvignon blancs at 15 years were light gold in color and had a fine bouquet. While preferences are personal, some of the best California white table wines have been made from this variety. One obtained the only grand prix for a white table wine in the San Francisco International judging of 1938.

Sauvignon blanc has a distinctive, somewhat grassy, weedy, or smoky aroma that is easily recognized. It has some of the so-called green olive and herbaceous odor found in Cabernet Sauvignon. If the grapes are mature and yellow, the wines will have this odor. This variety yields distinctively flavored wines in many regions of the world. When the grapes are grown in cooler regions, their aroma may be quite intense. Under milder climatic conditions, the strong aroma is attenuated but still easily recognized. When the vines are overcropped, the fruit has a less distinctive aroma.

The varietal aroma is not lost when the wine is aged in the bottle for several years. These wines retain their gold color for many years. We prefer the full California style to the smoky style of some California and many French Sauvignon blancs. The varietal name is used rather lightly in Argentina, Chile, Italy, and Yugoslavia. The grassy odor is attributed to methxyprazines and possibly to methional and methionol (Augustyn et al. 1982).

Mature Sémillon grapes can be identified by their slightly pink blush. At this stage, the fruit has a distinctive aroma that is transmitted to the wine. Its aroma has been characterized as figlike or melonlike and even cigarlike—descriptions that do not seem appropriate to us. Rather than confuse the semantics, we prefer to call it simply the Sémillon aroma. It is less spicy than those of Sauvignon blanc or Chardonnay.

Generally, the musts have a normal fermentation, and dry wines result. Both dry and slightly sweet (2%–5% sugar) Sémillon wines have been produced—by themselves in California and Australia and blended with Sauvignon blanc in Graves (France). A few dry Sémillons have been thin and acidulous (usually from over-cropped unripe grapes). Others have a rich, full flavor, though a slight bitterness may develop with age—inherent or bacterial? The wines should not be oaky.

Sylvaner (Franken Riesling by error) is not widely planted in California, and, even in Germany and Alsace, except in special areas, it occupies a secondary place to White Riesling. Its wines are not as distinctive. It is a good producer, but the wines are only moderately flowery, fruity, grapey, or distinctive. The fermentations are normal, and the producer seldom has problems with the wines, except the worst problem of all—they are only occasionally outstanding. In California, they are too low in acid (except in region I or II) unless picked early in the season. The aroma has been described as flowery, but this gives it too much credit.

Veltliner (Red and White Veltliner) is widely grown in Austria and has been tried experimentally and commercially in California. It is productive, but the wines are only slightly distinctive—not recommended but a pleasant wine that might form an alternative to Chenin blanc somewhere. But where? The clones tried in California have had a tendency to overcropping.

Walschriesling (Italian Riesling by error) is possibly a Central European native. It has, so far, not been recommended for California though it is widely grown in Bulgaria, Hungary, Italy, Romania, and Yugoslavia. The vine is not very big, but the crops are regular and the fermentations are good. We have not been able to find much distinctive aroma in its wines nor any compelling reason to recommend it for California.

White Riesling (Johannisberg Riesling and Rhine Riesling are less desirable) yields a wine with a fruity-floral, even spicy, apricotlike, or muscatlike aroma when ripe grapes are used. As Van Wyk et al. (1967) and others have shown, White Riesling does indeed contain terpineol alcohols and hence an aromatic floral aroma. If White Riesling is brought to full maturity in a warm season or region in Califorina, the berries may brown, and, in the warmer regions or seasons, the acidity of the juice is too low. California producers of a dry White Riesling wine should normally harvest the fruit before it reaches full maturity, even if the varietal aroma of the resulting wine is reduced. Use of late-harvested White Riesling has become a vogue in California in recent years. If the grapes are sound when attacked by the mold *Botrytis cinerea,* which causes shriveling and results in a high sugar content, high-quality sweet table wines may be produced. When the botrytis attacks unsound grapes, moldy-smelling wines result. Unfortunately some of both types have been produced in California. The German late-harvest types usually are only made when botrytis attacks sound grapes.

The whole gamut of White Riesling types is produced in California—from tart low-alcohol (10%–11%), dry wines to moderate-alcohol (12%), slightly sweet (2%–3% sugar) types, to low-alcohol (10%–11%) very sweet (10%–20% sugar) wines. These vary in color from light yellow, slightly greenish wines to gold. The drier types mature within a year or two. The sweeter types may last for 10 or more years. One accepts a slight, but not too pronounced, free sulfur dioxide odor in White Rieslings. The fermentations seldom cause trouble. Unfortunately, it is a relatively small producer, and the wines, especially of the late-harvest types, will be priced accordingly. The botrytis odor of the late-harvest types should not have a moldy odor.

2. White—having no distinguishable varietal aroma.

The following varieties do not appear to us to have sufficient varietal aroma to justify their wines being labeled with the name of the variety: Burger, Chasselas doré, Diamant, Feher Szagos, Green Hungarian, Malaga, Palomino, Thompson Seedless (Sultanina, Sultana [Australia], Kishmish), and Ugni blanc (Trebbiano in Italy). With favorable microclimates and special processing, some may be able to graduate to the previous group. Trebbiano is widely grown in Italy to produce *denominazione di origine controllata* (DOC) wines. We do not know why, because the wines are quite neutral.

In the United States, such wines are usually labeled with semigeneric names, such as California chablis and

New York rhine. In Europe, many such neutral wines have district or proprietary names—for example, many Portuguese, Spanish, Italian, Chilean, Argentinean, Australian, Russian, and Greek wines, including some with varietal labels. Contrary to the opinions of wine snobs, good and occasional fine wines can be found in this class. Many blended white table wines that are made from good varieties grown under proper climatic conditions, harvested at optimum maturity, and properly processed and aged can be of sound character and pleasant to drink. Unfortunately, how much will the public pay for a California chablis?

The main problem with these semigeneric wines is that there are usually no recognized standards to ensure that the wine has the desired typical character, except for the standards that the producers themselves may impose, more or less regularly. For example, several California wineries have blended a superior chablis for years. Other wineries produce chablis that taste flat and lack character or quality.

In an attempt to bring some order into this chaos, Amerine et al. (1980) recommended that California chablis be dry and California rhine be sweet. There is no evidence to date that this recommendation has been heeded. In fact, both California chablis and California rhine are now more likely to be sweet than dry. At present, many semigeneric type names are gradually disappearing in the United States. The names California or American white chianti, dry sauterne, hock, moselle, and the like are now rarely used.

3. Pink (or rosé).

At one time these were all dry pink wines. They have been labeled Grenache rosé or Gamay rosé or simply rosé.

Some California Pinot noirs also belong in this group. Occasionally a Cabernet or Zinfandel rosé has been produced. Aside from the attraction of the name, they are seldom of particular merit compared to the corresponding red wines. Rosés are produced in France (Loire, Tavel, and Provence), Italy, and elsewhere. Some Portuguese wines are really rosés, although they are not labeled as such.

The consumer's problem is how to distinguish the dry rosé from the sweet rosé. The best policy (already recommended, page 47) would be for the producer to state the sugar content on the label. Failing that, one can only guess whether the wine will be dry or sweet. We prefer the tart, fruity, dry rosés.

Unfortunately Grenache is not the best variety for producing a rosé in the Central Valley of California. Because of the prestige of the name Grenache, however, a great deal of this variety planted there has been made into rosé wine. In the hot climate of the Central Valley, the color of the wine is likely to be orange-pink and the taste distressingly flat. Rosé wines should be pink, not amber, orange, or purple. A fruity character is essential, and that requires a good total acidity in the must and the wine. For this reason, we doubt that the wines should be aged for more than a year or two. With few exceptions, we prefer rosés with 11% to 12% ethanol rather than 12% to 14%.

4. Red—having distinguishable varietal character.

As with the analogous white wines (section 1 above), the most important requirement for this group of wines is recognizable varietal character. Similarly, the main problem is the lack of that character due to too warm or too cool a climate for the grapes, overcropping, harvesting too soon, or excessive blending with neutral-flavored wines. A

Pinot noir with less than 10% ethanol can seldom have enough Pinot noir aroma to make a fine and recognizable wine. Growing the grapes in too warm a region or harvesting them too late often results in raisin flavors and an unpalatable dessert-wine or warm-climate character. These practices also yield wines that may never mature. We are not in sympathy with some California red table wines of 15% and 16% ethanol that have appeared on the market, nor with similar, high-ethanol wines produced in Yugoslavia (Dingač wines in Dalmatia) and Spain (Priorato region) when these wines are sold as table wines.

Another, more difficult, problem is deciding how long red table wines should be aged. Too many potentially fine red Bordeaux and Australian and California Cabernet Sauvignons have been and are being drunk too soon—long before they have reached their best quality from bottle aging. But who is to store the wines the requisite time? For the producers, it entails serious financial problems. Consumers often do not have the space to store the wines, or at least not at a suitable temperature. In Argentina and Chile, the problems are overcropping of good varieties, overblending, and often overaging of their wines.

a. *District named. France:* Beaujolais (Gamay), Bordeaux (blends), Burgundy (Pinot noir), Châteauneuf-du-Pape (blends), Hermitage (Syrah), Médoc (Cabernet Sauvignon, Merlot, etc. in blends), Pomerol (blends), Rhône (blends), Saint-Émilion (blends), and so on.

Italy: Barolo (Nebbiolo, etc.). Not distinctive.

Spain: Rioja (blends). Slightly distinctive.

Of the hundreds of Portuguese, Spanish, Italian, Yugoslavian, and Greek red table wines with district labels and without varietal labels, most do not have a distinguishable varietal character, or at least not consistently.

b. *Non–V. vinifera.* Red *V. labrusca* cultivars include Concord, Ives Seedling, and many others. The foxy flavor of their wines is strong. Alicante Bouschet (and Grand noir de la Calmette and Petite Bouschet) have all been grown in California, but in decreasing amounts. They are direct producers. The Alicante Bouschet produces well and its juice is red. If fermented with the skins, its wines can be very dark and high in bitter and astringent phenolics. Pressed off the skins before fermentation, it produces tart wines with a fruity herbaceous aroma. We have not found them to age well. It is significant that these varieties did not establish themselves in many countries—only in California, where their high color produced 700 gallons per ton of red wine during Prohibition (with sugar and water) and in the south of France, and Algeria (for blending). They are also good shipping grapes because of their thick skins and thus recommended themselves to the home winemaker who was more interested in volume than quality. Of the other red direct producers, Baco noir (herbaceous, astringent), De Chaunac, Foch, Royalty, Rubired (horehound), and Salvador (harsh) are commercially produced. (Descriptions from Amerine and Singleton, 1976.) Red cultivars of *V. rotundifolia* include Tarbell, Regale, and Noble.

c. *Muscats.* Aleatico and Muscat Hamburg are red muscat-flavored varieties. Few red table wines have been made from them, probably because they are too low in acidity.

d. *Varietal named.* The Cabernet family and others: Many varietal-labeled red table wines, both in the United States and abroad, have little recognizable aroma of the grape for which they are named. These include some of the direct-producer varieties and many

Italian so-called varietals. Even when the grape could have a recognizable varietal character, from being grown on trees or arbors or being too lightly pruned, it may be overcropped to the point of extinction of this character—for example, in Argentina. We have known some California producers to boast of their 10- to 12-ton-per-acre yields of Ruby Cabernet. Unfortunately, the wines smelled and tasted like it.

Barbera is a native of northern Italy, where it is responsible for wines of this name. The vines are only of moderate vigor and production, though under irrigated conditions in California it can be pushed to 6–8 tons per acre. In regions I and II, it has a high total acidity, which in Italy is protected and is found in the wine, sometimes to an acidulous taste. In regions IV and V in California, its wines are better balanced. They have not been very distinctive in aroma. Without the characteristic fruity–tart flavor they are not easy to recognize. Some region I and II wines in California that underwent a malolactic fermentation and have been aged in the wood and bottle acquire after 5 to 10 years a desirable bouquet. They are quite different from what would be considered characteristic Barbera wine in Italy.

Cabernet franc is a native of France. In the Graves, Pomerol, and St. Émilion regions, it is common, but less so in the Médoc. It is also grown in the Soviet Union (where its relative, Cabernet Sauvignon, is preferred). Some microclimate adaptation must account for its preference in certain areas because it produces less and has less color and possibly less flavor than Cabernet Sauvignon. The aroma is described as green-olive or weedy. It may be easier to train as it is less vigorous. It is seldom grown in California, where, we confess, we have seldom been able to distinguish it from Cabernet Sauvignon wines.

The wines of Cabernet Sauvignon grapes are generally considered by enologists to be the epitome of red wine quality (Lake 1977, Holzgang 1981). Cabernet Sauvignon has a distinctive, aromatic–spicy aroma in the grape, and this is transmitted to the wine. This odor has been described as black currant, grassy, green-olive, and herbaceous. It has been identified with 2-methoxy-3-isobutylpyrazine (Bayonove et al. 1975) and possibly n-octanol. However, Slingsby et al. (1980) were unable to find the former compound in extracts of Cabernet Sauvignon wines in California. They considered several other compounds to be of possible interest to the varietal aroma. Muller et al. (1971) also identified several compounds as possible contributors to the aroma of Cabernet Sauvignon and Ruby Cabernet wines. Augustyn and Marais (1982) identified ethyl-3-hydroxy-butyrate as a constituent of the aroma of Cabernet Sauvignon.

Once recognized by the consumer, it is not easily forgotten. The varietal aroma is distinctive under diverse climatic and production conditions, but it is by no means the same. In warm areas with irrigation, the grapes are larger and the aroma is less distinctive in the grapes and the wines. The wines will also be less red in color and flatter in taste.

Broad general regional flavor differences in the wines of Cabernet Sauvignon are easily recognized. In the Bordeaux region, this is not so clear because Cabernet Sauvignon there is usually grown and crushed with more or less of other varieties. Lake (1977) noted differences in Australia, and Amerine (1964) described four regional types in California: Napa– Sonoma, Livermore, Santa Clara, and Santa Cruz.

Recently Slingsby et al. (1980) described four types of California Cabernet: the wet–tea leaf or green-olive; the herbaceous, cooked-vegetable, or bell-pepper; the aromatic pepperminty, eucalyptus, or black-currant; and the flat, alcoholic, pyridine type. This classification creates several semantic problems, but we are, in general, in agreement with its intent. The first and third types would include most of the Cabernet Sauvignon wines produced from grapes grown in the Napa and Sonoma areas—that is, from regions II and III. The second type would be for the wines from grapes grown in the cooler parts of Monterey, Santa Barbara, Santa Cruz, and San Luis Obispo counties— that is, region I. And the last group would be for wines from grapes grown in the interior valleys and a few other locations—that is, from regions IV and V.

Correlations of headspace components and quantitative descriptive analyses of Cabernet Sauvignon wines were used to develop predictive equations (Noble 1978). Five attributes were rated: vegetative, woody, raisin, fruity, and Cabernet-like. Further developments can be expected in this field, possibly leading to identification of the components responsible for each of the attributes. See also pages 299–303.

The green-bell-pepper odor of the Monterey (etc.) region could be due to 2-methoxy-3-isobutylpyrazine, which has been described as having such an odor. So far as we know, this has not been proven. There are reports that the older vines and the less overcropped vines, drier soils, and more mature fruit have less of the bell-pepper odor, but more data are required.

Of course, growers pick early and late, and wine-makers prevent or induce the malolactic fermentation, clarify with different agents, and age for shorter or longer periods in smaller or larger cooperage of different kinds and ages of wood at different temperatures and humidities. One can ask, Is the admixture of other varieties with Cabernet Sauvignon in the Bordeaux region done to reduce the herbaceous odor, particularly in cooler years? Or, is it to reduce the tannin content of Cabernet Sauvignon wines and hasten maturity?

In recent years, a surplus of Cabernet Sauvignon grapes has developed from time to time in California and other areas. A number of rosé wines have been produced from this variety. When they are dry, they are not unpleasant. When sweet, we avoid them.

Carmine and Carnelian are new Cabernet-like hybrids recently released in California. They are good producers and have the green-olive aroma of Cabernet Sauvignon. Carnelian has produced very low red-colored wines of very moderate quality. Carmine is better colored and perhaps better flavored. Whether they will find a permanent place in the California wine industry is not now known.

Cinsaut, another variety from France, has the advantage of ripening well. The wines are moderately red and the taste somewhat flat. The aroma has been discussed as ripe-grape. It is no wonder that it is blended with other varieties at Châteauneuf-du-Pape in order to increase complexity. However, it does well in South Africa as a medium-quality variety.

Gamay is a native of the Beaujolais region of France. Its wines have been identified as roselike from 2-phenethanol. We have found this odor in few (very few) wines labeled California Gamay or Gamay Beaujolais. The raspberrylike odor claimed for it has generally escaped us. A fruity, tart, dry, slightly spicy, low-tannin wine is, for us, its best goal. This variety was once identified as being the same as the Napa Gamay in California, but this is apparently erroneous (see Antcliff 1976), and its name is probably Valdiguié (a variety of southwestern France). To complicate the complication, a clone of Pinot noir is grown as Gamay Beaujolais in some California vineyards! The zeal of California wineries for this name in either case is puzzling. Napa Gamay (Valdiguié?) is a splendid producer of late-ripening grapes of very little flavor or quality. If it undergoes a malolactic fermentation, it is flat tasting and off-colored. Even when properly made, it may be sweetened and (horrors) carbon dioxide added (deliberately or accidentally), and one gets a poor imitation of soda pop. The Gamay Beaujolais (i.e., from Pinot noir) could be a pleasant rosé wine if, again, it retained some acid. The true Gamay of Beaujolais does not seem to be grown commercially in California at present. We ask ourselves, why should it?

As for carbonic maceration Gamay wines, we have expressed elsewhere our doubts that the special flavors are so desirable as to go to the extra trouble. Where this leaves California Gamay, we do not know. In carbonic maceration, whole uncrushed grapes are placed in containers, where they undergo an intracellular fermentation of acids before alcoholic fermentation. There may be a place for early-maturing, light, red wines produced by at least a partial carbonic maceration.

Grenache is probably from Spain, but it is grown along the Rhone and in California, Australia, and elsewhere. Its fruit has a light purple-red color. The crops are irregular. In regions IV and V, it produces at best wines with a rosé color and a flat taste. It does better in regions II and III. The new wines have a tendency to oxidize and this is a defect. The flavor has not been studied, but it is only a slightly distinctive fruity, estery one. Perhaps rosé is its best use. Even in the Rioja in Spain, it is usually blended with better-colored varieties. From the grower's point of view, the fruit, what there is of it, always ripens.

Grignolino (several clones and perhaps some errors in naming) originated in Italy and is still grown there for making a wine of few pretensions. It is a good producer. The fermentations should not remain on the skins too long or the wines will be bitter (especially the pink-orange-colored clones). A clovelike odor has been reported.

Malbec is widely grown in the Bordeaux vineyards, though perhaps in diminishing proportions. The clones in California are irregular producers of very moderate quality (the malolactic fermentation must be carefully watched). Hence the description of some of its wines as being krautish (i.e., lactic) may be justified. At best, the wines have a fine color (turning too purple with an excessive malolactic fermentation). The familiar green-olive odor of the Cabernets is also sometimes noted. A ticklish variety to make wine from. Not recommended at present.

Merlot is a native Bordeaux variety. It is planted in Pomerol and St. Émilion but also in the Médoc. It has larger and thinner-skinned berries than Cabernet Sauvignon. In years of early rain, it may bunch rot, and pickers would have a hard time removing the moldy parts of the cluster. With mechanical harvesting, this would be impossible. However, since the larger-scale plantings have been made in California (since 1970), this has not been a major problem. The vine is vigorous and productive. The fermentations are normal.

Although Cabernet Sauvignon and Merlot have some of the same odor characteristics, they differ three to one and even five to one in the amounts of some components, as determined by gas–liquid chromatography (GLC) (Ribéreau-Gayon 1973). Of course, the size of the GLC peak need not be related to the strength of the odor, and other flavor components may be important. The varietal character of Merlot is not pronounced except under special conditions.

Merlot wines are less tannic and hence faster aging than those of Cabernet Sauvignon. In blind degustations, its wines are often identified as green-olive or Cabernet-like. This makes it a good blender with Cabernet Sauvignon to reduce the aging requirement. By themselves, the wines are well balanced, fine colored, and with a distinctive Cabernet-like aroma. They should age well. California producers differ in their enthusiasm for the wine of this variety, either by itself or in blends.

Mondeuse (or Refosco or Crabb's Black Burgundy) is a French variety but was once popular in California. The clusters are long and straggly so the fruit ripens without mold invasion. The colors are bright red, and the flavor is described as tart. Before Prohibition, it was favored as a blending grape.

Nebbiola (several clones) is the predominant grape in much of northwestern Italy. There it makes a variety of types of wine, none of which we find outstanding. The wines have been described as fruity-licorice. Barolo appears most often to be bitter-astringent when young and also when old. Even at 15 to 20 years, the aging does not produce an outstanding bouquet. We do not know whether it is grown elsewhere but apparently not (and justifiably so).

In experimental trials in California, it was often too flat in regions IV and V, and with insufficient color. A number of named clones were tried—none being sufficiently good to recommend the variety.

Petite Sirah, Durif, Shiraz, Serine, and Syrah are all apparently natives of the Rhône Valley of France. Their exact distinction from each other awaits the study of the ampelographers, but Shiraz and Syrah (see page 124) are apparently the grape of Hermitage. The others may not be identical and are apparently of lesser value. For now, we take Petite Sirah, Durif, and possibly Serine to be more or less equal and the most widely distributed variety (or varieties) in California. The disadvantage of this variety (or varieties) as planted in California is that it sunburns or raisins in hot seasons, and very high ethanol yields are common (up to 17% in 1936 and other hot years). The clusters are very tight, and excessive bunch rot is common after early rains or in high-humidity irrigated vineyards, especially where the variety is overcropped and cannot be harvested until very late.

In California, wines labeled Petite Sirah will have a full red color and moderate to high phenolics, thus requiring several years of bottle aging. Even with perfect maturity and careful fermentation and finishing, they remain hard and undistinguished; otherwise they are often astringent and even bitter. At worst, they are alcoholic and flat. At best, they have a ripe-grape odor and considerable bouquet. We do not believe the clone now used will make high enough quality to recommend growing it in the coastal counties for producing high quality Petite Sirah wines.

The description of Pinot noir wines as pepperminty, berrylike, strawberrylike, or blackberrylike is common. Boiled beetroot (Broadbent 1977) has also been suggested as the recognition symbol for Pinot noir aroma. None of these have touched off any vibrations in our olfactory systems, but perhaps we lack imagination. Of these words, we prefer the first. The aroma is not very distinctive—a ripe-grape odor seems appropriate. A number of papers on the chemical components of Pinot noir have been published—for example, Schreier (1980)—but none seem wholly to characterize the Pinot noir aroma.

The vines require care, and the timing of the harvest is critical, especially in a warm region, such as California. If harvested too soon, they lack adequate varietal aroma; if too late, the pH and sugar content can be excessively high, the acid too low, and the flavor may be burnt. They are also very finicky about climate. In regions warmer than III, the grapes lack color and acidity. The handling of the malolactic fermentation is difficult. We prefer a quick and complete one but would not be surprised if some future enological genius found a better way. At any rate, an excessive malolactic fermentation must be avoided.

Why there are not more fine Pinot noir wines outside of Burgundy is a mystery to us. It appears the climate must be cool (region I); the clone full-red colored; the fermentation warm ($20°-25°C$, $68-77°F$), but not hot ($>30°C$, $86°F$); the malolactic fermentation complete, perhaps simultaneously with the alcoholic fermentation; and the aging in about 300– 500 gallon oak containers in a cool condition ($<15\,°C$, $59\,°F$) for up to 2 years.

Pinot noir rosé wines leave us as unenthusiastic as Cabernet Sauvignon or Zinfandel rosés, especially if sweet.

Pinot St. George is grown in a few vineyards in California. Its European antecedent is not known. The berries are larger than those of Pinot noir. It has some relation to Pinot noir since some of its wines in blind judgings have been called like–Pinot noir; others describe it as not distinctive. It is not a vigorous grower but is a regular producer of moderate crops.

Ruby Cabernet, a California hybrid of Cabernet Sauvignon and Carignane, was developed by Professor H. P. Olmo of the University of California. It is an excellent producer and has fine color and a distinct Cabernet (green-olive) aroma. Virus-free wood is now available for propagation. It has been widely planted in the San Joaquin Valley in regions IV and V. The best microclimate for this variety may be region III since it has good acidity in the must.

The fermentations are rapid, sometimes too rapid when they are followed by an excessive malolactic fermentation. This has produced some flat wines of off-color and off-odor. When these lactic-sour wines were then aged in small cooperage in warm storage conditions, disaster resulted. Hopefully, future wines will be better. A weedy–tannic note appears in some wines and, occasionally, a bitter taste.

If Ruby Cabernet is to find a permanent place in the California industry, a technology that controls the extent of the malolactic fermentation will have to be developed. Perhaps in regions IV and V it would be best to prevent the malolactic fermentation.

Syrah is different from the California Petite Sirah (less tight clusters for one thing) (see page 121). The prototype was distributed from the University of California's experimental vineyard in the Napa Valley. Experimental wines were of fine color and a good grapey flavor and without the bitterness, astringency, and high ethanol of the Petite Sirah group. Commercial trials, with some success, are now underway in California.

Shiraz in South Australia has produced some fine wines, according to local enophiles. Those we have tested have been more memorable for bouquet than for aroma. The correct name of the variety appears to be Syrah. We think it worth testing in California if different from the clone mentioned above.

Valdepeñas (Tempranillo is correct), a heavy producing variety, is seldom grown in California. It originated in Spain and is grown in Argentina. The crushed grapes ferment well and completely (unless the grapes are too ripe). The new wines have a good color and a moderately distinctive spicelike odor. No one claims that it makes a great wine, but, with proper cropping, harvesting, and processing, it makes a pleasant wine. Some of the Argentinean wines are. The occupational disease is overcropping and flat-tasting wines.

Zinfandel has been commercially and successfully grown in California for about 125 years. We won't even speculate on where it came from or what its original name may have been! It bears well but has the unfortunate habit of setting a second and even third crop. These should normally not be harvested when the main crop is picked, as their fruit will still be too green. The exception may be when the harvest is late and more acid is required. Furthermore, the berries on a single cluster ripen unevenly, so it is always a question of when to harvest—when the greenest fruit in the cluster is ripe and the earliest ripening berries are shriveled or even raisined, or when the majority of the fruit in the cluster is ripe and the rest is still green. In the former case, very high apparent ethanol yields from the sugar from the shriveled berries will occur.

Nevertheless, Zinfandel bears well and produces its best wines in the lower-humidity parts of regions I, II, and III. In irrigated vineyards in regions IV and V, it may bunch rot. In dry seasons and dry areas of regions II and III, it may be attacked by red spiders. These cause leaf functioning to stop, and the fruit remains green—often called red-berry condition. Such fruit is worthless for wine.

The fermentations are good, and the new wines have a fine sharp-red color. The flavor is distinctive—berrylike, raspberrylike, sometimes black-pepperish, and so on. With a short experience with wines having a typical Zinfandel aroma, one should be able to recognize it without difficulty. The wines are aged in oak—larger tanks for the fruitier, less alcoholic (11%–12%) wines and 50–500 gallon cooperage for the more alcoholic (12%–13%) wines. These wines continue to develop in the bottle, particularly the latter type. Old Zinfandels (20+ years) often have a bouquet that is difficult to distinguish from old Cabernet Sauvignons.

A third type of Zinfandel has appeared on the market in recent years—the over-14%-ethanol wine. These wines result from very late harvesting of grapes containing many shriveled and raisined berries. Some are 15% to 17% in ethanol and retain 1% to 10% sugar. If sold as dessert wines, we would not object, though their flavor is not to our taste. But they are not table wines and may result in unpleasant consequences when consumed as if they were. Besides, as table wines, they are often flat and uninteresting.

Varieties that rarely yield wines with a recognizable varietal character are Aramon, Carignane, Charbono, Early Burgundy, Emperor, Flame Tokay, Mataro, Mission, Pagadebito, Portuguese Blue, Red Malaga, Sangioveto, Saperavi, and so on. We emphasize "rarely" because we have found a few that rose above the ordinary.

5. Red—having no distinguishable varietal character.

As with the analogous white wines (section 2 above), not all California red wines with semigeneric names (such as claret and burgundy) are of ordinary character. There is no law that prevents a producer from making a fine Cabernet Sauvignon and labeling it claret. He is most unlikely to do this, however, because the market price for Cabernet Sauvignon is much higher than for California claret. Moreover, a new blend of varieties could very well produce a fine wine that, because no variety amounted to at least 75%* of the total, would not be eligibile for a varietal label. Yet the wine might be of excellent, even unique, quality. Perhaps vineyard-district labeling, if it produced a consistent flavor, would be appropriate for such blends if typical of the vineyard or district.

B. Wines having more than 14% ethanol (dessert wines).

The variety of grape is probably less important for dessert wines (except muscatels) than for table wines, but it is not unimportant. For almost all types, riper grapes are needed, the acidity should not be too low, and the fruit should be an appropriate color (in the case of reds). These are almost all

---

*In 1983.

"It's a naive domestic burgundy without any breeding, but I think you'll be amused by its presumption."

fortified wines. However, where tradition rules and price is not a factor, some very sweet unfortified wines of less than or more than 14% ethanol that are clearly dessert types are produced. The number of types of dessert wines is small enough that each can be discussed here. The unfortified dessert wines are discussed above (pages 109 and 125).

1. Sherry—dry.

   a. *Baked process.* Some, but not all, California sherries are made by this process: about 60°C (140°F) for 60 to 90 days. If the wine is dry when baked, it will not have too much caramel character, but really dry shermats (sherry material) are seldom baked so some hydroxymethylfurfural and caramel are normally produced. Acetaldehyde content increases during heating. If, in addition, the wine is aged in small (140-gallon) cooperage for 1 to 5 years it acquires flavor complexity. A limit of 1.5% sugar would ensure that the "dry" sherries are indeed dry to most people's palates. Adding oxygen to the wine during heating (as in the Tressler process in New York state) hastens acetaldehyde accumulation and reduces the foxy flavor of the native varieties used.

b. *Yeast process.* Whether produced by the film-yeast (flor) or submerged-culture process, the wines should have a light color and a noticeable acetaldehyde odor. In the film-yeast process (used primarily in Spain, South Africa, and Australia), the acetaldehyde content builds up slowly. The longer the wine is under the film, the more complex the bouquet becomes. As the wine ages, the yeast film sinks to the bottom from time to time and undergoes autolysis (self-digestion by the action of autogenous enzymes), which also contributes to the complexity of the bouquet of the wine. In addition, the fractional blending in the solera system not only equalizes the character of the wine but makes it more complex. The volatile constituents of film-yeast sherries have been extensively studied by Fagan et al. (1981, 1982). They reported 14 new compounds. A biosynthetic pathway with ethyl 4-oxobutyrate as a key intermediate in the production of a number of lactones was proposed. Of these, 4-hydroxy-5-ketoheptanoic acid lactone and 4,5-dihydroxy acid γ-lactone were particularly noted as verifying the proposed pathway. Webb and Noble (1976) reported 130 volatile compounds in sherries: including 25 alcohols, 5 carbonyls, 10 acetals, 3 amides, 35 esters, and 5 lactones.

The difference in bouquet between film-yeast sherries and submerged-culture sherries (made in Canada, California, and the Soviet Union) is that the former are much more complex, with less free-acetal-dehyde odor. Webb et al. (1964) found submerged-culture wines to have more or less the same components as wines produced by film yeast. Baked sherries uniquely contained 2-furfuraldehyde. An aging period, such as is used in the solera system, is desirable in both processes. Old flor sherries develop into darker amontillados, which are much appreciated. Partly because of the concentration of the wine during aging, old amontillados may be slightly sweet.

In "Château Chalon" (Jura, France) film-yeast wines, 4,5-dimethyltetrahydro-2,3-furandione has been identified as the dominant odor (Dubois et al. 1976).

2. Sherry—sweet.

   a. *Baked process.* A number of California sweet baked sherries are marketed. They have a distinct caramel flavor. Most have 10% sugar or more, and an amber color. We doubt that aging would improve their quality except in small cooperage (less than 500 gallons).

   b. *Aging process.* Sweet sherries are also made in Spain and occasionally in California by aging in the warmer part of the bodega. In Spain, the *oloroso* wines so produced may have some flor character because of the complicated final solera blending. Too much caramel or raisin odor is considered a defect.

   It is worth noting that the use of the word *solera* on California sherries and ports is increasing—unfortunately. If the average age of the wine were increasing to a constant, as in a normal Spanish solera blending, we would not fault this. Sometimes the word seems to be used merely as an indication that the wines were aged in wood.

   A number of sherries of intermediate degrees of flor and nonflor character and of sweetness are produced. Otsuka et al. (1980), using principal component analysis, distinguished types of Spanish sherry: fino (aldehydes and higher alcohols); amontillado (lower ethyl acetate and high acetal); oloroso (none); and cream (aldehydes). Only types were distinguished, not quality.

3. Madeira.

This is another baked dessert wine. Its home is the island of Madeira off the north of Africa. It may be slightly sweet, medium sweet, or sweet; in Madeira, these variants are named Sercial, Boal (or Bual), and Malmsey, respectively. They are quite amber in color, owing to the use of Jacquez (red) grapes. Some have more of a baked character than others. We find most of them to be sweeter than we like, but the sweetness is obviously needed to mask the bitterness produced by baking. Some Madeiras have had an excessive amount of volatile acidity so it is advisable to sample the wine before purchasing any large amount.

We have shown elsewhere (Roessler and Amerine 1973) that one should take claims of great antiquity for Madeiras—especially at prices of $20 to $25 per bottle—with a grain of salt. In fact, we doubt that much commercial Madeira of the advertised ages exist, unless the law of compound interest has been repealed and someone has found a method of preventing the accumulation of fixed acids. We don't know what a California (or American in general) madeira should be. We have had some well-aged Russian *maderas* that tasted much like a respectable, aged, sweet sherry.

4. Málaga.

This is a Spanish, raisin-flavored wine that is traditionally made from raisins, or at least semi-raisins. It is very sweet, flat, and caramellike. We can't think of when or where it could be served in the United States. Because it is rather low in ethanol (about 15%) for a dessert wine, some of our students have suggested it as the wine to serve your "dry" maiden aunt when she comes to tea.

5. Marsala.

This Sicilian, blended, sweet dessert wine owes its primary character to the use of *cotto* (boiled-down grape juice). Whether one likes this bitter-burnt flavor or not, it is an essential part of Marsala and one that makes it useful in cooking. Marsalas are amber in color and sweet (despite what the label says). To drink them straight is more of a chore than a pleasure for us. In fact, we have never met a Marsala connoisseur except in the production and sales departments of Marsala producers or distributors. We don't know what a California (or American) marsala should be and, from those we have tasted, we don't *want* to know. Fortunately, very few have appeared on the market.

6. Muscatel.

A large number of dessert wines are produced from various muscat varieties. In California, the predominant variety is Muscat of Alexandria. In France, Italy, and the Soviet Union, Muscat blanc (the same as Muscat Frontignan or Muscat Canelli) is commonly used. These and other varieties are also used in Australia, South Africa, and elsewhere. In Italy, Aleatico (an orange-pink, muscat-flavored variety) is used to produce a white sweet dessert wine. Because of the low acidity of muscat varieties, the wines must be rather sweet to mask, at least partially, their flat taste. If the grapes are picked too early, they lack muscat flavor. If picked too late, they may raisin, and this will be reflected in the wine's caramel–raisin flavor and dark color. A little red muscatel from Muscat Hamburg has been made in California.

Should the wine be aged? If it is aged, it will almost certainly darken in color. If it is not aged, the flavor of the fortification spirits may be obvious and the wine may also be "hot" in taste and feel. All things considered, we favor picking the grapes not too late and aging the wine for not more than 2 to 5 years. Thus we prefer fruity, gold-colored muscatels. Others, however, prefer older and darker muscatels.

7. Port.

This sweet red dessert wine originated in the Douro Valley of Portugal, where it is still produced. There are three major types. Tawny ports owe their color to long aging or to the use of tawny-colored grapes (and sometimes, no doubt, to vineyard mixtures of red and white grapes). Ruby ports are ruby red and are aged for only a few years. The best (darkest) ruby ports are bottled after 2 years and aged to make vintage ports.

Most ports from the Douro Valley have a distinct odor (apparently by design) of higher alcohols from the spirits used for fortification. American consumers, however, prefer lower levels of the higher alcohols in their dessert wines than do the English and Portuguese. Tawny ports should not be too sweet. Ruby ports must be fruity and not astringent. After 10 to 20 years in the bottle, vintage ports develop a fine bouquet.

Similar, but by no means identical, types of sweet red wines are produced in Australia, California, Mexico, South Africa, the Soviet Union, and probably elsewhere. Some are of pleasant quality, whereas others appear to be produced from ordinary red varieties that lack flavor and/or acidity, color, and sugar. Such varieties yield wines with a neutral, flat flavor and low color. In some wines in California, the color is adjusted with lesser-quality varieties, such as Salvador or other hybrids (Royalty, Rubired), or high-colored varieties, such as Souzâo, are used for blending. Heating ruby-colored ports to give them a tawny color is illegal in Portugal and possibly should be elsewhere. The heated wines usually acquire a caramel odor and have a high hydroxymethylfurfural content (over 45 mg/l).

8. Tokaj (or Tokay).

In Hungary, the Aszu type of Tokaj is a sweet, unfortified wine that is more or less oxidized in odor. This is probably due to aging in small casks. We have found few such wines that were of exceptional quality, despite their price. This may be because the finer Tokajs are less often produced today than before World War II. We can report that they seem to be improving.

California "tokay" is a blend of angelica or white port (neutral white dessert wines), port, and sherry and is seldom aged. It is a type drunk more for the ethanol and sugar than for flavor or quality.

Wines with Added Flavors

From the Neolithic period, some wines have had flavors added. In such wines, one looks for a proper balance of the flavor and one that is characteristic of the type. Since the flavor is added deliberately, one should be critical when there is an excess or deficiency of the typical odor. Likewise, since these are wines that improve little with age (in fact, they often deteriorate), one may insist that they be brilliantly clear and of the precise color commercially attributed to the type.

I. Herb-based.

A. Vermouth—dry.

These wines are nowadays usually light yellow, but this is a commercial, not intrinsic, quality factor. "Dry" vermouths are not really dry—they have about 4% sugar. One should not tolerate any more than this, and one can hope that a drier type might be produced in the United States someday. The "occupational disease" of dry vermouths is excessive bitterness, and sometimes noticeable astringency. This is probably the reason for the relatively high sugar content: to mask the bitterness and astringency. They should have a complex herb character in odor and taste. As many as 20 to 50 different herbs and plant materials may be used. It is also possible to buy vermouth extracts.

B. Vermouth—sweet.

These wines are almost always a full amber color, but a detectable reddish hue is commercially acceptable. Since they are usually very sweet (10%–14% sugar), bitterness or astringency is seldom a problem. A few producers cannot resist the temptation to use too much vanilla or peppermint in their vermouth formulations. As with the dry type, complex herb flavors without any predominant odor are favored. Baked sweet sherries usually have too much caramellike odor to be used as base wines for sweet vermouths.

C. Byrrh.

Byrrh is a sweet, medium-red, French proprietary wine containing cinchona. The bitterness and astringency observed are normal. As a rule, the wine is not aged, but connoisseurs of Byrrh are reported to favor bottle aging for several years (to reduce the bitterness or astringency?). A sediment can be tolerated in aged samples but not in market samples.

D. Dubonnet.

Dubonnet is another French proprietary wine. It is less red than Byrrh (there is a white Dubonnet also), and the herb mixture is not bitter, nor is it as pronounced as in vermouth. For some years, Dubonnet has also been made in California for the American market. The flavor appears to be very similar, but the base wine seems to us less tart than that of the French product.

II. Fruit-based and fruit-flavor-based.

Fruit wines have been produced for many years. The chief factors in their sensory quality are the degree of specific fruit flavor and the balance of sugar and acid in the finished wines. Most (all?) fruit wines lose much of their specific fruit character within a year of production. Since the mature fruits (such as apples, blackberries, cherries, gooseberries, passion fruit, peaches, pears, and strawberries) contain too little sugar and too much (or too little) acid to produce a balanced wine, amelioration with sugar and water (and acid) is needed. The sugar increases the final ethanol content, and the water reduces the acidity. In order to mask the still-high acidity, some fruit wines are finished with 5% to 10% sugar. Fruit wine producers also claim, probably with justification, that the fruit character is improved by an increase in sugar content.

Since 1957, many fruit-flavored wines have been produced in the United States. Thunderbird, Silver Satin, and other proprietary wines have citrus flavors added. Wines with both less than and more than 14% ethanol are made, with varying amounts of sugar (from 5% to 14%). Passion fruit and other flavors are used in similar products, such as Bali Hai. For each of these wines, the distinctive proprietary character seems to be the first consideration. Is the fruit flavor distinctive but not too much so? In our opinion, some are too distinctive and the consumer is likely to lose interest. This is a problem with all flavored wines. Does the wine have a reasonable shelf life? We have found a number of such flavored wines that darkened and lost an appreciable amount of their fruit character in no more than 3 or 4 months of aging at room temperature. Others are stable for a year or more.

Improvement in quality could be achieved for these types of wines with greater complexity of flavor.

More recently, proprietary wines using grape- and apple-base wines and having more or less excess carbon dioxide have been produced, primarily in California. This shelf life is usually short. Perhaps the producers should call attention to this fact (at least to their retailers). As an example of what can be done, consider the dairy industry, which now regularly marks many of its products with a date beyond which freshness is not guaranteed. It is also worth noting the short shelf life that some conscientious beer producers permit their products, especially if sold in warm climates. If *vins nouveaus* continue to be produced (we wouldn't bet on it), we would also recommend that a date of 3 to 6 months following the vintage be given as the cutoff date for optimum quality.

The strawberry and other flavored wines are pleasant enough with the first taste, but they do not often maintain *our* interest (because they are difficult to hold at their low acidity). After the wine ages for a year or two, the typical fruit character is usually more or less attenuated. For those who do find such wines interesting, we believe the fruity flavor should be typical of the fruit named and not have any foreign character. Moreover, we see nothing inherently wrong with an artificial flavor if its presence is clearly stated. The labels on some of the imported cherry and plum wines do not make it clear to the ordinary consumer whether or not the fruit flavor is derived entirely from the fruit named.

There are only a few wines in which ripe fruits are used for flavoring. Originally in Spain, red wine, sugar, and citrus fruits (plus carbonated water or ice, sometimes) were used to produce sangria, especially as a summer drink. Several similar beverages have been produced in the United States and in Spain as bottled wines. We have found some of them to be lacking in freshness, to have an "off" citrus note, and to be disappointing in general. However, several have had limited consumer acceptance. Bottled kir is now available. It is based on a white table wine plus some concentrated red currant juice. In each case, we applaud their success but are unable to understand why such ordinary wines should enjoy it. Is it price? Or something new? Or?

Drinking the right wine at the right time is an art.

H. A. VACHELL

Le génie du vin est d'abord le cépage.

OLIVIER DE SERRES

A bottle of good wine, like a good act, shines ever in the retrospect.

R. L. STEVENSON

The wine which demands a second, third, . . . glass can never be a bad wine.
The wine of which you cannot finish one glass can never be a great wine.

E. GALLO

CHAPTER 6

The Sensory Examination

There is a good deal of difference between drinking and enjoying two red table wines at the dinner table and evaluating the same two wines in an international competition to decide which is the better. Of course, the same physiological limitations and psychological errors (Chapter 3) still plague both situations. Certain aspects of the sensory examination remain unaltered whether in the home or in a well-equipped sensory laboratory. In either place one must evaluate the appearance and color of the wine. Unless the dining room is dimly lit, a fairly good appraisal of the appearance can be made there. But it is practically impossible to make a reliable judgment of wine color in the normal dining room. The usual illumination casts a brownish tint on the wines, which distorts their true color and makes them look older than they really are. The more dimly lit the room, the more difficult it is to distinguish small differences in hue.

Furthermore, wine evaluation in the dining room suffers from extraneous food odors and the contrasting tastes of various foods. To which the consumer may respond that that is how most wines are consumed. But that misses the point: wine consumption at home is based on a preference decision, whereas wine evaluation in the laboratory is based on a difference decision or a difference–preference decision with experience with the full range of quality of the type. The latter are expressed in terms of some sort of scale, often as a rating of the intensity of some attribute.

There are other differences between the home and the laboratory. The normal dining room is not set up for serving wines "blind" in coded, identical glasses. This is just as well, because to do so would probably spoil the enjoyment of the wines, if not the whole meal. The number of possible psychological errors and the problem of adaptation make it extremely difficult to conduct a valid sensory examination of wines at the normal home dinner. In fact, competitive judgings at home are now sensibly done before sitting down to the dinner. There is the additional problem that some participants in a home wine judging do not arrive entirely free of alcohol and they obviously drink the wines. At some point during the judging, critical appraisal may become unreliable. For the best evaluation of relative quality or differences with maximum efficiency, the sensory examination should be conducted under specially prepared conditions.

Basic Considerations

The following questions need to be answered in any sensory quality examination: Where? With what? How many? How coded? Order of sampling? Time of day? Number of judges? Ability of the judges? Techniques to be used? Possible and necessary statistical analysis of the results?

Under private or commercial conditions, expert sensory evaluation is expensive because trained persons are required. In addition, carrying out the statistical analyses of the results may be time-consuming. Why is statistical analysis necessary? First of all, without proper statistical analysis, incorrect conclusions may be drawn from the data. Recently there has been a plethora of "comparative" tastings of wines. For example, five judges rank five wines for relative quality. Suppose the results are as shown in Table 6–1.

Table 6–1   Five wines ranked by 5 judges. (The best ranking is 1.)

Judge	Wine				
	X	Y	Z	R	S
1	3	4	5	1	2
2	4	2	5	3	1
3	5	4	1	3	2
4	2	5	3	1	4
5	5	2	3	1	4
Rank total	19	17	17	9	13

From these results one might conclude that wine R is the best, followed by wines S, Y or Z, and X. But is this a valid judgment and is it repeatable? Quite the contrary. As we will see from the discussion of ranking (page 279), there are, according to accepted levels of statistical significance, *no* differences among the five rankings. The statistical treatment (Appendixes O–1 and O–2) indicates that the judges do not exhibit a noticeable degree of agreement in their rankings, and it is therefore not appropriate to estimate an overall ranking for the wines.

Or consider the results of recent, widely publicized "judging." Fifteen judges scored five wines on a 20-point scale, with the results shown in Table 6–2.

The press release says that wine I is the winner, so the public rushes off to buy it. But is it significantly better than wine L? No. It can be shown by statistical analysis (page 279) that wines I and L are not significantly different from each other—that is, that they could not be distinguished on the basis of their scores, by this panel. It

Table 6-2 Five wines scored by 15 judges.
(The best score is 20.)

Judge	Wine				
	H	I	J	K	L
1	17	13	14	13	18
2	12	15	15	12	19
3	19	18	15	13	17
4	14	16	12	13	14
5	19	18	20	14	18
6	15	16	18	14	15
7	17	19	17	16	20
8	12	15	13	14	15
9	13	17	18	17	19
10	14	16	17	14	16
11	19	20	18	15	17
12	15	19	17	18	19
13	14	16	14	17	13
14	18	18	13	19	16
15	10	18	12	16	15
Total	228	254	233	225	251
Mean	15.2	16.9	15.5	15.0	16.7

can also be shown that wines, H, J, and K are significantly poorer than wines I and L, but that they are not significantly different from each other.

A statistical approach must always be employed in the analysis of sensory data because of the inherent variability of aesthetic judgments. (See also pages 174–178.) The *only* way to evaluate the results and reach reliable conclusions is by the use of appropriate statistical procedures. There is the possible exception when all the members of the panel agree on all ranks. We have never seen such a case with five judges and more than five wines.

It is therefore essential that the sensory examination be set up in such a way that we can obtain the required information with the greatest degree of statistical, physiological, and psychological confidence. We also wish to accomplish this with the fewest replications. Statistical confidence relates to the control of errors of the first and second kind (page 181); physiological and psychological confidence relate to the avoidance of sensory adaptation, psychological errors (Chapter 3), and so on.

Judges The number and type of judges depend on the nature of the test. In descriptive and quality assessments and in discrimination tests, judges of demonstrated ability should be used. But when measuring preference, potential consumers are required. If few judges are used, large differences between samples are required for statistical significance. On the other hand, if many judges are used, extremely small differences between samples may be statistically significant.

Sidel and Stone (1976) distinguish between trained judges for descriptive and quality assessments; experienced judges, selected on the basis of discrimination ability, for discrimination tests; and either experienced or inexperienced judges, qualified on the basis of acceptance attitudes, for affective (hedonic) tests. Weiss (1980) recommended sequential selection of judges for sensory tests because of the better performance of judges so selected (see page 203).

In the home there is nothing that one can do, normally, to qualify judges. They are guests and, as such, deserve the assumption that they are equally qualified to evaluate the wine presented. Hopefully they are there primarily to enjoy the wines, but, for some, evaluation may have its own hedonic and aesthetic value. See page 247. The results of their evaluations, however, must be taken with a certain healthy skepticism. The group is likely to have varying degrees of competence and acceptance for the wines served. This introduces a variable that increases the differences in response among the judges and reduces the reliability of the average results. The average results of five qualified wine judges can be accepted with a great deal more confidence than those of five wine dilettantes at a dinner, however interested and good-willed they may be.

No one should make critical sensory evaluations unless he or she is in good physical and mental condition. It is essential that the judge not feel rushed or under pressure. As much as possible, the judge should concentrate on the task at hand and be free of extraneous problems or distractions.

Much as the elderly dislike admitting it, our olfactory and gustatory sensitivities decrease up to about 65 years of age, with men and women not differing (Thumfart et al. 1980). Kare (1975) casts doubt on the reported decrease in taste discrimination in older persons (80–85) compared with younger persons (40–45). We have observed excellent judges over 70 years of age who were better than many younger judges. Perhaps the elderly look harder, are less thrown off by extraneous noises, and they may use clues younger judges do not recognize.

Tests Under laboratory conditions, it is possible to identify the judge who is "off" by comparing that judge's results on successive samples with those of the rest of the panel. But in the home, this is very difficult; if the test is not replicated, it is impossible. Therefore, if the test is to have commercial importance, it must be conducted under laboratory conditions, and it is necessary to attempt to qualify the judges.

The effect of training has been tested by Owen and Machamer (1979). There was improvement in accuracy, but some bias for reporting "different" judgments persisted. They believe that improvement in wine discrimination skills can be assessed. Training improved the accuracy of "same"/"different" judgments on white varietal wines by 14%. However, bias for "different" judgments persisted. Also training did not remove the problem of attending to irrelevant differences. Palmer (1974) reported that panelists who had previous experience in taste-profiling of foods (see page 289), but not of teas, were nearly as good as tea experts in discriminating among teas. Those with *no* sensory experience were considerably less discriminating.

To qualify a judge unequivocally for the sensory evaluation of wines is probably impossible. As we have said, a judge must be in

Plate 1 Wine glass painted black on the outside to prevent observation of appearance or color.

Plate 2 Lazy susan serving table. Note sections for separating samples. (Courtesy E. and J. Gallo Winery, Modesto, Ca.)

Plate 3 Panelist in booth. Note opening for serving.

Plate 4 Assistant serving samples. (Courtesy of E. and J. Gallo, Modesto, Ca.)

Plate 5   Glasses being served and
awaiting service.

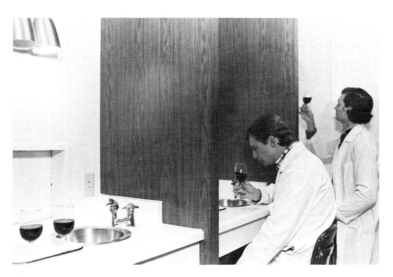

Plate 6   Two panelists in booths. Note spittoon basins and special lights.
(Courtesy of E. and J. Gallo, Modesto, Ca.)

Plate 7 Tulip-shaped, all-purpose wine glass.

Plate 8 Tulip-shaped glass for red table wines.

Plate 9 Tulip-shaped glass for white table wines.

Plate 10 Hollow-stem glass for sparkling wines.

Plate 11   Glasses hung upside down to avoid contact with wood.

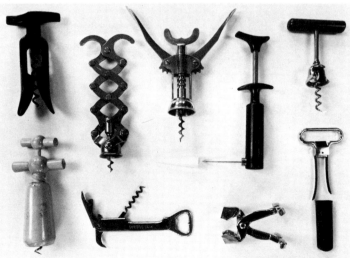

Plate 12   Corkscrews and other openers. Top row from left to right: three screw-type corkscrews, one hollow-needle pump opener, and screw type; lower row: two screw-type, champagne cork twister, and U-shaped puller. (© David Wakely, 1982.)

Plate 13 Tears of
a 12% solution of
ethanol in water.

Plate 14 Tears of
an 18% solution of
ethanol in water.

Plate 15 Herman Wente, one of the best of the post-Prohibition judges of California wines, examining the appearance and color of a white wine. (Courtesy of Wines & Vines.)

Plate 16 Two judges (M.A.A. and E.B.R.) evaluating wines. Note buckets used as spittoons.

good physical and mental condition. Some internal test to determine when a judge is "off" is desirable, but how to assess a judge's inherent ability is most difficult. Nevertheless, some basic hurdles can be erected to eliminate at least the grossly inadequate judge. First of all, we want to know what experience he or she has had in judging wines, particularly those of the type in question. Ask!

One of the biggest faults in wine judgings is that people with inadequate experience are thrust into situations in which they are asked to make quantitative and qualitative judgments on types of wines for which they are unqualified. Rather than bow out gracefully and risk a certain loss of face, they blunder ahead. Perhaps they are not even aware of their limitations. There is, of course, no perfectly qualified judge of all wines because no one can possibly have experienced all wines, much less developed critical judgment of them. However, the truly experienced wine judge can, to a certain extent, extrapolate experience with known wine types to *similar* types of wines. But such extrapolation is surely limited and is no substitute for experience with each type of wine being judged. In the beer studies of Clapperton and Piggott (1978), trained panelists used more descriptive terms than untrained panelists and were better able to distinguish between the beers. This accords with our observational experience. Lehrer (1975) showed that typical wine drinkers were inconsistent in how they applied words to wines. Subjects in the top third of a knowledge-of-wine quiz used more words than those in the bottom third of the quiz.

Sensitivity   Jakob and Matheir (1982) reported wide variation between individuals in their sensitivity to styrol (styrene). Wines stored in polyester resin tanks may acquire a sweetish plastic off-odor. The recognition threshold of different panelists varied from 0.01 to 5.0 mg/l. They recommend training of potential panelists and, indeed, have given a course for 400 students since 1976. Threshold and identification of off-odors were among the tests. The off-odors were asbestos, geraniumlike (from sorbic acid decomposition), bitter almond (from excess ferrocyanide), aerated, and sorbic acid per se.

Five dilutions of each were prepared: for geraniumlike, 20 to 100 mg/l of hexadienol; for bitter almond, 20 μg/l to 100 μg/l of potassium cyanide; for aerated, 5 to 40 mg/l of acetaldehyde; and for sorbic acid, 200 to 600 mg/l of sorbic acid. A series of solutions of asbestos was used for testing for the asbestos odor. As in many other experiments, the judges had changing thresholds over a 3-month period. Thresholds for sweetness and sourness were also determined. Jakob and Matheir recommended using analysis of variance (page 232) on actual wine judgments in selecting the best panelists. According to Mesnier (1981), the new Université du Vin in France will require 5 to 6 months of training for *dégustateurs qualifiés*.

One of us (M.A.A.) has seen judges in international competitions who were well qualified for judging European table wines but who made colossal errors in judging Portuguese ports, Spanish sherries, and eastern United States wines, precisely because they had limited or biased experience with these types. Schneyder (1982) suggests standard wine samples to be used for pretesting potential judges for international events.

The following few simple tests are not infallible. Everyone has an off-day or an off-test. Giving a test just before a judging puts a great deal of pressure on the judge, not to speak of embarrassment if he is disqualified. Qualification tests (perhaps the only ones!) were used for qualifying judges for the California State Fair some years ago (see Amerine and Ough 1964). They suggested wines of different sweetness, sulfur dioxide, acetic acid, and sourness; different varieties; varying quality or varietal flavor; identification of off-odors, and so on. Puisais (1978) has suggested white and rosé wines of complete and incomplete malolactic fermentation and of varying sugar, or red wines of varying levels of tannin. He also suggests the same variety from different regions, or several varieties from the same region, or several vintages from the same region.

The tests required that wines of known composition be placed in proper order: sugar (base wine [0.2% reducing sugar?], and base wine plus 0.5%, 1.0%, 1.75%, and 2.75% sucrose); acidity (base wine

[0.6% total acid], and base wine plus 0.05%, 0.1%, 0.175%, and 0.3% citric acid); sulfur dioxide (base wine [50 mg/l sulfur dioxide], and base wine plus 75, 100, 150, and 200 mg/l). Tests of varietal dilutions were also used. A wine with a strong and characteristic varietal aroma was diluted with a nonvarietal wine of similar color, acidity, sweetness, and alcohol content to produce a series of dilutions containing 80%, 60%, 40%, 20%, and 0% of the varietal wine (6 wines with the original varietal wine). The panelists' task is to place the wines in the correct order of varietal odor. Cabernet Sauvignon, Sauvignon blanc, Gewürztraminer, and Zinfandel could also be used for dilution tests. The blending wine should be as neutral flavor as possible and have a color and chemical composition as close to that of the varietal wine as possible.

Identification of varietal aromas is also a useful test, but one must be *sure* that the wines used do have distinguishable and typical varietal aromas. Amateurs cannot be expected to do well in such a test. Irrelevant differences in appearance or color can interfere with the aroma examination, but this problem can be overcome by using wine glasses that are painted black on the outside (see Plate 1). In the California State Fair tests, each reversal or error was a demerit. The judges with the least number of demerits were selected. The selection process took place 2 months before the actual judging.

Wines for such qualifying tests should be of generally recognized commercial quality. Finding such wines is not always as simple as it sounds. Certainly the wines should not be selected on the basis of price or popular reputation.

Variations of these tests could be used for international judgings, but the costs of arranging such a qualifying process would probably be prohibitive. In lieu of this, experience and reputation are used as criteria for the selection of judges. This practice has obvious deficiencies. A judge's reputation is not always based on accuracy and consistency. And even the most experienced judges for one type of wine may be inexperienced with other types. The selection committee should be sure that at least a majority of the judges for each panel are qualified for each type of wine they are to judge. It is also helpful if the judges have some respect for each other's abilities concerning the types they are best qualified to judge.

We admit that qualification tests for the selection of judges are sometimes impracticable and often impolitic. The solution is to use appropriate analytical procedures to determine statistical significance based on the combined assessments of the judges. In our experience, this sometimes reveals (more often than it should) that the combined scores of a panel of judges indicate no significant differences among the wines. This may be disappointing to the judges and those conducting the test, but it is far better to publish results that are really meaningful than results that are interesting but meaningless. The results may also reveal the anomalous data of one or two judges. Such judges should be included in later judgings, and their results must be included in all the tests, since they represent a part of the judges' universe.

Locale and Equipment

The best locale for judging wines is an area free of extraneous odors, colors, and sounds. Outdoor settings fail on all three counts. The wine cellar is the worst place. Normal temperature for sensory evaluation rooms is about 21°C (70°F). Food technologists find a gray background best. Certainly red and brown colors should be avoided. The room should be well lighted; natural northern light or its equivalent is preferred. Artificial light of the daylight type is satisfactory, but most fluorescent lamps and mercury-arc lamps are not. In some cases, it may be necessary to mask the color of the wine. Glasses painted black on the outside are one solution to this problem. Be sure that the special lighting does not mask the differences in hue (dominant wavelength), purity, and luminance. Also, the panelist should previously have demonstrated ability to perform sensory tests under the special lighting conditions (Sidel and Stone 1976).

To prevent the accumulation of odors, dentist-type spittoons are recommended. Air conditioning is also desirable to remove odors and to provide comfortable temperature and humidity. For judgings extending over several hours or days, physical comfort is an important factor. Naturally, the judges should not be able to see each other's score cards *nor each other* during the judging.

A lazy susan serving table in a modern wine-examination room is shown in Plate 2. Various aspects of separate booths for the sensory examination of wines are shown in Plates 3 through 6.

Glasses   The 8-oz-capacity (235 ml) tulip-shaped glass is preferred for comparative testings. In fact, for home use we find it better than the tiny glasses commonly used for sherry, the colored glasses sometimes used for German wines, the gigantic monstrosities recommended for Burgundy in some fancy restaurants, and other such aberrations. The tulip-shaped glass is also appropriate for sparkling wines, provided that a small, rough cross is scratched in the bottom of the glass to provide a site for the formation of bubbles. This can be done (not always with ease) with a steel file or, better yet, a scriber. The hollow-stem glass also gives a steady release of bubbles from the warmth of the hand on the hollow stem. The fluted glass is favored by some. It too works better if a small, rough cross is made in the bottom of the glass. An "ideal" glass has recently been recommended (Anon. 1973). It is shaped like a truncated, elongated egg and holds 215 ml. Four typical glasses used in wine evaluation are shown in Plates 7 through 10. The thinner the glass, the faster the wine warms up when the glass is held in the palm of the hand. The thinness of the glass is not a critical use factor, and thin glasses can be expensive. (They also break more easily.) The silver cup, much favored in Burgundy, does not seem to have much merit except as a means of detecting small differences in color (by reflections from the polished surface). Glasses, if always filled to the same level, serve this purpose equally well or better. Ideally the glasses should have a line etched at about one-third full. In critical judgings they should always be filled just to this level.

If traces of detergent are left in glasses after washing, they may impart a foreign odor and taste to the wines. We recommend *thorough* rinsing in hot, soft water. If a towel is used for drying, it must be specially washed so as to remove all detergent and sizing odors. Glasses stored in odorous surroundings (e.g., a new pine cupboard) will acquire the odor, especially if they stand upside down on a wood surface. The acquired odor may then be imparted to the wines. This problem can be avoided by hanging the glasses upside down (see Plate 11) and rinsing well with the wine to be tested before use.

Corkscrews and Other Openers   First the metal capsule must be removed. We recommend that it be cut off well below the rim of the bottle. The neck of the bottle and the top of the cork should then be carefully cleaned, preferably with a wet cloth followed by a dry cloth. This prevents any of the surface material getting into the wine.

Removing the cork can be a problem. Just after corking, the closure is rather hard and, unless paraffined, may stick. Corks that have been in bottles for many years may become spongy in the center and stick to the sides.

There are dozens of different types of openers; some basic types are shown in Plate 12. A corkscrew with a long (2-inch) screw that has a wide, flat (not round) surface is preferred. Corkscrews that work by some form of leverage are best, though with experience even a direct-pull corkscrew can be used. If the cork is very spongy, the hollow-needle pump opener is useful. The needle is pushed through the cork, and air is pumped into the space between the cork and the wine. Only a few strokes of the pump should be used. If the cork does not move, use a corkscrew. We do not recommend hollow-needle openers with carbon dioxide cylinders. If the cork is stuck and too much carbon dioxide is released, the bottle may explode.

Some people prefer the U-shaped puller. This consists of two flat, springy prongs that are pushed between the bottle and the cork. If the cork is good it is then easily withdrawn. However, if the cork is loose, it may be pushed into the bottle.

Should the wines be decanted before serving? The answer is "sometimes" with young wines with a slight off-odor or excess carbon dioxide and "never" for old, bottled-aged wines. See also p. 21. As Peynaud (1980) has written, *"Le conseil de décanter les vins vieux quelques heures avant de les consommer conduit à une véritable dégradation."* We would only say Amen.

Time of Day

Moore et al. (1964) failed to find increased sensitivity to sweetness before, as compared to after, meals. In fact, they found a diurnal increase in sensitivity. They claim that previous studies do not take into account the bias for finding less sweetness after meals. Nevertheless, there is almost universal prejudice against critical sensory evaluations within 2 or 3 hours after meals. Possibly the time of day is of less critical importance if the panelists are sufficiently motivated.

Temperature

Red table wines should be served at or near 20°C (68°F), which is slightly less than normal room temperature in the United States. For white table wines, about 16°C (60°F) is low enough to give the desired cool sensation and high enough to allow detection of most of the desirable (and undesirable) odors. For sparkling wines, about 13°C (55°F) is ideal. This again is high enough to allow detection of the bouquet. Most restaurants and many people at home serve white table wines and sparkling wines too cold. In the sparkling wines, this restricts the loss of carbon dioxide, and some odors (good and bad) cannot be detected. For dessert wines, about 18°C (65°F) seems to be a good compromise. At higher temperatures, dessert wines appear too alcoholic. On the other hand, dry sherries are certainly more appealing at 16–18°C (60–65°F) than at higher temperatures.

People differ in their reactions to the temperatures at which wines are served. If one is accustomed to testing wines at 16°C (60°F), it is probably best to stick with that temperature because some bias will surely be introduced if a significantly higher or lower temperature is used. However, we believe that pretesting conditioning is justified so that all the judges are accustomed to testing at a certain temperature. In big judgings, wines are usually served at the same (room) temperature because the logistics make it difficult to serve every wine at the proper temperature. This also helps ensure that some defects will not be overlooked.

To bring the wine to temperature, placing the bottle at the desired temperature for several hours before serving is the least objectionable procedure. For red wines, this is not a critical problem unless the cellar temperature is very cold Gyllensköld (1967) has measured the temperature of wines placed at room temperature, in ice, in water, or in a refrigerator. These conditions should bring the wine to within 1°C of the desired temperature within 1 to 3 hours. Room temperature is recommended for reds, but not above 20°C (68°F). For whites, the refrigerator is best, but ice and water is favored as more practical for keeping the wine cool. The desired refrigerator temperature is about 6°–8°C (43°–46°F). The deep freeze is not recommended.

What is to be avoided is (1) raising or lowering the temperature too precipitously (especially of reds with a sediment), (2) warming to too high a temperature, or (3) warming only a part of the bottle (as in front of a fire).

Number of Samples

We recommend not more than five samples, or ten if the differences between samples are large. The problem varies according to the nature of the test. If the test is simply to eliminate poor samples, a careful judge can test 20 to 50 samples without undue fatigue. This is because this particular task is comparatively easy. In establishing preference or relative preference, many comparisons are required, and the task is more complex and time-consuming. Adaptation is then a constant problem, and severe restriction of the number of samples is essential (page 59).

The number of samples can be increased if a wide variety of characteristics are represented, as, for example, in three dry white table wines, three sweet table wines, three rosés, three dry red table wines, three sherries, and three ports. Judges of normal competence and experience should be able to evaluate these 18 wines in about 2 hours in the order given. If all the wines are of the same type and of approximately the same quality, no more than five to ten samples should be judged at one time. If the wines are to be compared, the smaller number is preferable. If each sample is to be judged separately and only once, the larger number should cause no problems. Long (1982), for example, recommends only eight samples in commercial sensory tests.

When as many as 20 samples of the same type must be evaluated at one judging, either of two simplifying procedures can be adopted. The judges could first identify and eliminate those samples that they all agreed were poor or non-type-conforming. With luck, this would reduce the number of samples deemed worthy of detailed evaluation. It may be necessary when 100 or more samples of the same type are to be judged to have two qualified panels do the elimination. All wines eliminated should be checked by the other panel. Or, the judges could examine the samples in incomplete block arrangements (page 259).

The problems of having too many samples are often underestimated. Adaptation is a constant threat to accuracy. As the number of samples increases, psychological confusion due to an inability to remember the sensory impressions of previous samples becomes a major problem. If each sample is compared with every other sample one time, the numbers of necessary comparisons are as follows:

Number of samples	Number of comparisons
2	1
3	3
4	6
5	10
6	15

This is for one order of comparison only (i.e., sample 1, then sample 2, or vice versa, but not both). If the comparisons are to be made in *both* orders (i.e., sample 1, then sample 2, *and* vice versa), a judging of five samples would require at least 20 comparisons. If some of the samples are very similar, many more comparisons may be needed. The problems of physiological adaptation and psychological confusion then become severe and make it difficult to obtain meaningful results.

In large, formal judgings, some compromise has to be made unless the examination is to take an inordinate amount of time. One possibility is to have a preliminary judging solely for eliminating the poorer samples. (The judges must be careful not to eliminate any acceptable samples.) At subsequent sessions, scoring or ranking can be used on the wines that remain. This reduces the number of comparisons and increases the accuracy. In any event, the judges should not be kept at their task for more than about one hour at a time, with generous breaks (15 minutes) in between. Puisais (1978) recommended 10 samples for judging, but for very technical sessions 5 were sufficient; for simpler conditions, 20 samples were admissable.

Klenk (1972) says that German wine judges can and do evaluate 150 to 200 wines in a day. He estimates this as equivalent to drinking a bottle of wine per day even if most of each sample is not swallowed. In fact, he believes that, if the judge is careful not to swallow any of the wine, up to 300 wines can be evaluated in a day! No statistical evidence for the validity of this belief is given, and our observations indicate that errors will occur, more often in the afternoon than in the morning. Klenk also allows judges to evaluate up to 50 sparkling wines or brandies per day. He is right that sparkling wines and brandies are very fatiguing, but even 50 of them seems excessive to us, if they are to be ranked in order of relative preference or meaningful quality judgments made.

Procedures

Coding As we have already noted, knowing the identity of the wine has real advantages for appreciation. But when objective comparisons of wines are to be made (whether by difference or preference), it is necessary to eliminate, or at least minimize, all biases.

Thus it is essential to conceal the identity of the wines. Some form of coding must be used. In contrast to our previous recommendation (Amerine et al. 1959), we now prefer two-digit numbers from 14 to 99. If the number of samples is small, one can choose the code by pointing at random at a list of numbers from 14 to 99. However, in some complicated block designs entailing many samples, a preprinted list of random numbers should be used to avoid duplications. The code numbers used should not suggest any particular order or quality to the panel.

Systematics Inexperienced judges often attempt to do too many things at once in sensory evaluation. Important sensory qualities are often missed in this pell-mell examination. Professionals proceed systematically (and usually slowly).

The best system is to begin by observing the appearance. This may give valuable clues about possible defects in the wine. For example, the type of cloudiness may reveal the nature of the defect (page 30). Note also whether bubbles are present—they are usually evident as tiny bubbles at the glass/wine interface. This indicates excess carbon dioxide. In sparkling wines, the bubbles are larger, and they rise freely. The smaller the bubbles, however, the longer the wine will stay sparkling. If the bubbles are very large (usually in rapidly fermented or poorly carbonated sparkling wines), the wine may go flat in a few minutes. Persistence of the carbonation is considered a quality factor for bottle-fermented sparkling wines.

Some judges pay a good deal of attention to the "tears" of the wine. If a clean wine glass is half-filled with wine, one observes that a liquid film creeps slowly up the side of the glass. After a few minutes, some of the liquid at the ascending interface begins to form drops, which roll back down the glass in irregular columns. Thus the wine is said to be weeping, and the drops are its tears. (In Great Britain, they are called "legs"; in the technical literature, they are called "arches.")

The phenomenon is due to the Marangoni effects, but it was not first explained by Marangoni. Scriven and Sternling (1960) have given a history of the pertinent studies. They credit the British engineer and physicist James Thomson (the brother of Lord Kelvin) with the first correct explanation, in 1855. Briefly, the preferential evaporation of ethanol at the surface of the wine causes the surface film to be more aqueous than the liquid below. The maximum rate of ethanol evaporation is in the region of the air/liquid/glass interface at the top of the meniscus. Therefore the water concentration is a maximum in this region, and so is the surface tension. The vertical gradient in the surface tension causes the liquid film to creep up the side of the glass until it can no longer overcome the effect of gravity. As more liquid is dragged up the side of the glass by this "surface tension pump," it coalesces into drops (tears) at the top of the film, and flows back down again.

It is clear that the tears of wine are primarily water. The greater the ethanol content of the wine, the more tears there are. For the tears in 12% and 18% solutions of ethanol in water, see Plates 13 and 14.* The idea, still put forth in some popular texts, that the tears of

---

*Photographers will be interested in how these technically very difficult photographs were obtained. They were taken with an 8 × 10-inch view camera mounted with a 12-inch focal-length lens. The optimal background consisted of an out-of-focus black grid on a gray card, to provide visual edge refractions in the otherwise virtually invisible tears. This grid was placed 12 inches behind the principal plane of focus of the subject. The lens was closed down to f/11. Exposure was by flash, to freeze the motion. To obtain adequate contrast, it was necessary to print on ultrahigh-contrast Brovira #6 enlarging paper. The developer was heated to further increase the print contrast.

wine are glycerol is obviously erroneous. The boiling point of glycerol is 290°C (554°F) and its vapor pressure above the wine is negligibly low.

A careful consideration of the color and its appropriateness for the type of wine should follow the examination of the appearance. Abnormal colors may suggest defects in the wine. A brown-colored wine may be oxidized or unduly bitter (page 27). Of course, one must be wary of stimulus errors. A bluish-colored wine *may* have an undesirably high pH, but it could be a very young wine of certain varieties that is basically sound. Reducing the pH, aging, or fining and filtering the wine usually remove the bluish tint.

When finished wines are being considered for purchase, their appearance and color may be of critical importance (see Plate 15). At the present time, no one can sell a cloudy wine in the United States, much less a wine of abnormal color. This statement may be wishful thinking. We have seen some supposedly high quality white table wines with very little color from too high a level of sulfur dioxide. We have seen several Cabernet Sauvignons with purple-red color. These aberrations are unfortunate.

The experienced judge sets cloudy and off-color wines aside, thus saving his palate for wines without these defects. Of course, when a sensory examination of young wines is made in the winery to determine the appropriate finishing techniques, the appearance is of only secondary importance, since the finishing will surely eliminate any cloudiness. Slight defects in color may be corrected by appropriate aging, finishing, or blending with other wines.

Following the visual inspection, a careful olfactory examination should be made. This too should be done systematically. The wine in the glass should be swirled rather vigorously (three or four swirls should be enough) and then the glass brought quickly to the nose and sniffed. The purpose of the swirling is to expose as large a surface area of wine as possible so that evaporation of the volatile substances is enhanced. The released odors are concentrated by the tulip shape of the glass, with the more volatile components being lost first. If the swirling is too prolonged, more of the more volatile odors (both desirable and undesirable) will be lost, perhaps to below their absolute thresholds, and the character of the odor will change. We recommend a quick, strong sniff with full mental concentration on possible off-odors, which are usually identified first. Successive swirlings and sniffs follow only after a brief pause (15 to 30 seconds) to forestall the effects of adaptation and should be directed to the aroma and bouquet and their appropriateness for the type. If more than three or four such examination cycles are desired, one should empty the glass, pour some fresh wine, and repeat the process. Experienced judges try to quantify their impression at each stage—both for off-odors and the desirable aroma and bouquet.

Finally, some wine (about 10 ml, or ⅓ oz) is placed on the tongue and spread over its entire surface so as to make contact with as many taste buds as possible (see Plate 16). It is wise to try to identify each of the basic tastes successively. We prefer to evaluate the degree of sweetness first, followed by sourness and bitterness. Many other judges look for the degree of sourness first, followed by sweetness and bitterness. As already indicated (page 49), bitterness should not be confused with astringency, which is a tactile sensation. The degree of each taste should be noted, preferably in writing.

During the actual tasting, more odors are being released as the wine warms up in the mouth. These odors are often called *flavor*, and they should be looked for consciously.

How much wine, if any, should be swallowed? At home we drink the wine; that's what it's for! But in a judging of 5 to 20 wines, this is inadvisable. Nevertheless, even experienced judges consciously or unconsciously swallow a little wine to savor the aftertaste. We doubt that there are enough taste buds in the throat to make this worthwhile. But if a judge thinks this is important, it is probably wise to allow him to continue, provided he doesn't swallow too much! Even without swallowing, the senses become fatigued. Wise judges take frequent breaks.

The texture of the wine must also be noted. The tactile sensations of astringency and the thinness (alcoholicity and lack of sweetness) or thickness (related to sweetness and high ethanol) are easiest to recognize.

Theoretically, all of the sensory impressions should now be complete, except perhaps those of temperature. However, as the score cards indicate (page 212), there is one more attribute that must be taken into account. Apparently the sensory reactions together mediate a combined response, which we call general quality. This requires experience. General quality should not be used by the judge as a means of adjusting his quality score to what he considers "correct." General quality is a separate and distinctive factor. We have taught our students that it is the memorableness of the character of the wine, or its lasting come-hither appeal.

Selection of Test Procedure

In the home situation there will normally be one wine, and the usual discussion will reveal the good (and bad) aspects of the wine. No statistical analysis of the discussion is needed. Pleasure is the goal.

However, in the commercial world of wine making, judging and consumer testing in which comparisons between two or more samples are made, then selection of the correct test procedure, and finally statistical analysis of the results are necessary.

Pangborn (1980) gives a list of proper applications of sensory analyses of foods. Examples of misuse are the use of untrained judges doing elaborate semantic differential scaling of differences or similarities; the use of trained judges to rate hedonic responses in difference testing, assuming no preference if no statistical difference is found, and vice versa; and inappropriate scaling procedures (nonlinear scales, insufficient scalar points, and inappropriate scalar designations, etc.).

The experimental design for analysis of the results of a sensory test should be made before the test. It should provide (Sidel and Stone 1976): (1) "an unbiased estimate of the effect to be measured, (2) a valid estimate of the variability of the estimated effect, (3) an opportunity to use a simple mathematical model in the analyses of data and for testing a specific hypothesis concerning the true effects, and (4) efficiency in terms of cost per unit of information."

Table 6–3 gives a summary of a number of test procedures. They will be discussed further in the rest of this book.

Some Suggested Exercises

Serious amateur wine judges usually wish to improve their ability to distinguish between wines. How do they go about it? Obviously they practice. The main problem is finding a fixed frame of reference for each of the major odor and taste components of wines. What, for example, is low or high sourness? How does a low concentration of acetaldehyde smell compared with a high concentration? Can one distinguish low, moderate, and high concentrations of sulfur dioxide in wines?

The following exercises are intended to help answer these and similar questions. They should also prove useful in selecting the best judges for many sensory evaluation panels. However, there is certainly no direct relation between one's inherent taste or odor sensitivity and one's ability to evaluate wine quality. For each specific sensory characteristic, one must also know the level of intensity that is appropriate in the wine in question, and one must be able to recognize the proper balance among the various sensory characteristics. Experience is what really counts.

Obviously, most people do not have a ready supply of citric acid or glycerol or ethyl acetate, nor do they have the equipment for measuring or weighing such chemicals. We suggest that you solicit the interest and help of an enologically inclined chemist or pharma-

Table 6-3   Classification of sensory tests.

Psychological classification	Name of procedure	Type of judges	Statistical procedure	Text reference
Nominal	Single stimulus	Trained or consumer	A–not A	162
Nominal	Paired difference	Trained	Binomial ($p = \frac{1}{2}$) One-tailed	196
Nominal	Paired preference	Consumer	Binomial ($p = \frac{1}{2}$) Two-tailed	197
Nominal	Duo–trio	Trained	Binomial ($p = \frac{1}{2}$) One-tailed	198
Nominal	Triangle	Trained	Binomial ($p = \frac{1}{3}$) One-tailed	199
Interval	Ratio	Trained	Magnitude estimation	302
Ordinal	Ranking	Trained or consumer	Coeff. of concordance or analysis of variance	221 275
Interval	Hedonic	Trained or consumer	Analysis of variance	247
Interval	Scoring	Experienced	t or analysis of variance	225
Interval	Descriptive*	Highly trained	Varies, usually analysis of variance	289
Interval or ordinal	Complete block	Trained	Analysis of variance	240
Interval or ordinal	Incomplete block	Trained	Analysis of variance	259

*See pages 289–299 for a discussion.

cist. They do have the necessary chemicals and equipment, or can get them without difficulty. (See also Marcus 1974 and Rankine 1971.)

Thresholds   A suggested series of concentrations for testing sensitivity to sucrose (sweetness) in aqueous solution is 0.1%, 0.3%, 0.7%, and 1.2% by weight. The "A–not-A" type of test may be used, although other methods work equally well. In this test, a water blank (the standard) is tasted first. Then one of the sucrose solutions (in a random order) or another blank is tasted. The judge decides whether the sample presented is the same as or different from the standard. The test is repeated 6 times for each concentration, including the blank (30 times in all). Typical results for such a test are shown in Figure 6–1.

	Blank	0.1%	Sample (% sucrose) 0.3%	0.7%	1.2%
Correct decision	3	3	4	5	6
% Correct	50	50	66.7	83.3	100

Nature of difference _____

Taste (or smell) the standard (S) and the sample. Decide whether the sample is the same as or different from the standard.

Sample no.	Same as S	Different from S
_____	_____	_____
_____	_____	_____
_____	_____	_____
_____	_____	_____

Name _____ Date _____

Figure 6-1   Record form for an A–not-A test.

What is this judge's threshold for sucrose in water? Obviously 50% of the judge's decisions should be correct by chance alone. The percentage of correct decisions *above* chance is defined as $P_c = 2 \times (P_o - 50)$, where P_o is the percentage of correct decisions observed. In practice, the threshold is usually taken to be that concentration at which the judge makes 50% correct decisions above chance

($P_c = 50$)—that is, 75% correct decisions observed ($P_o = 75$), since $2(75 - 50) = 50$. In the present example, the sucrose threshold is therefore somewhere between 0.3% and 0.7%. A more exact threshold could be established by repeating the test with solutions between 0.3% and 0.7% sucrose—for example, 0.3%, 0.35%, 0.43%, 0.53%, and 0.68%.

The results can be plotted on log-probability paper, with P_c on the probability axis (ordinate) and concentration on the log axis (abscissa). Draw a straight line as close to the data points as possible. The intersection of this line with a horizontal line drawn from $P_c = 50$ defines the concentration threshold. For a still more accurate value, the line can be plotted by the method of least squares, either manually or with an electronic calculator or computer. For purposes of demonstration, we suggest that the group results be pooled and the average threshold calculated. However, it is instructive to compare the thresholds of various members of the group. For this purpose, the test should probably be repeated until there are at least 15 correct decisions for each individual.

This type of test can also be used to determine the thresholds for many other substances, in either wine or water. For example, the following amounts of various chemicals could be added to the base wine or water (the standards) that constitutes the first of five samples in the series: acetaldehyde (40, 80, 140, and 200 mg/l); acetic acid (3, 5, 9, and 14 g/l); diacetyl (4, 8, 12, and 20 mg/l, [Rankine et al. 1969a]); citric acid 0.2, 0.4, 0.8, and 1.6 g/l); ethyl acetate (30, 60, 100, and 150 mg/l); sorbic acid (50, 100, 175, and 275 mg/l); sulfur dioxide (40, 90, 150, and 250 mg/l); tartaric acid (0.03, 0.07, 0.10, and 0.15 g/l). The exact amounts to add will vary with the temperature, judge, and base wine. The sulfur dioxide test should be the last one attempted and should be made no more than once per day.

When water is used as the standard rather than a base wine, these tests establish the absolute thresholds of the judges (see page 69). When wines are used, the thresholds should be interpreted as difference thresholds (except for sorbic acid) because the concentration of the component in the base wine may already exceed that corresponding to the absolute threshold. Care should be exercised in selecting a fairly neutral wine of normal composition as the base wine. If testing time is limited, one may use four concentrations instead of five (omitting the lowest).

Thresholds can also be determined by the methods of just-noticeable difference (*jnd*) and just-not-noticeable difference (*jnnd*). In the former test, the samples are presented in order of increasing concentration, from below threshold to well above threshold. The judge indicates the first sample that he or she finds just noticeably different (sweeter, sourer, etc.) from the preceding sample. (For a record form see Figure 6–2.) This test can be used for determining absolute as well as difference thresholds. Because the errors of expectation and habituation may occur, the test should be done in both directions—that is, *jnd* and *jnnd*. In the latter test, the samples are presented in order of *decreasing* concentration; the judge indicates the first sample that he or she finds just *not* noticeably different from the preceding sample.

Nature of difference _____

Sample order: C H J K N R T

Taste (or smell) the samples, from the lowest concentration (left) to the highest (right). Indicate the first sample that is just noticeably different in taste (or smell) from the preceding sample.

Difference first noticed in sample _____

Name _____ Date _____

Figure 6–2　Record form for a just-noticeable-difference test.

For example, the test for a *jnd* is done five times with a series of wines containing citric acid. The base wine (nothing added) contains 0.50 g/100 ml; the amounts of citric acid added to make the remaining four samples are 0.02, 0.05, 0.10, and 0.25 g/100 ml, giving samples with 0.52, 0.55, 0.60, and 0.75 g/100 ml, respectively. In the *jnd* series, the actual *jnd* is 0.55 three times and 0.60 twice; in the corresponding *jnnd* series (also done five times) the actual *jnnd* is 0.55 three times and 0.52 twice. The weighted means of these two sets of data are given by

$$\frac{0.55(3) + 0.60(2)}{5} = 0.57 \, (jnd)$$

$$\frac{0.55(3) + 0.52(2)}{5} = 0.54 \, (jnnd)$$

and the overall mean value is therefore 0.56. Thus this judge's difference threshold for citric acid in wine is $0.56 - 0.50 = 0.06$ g/100 ml. The usual measures of central tendency, statistical significance, probable error, and so on, can be applied.

For determination of thresholds, Meilgaard and Reid (1979) recommended the ascending method of limits with the triangle system, with six increments of the compound being studied.

Off-Odors   The threshold tests for acetaldehyde, diacetyl, ethyl acetate, sorbic acid, and sulfur dioxide (listed above) can also be use for familiarizing the student with common off-odors. Other off-odors can be produced by adding a small amount of the substance in question to a neutral wine. For example, about 2 to 5 parts per billion of hydrogen sulfide will be detectable. For the higher alcohols, 400 mg/l of 3-methyl-1-butanol (isoamyl alcohol) will be adequate to give a fusel oil odor to the wine. Securing wines with typical and easily detectable off-odors of corkiness, moldiness, or woodiness may be difficult. One should inquire of wine merchants or wineries for help in locating such wines.

Other Exercises   Most of the procedures discussed previously can also be used in the training and selection of judges. For detecting differences of a nonspecific character (an unidentified off-odor, for example), the duo–trio test (page 198) and triangle test (page 199) are most useful. Judges who cannot distinguish the off-odor can be screened out. When potential judges are being trained, those who fail to detect the odor will know that they must practice to reach the requisite proficiency, or be disqualified. The duo–trio and triangle tests can also be used in blending wines to match a standard—an important winery operation. They are useful not only in winery operations but also in the training and selection of blenders.

Paired-sample tests (page 196) can be used for establishing quality differences. However, ranking (page 221) and scoring (page 211) are often the preferred procedures. Can an individual correctly rank a series of wines in increasing order of Cabernet aroma, sweetness, sourness, ethanol content, and so on? Those who are deficient in one or more such skills need further training and practice, or should simply not be used on a sensory evaluation panel for which the skill in question is a requirement.

Because individuals differ in their understanding of the tests, some preliminary training is desirable so that all the potential judges start the test series on an approximately equal basis. In all training tests, the statistical significance of the results must be calculated unless it is obvious from inspection of the data that the results are insignificant.

The procedures of descriptive analysis (page 289) should prove very useful in training students. Standard solutions that resemble certain varietal aromas could help to anchor the learner's use of certain terms.

Quality   Every amateur wine judge wants to be shown wines of varying quality. And he should be. But how are the wines of varying quality to be selected? Certainly not from the results of popular judgings or of many magazine articles. Probably not by comparing the wines of different vineyards since they differ so much in style. We now believe the best way to start is with the wines of a specific vineyard of different years (providing the vines are mature and not overcropped, that the method of fermentation remains the same, and that the wines are of nearly the same age). About four or five Zinfandels of vineyard X (say 1975, 1976, 1978, 1979, and 1980) may be scored (page 211) or ranked (page 221). The results of the more experienced judges can be compared with those of the less experienced, or the individual judges may be compared with each other, particularly if the judging is repeated several times.

But this is obviously not enough. The happiest solution is for the instructor to have had such a wide experience that he or she knows which vineyards and years to select. Failing this, one must consult reliable winemakers. Honest vinters will be glad to share their opinions regarding several vintages, of say, their Cabernet Sauvignons. They are not, obviously, completely disinterested guides (nor can they be).

Wine judgings have, especially in this country and in eastern Europe, grown to be very large and important public-relations-wise. This is unfortunate because the results of few judgings justify the attention given to them.

The reasons for the lack of significance are many: unqualified or variously qualified judges, too many wines, too little time for rejudging, poor judging conditions, complaints as to selection of wines (probably justified when the producer ships the wine), and comparison of wines of varying types in the same class (probably a justifiable complaint). However, not all the criticisms of judgings are unjustified. See Rankine's (1974) defense of the concentrated Australian judgings. Bassin (1981) complains that results of five panel members are averaged. Well, why not? Complaints as to preference for high-alcohol or high-colored wines are said to raise a question as to the skill of the panel. We have not noted it to be a problem. Bassin (1981) adds, "Any comparative tasting—regardless of how well intentioned and how well conducted—is nothing more than a tabulation of how a certain selection of wines impressed a certain group of people on a certain day. The very same wines on a different day with the same people or the same wines on the same day with different people may lead to different results." Long (1982) makes the same point. Unless one is using professionals with similiar standards and training, this is, sadly, true.

Should the wines be served "blind" or with the labels showing? For beginning students, we formerly favored the latter method because it gives the student the best chance to associate the label with the odor, taste, and flavor of the wine. However, this assumes that the students, and especially the instructor, are completely unprejudiced—a very risky assumption. For beginners, and certainly for more advanced students, "blind" judgings are much to be preferred. At home, the wines should be served with the labels showing unless some consensus opinion is desired. In this case, the wines should be served "blind." Ranking procedures are then usually preferred, but if the group has had experience in using a particular score card, scoring can be employed. (See also pages 211–221, 259–273, and 275–287.)

Just because we have tried to train *dégustateurs* does not mean that the training has been the objective of our teaching. For amateurs and professions, we hope that these exercises will show them what to look for. They are a means to an end, not the final objective. The final objectives are obviously (1) to produce the finest quality wines we can in California, or wherever, and (2) to recognize and appreciate the highest quality once we have produced it.

For some general nontechnical discussions, see Amerine et al. (1980), Buxbaum (1951), Cloquet (1906), Daepp (1968), Don (1977), Got (1955), Hagenow (1969), Hennig (1950), Lake (1969), Leglise (1976), Mareschalchi (1974), Marteau (1953), Mowbray (1981), Pittaro (1979), Puisais (1982), Troost (1972), Troost and Wanner (1962), and Yoxall (1972).

For more technical references, see Adda and Jounela-Eriksson (1979), Amerine et al. (1965a), Kiermeir and Haevecher (1972), Marie et al. (1962), Sauvageot (1982), Schöffling and Weiling (1973), and Schrodt and Jacob (1966).

SOME SUGGESTED EXERCISES

Malgré les habitudes et quoi qu'on en pense, l'endroit ou l'on déguste le moins bien, c'est le chai.

PIERRE POUPON

When you can measure what you are speaking about, and express it in numbers, you know something about it; but when you cannot measure it, when you cannot express it in numbers, your knowledge is of a meager and unsatisfactory kind: it may be the beginning of knowledge, but you have scarcely, in your thoughts, advanced to the stage of science.

LORD KELVIN

II
STATISTICAL
PROCEDURES

"Well, I'll be damned if I'll defend to the death your right to say something that's statistically incorrect."

CHAPTER 7

Terminology and Quick and Easy Analyses

For centuries, wine has been an integral part of the social and cultural life of most countries, and probably no fermented food product has a longer history of quality and sensory evaluation than wine. Homer, Pliny, and Horace wrote of wines that were famous long before, or at the beginning of, the Christian era. The fame of the wines they extolled was undoubtedly based on subjective comparisons, or perhaps even on some sort of deliberate sensory examinations.

Prior to 1940, many quality evaluations in the wine industry were performed by only one or two professionals. Even today, considerable quantities of wine are purchased by skilled wine brokers who base their selections solely on their own evaluations. However, with increasing consumer demand for better wines, greater competition among wine producers, and the development of appropriate statistical procedures for the analysis of sensory data, many wine professionals have concluded that it is unsound to rely on the quality and standards-of-identity judgments of only one or two individuals. This is particularly true in new product development and quality control.

Today it is standard practice in many wineries and wine-distributing companies and, indeed, throughout the entire food industry, to use regular panel evaluations, not only for quality control of their own products, but also for comparisons with competing products. The data obtained in such evaluations are then subjected to appropriate statistical analysis. Unfortunately, raw data indicating differences among wines in the popular press often imply significance when there is, in fact, no statistical justification for such a conclusion.

Recently, some wine distributors have in their advertising reported results of tastings comparing their own wines with those of other wineries. Results are the opinions of one or a group of judges, and, in most cases when the raw data are available and are analyzed statistically, the reported results have little or no validity. Unfortunately, in many cases of private and public judgings reported in the press, only averages or awards are recorded, with no indication of the scores or awards assigned by the individual judges.

In any judging, if the panel members agree, the results are conclusive, but, in the usual judgings, there are considerable differences of opinion among judges. The greater these differences, the less reliable are the results. When considerable disagreement among judges exists, one can only conclude that, with a different panel of judges, the scores might be considerably different. In any judging, samples of all wines should be obtained in the same way and should be treated identically. This has not always been the procedure followed in the case of wine samples compared in some of the judgings, the results of which have been highly advertised. No wine producer or distributor is apt to report the results of judgings not favorable to his products. Results of many of the judgings reported in advertising or in the press should be viewed with healthy skepticism.

It is the purpose of Part II of this book to describe and encourage the use of statistical procedures for the analysis of sensory data.

It is only in this way that the reliability of the results of judgings can be evaluated.

In this chapter, we shall present some fundamental statistical concepts and describe and illustrate the use of some quick and easy methods of analysis of sensory data making use of a minimum of mathematics and considerable use of tables for those people who do not wish to pursue more detailed mathematical procedures. The methods described will also be found useful in quality control when answers are needed immediately following sampling and also in the analysis of the results of judging panels when outcomes are desired immediately following the judging of each group of wines. The procedures are simple and yet agree surprisingly well with results obtained by use of more sophisticated methods. Before illustrating their uses, however, some explanation of customary statistical terms is necessary.

Terminology

In order to summarize a set of data and to simplify its presentation, certain measures that describe important features are employed. Two important measures are those of central tendency and dispersion. Any measure indicating a center of distribution is called a *measure of central tendency,* and a numerical value indicating the amount of scatter or spread about a central point is called a *measure of dispersion.* Three common measures of central tendency are the mean, the median, and the mode, and three important measures of dispersion are the range, the variance, and the standard deviation.

Mean (or Arithmetic Mean) For a set of n numbers X_1, X_2, X_3, ..., X_n, the mean commonly denoted by the Greek letter μ is defined as the arithmetic average—that is,

$$\mu = \frac{X_1 + X_2 + X_3 + \cdots + X_n}{n} = \frac{\Sigma X}{n} \quad (1)$$

where the Greek letter Σ is a short-cut indication for the summation process.

The mean is the most frequently used measure of central tendency. It is easy to compute, takes all numbers into consideration, and can be expressed mathematically so that it is well designed for algebraic manipulation.

Median   The median of a set of n numbers arranged in order of ascending or descending magnitude is the middle number of the set if n is odd and the average of the two middle numbers if n is even. The median is not influenced by extreme measurements. If, for some reason, it is desirable to ignore such values, then the median is useful. One disadvantage is that it can not be expressed algebraically.

Mode   The mode is the number of the set of n numbers that occurs most frequently. If there are no duplicate numbers in the set, there is no mode, or there may be several modes if there are several of the numbers that are repeated the same number of times. The mode is sometimes referred to as the most fashionable value. It is the least used of the measures of central tendency.

Range   For a set of numbers, the range is the difference between the largest and smallest numbers. Although the range does give some indication of the spread of the data about the mean, it depends entirely on extreme values and indicates nothing about the distribution of the data between these two extremes or the concentration of the data about the center. It is sometimes useful in quality control.

Variance   For a set of n numbers $X_1, X_2, X_3, \ldots, X_n$, the variance, denoted by v or σ^2, is defined as

$$\sigma^2 = \frac{(X_1 - \mu)^2 + (X_2 - \mu)^2 + (X_3 - \mu)^2 + \cdots + (X_n - \mu)^2}{n}$$

$$= \frac{\Sigma(X - \mu)^2}{n} \tag{2}$$

The variance is a widely used measure of dispersion. An important property of the variance is that of additivity. If several different and independent factors contribute to the dispersion in a set of data, the total variance is the sum of the variances due to the individual factors. Additivity of variance plays a part in many statistical methods, one of which, the analysis of variance, we shall use extensively in later discussions.

Standard Deviation   The standard deviation σ is defined as the square root of the variance—that is,

$$\sigma = \sqrt{\frac{\Sigma(X - \mu)^2}{n}} \quad \text{or} \quad \sigma = \sqrt{\frac{\Sigma X^2 - \frac{(\Sigma X)^2}{n}}{n}} \tag{3}$$

These expressions are numerically the same. Sometimes it is more convenient to use one or the other of the forms. The standard deviation is perhaps the most important and the most widely used measure of variability. A relatively small value of σ indicates close clustering about the mean and a relatively large value, wide scattering about the mean. At a glance, one can judge the reliability of the mean by observing the size of the standard deviation. The standard deviation constitutes a convenient statistical unit for use in the construction of other statistics and in the comparison of these with one another. Many measures are expressed in terms of the standard deviation.

EXAMPLE 1   For the set of numbers 3, 3, 5, 9, 10, what are the mean, median, mode, range, variance, and standard deviation?

(a) Mean $\mu = \dfrac{3 + 3 + 5 + 9 + 10}{5} = \dfrac{30}{5} = 6$

(b) Median $= 5$

(c) Mode $= 3$

(d) Range $= 10 - 3 = 7$

(e) Variance

$$\sigma^2 = \frac{(3 - 6)^2 + (3 - 6)^2 + (5 - 6)^2 + (9 - 6)^2 + (10 - 6)^2}{5}$$

$$= \frac{44}{5} = 8.8$$

(f) Standard deviation $\sigma = \sqrt{8.8} = 2.97$

Probability   In Part I of this book, we referred to the importance of statistical procedures in providing tests of significance. A discussion of significance of experimental data is usually based on a comparison of the actual results with those that would be obtained if chance alone were the determining factor. Since the interpretation of such tests depends upon the probabilities of the events in question, some understanding of the concept of probability is essential.

Briefly, the probability of an event can be defined as the relative frequency of that event in a large number of trials. From this definition it is clear that probability is a number between 0 and 1. An event with probability $p = 0$ cannot occur, and one with probability $p = 1$ is certain to occur. When we say that the probability of getting heads on the toss of a well-balanced coin is ½, we mean that one of every two tosses, *on the average*, will give heads. In other words, it is probable that in a large number of tosses 50% heads and 50% tails will be obtained. This does not mean that in 10 tosses of a coin we will get exactly 5 heads and 5 tails, nor that in 100 tosses we will get exactly 50 heads and 50 tails. However, if we continue tossing the coin indefinitely, the ratio of the number of heads (or tails) to the total number of tosses will approach the value ½ (0.5) ever more closely.

Imagine that a judge is presented with three glasses, two of which contain the same wine and the third a different but very similar wine. If the judge cannot, in fact, detect a difference among the three, chance alone will determine his or her ability to pick the odd wine. The probability of success in this instance is ⅓; the probability of failure is ⅔.

In a sequence of trials in each of which a certain result may or may not occur, the occurrence of the result is called a *success* and its nonoccurrence a *failure*. In a sequence of coin tosses, for example, getting heads might be designated a success; getting tails would therefore constitute a failure. This terminology is purely conventional, and the result called *success* need not necessarily be the desired one. The sum of the probabilities of success and failure for a given result is always equal to 1. Therefore, if the probability of success is p, the probability of failure is $1 - p$.

Problems requiring a statistical treatment of events (or results) often entail decisions based on a limited number of observations, the conclusions from which are to apply to a much larger category of events, of which those actually observed are only a part. The larger category about which we wish information is called the *population* (or universe), and the actual observations constitute the *sample*. If the sample is selected in such a way that all components of the population have an equal chance of being included, the sample is called a *random sample*. A quantity calculated from the sample—for example, its standard deviation (see page 226)—is called a *sample statistic*, or simply a *statistic*. Using a statistic to draw conclusions concerning a population from a sample of that population is called *statistical inference*. For such conclusions to be valid, the sample must be randomly selected out of the total population.

Null Hypothesis   The statistical method used in any scientific investigation originates with an investigator's idea, which leads to a tentative hypothesis about the population to be studied. This hypothesis, commonly called the *null hypothesis*, must be a specific assumption, made about some statistical measure of the population, with which to compare the experimental results. For example, in the toss of a fair coin, the null hypothesis $p = \frac{1}{2}$ states that, in a single toss, the chances are one in two (50:50) that a head will show.

In a consideration of a judge's ability to differentiate between two wine samples of differing quality, the null hypothesis $p = \frac{1}{2}$

states that the chances are 50:50 that the judge will make the correct decision; that is, it states that the judge does not have the sensory ability to detect a difference. In the previous example of the judge trying to select the odd wine sample from three, two of which are alike, the null hypothesis $p = \frac{1}{3}$ states that the chances are one in three that the judge will correctly select the odd sample; that is, it states that the judge does not have the sensory ability required for this particular task. In a comparison of the average quality ratings (scores) of two different wines, the null hypothesis $\mu_1 - \mu_2 = 0$ states that the difference between the mean scores μ_1 and μ_2 for the two populations is zero; that is, there are no quality differences between the two wine populations from which the samples were selected.

Statistical methods allow us to predict whether a null hypothesis is likely to be true or false. A *statistical test,* which is a decision rule or procedure, is then applied to the observed results to decide whether they agree sufficiently well with the expected values to support the null hypothesis or to suggest its rejection in favor of an *alternative hypothesis.* An alternative to the null hypothesis ($p = \frac{1}{2}$) of no sensory ability to differentiate between the two wine samples might be $p > \frac{1}{2}$. This alternative hypothesis states that, in a single trial, the probability of the judge's making the correct decision is greater than $\frac{1}{2}$; that is, it states that the judge does have some sensory ability to perform the task. If this hypothesis is true, the chances of the judge's being successful in detecting a difference are therefore better than 50:50. Analogously, an alternative to the null hypothesis $p = \frac{1}{3}$ might be $p > \frac{1}{3}$. The null hypothesis is usually designated H_0 and the alternative hypothesis H_1.

An alternative hypothesis is called a *one-sided alternative* and the corresponding test a *one-tailed test* if the hypothesis specifies a value on only one side of the value stated in the null hypothesis. The alternative hypotheses $p > \frac{1}{2}$ and $p > \frac{1}{3}$ are therefore both one-sided as are $p < \frac{1}{2}$ and $p < \frac{1}{3}$. If, however, an alternative hypothesis specifies values on both sides of the value stated in the null hypothesis, it is called a *two-sided alternative,* and the corresponding test is called a *two-tailed test.* The alternative hypotheses $p \neq$ ½ and $p \neq$ ⅓ are both two-sided since they may be greater than or less than ½ and ⅓ respectively. One- and two-tailed tests, illustrated in Figures 7–1 and 7–2, will be further discussed in the next chapter.

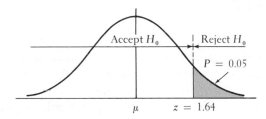

Figure 7-1 One-tailed test, 5% level.

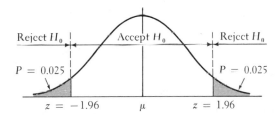

Figure 7-2 Two-tailed test, 5% level.

Types of Errors   Decision rules are seldom infallible and may lead to rejection of a true hypothesis, which is called an error of the first kind, or a *type I error.* Or, they may lead to acceptance of a false hypothesis, which is called an error of the second kind, or a *type II error.* The probabilities of occurrence of these errors can be minimized but never reduced to zero.

Experimental results rarely lead to obvious conclusions, and the question immediately arises as to the dividing line between acceptance and rejection of the null hypothesis. By a commonly accepted convention, the null hypothesis is rejected if, under the hypothesis, the result observed in the sample would occur by chance alone *at most* once in 20 trials ($P \leq 0.05$).* Such a result is called *significant*. If, under the null hypothesis and by chance alone, the result would occur at most once in 100 trials ($P \leq 0.01$), it is called *highly significant*, and, if it would occur at most once in 1,000 trials ($P \leq 0.001$), it is called *very highly significant*. These are known as the 5%, 1%, and 0.1% levels of significance, respectively. It should be understood, however, that, although we accept or reject the null hypothesis on the basis of these levels, we have not proved or disproved it, because there is always the possibility, however remote, that the difference between the observed result and that expected under the null hypothesis could have arisen by chance alone. At the 5% level of significance ($P = 0.05$), we wrongly reject the null hypothesis 5% of the time; at the 1% level ($P = 0.01$), we wrongly reject it 1% of the time; and, at the 0.1% level ($P = 0.001$), we wrongly reject it 0.1% of the time, or once every 1,000 times, on the average.

Correlation   The coefficient of correlation r (or R) is a measure of the degree of association between paired variables, such as corresponding scores of two judges for a group of wines. For k pairs of scores X and Y, r is calculated as follows:

$$r = \frac{\Sigma xy}{\sqrt{\Sigma x^2 \, \Sigma y^2}} \qquad \text{with } (k-2)\, df$$

---

*The small p introduced earlier is used to denote the probability of a simple event, such as getting heads in a single toss of a coin. The capital P is used to denote the probability of a composite of simple events, such as getting 3 heads in 5 tosses of a coin.

where $x = X - \overline{X}$ and $y = Y - \overline{Y}$. The value $r = -1$ indicates complete disagreement, and $r = 1$ indicates perfect agreement between judges. The value $r = 0$ indicates no relationship between the scores. In Appendix N, values of r (R) are given for various levels of significance and various degrees of freedom.

Quick and Easy Analyses

In sensory evaluation, we know that judges differ in the scores that they assign to various samples. If all judges evaluated all samples in exactly the same way, the total scores for all samples would be exactly the same, and no analysis would be needed. However, this is very rarely the case, and for each sample there is a range of scores, the *range* for each sample being the difference between the highest and lowest scores for the sample. In the usual analysis, we start with the assumption that all wines from which the samples are taken are the same, and, as a result, the total scores for all samples should be the same (null hypothesis). We can live with this assumption if differences among sample scores assigned by the judges are small, but the larger the differences become, the less faith we have in the assumption. At what point do sample total scores differ so much that we can no longer support the hypothesis of equality in the totals and become convinced that significant differences exist in the wines from which the samples are drawn? The 5% and 1% levels are the usual levels of rejection.

For analyses at these two levels, Kurtz et al. (1965) have developed tables based on ranges within samples, which can be adapted to permit a quick analysis of wine-judging scores, and Kramer (1973) has provided similar tables for ranked data. The use of these tables will be illustrated by means of several examples. The procedures used in the analyses of data based on scores follow those suggested by Tukey (1953).

EXAMPLE 2   Five scores for each of two wines are shown in Table 7-1. Is there a significant difference at the 5% level between the total scores of the two wines?

Table 7-1   Five scores for each of two wines.

	Wine	
	S_1	S_2
	6	6
	7	4
	7	5
	8	6
	9	7
Total	37	28
Range within sample	$9 - 6 = 3$	$7 - 4 = 3$
Total of ranges $= 3 + 3 = 6$		

(a) From Appendix A-1, for 2 samples of 5 scores each, the top entry is 1.53.

(b) For significance, the difference between total scores must exceed (total of ranges)(1.53) = 6(1.53) = 9.18.

(c) Since $37 - 28 = 9$ is less than 9.18, there is no reason to reject the hypothesis of no difference, and we can say that there is no evidence that the samples are significantly different at the 5% level.

EXAMPLE 3   Five scores for each of 4 wines are shown in Table 7-2. Are there significant differences at the 5% level among the sample totals?

(a) From Appendix A-1, for 5 scores and 4 wines, two values $\begin{cases} 0.96 \\ 0.72 \end{cases}$ are shown.

(b) For significance among totals, their range must exceed 12(0.96) = 11.52.

Table 7-2 Five scores for each of
four wines.

	Wine			
	S_1	S_2	S_3	S_4
	6	6	8	10
	7	4	7	8
	7	5	5	9
	8	6	6	8
	9	7	4	8
Total	37	28	30	43
Range	3	3	4	2
Total range $= 12$				

(c) Since $43 - 28 = 15$ is greater than 11.52, the null hypothesis is not supported, and significant differences among totals are indicated.
(d) For significant differences between pairs of samples differences between totals must exceed $12(0.72) = 8.6$. Differences among pairs of samples are shown below:

$43 - 28 = 15^*$ $\qquad$ $37 - 28 = 9^*$ $\qquad$ $30 - 28 = 2$

$43 - 30 = 13^*$ $\qquad$ $37 - 30 = 7$

$43 - 37 = 6$

*indicates significance.

Significance is indicated graphically as follows:

$\quad S_4 \quad S_1 \quad S_3 \quad S_2$

$\quad 43 \quad 37 \quad 30 \quad 28$

where samples underlined by the same line are not significantly different.

EXAMPLE 4   Five judges score 4 wines on a 20-point scale as shown in Table 7–3. Are there significant differences among wines and among judges at the 5% level of significance?

(a) In Appendix B–1, for 4 wines and 5 judges, two values $\begin{cases} 0.71 \\ 0.69 \end{cases}$ are shown.

(b) For significance, differences between wine totals must exceed $18(0.71) = 12.8$ For significance, differences between judge totals must exceed $18(0.69) = 12.4$

(c) No significant differences among judge totals are indicated.

(d) For wines, $85 - 52 = 33,$* $85 - 63 = 22,$* $85 - 67 = 18,$* $67 - 52 = 15,$* $67 - 63 = 4$, and $63 - 52 = 11$, where * indicates significance.

S_2	S_1	S_3	S_4
85	67	63	52

These results may be compared with those obtained by the analysis of variance in Example 6 (page 242).

In later chapters, more detailed analyses will be presented for those who wish to pursue further more sophisticated statistical procedures.

Hunches and intuitive impressions are essential for getting the work started, but it is only through the quality of the numbers at the end that the truth can be told.

LEWIS THOMAS

Table 7-3 Five judges score four wines on a 20-point scale.

Judge					Wine				
	S_1	$S_2 - S_1$	S_2	$S_3 - S_2$	S_3	$S_4 - S_3$	S_4	$S_1 - S_4$	Total
1	13	5	18	−3	15	−5	10	3	56
2	15	1	16	−4	12	−1	11	4	54
3	14	1	15	−4	11	−2	9	5	49
4	12	5	17	−4	13	−3	10	2	52
5	13	6	19	−7	12	0	12	1	56
Total	67		85		63		52		267
Range of differences		5		4		5		4	Total = 18

187

Indeed the intellectual basis of all empirical knowledge
may be said to be a matter of probability.

W. C. D. DAMPIER-WHETHAM

CHAPTER 8

Difference and Preference Testing

 For large sets of data comprising many values of a given variable, some form of summarization is needed so that the main features can be readily observed. The simplest method of arranging the data is to divide the whole range of values into a number of equal intervals called class intervals and to count the number of values falling within each such interval. The number of values within a class interval is called the class frequency, or simply the *frequency*. This set of frequencies is called a *frequency distribution*. If the actual frequencies are expressed as fractions of the total frequency, the resulting distribution is called a *probability distribution*. Before considering specific testing procedures, we will briefly discuss the usefulness of two frequency distributions—the normal and chi-square (χ^2) distributions—in problems concerning sensory evaluation.

Frequency Distributions

Normal Distribution   The normal distribution can be used to estimate the probabilities of chance results in a judge's performance, but *only* in a task in which there are only *two* possible events, such as picking the odd sample correctly (success) or picking it incorrectly (failure). Probabilities in the distribution are represented by areas under the *normal probability curve*, which is bell-shaped and symmetrical about the mean, μ, of the distribution. Because the value of any normally distributed variable *must* fall somewhere; that is, because the probability of its falling *anywhere* is 1, the total area (probability) under the curve is equal to 1. Tables for the normal probability curve list the values of the areas (probabilities) corresponding to various values of z, the *normal deviate*, which is defined as the deviation $X - \mu$ measured in terms of the standard deviation, σ:

$$z = \frac{X - \mu}{\sigma} \tag{4}$$

Here X is the value of any normally distributed variable with mean μ, and σ, the standard deviation, is a measure of the dispersion (scatter) in the distribution of X-values about the mean. The smaller the value of σ, the more tightly the X-values cluster about the mean; approximately ⅔ of them fall between $\mu - \sigma$ and $\mu + \sigma$. The probability of a chance result is a maximum (midpoint on the curve) when $z = 0$, i.e., when $X = \mu$.

In sensory evaluations in which the null hypothesis H_0 specifies the probability p of success (correct choice) in a single trial, the mean μ (expected number of successes) in n trials is equal to np, and the standard deviation σ can be shown to be $\sqrt{np(1 - p)}$. The *observed number* X of successes is obtained by counting and is therefore always a whole number (integer). When it is used in finding areas under the normal probability curve—which is continuous and therefore permits fractional as well as integral values—X, if it is greater than μ, must be reduced by the number 0.5. This is called a *correction for continuity*. For example, 5 or more on a counting scale is recorded as 4.5 or more on a continuous scale. Then the normal deviate becomes

$$z = \frac{(X - 0.5) - \mu}{\sigma} = \frac{(X - 0.5) - np}{\sqrt{np(1 - p)}} \tag{5}$$

Appendix C gives areas under the normal probability curve to the right of positive values of z or to the left of the corresponding negative values of z. Because the curve is symmetrical, the two areas are the same, so only the area to the right of a positive value of z is shown in the graph there, and only positive values of z are listed. For a one-tailed test, the notation $+z_{.05}$ is used to denote that value of z to the right of which 5% of the total area lies, as shown in Figure 7–1. Analogously, $-z_{.05}$ would be the value to the left of which 5% of the area lies. From Table 8–1, we see that, in a one-tailed test (page 180), $+z_{.05} = +1.64$ and $-z_{.01} = -2.33$. In a two-tailed test, the notation $z_{.05}$ denotes that value of z that defines *two* tail areas, each of which contains 2.5% of the total area, as shown in Figure 7–2. From Table 8–1, we see that, in a two-tailed test, $z_{.05} = 1.96$ and $z_{.01} = 2.58$.

Table 8-1   Values of z and χ^2 at three levels of significance.

Level of significance	Difference (one-tailed)		Preference (two-tailed)	
	$\pm z$	χ^2	z	χ^2
5% (significant)	± 1.64	2.71	1.96	3.84
1% (highly significant)	± 2.33	5.41	2.58	6.64
0.1% (very highly significant)	± 3.09	9.55	3.30	10.82

EXAMPLE 1   A judge is presented with three glasses of wine. Two glasses contain the same wine and the third glass a different but similar wine. The judge is asked to pick the odd sample. What is the probability that, by chance alone, the judge will be successful 9 or more times in 18 trials?

The formulation of the question ($9 \leq X \leq 18$) implies that we need to find the area under the normal probability curve between the z values corresponding to $X = 9$ and $X = 18$. Because the probability of the judge's being successful in all 18 trials is vanishingly small, however, the area under the curve to the right of the z value corresponding to $X = 18$ is so small that we can include it without introducing any significant error. We can therefore simply let $X = 9$ and find the entire area (to within the accuracy of 4 significant figures, as given in Appendix C) to the right of the corresponding z value.

The probability p of a correct choice in a single trial is ⅓, and the number of trials n is 18. Therefore $\mu = np = 6$, $\sigma = \sqrt{np(1 - p)} = \sqrt{18(⅓)(⅔)} = \sqrt{4} = 2$, and, since $X = 9$,

$$z = \frac{(X - 0.5) - \mu}{\sigma} = \frac{(9 - 0.5) - 6}{2} = \frac{2.5}{2} = 1.25$$

From Appendix C we see that, for $z = 1.25$, $P = 0.1056$. This is the probability (i.e., the chance is about 10 to 11%) that, by chance alone, the judge will correctly identify the odd sample 9 or more times in 18 trials.

Chi-Square (χ^2) Distribution   The chi-square distribution is useful in comparing a set of k observed frequencies (o) with a corresponding set of k expected or hypothesized frequencies (e), particularly when k is greater than 2. The appropriate statistic, which is called *chi-square*, is defined as

$$\chi^2 = \sum \frac{(o - e)^2}{e} \tag{6}$$

where the Greek letter Σ denotes the sum of the k terms $(o_1 - e_1)^2 / e_1 + (o_2 - e_2)^2/e_2 + \cdot \cdot \cdot + (o_k - e_k)^2/e_k$. If the events in question are those of success and failure, as in the examples we have been considering, then $k = 2$, so there are two observed frequencies and two expected frequencies. Chi-square is never negative because in each term the numerator is squared and the denominator is positive. If the observed and expected frequencies agree exactly in every one of the k terms, then $\chi^2 = 0$. It has a positive value if there is any difference between an observed and expected frequency, and it increases as the difference become greater.

The distribution of χ^2 depends upon the number of independent differences, called *degrees of freedom* (df). Since the sum of all the expected frequencies, Σe, must agree with the sum of all the observed frequencies, Σo, the sum of all the differences is $\Sigma(o - e) = 0$. Therefore only $k - 1$ of the expected values are independent, and the remaining one can be calculated from the relation $\Sigma(o - e) = 0$. The number of degrees of freedom is therefore, $k - 1$. Values of χ^2 for various combinations of probabilities and numbers of degrees of freedom are given in Appendix D.

Imagine a series of n trials, with X observed successes and $n - X$ failures. If the null hypothesis specifies the probability of success in a single trial as p, and therefore that of failure as $1 - p$, χ^2 takes the form

$$\chi^2 = \frac{(|X - np| - 0.5)^2}{np} + \frac{[|(n - X) - n(1 - p)| - 0.5]^2}{n(1 - p)}$$

$$= (|X - np| - 0.5)^2[1/np + 1/n(1 - p)]$$

$$= \frac{(|X - np| - 0.5)^2}{np(1 - p)} \tag{7}$$

where $|X - np|$ is the *absolute value* of the expression $X - np$; that is, it is the value without regard to algebraic sign (it can therefore be interpreted as a positive quantity). As in the normal distribution, the number -0.5 is a correction for continuity because the χ^2 curve is also continuous, whereas the observed frequencies can only be integers. This correction is applicable only for 1 df, which holds for the examples we have been considering, because $k = 2$ (success and failure). In this case the one-tailed probability associated with a value of χ^2 equals the two-tailed probability associated with the corresponding value of z, the normal deviate.

EXAMPLE 2   Use χ^2 to estimate the probability in Example 1.

$$\chi^2 = \frac{(|X - np| - 0.5)^2}{np(1 - p)} = \frac{(|9 - 6| - 0.5)^2}{18(\frac{1}{3})(\frac{2}{3})} = \frac{(2.5)^2}{4}$$

$$= 1.56$$

From Appendix D, we see that, for 1 df, $\chi^2 = 1.56$ is very close to the value 1.64, which corresponds to a probability of 0.20. Since this equals the total probability for both tails of the normal distribution, the one-tailed probability is close to 0.10, which agrees with the result obtained in Example 1.

The applications and appropriateness of the statistical terms and reasoning outlined above will be evident in the discussions and examples that follow.

Difference Tests

Difference tests are used in the comparison of two wines to evaluate objectively the differences between them, to test the ability of judges to make comparisons of chemical constituents or sensory characteristics, and, on the basis of preference ratings, to establish quality differences.

Sensory evaluations are usually conducted by a small laboratory panel of judges or by members of the consuming public. The number of panelists in laboratory testing varies with conditions, such as the number of qualified persons available. Many investigators recommend panels of 5 to 10 members; we agree. Large panels are customary in preference tests in which the only criterion for the selection of members is representativeness of some consumer population. Laboratory panels can suggest probable consumer reactions, but any resulting conclusions relating to the consuming public should be very carefully evaluated. We view such conclusions with considerable skepticism because the relation of the laboratory panel to the consuming public is generally not clear.

The results of a sensory evaluation have little meaning unless the panelists have demonstrated the ability to detect differences that *can* be detected, and to do so consistently. These differences are often very subtle and difficult to detect. Obviously the panel should consist of individuals with the greatest sensitivity and experience. When no difference between samples for a single odor or taste can be established, the question of preference based on this difference is obviously irrelevant. Not everyone agrees.

There is the possibility that judges may use different criteria and motivation in making difference compared to preference judgments. In fact, judges may be willing to commit themselves to a preference decision (since it is personal) before making a difference decision (where there is competition with the rest of the panel).

Although in the usual statistical analysis the assumptions and test procedures used for one judge making n comparisons are the same as those used for n judges making a single comparison each, these two experiments are not the same. In all difference tests, it is customary to assume an unchanging fundamental probability. Tests based on this assumption are more reliable when performed by one "competent" judge, but even then their validity is doubtful owing to the possibility of fatigue and the effects of various psychological factors (see page 59). The problems encountered in panel or consumer tests are even more complicated because of varying thresholds and differing directions of preference. To conform to basic assumptions in detecting possible differences, it is clearly important to use the best judge or judges available except in market-testing research, in which the preferences of a large number of people need to be taken into account.

It has already been pointed out (page 151) that, in all trials in wine evaluations, the samples should be presented as uniformly as possible—at the same temperature, in identical glasses, but in different orders. Testing procedures in common use are the paired-difference, paired-preference, duo-trio, and triangle tests.

Paired-Difference and Paired-Preference Tests   In the paired-difference test, the judge is presented with two samples and asked to identify the one with the greater intensity of a specific constituent or well-defined characteristic (see Figure 8–1). In the paired-preference test, the judge is asked to express a preference for one of the samples. In either case, the judge may be required to make a choice. This is called the forced-choice procedure and is generally preferred. If the judges object to a forced-choice procedure, then a "no difference" reply may be accepted. If one ignores the "no difference" replies, the chance of obtaining a significant result is increased. If the "no difference" replies are divided equally between the two categories, the chance of obtaining a significant result is reduced.

Type of test
(e.g., sweetness of wine)

Taste both samples. Circle the sweeter of the two.

Test	Samples	
1	_____	_____
2	_____	_____
3	_____	_____
4	_____	_____

Name _____ Date _____

Figure 8–1   Record form for paired-difference test.

These procedures may be carried out by one judge several times or by a panel of judges one or more times. Based on the null hypothesis of no difference, about one-half of the responses should be correct by chance alone—that is, $H_0: p = \frac{1}{2}$.

The paired-difference test is useful in quality control and in the selection of judges. The presence of more or less of some constituent in one of the samples may already be known to the experimenter, or it can be determined by a specific chemical test. If, in several trials, the judge makes the correct differentiation significantly more often than would be expected by chance ($p = \frac{1}{2}$), the experimenter can infer that the judge does possess some ability to detect that particular constituent. In this case, a one-tailed test is applicable, and the alternative hypothesis is $H_1: p > \frac{1}{2}$ because the judge shows ability only by making the correct choice more often than possible by guessing. The one-tailed *region of significance* in the normal distribution is shown in Figure 8–2 for the 5% level. Calculated values of z (page 191) that exceed $+1.64$, the value at the 5% level ($+z_{.05}$), indicate a significant differentiation ability.

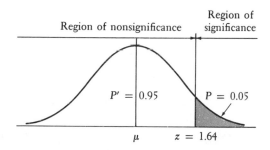

Figure 8–2   One-tailed test, 5% level. $H_0: p = \frac{1}{2}$. $H_1:$ $p > \frac{1}{2}$.

In paired-preference testing, the judge is asked to express a preference between two wines. A statistically significant preponderance of selections of one wine over the other then indicates a significant preference difference and, therefore (assuming the judge's tastes are conventional), a significant, objective quality difference. Since either wine may be the preferred one (i.e., since the selection of a given wine very infrequently is just as meaningful as its selection very frequently), the alternative hypothesis here is $H_1: p \neq$ ½, and the two-tailed test is applicable. The two-tailed region of significance in the normal distribution is shown in Figure 8-3 for the 5% level. Calculated values of z that numerically exceed 1.96, the value at the 5% level ($z_{.05}$), indicate a significant preference or quality difference.

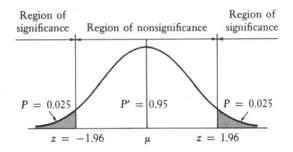

Figure 8-3 Two-tailed test, 5% level.
$H_0: p =$ ½. $H_1: p \neq$ ½.

Duo–Trio Test This test is a modified paired-sample test, in which a reference sample is identified and presented first, followed by two coded samples, one of which is identical to the reference sample. The judge is asked to decide which of the two coded samples is the same as the reference sample (see Figure 8-4). As in the paired-sample test, the null hypothesis is $H_0: p =$ ½ because, by chance alone, the judge will pick the correct sample about one-half of the time. Since this is a difference test, it is one-tailed. It is especially applicable in quality control, in which a sample is to be compared with a reference standard.

Type of test
(e.g., comparison of old and new blends)

Taste or smell (or both) the reference sample and the two coded samples. Decide which of the latter is the same as the reference sample.

Test	Coded samples		Sample same as reference sample
1	————	————	————
2	————	————	————
3	————	————	————
4	————	————	————

Name ——————————————— Date ———————————

Figure 8-4   Record form for duo–trio test.

Triangle Test   In the triangle test, the judge is presented with three samples, two of which are identical, and is asked to select the odd sample (see Figure 8–5). The probability of a correct choice by chance alone is one-third; that is, the null hypothesis is $H_0: p - \frac{1}{3}$. The test is easy to administer and is also useful in quality control.

Type of test
(e.g., difference in wine flavored by two agents)

Taste or smell (or both) all three samples. Decide which of the three is unlike the other two.

Test	Samples			Sample unlike the other two
1	————	————	————	————
2	————	————	————	————
3	————	————	————	————
4	————	————	————	————

Name ——————————————— Date ———————————

Figure 8-5   Record form for triangle test.

Use of the triangle test in the selection of judges was proposed by Seldon (1979). Unfortunately, only one trial was suggested so a poor judge could be included by chance one-third of the time. The test must be repeated at least five times for significant elimination of unqualified judges.

If three or more stimuli are available with the same or different concentrations, a series of triangle tests can be run to provide a measure of sensory difference if a significant result has been obtained. Frijters (1982) discussed three procedures: the triangular constant-method model, the Thurstone–Ura model for the triangular method, and the three-alternative method. He pointed out that both of the latter methods perform equally well in measuring a sensory difference. For both methods, he provided tables for use in converting the proportion of correct responses (P_c) to the measure of sensory difference (d') and provided a worked example.

The duo–trio and triangle procedures should be used only for difference (one-tailed) testing, as described above, because it has been shown that having two samples of one wine and one sample of the other tends to cause bias in preference judgments.

Summary   For various numbers of trials in the paired-sample and duo–trio tests, Appendix E gives the minimum numbers of correct judgments required to establish a significant difference (one-tailed test) at various significance levels. Appendix F gives, for the paired-sample test, the minimum numbers of agreeing judgments required to establish a significant preference (two-tailed test). Appendix G gives analogous information for establishing a significant difference in the triangle test. Values for $X > \mu$ that are not in the tables can be found by solving the following equations:

$$X = \frac{n + z\sqrt{n} + 1}{2} \quad \text{or} \quad X = \frac{n + \sqrt{n\chi^2} + 1}{2}$$

$$\text{for } p = \tfrac{1}{2} \text{ (one- or two-tailed)} \qquad (8)$$

and

$$X = \frac{2n + 2.83z\sqrt{n} + 3}{6} \quad \text{or} \quad X = \frac{2n + 2.83\sqrt{n\chi^2} + 3}{6}$$

for $p = \frac{1}{3}$ (one-tailed only) (9)

In n trials (number of judges or judgments), the minimum number of correct or agreeing judgments required for significance is the next greater integer above the value of X obtained from the appropriate equation above, for the value of z or χ^2 found in Table 8–1. Values of z for other levels of significance can be found in Appendix C, and values of χ^2 in Appendix D.

Appendixes H and I give the probabilities of X or more correct judgments in n trials for the paired-difference and triangle tests respectively. Appendix J gives the probabilities of X or more agreeing judgments in n trials.

EXAMPLE 3   In a paired-sample test, a judge is given two glasses containing a dry white table wine, to one of which a small amount of ethyl acetate has been added. Fourteen times in 20 trials the judge correctly identifies the adulterated sample. From Appendix E, we see that in 20 trials at least 15 correct judgments are required for significance at the 5% level. On the basis of this test, therefore, the judge is not able to detect the ethyl acetate that has been added.

EXAMPLE 4   In a paired-sample test, 50 judges are asked to express their preference for one of two wines. Thirty-six preferences are expressed for wine S_1 and 14 for wine S_2. From Appendix F, we see that the minimum number of agreeing judgments required for significance at the 5% level in a two-tailed test is 33, and at the 1% level, 35. On the basis of this test, wine S_1 is judged better than wine S_2 at both the 5% (significant) and 1% (highly significant) levels. Therefore the chances of being wrong in rejecting the null hypothesis (H_0:

$p = \frac{1}{2}$) of there being no difference between the wines are less than one in 100.

EXAMPLE 5 In a duo–trio test of 24 trials, how many correct identifications of the identical samples are required for significance at the 5% and 1% levels? From Appendix E we see that, for a one-tailed test, at least 17 and 19 correct identifications are required for significance at the 5% and 1% levels, respectively.

EXAMPLE 6 In a triangle test, a judge correctly identifies the odd sample in 13 of 23 trials. The judge therefore indicates ability at the 5% level of significance because, from Appendix G, at least 12 correct identifications are required at this level.

EXAMPLE 7 In a paired-sample preference test with 64 trials, how many agreeing judgments are required for significance at the 5% level? Since $n = 64$ does not appear in Appendix F, we use Equation 5 to determine X, the number of agreeing judgments required.

$$X = \frac{64 + 1.96\sqrt{64} + 1}{2} = \frac{64 + 1.96(8) + 1}{2} = 40.3$$

Therefore at least 41 agreeing judgments are required at the 5% level of significance.

The number of judges used in taste difference tests varies depending on the ability and training of the judges, the test to be used, the quality difference considered to be of practical importance, and the adopted significance level. Basker (1981) supplied information on the required number of judges in such cases.

In testing procedures involving two or more wines, differences between wine samples can be established by quantitative measures obtained from score cards or other means of scoring, by ranking, or by hedonic rating. Each of these procedures will be discussed in the following chapters.

Sequential Procedure for Selection of Judges

When paired-sample, duo–trio, and triangle tests are used in the selection of judges, a predetermined number of trials is employed and those candidates showing the greatest ability are selected. Questions have been raised regarding the number of trials needed and the quality of the judges thus obtained. Often too little testing is done because of limitations of time and suitable experimental material.

Sequential procedures can provide considerable improvement over other selection procedures and can save valuable time and materials. In a sequential testing plan, the number of trials is not predetermined, and the decision to terminate the experiment at any time depends upon the previous results. The sequential procedure described here is a modification of that developed by Wald (1947) and adapted by Bradley (1953).

Let p be the true proportion of correct decisions that would be obtained in paired-sample, duo–trio, or triangle tests if the potential judge were to continue testing indefinitely. This is a measure of the judge's inherent ability in the test in question. Values of p_0 and p_1 are specified such that individuals having abilities equal to or greater than p_1 will be accepted as judges, and those with abilities equal to or less than p_0 will be rejected. The testing plan depends on the values assigned to p_0 and p_1 and also on the values of α and β, the probabilities of committing errors of the first and second kind, respectively (α is the probability of rejecting a qualified judge, and β is the probability of accepting an unqualified one). Potential judges are accepted or rejected on the basis of their performance with respect to a chart of two parallel straight lines L_0 and L_1, which are uniquely determined by the assigned values of p_0, p_1, α, and β. These lines divide the plane into three regions: one of acceptance, one of rejection, and one of indecision, as shown in Figure 8-6.

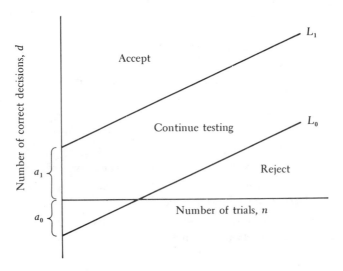

Figure 8-6   Sequential test chart.

The equations of the lines are

$$L_0: d_0 = a_0 + bn \quad \text{and} \quad L_1: d_1 = a_1 + bn \tag{10}$$

where n is the total number of trials, d (either one) is the accumulated number of correct decisions, b is the common slope of the two lines, and a_0 and a_1 are the intercepts on the vertical axis. The common slope b of L_0 and L_1 is

$$b = k_2/(k_1 + k_2) \tag{11}$$

and the intercepts a_0 and a_1 are

$$a_0 = -e_1/(k_1 + k_2) \quad \text{and} \quad a_1 = e_2/(k_1 + k_2) \tag{12}$$

where

$$k_1 = \log(p_1/p_0) = \log p_1 - \log p_0$$
$$k_2 = \log[(1 - p_0)/(1 - p_1)] = \log(1 - p_0) - \log(1 - p_1)$$
$$e_1 = \log[(1 - \beta)/\alpha] = \log(1 - \beta) - \log \alpha$$
$$e_2 = \log[(1 - \alpha)/\beta] = \log(1 - \alpha) - \log \beta$$

After each trial, the experimenter plots the point (d, n), representing the accumulated number of correct decisions (vertical scale) versus the total number of trials (horizontal scale). Each plotted point is therefore one n unit to the right of the preceding point, and is either one d unit above the preceding point or on the same horizontal level, depending on whether the decision was correct or incorrect, respectively. Testing continues until a plotted point falls on or above the upper line, resulting in acceptance of the candidate as a judge, or on or below the lower line, resulting in rejection.

The number of trials required depends upon the ability of the potential judge and on the assigned values of p_0, p_1, α, and β, which are determined by the experimenter. Before making a commitment to a given set of values, the experimenter may wish to know the average number of trials that can be expected for that set of values. The number of trials required can be decreased by increasing the difference between p_0 and p_1 or by increasing α or β, or both. If competent judges are in good supply, the experimenter may wish to increase α and accept a greater risk of rejecting a competent judge.

The average number of trials to be expected, $\bar{n}$, can be obtained from among four calculated values corresponding to special values of p, as shown below and on the next page.

$p = 0$ (no ability)

$$\bar{n}_0 = e_1/k_2$$

$p = p_0$ (maximum unacceptable ability)

$$\overline{n}_{p_0} = \frac{(1 - \beta)e_1 - \beta e_2}{(1 - p_0)k_2 - p_0 k_1}$$

$p = p_1$ (minimum acceptable ability)

$$\overline{n}_{p_1} = \frac{(1 - \alpha)e_2 - \alpha e_1}{p_1 k_1 - (1 - p_1)k_2}$$

$p = 1$ (infallible ability)

$$\overline{n}_1 = e_2/k_1$$

The average number of trials to be expected is the largest of these four values.

EXAMPLE 8   Suppose that a triangle test is used as a basis for selecting judges in a sequential procedure. For the assigned values $p_0 = 0.45$, $p_1 = 0.70$, $\alpha = 0.10$, and $\beta = 0.05$, find the average number of trials to be expected. (Competent judges are in good supply, so α is being taken as 0.10.)

We begin by finding the values of k and e:

$$k_1 = \log(0.70/0.45) = 0.1919$$

$$k_2 = \log(0.55/0.30) = 0.2632$$

$$e_1 = \log(0.95/0.10) = 0.9777$$

$$e_2 = \log(0.90/0.05) = 1.2553$$

We then use these values in the four equations for $\overline{n}$:

$$\overline{n}_0 = 0.9777/0.2632 = 3.7$$

$$\bar{n}_{p_0} = \frac{(0.95)(0.9777) - (0.05)(1.2553)}{(0.55)(0.2632) - (0.45)(0.1919)} = \frac{0.866}{0.058} = 14.9$$

$$\bar{n}_{p_1} = \frac{(0.90)(1.2553) - (0.10)(0.9777)}{(0.70)(0.1919) - (0.30)(0.2632)} = \frac{1.032}{0.055} = 18.8$$

$$\bar{n}_1 = 1.2553/0.1919 = 6.5$$

We see that the test will require an average of 19 trials. The number required for each candidate will, of course, depend upon his inherent ability, p.

EXAMPLE 9 Using the values of k and e calculated in Example 8, find the equations of the lines L_0 and L_1.

From Equations 11 and 12 we obtain

$$b = 0.2632/0.4551 = 0.578$$

$$a_0 = -0.9777/0.4551 = -2.15$$

$$a_1 = 1.2553/0.4551 = 2.76$$

The equations of the lines are therefore

$$L_0 : d_0 = -2.15 + 0.578n$$

$$L_1 : d_1 = 2.76 + 0.578n$$

EXAMPLE 10 The performances of two candidates for wine judge, A and B, are shown in the table below, where a 1 indicates a correct decision and a 0 an incorrect decision. Evaluate their performances with respect to the lines L_0 and L_1 and determine the number of trials after which each candidate is either accepted or rejected.

No. of trials n: 1 2 3 4 5 6 7 8 9 10 11 12 13 14 15 16 17 18 19

Decisions	A:	1 0 1 0 0 0 1 0 1 1 0 0 0
	B:	1 1 1 0 1 0 0 1 1 1 0 1 1 1 0 1 1 1 1

No. of correct	A:	1 1 2 2 2 2 3 3 4 5 5 5 5
decisions, d	B:	1 2 3 3 4 4 4 5 6 7 7 8 9 10 10 11 12 13 14

The performances of A and B are shown in Figure 8–7, in which the number of correct decisions is plotted against the total number of trials. By the criteria specified for the sequential procedure, we see that A is rejected as a judge after 13 trials and B is accepted after 19 trials.

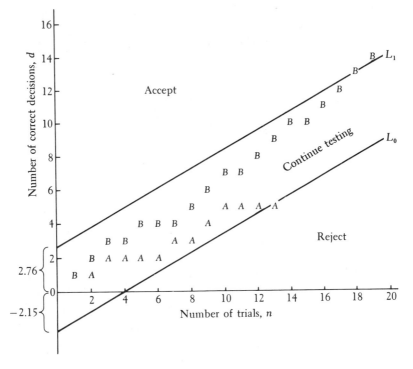

Figure 8-7   Performances of candidates A and B in a sequential test procedure.

And where a Mathematical Reasoning can be had, it is as great a Folly to make use of any other, as to grope for a Thing in the Dark, when you have a Candle standing by you.

JOHN ARBUTHNOT

With respect to small differences between large groups, I would suggest that the crucial question is not, Is the difference statistically significant? but rather, Is the difference practically important?

R. D. ILIFF

*Every judicious person will be sensible that the problem now mentioned
is by no means a curious speculation in the doctrine of chances,
but necessary to be solved in order to assure foundation for all our reasonings
concerning the facts, and what is likely to be hereafter.*

REV. RICHARD PRICE

CHAPTER 9

Scoring

 There are various scaling procedures for identifying and measuring the degree of difference between sounds, odors, or wine quality. Nominal scales simply identify without implying any relationship. The description of wines as oaky, astringent, red, and so on is nominal. Ordinal scales imply some sort of greater or lesser degree, but the levels between steps may be different. Therefore, when we say low, medium, or high red, we are using an ordinal scale. Ranking tests are also ordinal. An interval scale means that there are equal intervals between the steps of the scale. Hedonic scorecards are believed to be interval scales, but this has not been proven. Finally, there are ratio scales, in which the ratios between two aspects of the wine are used to arrange the wines in order—that is, the sweetness of one wine as a function of a standard. Nelson (1980) has pointed out that the Davis scorecard is nominal (10 categories), ordinal (some categories have greater weight than others), and interval (each category is scored using an equal interval scale).

The major defect of all scorecards is that the importance of certain characteristics varies with the type of wine and (probably)

with the judges. Everyone using scorecards recognizes that different judges weight the various parameters differently. Using the least-squares multilinear regression method, van Rooyen (1982) verified that this was so. Certain parameters were not properly used, and others were weighted out of proportion to actual scorecard weights. With the scorecard used (that of Tromp and Conradie 1979), harmony, flavor, typicality, and to a lesser extent purity correlated highly with overall quality. This may have resulted from the wines being very similar to one another in the other parameters of the scorecard: clarity, color, maturation bouquet, acidity, astringence, bitterness, and fullness. Obviously, the last word has not been said regarding scorecards and their proper construction. Dissimilar wines being judged in the same group probably present insurmountable problems for a single scorecard.

We have observed that experienced judges do not evaluate all the categories of the scorecard but simply indicate a total score according to the anchored scorecard guidelines: in the Davis scorecard, 12 or below for defective wines, 13 to 16 for standard wines, and 17 to 20 for superior wines.

With experienced judges, scoring is usually the most acceptable procedure for establishing differences between wine samples because it measures the magnitudes of the differences. The scoring scale to be used must be clearly defined and understood by all the judges. A 9-point quality scale (see Figure 9–1) has been widely used. The judge checks the appropriate quality, which is converted to a numerical score: 1 for extremely poor, to 9 for excellent.

Types of Scorecards

A 9-point anchored scorecard was favored by Ough and Baker (1961) over a 20-point unanchored scorecard since it forced the judges to use the entire range. The divisions were as follows: unacceptable (1); average with some defects (2, 3); average quality (4 to

Wine sample _____

Check the appropriate quality.

_____ Excellent
_____ Very good
_____ Good
_____ Below good, above fair
_____ Fair
_____ Below fair, above poor
_____ Poor
_____ Very poor
_____ Extremely poor

Name _____ Date _____

Figure 9-1 A 9-point quality scale.

6); above average with some superior qualities (7, 8); and superior quality (9). Ough and Winton (1976) also preferred the 9-point scorecard for its more effective use of the extremities of the scale. This scale was also used by Tromp and Conradie (1979) for young experimental wines, but no direct comparison with the 20-point scale was given. They found the 9-point scale to be readily learned so that new subjects could be easily introduced to its use. A 3-day training period was used, and, with the tasks assigned, experienced judges appeared no more proficient than inexperienced ones.

In the evaluation of overall wine quality, scorecards usually provide for 9-, 10-, or 20-point rating scales. On the basis of a 20-point scale, the following groupings are suggested: (a) *superior* (17–20 points)—wines of fine quality, well-balanced, no pronounced defects, and free of excess "young" character; (b) *standard* (13–16 points)—the wines of commerce (including ordinary bottled wines), not deficient in any important characteristic, but lacking proper age or the balance required for fine quality; (c) *below standard* (9–12 points)—wines lacking some required characteristic or suffering from some malady (wines with off odors or off taste or high volatile acidity);

(d) *unacceptable,* or *spoiled* (1–8 points)—wines so spoiled that they must be discarded. See pages 225–273 for methods of analyzing the results.

Davis Scorecard   The original, so-called Davis scorecard (see Figure 9–2) was developed by the staff of the Department of Viticulture and Enology at the University of California, Davis, as a method of rating the large number of experimental wines that were produced there. Later it was used as a training device for students who were beginning their education in the sensory evaluation of wines. This scorecard overemphasized some factors (acescence, for example) and underemphasized others (aroma and bouquet being the worst examples). Among its other defects was that it did not differentiate between bitterness and astringency (page 49). The concepts of flavor (now generally regarded as odor perceived via the mouth) and gen-

Wine sample _____

Characteristic	Weight
Appearance	2
Color	2
Aroma and bouquet	4
Volatile acidity	2
Total acidity	2
Sweetness	1
Body	1
Flavor	2
Bitterness	2
General quality	2

Ratings: *superior* (17–20); *standard* (13–16); *below standard* (9–12); *unacceptable,* or *spoiled* (1–8).

Name _____ Date _____

Figure 9-2   The Davis scorecard. (The meanings specified for the total scores serve to assure relative uniformity of the judges' interpretations of these terms.)

eral quality were not clearly defined. It also became apparent that the definitions of superior (17–20 points), standard (13–16 points), below standard (9–12 points), and unacceptable, or spoiled (1–8 points) varied from judge to judge, depending on the judge's experience and severity of judgment.

Kiermeir and Haevecker (1972) pointed out that, in the Davis scorecard, there is no apparent place for the degree of carbon dioxide retention in sparkling wines. The 20-point scorecard for German sparkling wines provides 2 points for this and 3 points for the dosage balance, reducing the points for total taste by 5 points.

Holzgang (1981) rejected the Davis scorecard as not allowing sufficient room for subjective evaluation of overall quality. His scorecard allows 5 points for overall quality. The question is whether this allows too much leeway for subjective opinions.

Despite these objections, the Davis scorecard has been successfully used by trained judges at Davis without serious difficulty. In fact, the staff has learned to use it with remarkable precision in the results and their interpretation. As a pedagogical tool, it has proved useful for both regularly enrolled students and those taking adult wine-appreciation courses. Any problems are always explained to the students. A modified Davis scorecard, which avoids some but not all problems, is shown in Figure 9–3.

In recent years, the Davis scorecard has been used (or misused) by professional and amateur groups with less success. Most of the difficulty arises from varying interpretations of the relative values of the different sections of the scorecard (see page 214). Some amateurs assign high scores to all the wines, whereas professionals usually spread their scores over a larger range. Disaster occurs when amateurs and professionals judge together and the average scores for the individual wines are used to rank the wines. This cannot be done safely, sometimes even with appropriate statistical procedures.

One solution to this problem would be to hold one or more practice sessions of the group and discuss the meaning of the scores. Another possible solution would be to use the shorter, 9-point scorecard devised by Ough and Baker (1961). However, bunching of the

Wine sample _____

Characteristic	Weight
Appearance	2
Color	2
Aroma and bouquet	6
Total acidity	2
Sweetness	1
Body	1
Flavor	2
Bitterness	1
Astringency	1
General quality	2

Ratings: *superior* (17–20); *standard* (13–16); *below standard* (9–12); *unacceptable,* or *spoiled* (1–8).

Name _____ Date _____

Figure 9-3 A modified Davis scorecard.

scores in the 8- to 9-point range would then be even more acute than bunching in the 17- to 20-point range of the 20-point scale. See also van Rooyen (1982) for a detailed analysis of the use of a 9-point scorecard, anchored to five quality steps and eleven descriptors (clarity, color, etc.).

We recommend using only professional judges if the objective is to rank a group of wines in order of merit *by their scores*. The judges, though experienced, will still require one or more practice sessions in which their scores are compared. Although it may embarrass a judge to be found scoring too high or too low, it is essential that this be revealed if the average scores are to be meaningful. Also, judges may have very different standards of excellence for different types of wines. With samples before them, the judges should discuss the various types of wines to be evaluated. Questions such as the following must be discussed: What range of color will be tolerated in a given type of wine? What is the typical varietal aroma? How much fermentation bouquet can be allowed (especially in young white wines)? Are dry and sweet wines to be judged together? How much credit should be given for bottle bouquet (as in a well-aged red wine)? With respect to these and similar questions, the differences between superior and standard wines must be clear to all the judges.

Other Scorecards   A 20-point scorecard that avoids the detailed evaluation required for the Davis scorecard is shown in Figure 9–4 and appears very useful. Two noteworthy features of this scorecard are the provision for listing specific defects and the specification of the minimum acceptable number of points for each of the three categories. One disadvantage is the heavy weight given to taste in evaluating the wine. Paul (1964) and Peynaud (1980) also used 20-point scorecards. Paul weighted the scorecard heavier on odor and Peynaud on flavor.

Klenk (1972) has used the following, very similar 20-point scorecard: color, 2; appearance, 2; odor, 4; taste, 12. Again, the taste contribution to quality seems to us to be greatly overemphasized. In competitions in which this scale was used, the gold medal was given to wines that scored 19.6 to 20, the silver medal to wines scoring 18.6 to 19.5, and the bronze medal to wines scoring 17.6 to 18.5. For example, Klenk gives data for 8 wines, each of which was judged by 4 judges. The averages were 20 and 19.9 (gold medal), 19.0, 19.0, and 18.8 (silver medal), and 18.5, 18.5, and 17.8 (bronze medal). Statistical analysis of Klenk's data shows that differences of less than 0.51 between average scores were not significant. Therefore the silver-medal wines and the first two bronze-medal wines were not significantly different from one another.

Klenk has also used a 40-point scorecard scaled as follows: color, 3; appearance, 3; odor, 10; taste, 24. We believe that this is too great a range for normal use because judges cannot differentiate 40 levels of quality.

The Klenk scorecard is now official for the control of wine quality in the Federal Republic of Germany (Schöffling et al. 1980). It has been partially anchored as shown on p. 219.

Wine Evaluation
Seagram Wine Quality Laboratory

To: _____   Date: _____ Sample no.: _____

From: _____   Location: _____

Brand: _____   Type: _____

Producer: _____   Country: _____

Age: _____ % Ethanol: _____   No. of bottles: _____

Samples recd. from: _____   Date evaluated: _____

Identification of case, bottle, date, etc.: _____

Appearance	*Points*
Ordinary sound wine _____	3
Outstanding color and clarity (+1) _____	
_____	
Defects (−1 to −3) _____	
_____	
Total appearance points (Maximum 4; minimum acceptable 2)	☐

Odor	*Points*
Ordinary sound wine _____	2
Positive attributes (+1 to +2) _____	
_____	
Defects (−1 to −2) _____	
_____	
Total odor points (Maximum 4; minimum acceptable 1)	☐

Taste	*Points*
Ordinary sound wine _____	7
Positive attributes (+1 to +5) _____	
_____	
Defects (−1 to −7) _____	
_____	
Total taste points (Maximum 12; minimum acceptable 5)	☐
Total wine rating (Maximum 20; minimum acceptable 9)	☐

Ratings: *great* (18–20); *fine* (15–17); *good* (12–14); *fair* (9–11); *poor,* or *unacceptable* (below 9). Wine is also unacceptable if it does not meet the minimum in all three categories. Unless it also *exceeds* the minimum in at least one category, it cannot meet the overall minimum of 9 points.

Figure 9-4 A 20-point scorecard. (Courtesy of Joseph E. Seagram & Sons, Inc.)

color: pale or dark, 0; bright yellow, 1; typical, 2.

clarity: cloudy, 0; bright, 1; crystal clear, 2.

odor: unsound, 0; lacking character, 1; clean, 2; fragrant-flowery, 3; fruit and perfume, 4.

taste: unsound, 0; sound, 1–3; clean and vinous, 4–6; matured and harmonious, 7–9; well matured and noble, 10–12.

It is not clear to us that unsound, sound, clean and vinous, matured and harmonious, and well matured and noble really represent five steps of quality. The same remark applies to several other odor and taste descriptions. This criticism would seem to be all the more important since untrained consumers were using the scorecards. It is significant that, in the Schöffling et al. (1980) tests, the experts had significantly higher scores than the nonexpert consumers. The sweeter wines were favored by both groups.

The typical 20-point scorecard is well suited for the evaluation of still table wines, but it requires modification for other types of wines. For example, the persistence of the sparkle in sparkling wines must be taken into account; either flavor or general quality may be invoked as a means of subtracting points for lack of persistence of the gassiness. In dessert wines (except muscatels), aroma is not a prominent characteristic; greater emphasis must be given to bouquet.

Another scorecard that has been used in international judgings is that of the Office International de la Vigne et du Vin in Paris (see Figure 9–5). The perfect score is 0. Defects are marked on an increasing scale for each category as a multiplying factor ($\times 0$, $\times 1$, $\times 4$, $\times 9$, $\times 16$). As with all scorecards, some degree of familiarity with the terms is necessary. Odor intensity and odor quality seem clear enough. The difference between taste intensity and taste quality is by no means so clear. Taste intensity would *seem* to pertain to the positive aspects of sweetness, sourness, and bitterness—that is, the ideal intensity of each. Taste quality would then pertain to the balance (or lack of it) in the overall taste character. This scorecard introduced the concept of caudality—that is, the persistence of odor as a measure of

Characteristic	Weight	Multiplying factor for increasing defects				
		×0	×1	×4	×9	×16
Appearance	1	___	___	___	___	___
Color	1	___	___	___	___	___
Odor intensity	1	___	___	___	___	___
Odor quality	2	___	___	___	___	___
Taste intensity	2	___	___	___	___	___
Taste quality	3	___	___	___	___	___
Harmony or balance	2	___	___	___	___	___

Multiplying factors: *outstanding* (0); *very good* (1); *good* (4); *acceptable* (9); *unacceptable* (16).

Name _____ Date _____

Figure 9–5   Scorecard of the Office International de la Vigne et du Vin, Paris.

quality. Puisais (1982) gives considerable attention to this concept. Whether it is a reproducible measure is one problem. There does not seem to be adequate published information on this subject. Whether it is related to the quality of the wine is another problem. More research on this would be welcome.

The Associazione Enotecnici Italiani (1975) in Milan has proposed a 100-point scorecard (see Figure 9–6). This system will probably work as well as most others, although it has several disadvantages: a 100-point scale is too large (in our opinion, there are simply not 100 different quality levels), the words *finesse* and *harmony* are difficult to define in sensory terms, and old red wines and most dessert wines would score low in freshness. It does have the advantage, however, of forcing judges to quantify their judgments, from *bad* to *excellent*, on several wine attributes. See also Sernagiotto (1969).

When other evaluation methods are used, such as ranking or hedonic rating, it is still necessary that the judges understand the problems discussed above and that they agree as closely as possible on the

	Weight	Excellent 4	Good 3	Average 2	Mediocre 1	Bad 0
Visual						
Appearance	2	___	___	___	___	___
Color	2	___	___	___	___	___
Olfactory						
Finesse	2	___	___	___	___	___
Intensity	2	___	___	___	___	___
Freshness	2	___	___	___	___	___
Taste						
Body	2	___	___	___	___	___
Harmony	2	___	___	___	___	___
Intensity	2	___	___	___	___	___
Final taste-odor sensation	3	___	___	___	___	___
Typicalness	3	___	___	___	___	___
General impression	3	___	___	___	___	___

Name _____ Date _____

Figure 9-6   Scorecard adapted from that published by the Associazione Enotecnici Italiani (1975), Milan.

definitions and interpretations of the terms to be used in describing the wines.

Ranking

In the ranking procedure (a type of scoring), the judges are asked to arrange a series of two or more samples in increasing or decreasing order with respect either to the intensity of a particular characteristic (see Figure 9–7) or to their own preference (Paul 1967). Long (1982) recommends ranking in the evaluation of wines since the test is simple to administer, may not require highly skilled judges, and makes possible a distribution-free analysis. It does, however, disre-

Rank the 6 samples in order of increasing ethanol content.

Highest _____

_____

_____

_____

_____

Lowest _____

Name _____ Date _____

Figure 9-7   Ranking wines in order of percent ethanol.

gard degrees of difference among the wines and is therefore usually less sensitive to the effects of such differences than tests based on scoring. See Chapter 12 for methods of analyzing ranking results.

Hedonic Rating

Hedonic rating is what the name implies: quality evaluation based on the pleasure that the judge finds in the wine. The evaluations are usually made on 5- to 9-point balanced scales ranging from extreme disapproval to extreme approval, such as the one shown in Figure 9-1. The results are converted to numerical scores, which are then treated by rank analysis or the analysis of variance (these topics are discussed later). The procedure is used by both experts and untrained consumers, but is more appropriate for the latter group. Consumer tests are very important in winery development programs of new products. If significant preferences are established, more elaborate consumer testing (interviews, etc.) should be carried out to establish which characteristics please or displease the public.

What do the results of hedonic rating mean? Are they merely a subjective preference opinion? If so, averaging the scores is not very meaningful. However, if they denote a degree of quality relative to some theoretical, agreed-on standard of perfection, then the average score may have objective value. In fact, if tested by appropriate statistical procedures, the differences among the average scores of the various wines may reveal significant differences among the wines, or they may indicate no significant differences. See pages 247–249 for methods of analyzing the results.

Everywhere one observes the unfortunate habit of generalizing, without demonstration, from special cases.

NIELS ABEL

A statistically significant difference is not necessarily an important difference, and a difference that is not statistically significant may be an important difference.

R. P. CARVER

CHAPTER 10

Tests of Significance of Scores

 Regardless of the type of evaluation procedure used, the overall results for each wine in the test are usually expressed in terms of a single numerical score. These scores can be analyzed statistically to determine if significant differences exist. Although the usual statistical procedures presuppose a normal distribution of scores, moderate deviations from such a distribution do not invalidate the results. Studies have shown that the distribution of scores in most tests is only moderately asymmetrical, and the usual test procedures are valid. Sometimes the scores fit a *bimodal distribution* (one with two peaks in its graph), which means that we may be dealing with two types of judges who differ significantly in their quality standards or preferences. It may then be desirable to separate and compare the scores for the two groups making up the bimodal distribution.

Variability

Tests of significance entailing means (averages) of scores are based on estimates of the variability of that population of which the scores constitute a random sample (see page 179). The customarily used estimates of the variability are the variance, v, of a sample distribution of scores and its square root, $s = \sqrt{v}$. The latter represents what is usually taken as an estimate of the standard deviation (σ) of the population, as determined from a sample of that population.* The variance is thus a measure of the dispersion of the observed values of a variable (here, the score) about the mean value. If X_1, X_2, X_3, $\cdots$, X_n represent n sample scores, their mean value is

$$\overline{X} = \frac{X_1 + X_2 + X_3 + \cdots + X_n}{n} = \frac{\Sigma X}{n} \tag{13}$$

where, in analogy with our previous usage, the Greek letter Σ denotes the sum of the n values of X.

An unbiased estimate of the variance (σ) of the population of which the n scores are a random sample is defined as

$$v = s^2 = \frac{\Sigma(X - \overline{X})^2}{n - 1} = \frac{\Sigma X^2 - (\Sigma X)^2/n}{n - 1} = \frac{\Sigma X^2 - C}{n - 1} \tag{14}$$

where $C = (\Sigma X)^2/n$ is a correction term that converts the sum of the squares of the deviations of the scores from 0, $\Sigma(X - 0)^2 = \Sigma X^2$, into the sum of the squares of the deviations of the scores from their mean value, $\overline{X}$, $\Sigma(X - \overline{X})^2$. It is customary to refer to the numerator of the expression for v as the *sum of squares* (SS) and to the denominator as the corresponding number of *degrees of freedom* (*df*). The latter is $n - 1$ because $\Sigma(X - \overline{X}) = 0$ and therefore only $n - 1$ of the differences $X - \overline{X}$ are independent. A sum of squares divided by the number of degrees of freedom gives an unbiased estimate of the variance of the population.

---

*Note that the standard deviation of the population is denoted by σ (see page 177), but the estimate of it, based on the actual sample, is denoted by s.

EXAMPLE 1   From the 8 sample scores $X = 8$, 7, 6, 5, 5, 6, 8, and 7, verify numerically that $\Sigma(X - \overline{X}) = 0$ and that $\Sigma(X - \overline{X})^2 = \Sigma X^2 - C$. Find the value of s, which is an estimate of the standard deviation of the population from which the sample was selected.

Partial calculations are shown in Table 10–1, from which we see immediately that $\Sigma(X - \overline{X}) = 0$. Using the other sums shown there, we obtain $C = (52)^2/8 = 338$, so

$$\Sigma X^2 - C = 348 - 338 = 10 = \Sigma(X - \overline{X})^2$$

From Equation 14 we obtain $v = 10/7 = 1.43$, so

$$s = \sqrt{v} = \sqrt{1.43} = 1.20$$

We will encounter calculations of this kind again (see page 233) in the discussion of analysis of variance.

Table 10–1   Partial calculations for the scores given in Example 1.

	X	$X - \overline{X}$	$(X - \overline{X})^2$	X^2
	8	1.5	2.25	64
	7	0.5	0.25	49
	6	−0.5	0.25	36
	5	−1.5	2.25	25
	5	−1.5	2.25	25
	6	−0.5	0.25	36
	8	1.5	2.25	64
	7	0.5	0.25	49
Total	52	0	10.00	348
Mean	6.5			

The *t*-Distribution

When the standard deviation σ of the population is known, the normal distribution is applicable in "either–or" decision problems, such as: is there a significant difference between these two mean scores or not? If σ is unknown and must be estimated from a sample by calculating s, the sampling distribution of the resulting statistic (see page 226) is no longer a normal one. The appropriate test statistic in this case is denoted by t. Like χ^2, t has a different distribution for each value of the number of degrees of freedom. When the population is normal, the t-curve is also symmetrical and bell-shaped, but non-normal. As the size of the sample from which s is calculated increases, the t-curve approaches the normal curve as a limiting form.

Values of t for various combinations of probabilities and numbers of degrees of freedom are given in Appendix K. The probabilities shown at the top of the table pertain to a two-tailed test, and those shown at the bottom of the table are the corresponding values for a one-tailed test. See Figures 7–1 and 7–2.

Two Sets of Scores (Unpaired) Statistical tests for significant difference are based on the null hypothesis that no difference exists. This assumption applies both to population mean scores and standard deviations. The statistic t is useful in determining significance in such tests. If, for two sets of scores, no score from one set corresponds to any particular score from the other set (as, e.g., in the sets of scores obtained for one wine by two different panels of judges), the scores are independent, or *unpaired*, and the t-distribution furnishes the appropriate test of significance for comparing the mean scores of the two sets. Suppose there are n_1 X-scores and n_2 Y-scores (n_1 may or may not equal n_2); t is then defined as

$$t = \frac{\overline{X} - \overline{Y}}{\sqrt{\left(\dfrac{n_1 + n_2}{n_1 n_2}\right)\left[\dfrac{\Sigma X^2 + \Sigma Y^2 - (\Sigma X)^2/n_1 - (\Sigma Y)^2/n_2}{n_1 + n_2 - 2}\right]}} \tag{15}$$

$$(df = n_1 + n_2 - 2)$$

The significance of the result is determined by comparing the calculated value of *t* with the two-tailed values given in Appendix K, for the appropriate number of degrees of freedom. Calculated values of *t* that exceed those in the table indicate significant differences between the mean scores $\overline{X}$ and $\overline{Y}$, at the level of significance in question. In other words, such values of *t* lead to rejection of the null hypothesis of no difference.

EXAMPLE 2 A panel of six judges scores a wine on a 10-point scale (see *X*-scores in Table 10–2), and a second panel of eight judges scores the same wine, using the same scale (see *Y*-scores in Table 10–2). Is there a significant difference at the 5% level between the mean scores for the two panels?

Using the total and mean values obtained in Table 10–2 on page 230, we solve Equation 15:

$$t = \frac{8.0 - 6.5}{\sqrt{\left[\dfrac{6 + 8}{6(8)}\right]\left[\dfrac{388 + 348 - (48)^2/6 - (52)^2/8}{6 + 8 - 2}\right]}}$$

$$= \frac{1.5}{\sqrt{0.340}} = \frac{1.5}{0.583} = 2.57$$

From Appendix K, we see that $t_{.05}(12 \ df) = 2.179$. Since the calculated value $t = 2.57$ is greater than the tabular value 2.179, the null hypothesis of no difference must be rejected, and the analysis indicates that the mean scores for the two panels are significantly different. The two panels are therefore not using the same standards of judgment in evaluating the wine.

Two Sets of Scores (Paired) If one judge compares the same two wines on several different occasions, or if each member of a panel of judges compares the same two wines, a set of *paired* scores results. For the *n* paired scores *X* and *Y*, the differences $D = X - Y$ are then computed, and the mean difference $\overline{D} = \Sigma D/n$ between

Table 10-2 A wine scored by two panels of judges (see Example 2).

| | Panel | | | |
	X	Y	X^2	Y^2
	9	8	81	64
	8	7	64	49
	7	6	49	36
	9	5	81	25
	7	5	49	25
	8	6	64	36
		8		64
		7		49
Total	48	52	388	348
Mean	8.0	6.5		

the mean scores $\overline{X}$ and $\overline{Y}$ is tested with the *t*-distribution. The expression for *t* in this case is

$$t = \frac{\overline{D}}{\left(\dfrac{1}{n}\right)\sqrt{\dfrac{n\Sigma D^2 - (\Sigma D)^2}{n-1}}} = \frac{\Sigma D}{\sqrt{\dfrac{n\Sigma D^2 - (\Sigma D)^2}{n-1}}} \qquad (16)$$

$$(df = n - 1)$$

Again, the calculated value of *t* is compared with the two-tailed values given in Appendix K to determine the significance of the result.

EXAMPLE 3 A panel of seven judges scores two wines on a 20-point scale, as shown in Table 10–3. Is there a significant difference at the 5% level between the mean scores of the wines?

Using the total values for D and D^2 obtained in Table 10–3, we solve Equation 16:

Table 10-3 Two wines scored by seven judges (see Example 3).

Judge	Wine		D	D²
	X	Y		
A	15	14	1	1
B	12	14	−2	4
C	14	15	−1	1
D	17	14	3	9
E	11	11	0	0
F	16	14	2	4
G	15	13	2	4
Total	100	95	5	23
Mean	14.3	13.6	0.714	

$$t = \frac{5}{\sqrt{\dfrac{7(23) - (5)^2}{7 - 1}}} = \frac{5}{\sqrt{22.7}} = \frac{5}{4.76} = 1.05$$

From Appendix K, we see that $t_{.05}(6\ df) = 2.447$. Since the calculated value $t = 1.05$ is less than the tabular value 2.447, there is no reason to reject the null hypothesis. Therefore the mean scores of the wines are not significantly different, i.e., this panel of judges cannot distinguish between the two wines.

Note that in the case of more than two wine samples it is not proper in testing for significance among sample means to consider pairs of individual samples and apply the *t*-test repeatedly to these pairs. If this procedure is followed, the chance of obtaining erroneous conclusions will be very great. For example, in a widely reported comparison of 14 California Chardonnays scored by 11 judges, the mean scores of wines by pairs were compared by the use of the *t*-test. In the case of 14 wine samples taken from populations with identical means, 91 pairs of samples must be tested separately to determine whether their means differ significantly. Of these pairs, by chance alone, 5% would be expected to yield absolute value of t exceeding $t_{.05}$ and thus indicating significant differences. The probability that one or more of these 91 pairs of samples will give a t-value whose absolute value exceeds $t_{.05}$ is

$$1 - \left(\frac{19}{20}\right)^{91} = 1 - 0.0094 = 0.9906$$

Therefore, 99% of the time, on the basis of the 5% level of significance, a wrong conclusion will result by calling one or more pair of mean scores significantly different. The appropriate procedure is the use of the analysis of variance, which considers all mean scores together.

Analysis of Variance

Scores for Several Wines   In comparing the mean scores of more than two wines, the t-distribution is no longer appropriate. Instead, the statistical technique called *analysis of variance* is used to determine whether there are significant differences in the mean scores of the wines. The analysis of variance is essentially an arithmetic process for partitioning a total sum of squares (page 226) into components associated with various sources of variation.

To analyze a number, say k, of wines, for each of which n scores are available, a so-called *one-way*, or single-classification, analysis of variance is appropriate. Such a classification is shown in Table 10–4, where X_{ij} represents the j-th score of the i-th wine sample (i can have any value from 1 to k, and j can have any value from 1 to n).

The variance of this classification of scores can be estimated in three ways, from three sums of squares (two of which include a rele-

Table 10-4 One-way analysis of variance.

	Wine					
	1	2	3	$\cdots$	k	
	X_{11}	X_{21}	X_{31}	$\cdots$	X_{k1}	
	X_{12}	X_{22}	X_{32}	$\cdots$	X_{k2}	
	X_{13}	X_{23}	X_{33}	$\cdots$	X_{k3}	
	$\vdots$	$\vdots$	$\vdots$	X_{ij}	$\vdots$	
	X_{1n}	X_{2n}	X_{3n}	$\cdots$	X_{kn}	
Total	W_1	W_2	W_3	$\cdots$	W_k	Grand total $G = \Sigma W_i$
Mean	$\overline{X}_1$	$\overline{X}_2$	$\overline{X}_3$	$\cdots$	$\overline{X}_k$	Total no. of scores $= kn$

vant correction term, C) and their corresponding numbers of degrees of freedom. The three sums of squares in question are the *total* sum of squares, the *sample* sum of squares (i.e., the sum of squares between means of wine samples), and the *error* sum of squares (i.e., the sum of squares within samples). The correction term and the three sums of squares are defined as follows:

$$C = (\text{Grand total})^2/kn = G^2/kn \qquad (17)$$

$$\text{Total } SS = \sum_{ij} X_{ij}^2 - C \qquad (df = kn - 1) \qquad (18)$$

$$\text{Sample } SS = n\left(\sum_i \overline{X}_i^2 - G^2/kn^2\right)$$

$$= (W_1^2 + W_2^2 + \cdots + W_k^2)/n - C$$

$$= \sum_i W_i^2/n - C \qquad (df = k - 1) \qquad (19)$$

$$\text{Error } SS = \left(\sum_j X_{1j}^2 - W_1^2/n \right) + \left(\sum_j X_{2j}^2 - W_2^2/n \right) + \cdots$$

$$+ \left(\sum_j X_{kj}^2 - W_k^2/n \right)$$

$$= \sum_{ij} X_{ij}^2 - \sum_i W_i^2/n \qquad [df = k(n-1) \qquad (20)$$

From these relations it follows that

$$\text{Total } SS = \text{Sample } SS + \text{Error } SS \qquad (21)$$

and

$$\text{Total } df = \text{Sample } df + \text{Error } df \qquad (22)$$

The within-sample sum of squares (Error SS) is usually calculated by subtracting the between-sample sum of squares (Sample SS) from the total sum of squares (Total SS). The Error SS is the residual sum of squares. The value of the *error mean square* (the error variance) is given by $v = \text{Error } SS/\text{Error } df$. It is often referred to as a *generalized error term* because it is a measure of the error variation contributed by all the samples. It is independent of any differences that might exist among the sample means. The value of the *sample mean square* (Sample SS/Sample df), on the other hand, is a measure of the differences among the sample means; the larger the differences, the larger the sample mean square. The null hypothesis is that the samples come from k populations, all having the same means μ and the same variances v. This implies equality among the sample means.

The results of an analysis of variance are usually summarized in a table similar to Table 10–5.

Table 10-5 Analysis of variance for the data of Table 10–4.

Source	SS	df	ms	F
Total	$(1) = \Sigma X_{ij}^2 - C$	$kn - 1$		
Wines	$(2) = \Sigma W_i^2/n - C$	$k - 1$	$(2)/(k - 1)$	Wine ms/Error ms
Error	$(3) = \Sigma X_{ij}^2 - \Sigma W_i^2/n$	$k(n - 1)$	$(3)/k(n - 1)$	

The sample mean square and the error mean square provide two independent estimates of the common population variance. They are compared by calculating their ratio, which is a statistic called F:

$$F = \frac{\text{Sample mean square}}{\text{Error mean square}} \tag{23}$$

This calculated F-value is compared with the tabular values given in Appendixes L–1, L–2, or L–3. The F-distribution is represented by double-entry tables with respect to the degrees of freedom. The degrees of freedom for the numerator are shown in the top rows of the tables, and the degrees of freedom for the denominator are shown in the left-hand columns. Calculated F-values that exceed the tabular values for the appropriate values of *df* indicate rejection of the null hypothesis of no differences among the sample means; that is, there are significant differences. (If the sample mean square is less than the error mean square, $F < 1$ and the result is nonsignificant by definition. The null hypothesis is then accepted without the need to refer to the table.) A significant F-value implies that the evidence is sufficiently strong to indicate differences among the sample means, but it does not reveal *which* of the various differences among the sample means may be statistically significant. To determine these differences is the next step in the analysis.

Least Significant Difference One procedure for determining which wine-sample means are significantly different, following the demonstration of a significant F-value, is to calculate the *least significant difference* (*LSD*), which is the smallest difference that could exist between two significantly different sample means:

$$LSD = t_\alpha \sqrt{2v/n} \qquad [df = k(n - 1)] \qquad (24)$$

where t_α is the t-value, with $k(n - 1)$ degrees of freedom, at the significance level α, v is the error variance, and n is the number of scores on which each mean is based. For the difference between two means to be significant at the level of significance selected, the observed difference must exceed the LSD-value.

EXAMPLE 4   Given 5 scores for each of 4 wines, as shown in Table 10–6, analyze the results for significance:

$$C = (142)^2/20 = 1008.2$$

$$\text{Total } SS = (10)^2 + (8)^2 + \cdots + (6)^2 - C$$

$$= 1066 - 1008.2 = 57.8 \qquad (19 \ df)$$

$$\text{Wine } SS = \frac{(42)^2 + (43)^2 + (31)^2 + (26)^2}{5} - C$$

$$= 5250/5 - 1008.2 = 41.8 \qquad (3 \ df)$$

$$\text{Error } SS = 57.8 - 41.8 = 16.0 \qquad (16 \ df)$$

These results are combined into an *analysis of variance table*, as shown in Table 10–7.

Since the calculated F-value is larger than any of the three tabular values from Appendix Tables L–1, L–2, and L–3, significant differences among the means of the wine scores are indicated at all three levels. The level of significance of a calculated F-value is often denoted by one or more asterisks: one for the 5% level, two for the 1% level, and three for the 0.1% level. In this example, the significance of the calculated F-value is denoted by 13.9***. Significance at any given level obviously implies significance at all lower levels.

Table 10-6 Five scores for each of four wines (see Example 4).

	Wine				
	S_1	S_2	S_3	S_4	
	10	9	7	6	
	8	9	5	5	
	7	8	6	4	
	9	10	7	5	
	8	7	6	6	
Total	42	43	31	26	$G = 142$
Mean	8.4	8.6	6.2	5.2	

Table 10-7 Analysis of variance table for the data in Example 4.

Source	SS	df	ms	F	$F_{.05}$	$F_{.01}$	$F_{.001}$
Total	57.8	19					
Wines	41.8	3	13.9	13.9***	3.24	5.29	9.00
Error	16.0	16	1.0				

For the 1% level we use the *t*-value from Appendix K to calculate the *LSD* by Equation 21:

$$LSD = t_{.01}(16 \; df)\sqrt{2(1.0)/5} = 2.921\sqrt{0.40} = 1.85$$

Significance is usually shown by ranking the mean scores and underlining those that are *not* significantly different. The difference between any two scores that are not connected by an underline is therefore significant. For the mean scores in the present example we would write

Wine

	S_2	S_1	S_3	S_4
Mean	8.6	8.4	6.2	5.2

Thus there is no significant difference between wines S_1 and S_2 because the difference between their mean scores, 0.2, is less than 1.85, the calculated *LSD*. However, each of these wines is significantly better than wines S_3 and S_4. Wines S_3 and S_4 are not significantly different from each other.

Duncan's New Multiple-Range Test   Some experimenters prefer *Duncan's new multiple-range test* (Duncan 1955, Harter 1960), in which, after ranking, each sample mean is compared with every other sample mean, using a set of significant differences that depend on, and increase with, the increase in the range between the ranked means. The smallest value is obtained for adjacent means, and the largest value for the extremes. In Duncan's test, the shortest significant range R_p for comparing the largest and smallest of p mean scores, after they have been ranked, is given by

$$R_p = Q_p \sqrt{v/n} \qquad [df = k(n-1)] \tag{25}$$

where the number of degrees of freedom is that for the error variance v. The appropriate value of Q_p can be obtained from Appendixes M–1, M–2, or M–3.

EXAMPLE 5   Use Duncan's new multiple-range test to establish significance for the data in Example 4.

For the 1% level, $\sqrt{v/n} = \sqrt{1.0/5} = \sqrt{0.2} = 0.447$, and the values of Q_p for $p = 2$, 3, and 4 are obtained from Appendix M–2. The results are summarized in Table 10–8. We see that the R_p-values are appropriate for making the following comparisons:

Table 10-8 Duncan's new multiple-range test (1% level) for the data in Example 4.

Shortest significant range			Comparison				
p	2	3	4					
Q_p	4.13	4.31	4.42	Wine	S_2	S_1	S_3	S_4
R_p	1.85	1.93	1.98	Mean	8.6	8.4	6.2	5.2

$$R_2 = 1.85 \quad S_2 \text{ with } S_1, S_1 \text{ with } S_3, \text{ and } S_3 \text{ with } S_4$$

$$R_3 = 1.93 \quad S_2 \text{ with } S_3, \text{ and } S_1 \text{ with } S_4$$

$$R_4 = 1.98 \quad S_2 \text{ with } S_4$$

The results are the same as those obtained in Example 4. There is no significant difference between wines S_1 and S_2, but each of these wines is significantly better than wines S_3 and S_4. Wines S_3 and S_4 are not significantly different from each other.

If the mean scores of the wines are based on different numbers of individual scores, that is, n_1 scores for the first wine, n_2 scores for the second wine, . . . , n_k scores for the k-th wine, the analysis is very similar but the following modifications must be made:

1. Sample $SS = W_1^2/n_1 + W_2^2/n_2 + \cdots + W_k^2/n_k - C$

2. Effective number of replications n_{eff} replaces n:

$$n_{\text{eff}} = \left(\frac{1}{k-1}\right)\left(\frac{\Sigma n_j - \Sigma n_j^2}{\Sigma n_j}\right)$$

where Σn_j is the total number of wine samples in the experiment.

3. $LSD = t_\alpha \sqrt{2v/n_{\text{eff}}}$ and $R_p = Q_p \sqrt{v/n_{\text{eff}}}$
where t_α and Q_p are based on $\Sigma n_j - k$ degrees of freedom.

Scoring of Several Wines by Several Judges   In the customary sensory evaluation in which a panel of n judges scores each of k wines, the so-called *two-way*, or double-classification, analysis of variance is appropriate in testing for significance. In this classification, the total sum of squares, calculated as the variation among all scores, is subdivided into three parts: a sum of squares based on the variation among wines, a sum of squares based on the variation among judges, and a remainder sum of squares. The latter is not the result of variation among wines or judges but is a measure of the unexplained variation, or error variation. The degrees of freedom are subdivided in the same way. This is known as a *randomized complete-block design;* its pattern is shown in Table 10–9, and a schematic representation of the analysis is shown in Figure 10–1. The definitions are as follows (compare them with Equations 17–22):

(a) $C = G^2/kn$ $\qquad\qquad\qquad\qquad\qquad$ df

(b) Total $SS = \Sigma X_{ij}^2 - C$ $\qquad\qquad\qquad$ $kn - 1$

(c) Wine $SS = \Sigma W_i^2/n - C$ $\qquad\qquad$ $k - 1$

(d) Judge $SS = \Sigma T_j^2/k - C$ $\qquad\qquad$ $n - 1$

(e) Error $SS =$

$\qquad$ (b) $-$ (c) $-$ (d) $\qquad\qquad$ $(kn - 1) - (k - 1) - (n - 1)$

$\qquad\qquad\qquad\qquad\qquad\qquad\qquad\qquad$ $= (k - 1)(n - 1)$

From these sums of squares and the corresponding numbers of degrees of freedom, three independent estimates of the population variance are computed. On the assumption that the groups making up the total set of measurements (scores) are random samples from populations with the same means, the three estimates of the population variance can be expected to differ only within the limits of chance fluctuation. There are two null hypotheses here, namely, that the population means for the wines are all the same and that those for the judges are all the same. These hypotheses are tested by comparing the among-wine variance and the among-judge variance, respectively, with the error variance. The comparisons consist of calculating the variance ratios

$$F = \frac{\text{variance for wines}}{\text{error variance}} \quad \text{and} \quad F = \frac{\text{variance for judges}}{\text{error variance}} \quad (26)$$

To establish significance, as before, the calculated values of F are compared with the tabular values at the three levels of significance.

Table 10-9   Two-way analysis of variance (randomized complete-block design).

Judge	Wine					Total
	1	2	3	$\cdots$	k	
1	X_{11}	X_{21}	X_{31}	$\cdots$	X_{k1}	T_1
2	X_{12}	X_{22}	X_{32}	$\cdots$	X_{k2}	T_2
3	X_{13}	X_{23}	X_{33}	$\cdots$	X_{k3}	T_3
$\cdot$	$\cdot$	$\cdot$	$\cdot$	X_{ij}	$\cdot$	$\cdot$
n	X_{1n}	X_{2n}	X_{3n}	$\cdots$	X_{kn}	T_n
Total	W_1	W_2	W_3	$\cdots$	W_k	$G = \Sigma T_j = \Sigma W_i$
Mean	$\overline{X}_1$	$\overline{X}_2$	$\overline{X}_3$	$\cdots$	$\overline{X}_k$	Total no. of scores $= kn$

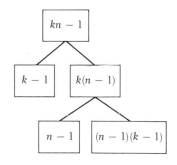

Partition of the total variation

Total variation → Between-wine variation, Within-wine variation → Between-judge variation, Residual variation

Partition of the degrees of freedom

$kn - 1$ → $k - 1$, $k(n - 1)$ → $n - 1$, $(n - 1)(k - 1)$

Figure 10-1   Schematic representation of randomized block design analysis.

A summary of the analysis of variance for the data of Table 10–9 is shown in Table 10–10.

Table 10-10 Analysis of variance for the data of Table 10–9.

Source	SS	df	ms	F
Total	$(1) = \Sigma X_{ij}^2 - C$	$kn - 1$		
Wines	$(2) = \Sigma W_i^2/n - C$	$k - 1$	$(5) = (2)/(k - 1)$	$(5)/(7)$
Judges	$(3) = \Sigma T_j^2/k - C$	$n - 1$	$(6) = (3)/(n - 1)$	$(6)/(7)$
Error	$(4) = (1) - (2) - (3)$	$(k - 1)(n - 1)$	$(7) = (4)/(k - 1)(n - 1)$	

EXAMPLE 6 Five judges score four wines on a 20-point scale, as shown in Table 10–11. Are there significant differences among the sample means at the 1% level?

Substituting the data into the equations given in Table 10–10, we obtain

$$C = (267)^2/20 = 3564.45$$

$$\text{Total } SS = (13)^2 + \cdots + (12)^2 - C = 142.55 \qquad (19 \; df)$$

$$\text{Wine } SS = \frac{(67)^2 + \cdots + (52)^2}{5} - C = 112.95 \qquad (3 \; df)$$

$$\text{Judge } SS = \frac{(56)^2 + \cdots + (56)^2}{4} - C = 8.80 \qquad (4 \; df)$$

$$\text{Error } SS = 142.55 - 112.95 - 8.80 = 20.80$$

$$(19 - 3 - 4 = 12 \; df)$$

These results and the remaining calculations are shown in Table 10–12.

Since the calculated *F*-value for wines is greater than the tabular value, significant differences between the means of the wine scores do exist at the 1% level. (In fact, they exist at the 0.1% level, as implied by the three asterisks on the calculated *F*-value.) The calcu-

Table 10-11 Five judges score four wines on a 20-point scale (see Example 6).

Judge	Wine				Total
	S_1	S_2	S_3	S_4	
1	13	18	15	10	56
2	15	16	12	11	54
3	14	15	11	9	49
4	12	17	13	10	52
5	13	19	12	12	56
Total	67	85	63	52	$267 = G$
Mean	13.4	17.0	12.6	10.4	

Table 10-12 Analysis of variance table for the data in Example 6.

Source	SS	df	ms	F	$F_{.01}$	$F_{.001}$
Total	142.55	19				
Wines	112.95	3	37.65	21.76***	5.95	10.80
Judges	8.80	4	2.20	1.27	5.41	
Error	20.80	12	1.73			

lated F-value for judges is less than the tabular value, so there are no significant differences among the judges; that is, they have been consistent in their scoring.

Specific differences among the wines can be tested by calculating the least significant difference:

$$LSD = t_\alpha \sqrt{2v/n} = t_{.01}(12 \; df) \sqrt{2(1.73)/5} = 3.055 \sqrt{0.692} = 2.54$$

Therefore 2.54 is the smallest difference that can exist between two significantly different sample means. Again, using the method of underlining mean scores that are not significantly different, we write

	Wine			
	S_2	S_1	S_3	S_4
Mean	17.0	13.4	12.6	10.4

We see that wine S_2 is significantly better than wines S_1, S_3, and S_4. Wine S_1 is significantly better than wine S_4. Wines S_1 and S_3 are not significantly different, and wines S_3 and S_4 are not significantly different.

Computers Calculations for the one- and two-way analyses of variance as well as for other statistical procedures are readily carried out on a computer, and most computer centers have program libraries with prepared programs available. Calculations by a computer are not only much faster but also much more reliable than those carried out using an ordinary desk calculator. Delays resulting from having to prepare data cards, submitting them to the computer center and awaiting the returned output have been eliminated by the installation in laboratories and offices of remote control terminals that provide input and output information to and from a computer at a remote site, which in some cases may be hundreds of miles away.

Computer programs may not always be available, and occasionally results of tastings are desired immediately following the judging. In such cases, the small hand-held calculators provide a means of analyzing results without much difficulty. In Appendixes Q and R, procedures are presented for carrying out two-way analyses of variance using calculators manufactured by two well-known companies. Some of the more sophisticated models have cards with prepared programs that can be inserted in the calculator further simplifying the calculations. For some models, printers are available to provide taped records.

Estimation of Reliability When k wines are scored by n judges, the reliability of a single score can be estimated by the average of intercorrelations between the scores when a pooled estimate of the variance is used in the denominator of each of the correlations. This estimate of reliability can be shown to be

$$r_1 = \frac{ms \text{ between wines} - ms \text{ within wines}}{ms \text{ between wines} + (n-1) \, ms \text{ within wines}} \quad \text{and} \quad (27)$$

$$ms \text{ within wines} = \frac{SS \text{ for judges} + SS \text{ for error}}{df \text{ for judges} + df \text{ for error}} \quad (28)$$

The reliability of the average of n scores may be expressed in terms of the reliability of a single score as follows:

$$r_n = \frac{nr_1}{1 + (n-1) \, r_1} \quad (29)$$

This reliability may be interpreted as follows: If the judging of the same wines were to be repeated with another similar group of n judges, the correlation between the mean ratings obtained from the two sets of data would be approximately equal to r_n. The procedure will be illustrated with data from a recent judging of five Pinot noir wines by a panel of seven judges. The results of the scoring are shown in Table 10–13, and the results of the analysis in Table 10–14.

Table 10-13 Seven judges scored five samples of Pinot noir wines on a 10-point scale.

Judge	S_1	S_2	S_3	S_4	S_5	Total
1	8	4	2	5	4	23.0
2	6	4	5	6	5	26.0
3	6.5	3	8.5	7	5.5	30.5
4	3	4	5	6	7	25.0
5	8	7	5.5	8	6.5	35.0
6	3	3.5	7	9	8	30.5
7	7.5	5	4.5	5.5	8.5	31.0
Total	42.0	30.5	37.5	46.5	44.5	201.0

Table 10-14   Analysis of variance table for the data in Table 10–13.

Source		SS	df	ms	F	$F_{.05}$
Total		115.19	34			
Between wines		23.26	4	5.82	1.97	2.78
Within wines		91.93	30	3.06		
Between judges	20.99		6	3.50	1.18	
Error (residual)	70.94		24	2.96		

On the basis of these data there is no reason to reject the null hypothesis of no difference between the wine scores. It is not hard to see why this is true when one looks at the correlations of judges' scores in Table 10–15. The average of these correlations is 0.114. This same value can be more easily calculated from r_1.

$$r_1 = \frac{5.82 - 3.06}{5.82 + 6(3.06)} = \frac{2.76}{24.18} = 0.114$$

The reliability of the average of 7 scores is

$$r_7 = \frac{7(0.114)}{1 + 6(0.114)} = 0.47$$

Table 10-15   Correlations between judges' scores.

Judge	Judge						
	1	2	3	4	5	6	7
1		0.33	−0.11	−0.52	0.59	−0.84	0.59
2			0.33	0	0.15	0.12	0.13
3				0.15	−0.15	0.78	−0.14
4					−0.15	1.00	0.19
5						−0.19	0.15
6							−0.01

This low value results from the inconsistencies among the judges' scores.

Hedonic Rating Hedonic rating of wines is usually done with a scale of 5, 7, or 9 points. The usual 9-point scale comprises the following categories: *like extremely* (4); *like very much* (3); *like moderately* (2); *like slightly* (1); *neither like nor dislike* (0); *dislike slightly* (−1); *dislike moderately* (−2); *dislike very much* (−3); *dislike extremely* (−4). (See also Figure 9–1.) To analyze the results, the numerical values shown in parentheses are used and the analysis of variance is applied. Any set of consecutive integers could be used instead of these numbers, but those used here result in the smallest intermediate values.

EXAMPLE 7 Fifty judges rate four wines on a 7-point hedonic scale, as shown in Table 10–16. Are there significant differences in the judges' preference among the wines?

$$C = (227)^2/200 = 257.64$$

$$\text{Total } SS = 729 - 257.64 = 471.36 \qquad (199 \; df)$$

$$\text{Wine } SS = \frac{(109)^2 + (89)^2 + (28)^2 + (1)^2}{50} - C$$

$$= 411.74 - 257.64 = 154.10 \qquad (3 \; df)$$

$$\text{Error } SS = 471.36 - 154.10 = 317.26 \qquad (196 \; df)$$

These results and the remaining calculations are shown in Table 10–17. (Since *F*-values for 196 degrees of freedom [denominator] are not given in Appendix L–3, the values for $df = \infty$ are used.)

Since $F = 31.7$ (calculated) exceeds $F_{.001} = 5.42$ (tabular), very highly significant differences among the mean scores of the wines are indicated. If Duncan's new multiple-range test is applied, we have

$$R_p = Q_p \sqrt{v/n} = Q_p \sqrt{1.62/50} = Q_p(0.18)$$

Table 10-16 Fifty judges assign hedonic ratings to four wines (see Example 7).

Rating	X	S_1	S_2	S_3	S_4	Σf	$(\Sigma f)X$	$(\Sigma f)X^2$
			Frequency of response, f					
			Wine					
Like very much	3	22	8	2	5	37	111	333
Like moderately	2	17	25	13	8	63	126	252
Like slightly	1	10	15	18	3	46	46	46
Neither like nor dislike	0	0	2	5	10	17	0	0
Dislike slightly	-1	1	0	4	15	20	-20	20
Dislike moderately	-2	0	0	6	9	15	-30	60
Dislike very much	-3	0	0	2	0	2	-6	18
Total Σf		50	50	50	50	200		
ΣfX		109	89	28	1		$227 = G$	
ΣfX^2								729
Mean $\Sigma fX/\Sigma f$		2.18	1.78	0.56	0.02			

Table 10-17 Analysis of variance table for the data in Example 7.

Source	SS	df	ms	F	$F_{.05}$	$F_{.01}$	$F_{.001}$
Total	471.36	199					
Wines	154.10	3	51.4	31.7***	2.60	3.78	5.42
Error	317.26	196	1.62				

The results are summarized in Table 10–18. (Again, the numbers for $df = \infty$ are used.)

In this example, we see that wines S_1 and S_2 are significantly better than wines S_3 and S_4. Wine S_1 is not significantly different from wine S_2, and wine S_3 is not significantly different from wine S_4.

Table 10-18   Duncan's new multiple-range test (0.1% level) for the data in Example 7.

Shortest Significant Range				Comparison				
p	2	3	4					
Q_p	4.65	4.80	4.90	Wine	S_1	S_2	S_3	S_4
R_p	0.837	0.864	0.882	Mean	2.18	1.78	0.56	0.02

Interaction   The term *interaction* is used in statistics to describe a differential response to two variables, usually referred to as *factors*, which may or may not act independently of each other. In the analysis of variance, interaction is expressed by a so-called residual term, which provides another estimate of variance. It reflects the relations between experimental factors or the failure of one factor to vary in accord with variations in the second factor. For example, judges differ in their susceptibility to physical and mental fatigue and in their reactions to the foods they consume. Such differences can lead to interaction effects when the same judges evaluate the same wines at two different times. (Time is always one of the factors in interaction effects in wine evaluation.)

Some possible situations are shown in Figure 10–2, which relates the scoring of two wines by two judges to the time of day. If the lines joining the morning and afternoon scores for each judge are parallel, there is no interaction. The greater the departure from parallelism, the greater the interaction, owing to the differential response of the judges to the factors time and, say, fatigue. Small departures from parallelism may be caused by variation in, or treatment of, wine samples or as a result of random sampling errors. The problem is to test statistically whether an observed departure from parallelism is greater than could reasonably be expected to occur by chance alone.

The significance of an interaction is determined by comparing its estimate of variance with that of experimental error. A significant

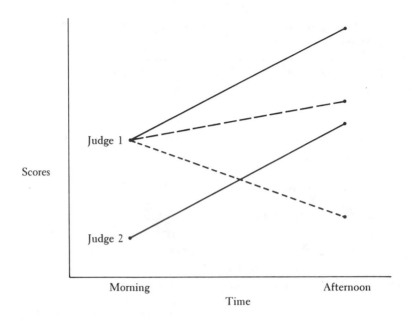

Figure 10-2 Changes in scores with time. The two solid lines show no interaction between the judges' scores and time. The lower solid line and the two dashed lines show different degrees of interaction.

interaction is one that is too large to be explained on the basis of chance alone, under the null hypothesis of no interaction. A nonsignificant interaction leads to the conclusion that the factors in question act independently of each other. The existence or nonexistence of interactions can only be determined when scores are replicated.

EXAMPLE 8 Five judges score four wines on two successive days, called time I and time II. The results are shown in Table 10–19. Analyze the results for significance, to determine whether there is interaction.

Table 10-19 Five judges score four wines on two successive days (see Example 8).

Judge	\multicolumn{4}{Wine}				Total	Judge	Wine				Total

		Time I						Time II				
		Wine						Wine				
Judge	S_1	S_2	S_3	S_4	Total	Judge	S_1	S_2	S_3	S_4	Total
1	10	10	8	6	34	1	8	9	6	7	30
2	9	9	6	8	32	2	7	8	6	6	27
3	10	10	9	8	37	3	9	8	7	9	33
4	8	8	8	5	29	4	10	9	8	5	32
5	8	7	6	4	25	5	9	10	7	5	31
Total	45	44	37	31	157	Total	43	44	34	32	153

For the 40 individual scores we have

$$C - (310)^2/40 = 2402.5$$

$$\text{Total } SS = (10)^2 + (9)^2 + \cdots + (5)^2 - C$$
$$= 2504 - 2402.5 = 101.5 \qquad (39 \; df)$$

If the individual scores for the two times are added, as shown in Table 10–20, the result is a classification of wines and judges called a *two-way pattern*. Since the entries in the table are the totals of two scores, the denominators of the equations for the sums of squares are twice as great as in the usual analysis, and the means are obtained by dividing the totals by 10 (5 judges $\times$ 2 times). The correction term remains the same because it always pertains to the same totals. The total sum of squares for this pattern is called a *subtotal sum of squares* to distinguish it from the total sum of squares for the independent scores. The calculations follow.

Table 10–20 Combined (two-way) scores for times for the data in Table 10–19.

			Wine		
Judge	S_1	S_2	S_3	S_4	Total
1	18	19	14	13	64
2	16	17	12	14	59
3	19	18	16	17	70
4	18	17	16	10	61
5	17	17	13	9	56
Total	88	88	71	63	310 $= G$
Mean	8.80	8.80	7.10	6.30	

Wines $\times$ Judges (disregard times)

$$\text{Subtotal } SS = \frac{(18)^2 + (16)^2 + \cdots + (9)^2}{2} - C$$

$$= 2481 - 2402.5 = 78.5 \qquad (19 \; df)$$

$$\text{Wine } SS = \frac{(88)^2 + (88)^2 + (71)^2 + (63)^2}{10} - C$$

$$= 2449.8 - 2402.5 = 47.3 \qquad (3 \; df)$$

$$\text{Judge } SS = \frac{(64)^2 + (59)^2 + \cdots + (56)^2}{8} - C$$

$$= 2416.75 - 2402.5 = 14.25 \qquad (4 \; df)$$

$$\text{Interaction } SS = 78.5 - 47.3 - 14.25 = 16.95$$
$$\text{(Wine} \times \text{Judge)} \qquad (19 - 3 - 4 = 12 \; df)$$

The next step in the analysis is to combine the total scores for the 5 judges, which results in a two-way pattern of wines and times, as shown in Table 10–21. Since the entries in the table are the totals of 5 individual scores, the denominators of the equations are 5 times as great as in the usual analysis. The calculations follow.

Table 10-21 Combined (two-way) scores for judges for the data in Table 10–19.

	Wines × Times (disregard judges)				
	Wine				
Time	S_1	S_2	S_3	S_4	Total
I	45	44	37	31	157
II	43	44	34	32	153
Total	88	88	71	63	$310 = G$
Mean	8.80	8.80	7.10	6.30	

$$\text{Subtotal } SS = \frac{(45)^2 + (43)^2 + \cdots + (32)^2}{5} - C$$

$$= 2451.2 - 2402.5 = 48.7 \qquad (7 \; df)$$

$$\text{Wine } SS = 47.3 \text{ (from preceding pattern)} \qquad (3 \; df)$$

$$\text{Time } SS = \frac{(157)^2 + (153)^2}{20} - C$$

$$= 2402.9 - 2402.5 = 0.4 \qquad (1 \; df)$$

$$\text{Interaction } SS = 48.7 - 47.3 - 0.4 = 1.0$$
$$\text{(Wine × Time)} \qquad (7 - 3 - 1 = 3 \; df)$$

Next the total scores for the 4 wines are combined to give a two-way pattern of judges and times, as shown in Table 10–22. Since the entries in the table are the totals of 4 individual scores, the denominators of the equations are 4 times as great as in the usual analysis. The calculations follow.

$$\text{Subtotal } SS = \frac{(34)^2 + (30)^2 + \cdots + (31)^2}{4} - C$$

$$= 2429.5 - 2402.5 = 27.0 \qquad (9 \; df)$$

Table 10-22 Combined (two-way) scores for wines for the data in Table 10–19.

Time	Judges × Times (disregard wines)					
	Judge					
	1	‑2	3	4	5	Total
I	34	32	37	29	25	157
II	30	27	33	32	31	153
Total	64	59	70	61	56	$310 = G$
Mean	8.00	7.38	8.75	7.62	7.00	

$$\text{Judge } SS = 14.25 \qquad\qquad (4\ df)$$

$$\text{Time } SS = 0.4 \qquad\qquad (1\ df)$$

$$\text{Interaction } SS = 27.0 - 14.25 - 0.4 = 12.35$$
$$(\text{Judge} \times \text{Time}) \qquad\qquad (9 - 4 - 1 = 4\ df)$$

These results and the remaining calculations are shown in Table 10–23. (Recall the meaning of the asterisks on the calculated F-values, mentioned in Example 4.)

We see that the wines are significantly different at all three levels, and that the values for the judges and the judge × time interaction are significant at the 5% level. The significant interaction indicates that the judges have reacted differently at the two times, as can be seen from their total scores at the two times. The total scores for the first three judges are less at time II than at time I, but the last two judges have total scores greater at time II than at time I. This might mean that we are dealing with two different types of judges. It could be the result of different foods consumed on the two days, varying mental or physical conditions, temperature differences, or other causes.

Table 10-23   Analysis of variance table for the data in Example 8.

Source	SS	df	ms	F	$F_{.05}$	$F_{.01}$	$F_{.001}$
Total	101.50	39					
Wines	47.30	3	15.77	20.48***	3.49	5.95	10.80
Judges	14.25	4	3.56	4.62*	3.26	5.41	
Times	0.40	1	0.40				
Interactions							
W × J	16.95	12	1.41	1.83	2.69		
W × T	1.00	3	0.33				
J × T	12.35	4	3.09	4.01*	3.26	5.41	
Error	9.25	12	0.77				

The least significant differences can now be used to make specific comparisons of the mean scores for the wines and for the judges.

$$\text{Wines: } LSD = t_{.001}(12 \ df)\sqrt{2(0.77)/10} = 4.318\sqrt{0.154}$$
$$= 1.69$$

	Wine			
	S_1	S_2	S_3	S_4
Mean	8.80	8.80	7.10	6.30

$$\text{Judges: } LSD = t_{.05}(12 \ df)\sqrt{2(0.77)/8} = 2.179\sqrt{0.192}$$
$$= 0.96$$

	Judge				
	3	1	4	2	5
Mean	8.75	8.00	7.62	7.38	7.00

Some experimenters combine the sum of squares and number of degrees of freedom for nonsignificant interactions with the sum of squares and number of degrees of freedom, respectively, for the error, and use the resulting value as a revised error term. This increases the number of degrees of freedom on which the error is based. The results of these calculations for the data in Example 8 are shown in Table 10–24. The corresponding *LSD* values are shown below.

Table 10-24   Analysis of variance table for the data in Example 8, with nonsignificant interactions combined with error.

Source	SS	df	ms	F	$F_{.05}$	$F_{.01}$	$F_{.001}$
Total	101.50	39					
Wines	47.30	3	15.77	15.46***	2.96	4.60	7.27
Judges	14.25	4	3.56	3.49*	2.73	4.11	
Times	0.40	1	0.40				
J × T	12.35	4	3.09	3.06*	2.73	4.11	
Error	27.20	27	1.01				

This procedure results in slight changes in the significance patterns when the *F*-values are close to the borderline between significance and nonsignificance. It often yields a smaller value for the error variance, although in Example 8 it yields a larger value.

I believe in the wisdom of often saying "probably" and "perhaps."

JAMES HILTON

Figures may not lie, but statistics compiled unscientifically and analyzed incompletely are almost sure to be misleading, and when this condition is unnecessarily chronic the so-called statisticians may well be called liars.

E. B. WILSON

CHAPTER 11

Incomplete Blocks

 In wine judging, if each judge scores all the samples at the same session, the randomized complete-block design discussed previously (page 240) is appropriate. However, judges find it increasingly difficult to make satisfactory ratings as the number of wines presented to them becomes larger. The number of samples that can be reliably scored at any one session depends on several factors, including the type of wine being evaluated. Taste fatigue, when too many samples are judged at a single session, can result in biased opinions and cause heterogeneity of scoring to be so great that any comparisons are practically useless. When the number of samples is large and exceeds the number that can be reliably differentiated at a single trial, then the *incomplete-block design*, in which a judge scores only a portion of the samples at one time, is useful. This design was introduced by Yates (1936) to overcome heterogeneity in field plots in connection with agricultural experimentation. The procedure is applicable in sensory testing where the block represents the scores assigned by an individual judge in a single trial, and the score for a single sample replaces the plot yield. Incomplete-block designs reduce the need for the judge to have long-time memory retention since consistency is necessary only within the incomplete-block limit.

Balanced Incomplete-Block Design

An incomplete-block design in which each block contains the same number of samples k, and in which each pair of samples appears together in the same block the same number of times λ, is called a balanced incomplete-block design. In such designs, all pairs of samples are compared with approximately the same precision even though block sizes may be small and differences between blocks may be large.

Since only some of the wines are judged at the same time, and since each wine is compared with every other wine, only certain arrangements of blocks, samples within blocks, and replications are possible. The relevant procedures and possible incomplete-block designs for specific numbers of samples and judges can be found in Fisher and Yates (1974) and Cochran and Cox (1957).

A balanced incomplete-block design is specified by the following design parameters in common use:

t = number of wine samples
k = number of wine samples scored by each judge at each session
b = number of judges (blocks)
r = number of scores for each wine sample
n = total number of scores in the design
λ = number of times each pair of wine samples appears in the same block

These six parameters are not independent. They are integers subject to the following restrictions:

(1) $b \geq t$ and $k < t$
(2) $tr = bk = n$
(3) $\lambda(t - 1) = r(k - 1)$, or $\lambda = r(k - 1)/(t - 1)$

A design with $b = t$ and $r = k$ is said to be symmetric, and n is a square. For practical reasons there should not be too many replications, that is, $r \leq 10$. Because of the above restrictions, only certain designs are possible, many of which are listed by Fisher and Yates (1974) and Cochran and Cox (1957).

Additional notation that will be used in the following examples is as follows:

W_i = total score for wine sample i

B_i = sum of totals for blocks in which sample i appears

$A_i = kW_i - B_i$ represents for wine sample i, the sample effect adjusted for, and free of, the effects of the blocks in which it appears $(\Sigma A_i = 0)$

The calculations and the analysis of variance follow the usual patterns except for the sample sum of squares adjusted for blocks, which is defined as

$$\text{Wine } SS \text{ (adj.)} = \frac{\Sigma A_i^2}{kt\lambda} \qquad (30)$$

Since each A_i is free of block effects, it represents, for sample i, an estimated sample effect w_i that provides an adjustment to the general mean score, namely, an adjusted mean score for the sample. The adjusted mean for each sample is $\widehat{X}_i = \mu + w_i$, where $w_i = A_i / t\lambda$; $(\Sigma w_i = 0)$. In using the LSD or Duncan's new multiple-range test to compare adjusted mean scores for samples, the value of the effective error variance to be used instead of v is

$$v_{\text{eff}} = v \left[\frac{k(t-1)}{t(k-1)} \right] \qquad (31)$$

The pattern for a balanced incomplete-block design for seven judges scoring seven wines is shown in Table 11–1, and the corresponding analysis of variance is shown in Table 11–2.

Table 11-1 Balanced incomplete-block design:
$t = b = 7$ $k = r = 3$ $\lambda = 3(2)/6 = 1$

Block (judge)	Wine							Total
	S_1	S_2	S_3	S_4	S_5	S_6	S_7	
1	X	X		X				T_1
2		X	X		X			T_2
3			X	X		X		T_3
4				X	X		X	T_4
5	X				X	X		T_5
6		X				X	X	T_6
7	X		X				X	T_7
Total	W_1	W_2	W_3	W_4	W_5	W_6	W_7	G

Table 11-2 Analysis of variance for Table 11-1.

Source	SS	df	ms
Total	$(1) = \Sigma X_{ij}^2 - C$	$kb - 1$	
Blocks	$(2) = \Sigma T_j^2/k - C$	$b - 1$	$(2)/(b - 1)$
Wines (adj.)	$(3) = \Sigma A_i^2/tk\lambda = \Sigma A_i w_i/k$	$t - 1$	$(3)/(t - 1)$
Error	$(4) = (1) - (2) - (3)$	$kb - b - t + 1$	$(4)/(kb - b - t + 1)$

$A_i = kW_i - B_i$; Wine 1 appears in blocks 1, 5 and 7; Therefore $B_1 = T_1 + T_5 + T_7$.

$w_i = A_i/t\lambda$; Adjusted wine mean $\hat{\bar{X}}_i = G/kb + w_i = G/kb + A_i/t\lambda$.

$v_i =$ variance for adjusted wine mean $\hat{\bar{X}}_i = \dfrac{k(t - 1)v}{t(k - 1)r}$; $C = G^2/kb$.

EXAMPLE 1   Six wines are scored on a 10-point scale by judges in 10 blocks of 3 samples each. There are 5 scores for each wine sample, each of which is compared twice with every other sample in the same block. The pattern is shown in Table 11–3. Analyze the data for significance.

Table 11-3   Six wines scored on a 10-point scale by judges in 10 blocks of 3 samples each (incomplete-block design; see Example 1).

Block	Wine						
(judge)	S_1	S_2	S_3	S_4	S_5	S_6	Total
1	4	5			5		14
2	6	7				6	19
3	6		7	5			18
4	7		5			7	19
5	4			6	4		14
6			6		4	10	20
7		8	7	5			20
8		10	4		6		20
9		6		4		9	19
10				4	5	8	17
Total W_i	27	36	29	24	24	40	$180 = G$
kW_i	81	108	87	72	72	120	$\mu = 180/30$
B_i	84	92	97	88	85	94	$= 6.00$
A_i	-3	16	-10	-16	-13	26	
w_i	-0.25	1.33	-0.83	-1.33	-1.08	2.17	
$\mu + w_i$	5.75	7.33	5.17	4.67	4.92	8.17	

In this design $t = 6$, $b = 10$, $k = 3$, $r = 5$, and $\lambda = 2$. The calculations are shown below.

$$C = (180)^2/30 = 1080$$
$$\text{Total } SS = (4)^2 + (5)^2 + \cdots + (8)^2 - C$$
$$= 1168 - 1080 = 88 \qquad (29\ df)$$

$$\text{Block } SS = \frac{(14)^2 + (19)^2 + \cdots + (17)^2}{3} - C$$

$$= 1096 - 1080 = 16 \qquad\qquad (9\ df)$$

$$\text{Wine } SS\,(\text{adj.}) = \frac{\Sigma A_i^2}{kt\lambda} = \frac{(-3)^2 + (16)^2 + \cdots + (26)^2}{3(6)(2)}$$

$$= 1466/36 = 40.72 \qquad\qquad (5\ df)$$

$$\text{Error } SS = 88 - 16 - 40.72$$

$$= 31.28 \quad (\text{intra-block error}) \qquad\qquad (15\ df)$$

These results and the remaining calculations are shown in Table 11–4.

Table 11-4   Analysis of variance table for the data in Example 1.

Source	SS	df	ms	F	$F_{.05}$	$F_{.01}$
Total	88.00	29				
Blocks	16.00	9	1.78			
Wines (adj.)	40.72	5	8.14	3.89*	2.90	4.56
Error	31.28	15	2.09			

The analysis indicates significant differences among the sample means at the 5% level because the calculated value $F = 3.89$ exceeds the tabular value $F_{.05} = 2.90$. If the *LSD* is used to test for specific differences among the wines, we have

$$LSD = t_{.05}(15\ df)\sqrt{\frac{2v}{r}\left[\frac{k(t-1)}{t(k-1)}\right]}$$

$$= 2.131\sqrt{\left[\frac{2(2.09)}{5}\right]\left[\frac{3(5)}{6(2)}\right]} = 2.131\sqrt{(0.836)(1.25)}$$

$$= 2.131\sqrt{1.04} = 2.17$$

			Wine			
	S_6	S_2	S_1	S_3	S_5	S_4
Mean	8.17	7.33	5.75	5.17	4.92	4.67

We see that there is no significant difference between wines S_6 and S_2. Wine S_6 is significantly better than wines S_1, S_3, S_5, and S_4. Wine S_2 is not significantly different from wines S_1 and S_3 but is significantly better than wines S_5 and S_4. There are no significant differences among wines S_1, S_3, S_5, and S_4.

Reference Sample in Each Block

The sensory score assigned to any sample is influenced by the quality of the samples with which it is compared. Where only a portion of the samples are scored at any one time consistency in scoring is difficult. In order to assure greater uniformity in scoring, a design incorporating a control or reference sample in each block has been suggested. Gacula (1978) has outlined the procedure.

The parameters for such a design are the same as those for the case where no reference sample is included, except that the number of wines is $t + 1$ and the number of samples in each block is $k + 1$. If the basic design is repeated p times to increase replication, the parameters b, r and λ are multiplied by p. The adjusted means for the wine samples are $\widehat{W}_R = \mu + w_R$ and $\widehat{W}_i = \mu + w_i$ where μ is the grand mean excluding the reference sample. Comparisons of adjusted sample means may be made by any of the multiple comparison procedures, such as the LSD and Duncan's tests.

Gacula (1978) discusses the analysis of balanced incomplete blocks with reference samples when there are repetitions of the pattern. Cornell and Knapp (1972) and Cornell and Schreckengost (1975) developed composite complete–incomplete block designs for use in sensory evaluation. In these designs, however, increase in block size tends to defeat the purpose of incomplete block design.

Following the procedure outlined by Gacula, the pattern and analysis for 7 wines in blocks of 3 samples with a reference sample in each block is shown in Table 11–5, and the corresponding analysis of variance is shown in Table 11–6.

$$A_R = (k + 1)W_R - G \quad \text{and} \quad A_i = (k + 1)W_i - B_i$$

Wine 1 appears in blocks 1, 5, and 7; therefore $B_i = T_1 + T_5 + T_7$.

$$w_R = \frac{A_R}{bk} \text{ with variance } \left[\frac{k + 1}{bk}\right]v \quad \text{where } v \text{ is the error variance}$$

$$w_i = \frac{tA_i + A_R}{t(rk + \lambda)} \text{ with variance } \left[\frac{(t - 1)^2(k + 1)}{tr(kt - 1)}\right]v$$

Variance for contrasts between i and R means is $\left[\dfrac{(k + 1)(k + t - 2)}{r(kt - 1)}\right]v$

Table 11-5 Incomplete blocks with reference sample:
$$t = b = 7 \qquad k = r = 3 \qquad \lambda = 3(2)/6 = 1$$

Judge	R	1	2	3	4	5	6	7	Total
				Wine					
1	X	X	X		X				T_1
2	X		X	X		X			T_2
3	X			X	X		X		T_3
4	X				X	X		X	T_4
5	X	X				X	X		T_5
6	X		X				X	X	T_6
7	X	X		X				X	T_7
	W_R	W_1	W_2	W_3	W_4	W_5	W_6	W_7	G

Table 11-6 Analysis of variance for Table 11-5.

Source	SS	df	ms
Total	$(1) = \Sigma X_{ij}^2 - C$	$(k+1)b - 1$	
Blocks	$(2) = \Sigma T_j^2/k - C$	$b - 1$	$(2)/(b-1)$
Wines (adj.)	$(3) = \Sigma A_i w_i/(k+1)$	t	$(3)/t$
Error	$(4) = (1) - (2) - (3)$	$kb - t$	$(4)/(kb - t)$

EXAMPLE 2 Six wines are scored on a 10-point scale by judges in 10 blocks with 3 samples and a reference sample in each block. The pattern is shown in Table 11-7 and the results in Table 11-8. Analyze the data for significance.

In this design $t + 1 = 7$, $k + 1 = 4$, $b = 10$, $r = 5$ and $\lambda = 2$.

$$C = (250)^2/40 = 1562.5$$

$$\text{Total } SS = (6)^2 + (4)^2 + \cdots + (8)^2 - C$$
$$= 1672 - 1562.5 = 109.5$$

$$\text{Block } SS = \frac{(20)^2 + (26)^2 + \cdots + (23)^2}{4} - C$$
$$= 1588.5 - 1562.5 = 26$$

$$\text{Wine } SS \text{ (adj.)} = \frac{\Sigma A_i w_i}{k + 1}$$

$$= \frac{30(1.00) + (-8)(-0.18) + \cdots + 28(1.94)}{4}$$

$$= 43.17$$

$$\text{Error } SS = 109.5 - 26 - 43.17 = 40.33$$

Table 11-7 Six wines scored on a 10-point scale by judges in 10 blocks of 3 samples each with a reference sample in each block.

Block (judge)	Wine							Total
	S_R	S_1	S_2	S_3	S_4	S_5	S_6	
1	6	4	5			5		20
2	7	6	7				6	26
3	6	6		7	5			24
4	8	7		5			7	27
5	5	4			6	4		19
6	9			6		4	10	29
7	8		8	7	5			28
8	7		10	4		6		27
9	8		6		4		9	27
10	6				4	5	8	23
Total W_i	70	27	36	29	24	24	40	$250 = G$
$(k + 1)W_i$	280	108	144	116	96	96	160	$\mu = 180/30$
B_i	250	116	128	135	121	118	132	$= 6.00$
A_i	30	−8	16	−19	−25	−22	28	
w_i	1.00	−0.18	1.24	−0.82	−1.18	−1.00	1.94	
$\mu + w_i$	7.00	5.82	7.24	5.18	4.82	5.00	7.94	

Table 11-8 Analysis of variance table for the data in Example 2.

Source	SS	df	ms	F	$F_{.05}$	$F_{.01}$
Total	109.50	39				
Blocks	26.00	9	2.89			
Wines (adj.)	43.17	6	7.20	4.29**	2.51	3.67
Error	40.33	24	1.68			

The analysis indicates significant differences among the sample means at both the 5% and 1% levels. If the LSD is used to test for specific differences among the wines other than the reference wine, we have at the 5% level

$$LSD = t_{.05}(24 \; df) \sqrt{2v \left[\frac{(t-1)^2(k+1)}{tr(kt-1)} \right]}$$

$$= 2.064 \sqrt{2(1.68) \left[\frac{25(4)}{6(5)(18-1)} \right]} = 1.68$$

This leads to the following results:

	Wine					
	S_6	S_2	S_1	S_3	S_5	S_4
Adj. mean	7.94	7.24	5.82	5.18	5.00	4.82

Thus, S_6 is not significantly different from S_2, etc.

If the LSD is used to test for the difference between the reference wine and the other wines, we have

$$LSD = t_{.05}(24 \; df) \sqrt{v \left[\frac{k+1}{bk} + \frac{(t-1)^2(k+1)}{tr(kt-1)} \right]}$$

$$= 2.064 \sqrt{1.68 \left[\frac{4}{30} + \frac{100}{30(17)} \right]} = 1.54$$

At the 5% level the reference wine is not significantly different from wines S_1, S_2, and S_6, but it is significantly better than wines S_3, S_4, and S_5.

Balanced Lattices

Sometimes it is possible to have the judges score each of the wines in an incomplete-block design, scoring a part of the total number at different times. For each judge the incomplete blocks are grouped to form a replication. This design permits the removal of variations in replications from the block sum of squares. Balanced lattices are of this type of design. They are useful and the calculations are simple. The number of such designs is limited because the number of samples must be a perfect square, k^2 (that is, 4, 9, 16, etc.), grouped in blocks of k samples with $k + 1$ replications.

EXAMPLE 3 Nine wines are scored on a 10-point scale by 4 judges, each judge scoring all 9 samples in 3 incomplete blocks of 3 samples each, as shown in Table 11–9. Test the wine scores for significance.

In this design $k = 3, t = k^2 = 9, r = k + 1 = 4$, and $\lambda = 1$. The calculations are shown below.

$$C = (211)^2/36 = 1236.69$$

$$\text{Total } SS = (9)^2 + (3)^2 + \cdots + (3)^2 - C$$
$$= 1399 - 1236.69 = 162.31 \qquad (35 \; df)$$

$$\text{Block } SS = \frac{(19)^2 + (16)^2 + \cdots + (14)^2}{3} - C$$
$$= 1255 - 1236.69 = 18.31 \qquad (11 \; df)$$

$$\text{Replication } SS = \frac{(53)^2 + (50)^2 + (55)^2 + (53)^2}{9} - C$$
$$= 1238.11 - 1236.69 = 1.42 \qquad (3 \; df)$$

$$\text{Block (in repl.) } SS = 18.31 - 1.42 = 16.89 \qquad (8 \; df)$$

Table 11-9 Nine wines scored on a 10-point scale by four judges in blocks of 3 samples each (balanced lattice; see Example 3).

Replication (judge)	Block	S_1	S_2	S_3	S_4	S_5	S_6	S_7	S_8	S_9	Total
I	1	9	3	7							19
	2				5	4	7				16
	3							9	7	2	18 53
II	4	8			4			8			20
	5		5			3			7		15
	6			8			4			3	15 50
III	7	9				4				3	16
	8			7	4				8		19
	9		5				6	9			20 55
IV	10			7		3		9			19
	11	7					7		6		20
	12		5		6					3	14 53
Total W_i		33	18	29	19	14	24	35	28	11	211 = G
kW_i		99	54	87	57	42	72	105	84	33	633
B_i		75	68	72	69	56	71	77	72	63	633
A_i		24	-14	15	-12	-24	1	28	12	-30	0
w_i		2.67	-1.56	1.67	-1.33	-2.67	0.11	3.11	1.33	-3.33	0
$\mu + w_i$		8.53	4.30	7.53	4.53	3.19	5.97	8.97	7.19	2.53	$\mu = 211/36$ $= 5.86$

271

$$\text{Wine } SS \text{ (adj.)} = \frac{\Sigma A_i^2}{kt\lambda}$$

$$= \frac{(24)^2 + (-14)^2 + \cdots + (-30)^2}{3(9)(1)}$$

$$= 131.33 \qquad\qquad (8\ df)$$

$$\text{Error } SS = 162.31 - 18.31 - 131.33$$

$$= 12.67 \quad \text{(intra-block error)} \qquad (16\ df)$$

These results and the remaining calculations are shown in Table 11–10.

Table 11-10 Analysis of variance table for the data in Example 3.

Source	SS	df	ms	F	$F_{.001}$
Total	162.31	35			
Blocks	18.31	11			
Replications	1.42	3			
Blocks (in repl.)	16.89	8	2.11	2.67	
Wines (adj.)	131.33	8	16.42	20.78***	6.19
Error	12.67	16	0.79		

We will use Duncan's new multiple-range test to compare the adjusted mean scores of the wines. The standard error of an adjusted mean score is

$$\frac{R_p}{Q_p} = \sqrt{\frac{v}{r}\left[\frac{k(t-1)}{t(k-1)}\right]} = \sqrt{\frac{0.79}{4}\left[\frac{3(8)}{9(2)}\right]} = \sqrt{.026} = 0.51$$

The results are summarized in Table 11–11.

Table 11-11   Duncan's new multiple-range test (1% level) for the data in Example 3.

			Shortest significant range					
p	2	3	4	5	6	7	8	9
Q_p	4.13	4.31	4.42	4.51	4.57	4.62	4.66	4.70
R_p	2.11	2.20	2.25	2.30	2.33	2.36	2.38	2.40

				Comparison				
Wine	S_7	S_1	S_3	S_8	S_6	S_4	S_2	S_5	S_9
Mean	8.97	8.53	7.53	7.19	5.97	4.53	4.30	3.19	2.53

The incomplete-block designs that we have described involve only what is known as the *intra-block error* and are based on the assumption that the blocks are fixed. If the block effects are assumed to be random, however, more efficient estimates of the treatment means can sometimes be obtained by a procedure called *recovery of inter-block information*. This procedure is described in Cochran and Cox (1957). It is recommended only for large experiments in which the numbers of degrees of freedom for blocks and error exceed 25.

Statistics wipes out the comments of men's opinions, but it confirms the judgments of nature.

But if probability is a measure of the importance of our state of ignorance, it must change its value whenever we add new knowledge. And so it does.

T. C. FRY

CHAPTER 12

Ranking Procedures

In difference and preference testing, scoring according to some numerical scale is the usual and generally preferable procedure, especially with experienced judges, since the procedure indicates not only differences but also provides a measure of their magnitudes. Sometimes, however, judges, especially inexperienced ones, find it difficult to express preferences in terms of quantitative measures. They find it much easier to rank wines in order of preference or in order of some odor or taste component. On a numerical scale, such as 1 to 10, judges frequently differ as to the proper location and spread of scores, with the result that they may use the potential range quite differently. The use of ranks eliminates these inconsistencies in location and spread. Ranking is usually easier, quicker, and less expensive to administer and analyze than more sophisticated procedures.

Pairs of Ranks

When only two wines are being compared, pairs of ranks are obtained. One test that is then used is based on the signs of the differences between the paired values. The procedure is identical to that used in preference testing of paired samples. The null hypothesis of equal numbers of positive and negative differences (H_0: $p = 0.5$) is tested approximately by calculating

$$\chi^2 = \frac{(|n_1 - n_2| - 1)^2}{n_1 + n_2} \tag{32}$$

where n_1 and n_2 are the numbers of positive and negative differences, respectively, $|n_1 - n_2|$ represents the numerical (non-negative) value of the difference between them, and χ^2 is based on one degree of freedom.

EXAMPLE 1   Two wines, S_1 and S_2, are ranked 15 times, as shown below. Is there a significant difference between them?

S_1	1	1	2	1	2	1	1	2	1	1	1	2	1	1	1
S_2	2	2	1	2	1	1	1	1	2	2	2	1	2	2	2
Sign	+	+	−	+	−	0	0	−	+	+	+	−	+	+	+

The $+$ sign means that wine S_1 was ranked above wine S_2 and the $-$ sign means that wine S_2 was ranked above wine S_1. Ties (denoted by 0) are disregarded in the analysis. The $+$ sign appears 9 times and the $-$ sign 4 times. Therefore

$$\chi^2 = \frac{(|9 - 4| - 1)^2}{13} = 16/13 = 1.23$$

Appendix D shows that $\chi^2_{.05}(1\ df) = 3.84$, which is larger than the calculated value. There is therefore no reason to reject the null hypothesis, and no significant difference between the two wines is indicated.

The advantages of this test are simplicity, no requirement of equal variances, and relative insensitivity to recording errors. The disadvantage, however, is that it disregards the magnitude of the difference, if any, between the wines. This problem is inherent in ranking procedures.

Ranking of Several Wines by Two Judges

To determine whether two judges are significantly different in their rankings of several wines, *Spearman's rank correlation coefficient* can be used to test the agreement between the rankings. This correlation coefficient is defined as

$$R = 1 - \frac{6\Sigma d^2}{k(k^2 - 1)} \tag{33}$$

where Σd^2 is the sum of the squares of the differences between the rank values given by the two judges to each of k wine samples. (If any wines in one ranking are tied, each is assigned the mean of the rank values they would otherwise have had.) The value of R can vary from -1 (totally opposite rankings by the two judges) to $+1$ (perfect agreement between the judges). The intermediate value $R = 0$ indicates that the two rankings are totally unrelated; that is, they are entirely the result of chance. This, in fact, is the null hypothesis, which can be written H_0: $\rho = 0$, where ρ is the *population rank correlation*.

Little reliability can be placed on a value of R obtained from the rankings of fewer than 10 samples. The significance of a calculated value of R can be determined by comparing the value of

$$t = R\sqrt{\frac{k - 2}{1 - R^2}} \tag{34}$$

with the appropriate t-value, based on $k - 2$ degrees of freedom, in Appendix K. For significance the calculated t-value must exceed the tabular value. A significant positive t-value indicates that the judges agree in their rankings. The significance of calculated R-values can also be determined by the use of Appendix N. Calculated values that exceed those in the table are significantly different from zero and indicate agreement in the rankings.

EXAMPLE 2 Two judges rank 10 wines, as shown below. Is there a significant difference in their rankings?

	Wine									
Judge	1	2	3	4	5	6	7	8	9	10
J_1	2	1	10	7	8	6	3	4	5	9
J_2	3	1	8	9	10	7	4	2	5	6
Difference										
d	-1	0	2	-2	-2	-1	-1	2	0	3
d^2	1	0	4	4	4	1	1	4	0	9

$$\Sigma d^2 = 28$$

The null hypothesis (H_0: $\rho = 0$) is that there is no correlation between the rankings. Solving Equations 33 and 34, we obtain

$$R = 1 - \frac{6(28)}{10(99)} = 0.830$$

$$t = 0.830 \sqrt{\frac{8}{1 - 0.689}} = 4.21$$

From Appendix K we see that $t_{.01}(8 \ df) = 3.355$. Since the calculated value $t = 4.21$ exceeds the tabular value, we reject (at the 1% level) the null hypothesis and conclude that the value $R = 0.830$ is highly significantly different from 0. The agreement between the rankings of the two judges is therefore highly significant. If we use Appendix N (recalling that $df = 10 - 2 = 8$) we see that any value of R greater than 0.7646 is significant at the 1% level. Therefore $R = 0.830$ is highly significant. Using Appendix N eliminates the need to calculate t.

This procedure can also be applied in the evaluation of judging ability. Adding increasing amounts of some constituent to a wine provides a set of samples of known order. If a panelist is asked to rank the set for increasing amounts of the constituent, we have an accurate standard with which to compare his ranking, and Spearman's rank correlation coefficient is appropriate for rating his competence.

Ranking of Several Wines by More Than Two Judges

The ranking of k wines by n judges is a very common procedure. In Chapter 7, a quick appraisal of possible significant differences among a set of rankings was made by the use of Appendixes O-1 and O-2. These tables prepared by Kramer (1973) list ranges of *rank totals*, which are the sums of the n individual rank values for a given wine. Rank totals that lie *outside* the ranges shown in the tables indicate results significantly different from those that would be obtained by chance alone. See the original Kramer tables for special cases. These tables do provide a quick and simple way of identifying significantly good and significantly poor samples, but they do not assist in identifying relationships between the rank totals of the remaining samples. Kramer suggests reranking the remaining rank totals and repeating the procedure. We do not recommend this reranking.

EXAMPLE 3   Twelve judges rank five wines, yielding the following rank totals: S_1 (34), S_2 (20), S_3 (52), S_4 (26), S_5 (48). Use Appendixes O to determine whether there are significant differences among these rankings.

Appendix O–1 shows that for 12 rankings of five samples there are significant differences at the 5% level for rank totals not within the range 25–47. Thus we see that wine S_2 is ranked significantly low, and wines S_3 and S_5 are ranked significantly high. At the 1% level the range is 22–50, so at this level wine S_2 is ranked significantly low and wine S_3 is ranked significantly high.

Fisher and Yates Procedure   Fisher and Yates (1974) provided tables for transforming ranks into normal scores to which they suggested the application of conventional analysis of variance. This procedure is frequently used, and it does provide for multiple comparisons among all rank totals. Bradley (1968) pointed out that the resulting F test is really a test for identical populations, and in using it to compare means one must assume identical population shapes and variances. The distribution of F based on normal scores is not exactly the same as the tabled F. In spite of these shortcomings, it does provide a test which, even though approximate, gives reasonably good results.

Appendix P shows that, for six ranked wines, the normal scores that replace the rank values 1, 2, 3, 4, 5, and 6 are 1.267, 0.642, 0.202, -0.202, -0.642, and -1.267, respectively. This transformation converts the ranking into a normal population, and the usual analysis of variance procedure is applied. Since the positive and negative values of the normal scores are distributed symmetrically about their mean value, 0, the total for each judge is zero and therefore the grand total, G, is also zero. This greatly simplifies the computations.

EXAMPLE 4   Five judges rank six wines, as shown in Table 12–1. Use Appendix P to convert ranks to normal scores as shown in Table 12–2, and analyze the results.

$$C = 0$$

$$\text{Total } SS = 10\left[(1.267)^2 + (0.642)^2 + (0.202)^2\right]$$

$$= 20.583 \qquad\qquad (29\ df)$$

Table 12-1 Six wines ranked by five judges (see Example 4).

Judge	Wine					
	S_1	S_2	S_3	S_4	S_5	S_6
1	6	4	2	3	5	1
2	3	6	4	1	5	2
3	1	2	5	3	6	4
4	5	6	3	1	4	2
5	6	5	4	2	3	1
Rank total	21	23	18	10	23	10

Table 12-2 Normal scores for the rankings in Table 12-1.

Judge	Wine						Total
	S_1	S_2	S_3	S_4	S_5	S_6	
1	−1.267	−0.202	0.642	0.202	−0.642	1.267	0
2	0.202	−1.267	−0.202	1.267	−0.642	0.642	0
3	1.267	0.642	−0.642	0.202	−1.267	−0.202	0
4	−0.642	−1.267	0.202	1.267	−0.202	0.642	0
5	−1.267	−0.642	−0.202	0.642	0.202	1.267	0
Total	−1.707	−2.736	−0.202	3.580	−2.551	3.616	$0 = G$
Mean	−0.341	−0.547	−0.040	0.716	−0.510	0.723	

$$\text{Wine } SS = [(-1.707)^2 + (-2.736)^2 + \cdots + (3.606)^2]/5$$
$$= 8.568 \qquad\qquad (5\ df)$$

$$\text{Judge } SS = 0 \qquad\qquad (4\ df)$$

$$\text{Error } SS = 20.583 - 8.568 = 12.015 \qquad\qquad (20\ df)$$

These results and the remaining calculations are shown in Table 12-3.

Table 12-3 Analysis of variance table for the data
in Example 4.

Source	SS	df	ms	F	$F_{.05}$	$F_{.01}$
Total	20.583	29				
Wines	8.568	5	1.71	2.85*	2.71	4.10
Judges	0	4				
Error	12.015	20	0.601			

Since the calculated F-value of 3.41 exceeds the tabular value of 2.62, significant differences at the 5% level are indicated, and the *LSD* can be used to determine which wines are significantly different from each other.

$$LSD = t_{.05}(20 \ df) \sqrt{2(0.601)/5} = 2.086 \sqrt{0.240} = 1.02$$

Friedman Procedure Friedman (1937) proposed for ranked data a test that is still widely used. His test for k wines ranked by n judges measures the homogeneity of the k rank sums R_i. It also tests the concordance among the judges and therefore, by implication, differences among the ranked wines. Friedman's test statistic is

$$T = \frac{n(k-1)(B-C)}{A-C} \tag{35}$$

where $A = \Sigma r_{ij}^2$, $B = \dfrac{1}{n} \Sigma R_i^2$, $C = \dfrac{(\Sigma r_{ij})^2}{nk} = \dfrac{nk(k+1)^2}{4}$, and r_{ij} is the rank assigned to the ith wine by the jth judge. T is distributed as χ^2 with $(k-1)$ degrees of freedom. If there are no ties, $A = \dfrac{nk(k+1)(2k+1)}{6}$, and Friedman's test statistic becomes

$$T = \frac{12}{nk(k+1)} (\Sigma R_i^2) - 3n(k+1). \qquad (36)$$

The value of T can also be obtained from an analysis of variance table by means of the relationship

$$T = \frac{n(k-1) \text{ Wine } SS}{\text{Total } SS}. \qquad (37)$$

Iman and Davenport Procedure   Recent studies by Iman and Davenport (1980) use a statistic

$$T' = \frac{(n-1)(B-C)}{A-B}. \qquad (38)$$

They conclude that the F approximation to T' is superior to the χ^2 approximation to T. The value of T' can be shown to be identical to the F-value for wines as computed in the analysis of variance applied directly to the ranked data. Conover (1980) also recommends the use of the statistic T' in the analysis of ranked data. If, and only if, the value of T' is significant, should the rank totals of individual wines be compared by calculating the LSD.

$$LSD = t_\alpha \left[\frac{2n(A-B)}{(n-1)(k-1)} \right]^{1/2} = t_\alpha \sqrt{2n \text{ (error mean square)}} \quad (39)$$

EXAMPLE 5   In a judging comparing samples of Australian and California Chardonnays, seven samples were ranked by six judges as shown in Table 12–4.

$$A = \Sigma r_{ij}^2 = 6[(1)^2 + (2)^2 + \cdots + (7)^2] = nk(k+1)(2k+1)/6$$
$$= 6(7)(8)(15)/6 = 840$$

$$B = \frac{1}{n} \Sigma R_i^2 = \frac{1}{6} [(18)^2 + (28)^2 + \cdots + (34)^2] = \frac{4464}{6} = 744$$

Table 12-4 Seven Chardonnays ranked by six judges.

Judge	S_1	S_2	S_3	S_4	S_5	S_6	S_7
				Wine			
1	3	7	2	1	5	4	6
2	2	3	5	1	4	7	6
3	4	2	7	1	3	6	5
4	2	3	1	5	7	4	6
5	4	6	3	1	2	7	5
6	3	7	2	1	5	4	6
Total R_j	18	28	20	10	26	32	34

$$T' = \frac{5[744 - 6(7)(8)^2/4]}{840 - 744} = \frac{5(744 - 672)}{96} = 3.75$$

$F_{.05}$ (with 6 and 30 df) $= 2.42$. Since $T' > 2.42$, there is reason to reject the null hypothesis of no difference, and therefore significant differences among rank totals are indicated at the 5% level. We can proceed to compare totals between pairs of ranks.

$$LSD = t_{.05}(30\ df)\left[\frac{2n(A - B)}{(n - 1)(k - 1)}\right]^{1/2} = 2.042\sqrt{\frac{12(96)}{5(6)}} = 12.65$$

and

	S_4	S_1	S_3	S_5	S_2	S_6	S_7
				Wine			
Rank	10	18	20	26	28	32	34

Analysis of variance of original ranked data is shown in Table 12-5 and may be compared with the Iman and Davenport procedure. $F = T'$ and the two procedures are identical.

Table 12-5 Analysis of variance for the data of Table 12–4.

Source	SS	df	ms	F
Total	168	41		
Wines	72	6	12	3.75
Judges	0	5		
Error	96	30	3.2	

Since the Iman and Davenport procedure is equivalent to applying the analysis of variance directly to the ranked data, it is subject to some of the same criticisms as the Fisher and Yates procedure. Both are approximate procedures that agree surprisingly well and provide comparisons for the rank totals of all wines. The Fisher and Yates procedure, when applied to the data of Table 12–4, gives the same results as the Iman and Davenport procedure.

Kramer's tables for six judges and seven wines gives the range 12–36 for nonsignificance at the 5% level, indicating that sample S_4 is significantly better than the other samples, but supplies no additional information.

According to Friedman's procedure

$$T = \frac{12}{nk(k+1)} (\Sigma R_i^2) - 3n(k+1) = 15.43$$

From Appendix J, $\chi^2_{.05}$ (6 df) = 12.59. Since $T > 12.59$, significant differences among samples are indicated, but there is no indication where these differences may be. T could have been calculated from

$$T = \frac{n(k-1) \text{ Wine } SS}{\text{Total } SS} = \frac{6(6)(72)}{168} = 15.43$$

In all these tests, if there are ties, average ranks are assigned.

Incomplete Blocks for Ranked Data

Durbin (1951) developed a procedure for testing the null hypothesis of no differences among samples in a balanced incomplete-block design when the data consist of ranked scores.

The same notation will be used as in the case of the balanced incomplete-block design for data consisting of numerical scores.

t = number of wine samples
k = number of wine samples scored by each judge at each session
b = number of judges (blocks)
r = number of scores for each wine sample
λ = number of times each pair of wine samples appears in the same block
R_i = sum of ranks for wine sample S_i

The test statistic is similar to that in the Friedman test for data expressed as numerical scores and is given by

$$T = \frac{12(t-1)}{rt(k-1)(k+1)} \Sigma R_i^2 - \frac{3r(t-1)(k+1)}{k-1} \qquad (40)$$

which is distributed as χ^2 with $(t-1)$ degrees of freedom. If the value of T exceeds the tabular value of χ^2 at the adopted level of significance, the null hypothesis is rejected, and significant differences among rank sums are suggested. We can proceed to compare rank totals between pairs of samples by calculating

$$LSD = t_\alpha \left\{ \frac{r(k+1)(k-1)[bk(t-1) - tT]}{6(t-1)(bk-t-b+1)} \right\} \qquad (41)$$

where t_α is obtained from Appendix K with $(bk - t - b + 1)$ degrees of freedom. Differences that exceed this value are significant.

EXAMPLE 6   Seven judges rank seven wines in a balanced-incomplete block design in which three wine samples are compared by each judge as shown in Table 12-6.

Table 12-6   Seven judges rank seven wines in lots of three in a balanced incomplete-block design. (See Table 11-1.)

$$t = b = 7 \qquad k = r = 3 \qquad \lambda = 1$$

Judge	\multicolumn{7}{c}{Wine}
	S_1	S_2	S_3	S_4	S_5	S_6	S_7
1	3	2		1			
2		2	1		3		
3			1	2		3	
4				1	3		2
5	1				2	3	
6		2				3	1
7	3		1				2
Total R_i	7	6	3	4	8	9	5

$$\Sigma R_i^2 = (7)^2 + (6)^2 + \cdots + (5)^2 = 280$$

$$T = \frac{12(6)}{3(7)(2)(4)}(280) - \frac{3(3)(6)(4)}{2} = 120 - 108 = 12$$

From Appendix D, $\chi_{.05}^2$ (6 df) = 12.59. Since the value of T is less than 12.59, there is no reason to reject at the 5% level of significance the null hypothesis of no differences among rank totals.

G. J. Newell (1982) has proposed a new procedure involving the linear logistic model for the analysis of sensory data. The procedure does not require the use of any category scaling, such as a hedonic scale, but uses the ordinal nature of the data. The major advantage that the procedure provides is the facility to treat data as ordinal rather than having to attach scores to each response. Tomassone and Flanzy (1977) have summarized various procedures for analyzing results of ranked data.

An equation is the most serious and important thing in mathematics.

SIR OLIVER LODGE

CHAPTER 13

Descriptive Sensory Analysis

Descriptive sensory analysis, first called *flavor profile*, was developed by the Arthur D. Little Company of Cambridge, Massachusetts. It has been used in product development, quality control, and laboratory research by numerous food and drug companies (Amerine et al. 1965a). In this method, a panel of highly trained judges is used to identify the individual and overall odor and flavor characteristics of a food in terms of the sensory impressions they create. Properly trained panels achieve considerable agreement, after group discussion, on overall sensory impressions and intensities and order of detection of the various sensory factors. Disadvantages of the flavor profile method are the expense of training the judges, the possible bias introduced by a dominant (assertive) member of the panel during the group discussion, and the difficulty of statistical analysis of the results.

For an example of a record form for the descriptive sensory analysis of wines, see Figure 13–1. As in the flavor profile method, many winery staff members and private groups make their decisions on the quality of a wine after group discussion of the results obtained in the individual sensory examinations. Is group discussion beneficial

DESCRIPTIVE SENSORY ANALYSIS

	Identification	Intensity 0 to 10	Quality −5 to +5
Prior to Tasting			
1. *Visual*			
Appearance: cloudy, dull (hazy), clear, brilliant			
Color: straw yellow, greenish yellow, yellow, gold, amber; pink, violet-pink, eye-of-the-partridge (light brownish red), ruby red, violet-red, brownish red (tawny)			
Intensity: light, strong			
Gas release: none, fine bubbles, medium bubbles, large bubbles			
2. *Olfactory**			
Complex: vinous, distinct, varietal, flowery, musty(?), oxidized			
Specific: ethyl acetate, fusel oils, hydrogen sulfide, mercaptan, sulfur dioxide			
In-Mouth			
3. *Gustatory*			
Balanced: thin, full-bodied			
Specific: sweet, sour, bitter, salty			
4. *Olfactory (flavor)**			
Complex: earthy, fruity, herbaceous, woody			
Specific (identify)			
5. *Texture:* astringent, burning, prickly, foreign*			

*The chemical origin of the sensory impression should be specified if possible.

Name _____ Date _____

Figure 13-1 Record form for descriptive sensory analysis of wines. (Adapted from J. Puisais et al. 1974.)

or does it entail too great a risk of prejudicial influences? Meyers and Lamm (1975) have studied this problem; the answer is by no means as unequivocal as one would wish. There is first of all the danger of a dominant individual's imposing his or her judgment on the group, by either reputation or force of personality. If this occurs, group discussion is useless except as an ego-cultivating exercise for the dominant individual (e.g., the winery owner), or over-aggressive individuals trying to mask an inferiority complex, etc. The influence of a supposedly learned judge is called the "halo" effect. Jones (1958) and Foster et al. (1955) have noted that a group judgment is not the same as a group of judgments, because an individual can sway the group judgment. (The obvious analogy with trial juries here is inescapable.) See Kalven and Ziesel (1966).

Even if there is no dominant individual, the group influence itself may be detrimental. As Meyers and Lamm say, "What people learn from discussion is mostly in the direction supporting the majority's initial preference." The problem is that, probably subconsciously, members of the group usually show a disproportionate interest in facts and opinions that support their initial preferences and tend to ignore those facts and opinions that do not. This appears to be true for both verbal and written opinions. If knowledge of the positions of other members of the panel has a polarizing effect (and how can it help but do so if the owner or winemaker is present?), we recommend that all the panelists withhold information on their initial preferences or opinions.

For cider and perry evaluation, Williams (1975, 1977, 1978), Williams and Carter (1977), Williams and Lewis (1978), and Williams et al. (1977) developed a profile assessment procedure. A vocabulary was developed first (163 words or phrases: 10 for appearance, 125 for odor, and 28 for taste). During the development of a vocabulary, samples of standard odors were available (see Table 13–1). In the final assessment forms, 46 odor terms grouped into 11 classes remained adjectives. These classes and the terms used were under continuous development.

Table 13-1 Adjectives selected for describing cider and perry aromas and compositions of standards* used to represent them grouped according to classes into which they were placed.

Odor class	Profile sheet adjective number and description	Composition
I. Cough provoking/ irritating	1. Choking, like SO_2	75 μl 5% sulfur dioxide solution
	2. Like high concentration of acetaldehyde	75 μl acetaldehyde
	3. Like high concentration of amyl alcohol	75 μl 3-methyl-1-butanol
	4. Like high concentration of acetic acid	75 μl acetic acid
II. Sharp	6. Like rhubarb	500 μl ethanolic extract natural rhubarb
	7. Like acetic acid	15 μl acetic acid
III. Dry/alcoholic/ fuselly	8. Like ethanol	500–1000 μl ethanol
	9. Like higher alcohols	5–10 μl 3-methyl-1-butanol
	10. Like ethyl acetate	5–10 μl ethyl acetate
	11. Like low concentration of acetaldehyde	5–10 μl acetaldehyde
	12/13. Green	2–5 μl hex-3-enol or 10–20 μl hexanol
IV. Musty	14. Earthy	—
	15. Cardboard	—
	16. Mousy/biscuity	2–5 μl concentrated ether extract of acetamide
V. Sour/stale	17. Like acetic acid (sour character)	10–15 μl acetic acid
	18. Rancid	2–5 μl butyric acid
	19. Old horse	5 mg 2-phenylacetic acid
	20. Fatty	5 μl 2,4-decadienal solution
	21. Soapy	500 mg unperfumed soap

Odor class	Profile sheet adjective number and description	Composition
VI. Sulfury	22. Rubbery	2 ml water in which rubber tubing had been boiled
	23. Like bad eggs	Hydrogen sulfide bubbled through molten paraffin wax
	24. Like cooked cabbage	5–10 μl methyl mercaptan
	25. Catty	(i) Catty cider distillate (ii) 10–15 μl p-menthion-8-thiol
	26. Like onions	2–5 μl allyl disulfide
	27. Like shrimps	2–5 ml dimethyl sulfide
VII. Yeasty	28. Like mushrooms	20 μl commercial essence
	29. Like yeast extract	500 mg of "Marmite"
	30. Like dough	500 μl decanted liquor from yeast culture
VIII. Scented	31. Like cucumber (fragrant character)	2–5 μl commercial cucumber essence
	32. Like roses	25–50 μl 2-phenethanol
	33. Like flowers	not characterized
IX. Fruity	34. Like strawberries	2–5 μl commercial essence
	35. Like bananas	2–5 μl commercial essence
	36. Like pineapples	2–5 μl commercial essence
	37. Like pears	2–5 μl commercial essence
	38. Like peardrops	5–10 μl 3-methylbutyl acetate
	39. Like apples	(i) 5–10 μl hexyl acetate (ii) 2–5 μl ethyl 2-methyl butyrate (iii) 5–10 μl natural apple essence

Table 13-1   (Continued)

Odor class	Profile sheet adjective number and description	Composition
X. Sugary/cooked	41. Like raisins/sweet sherry	10–20 µl commercial red grape essence
	42. Like diacetyl	5–10 µl diacetyl
	43. Like caramel	1 g commercial caramel essence
	44. Like black treacle	1 g commercial black treacle
XI. Phenolic/spicy/ bittersweet	45. Phenolic/ carbolic	10–20 µl phenol
	46. Pharmaceutical	2–5 ml methyl salicylate
	47. Like bittersweet cider	(i) 2–5 µl 4-ethylphenol (ii) Natural bittersweet cider
	48. Spicy (1) ethyl guaiacol	2–5 µl 4-ethyl guaiacol
	49. Spicy (2) allspice	250 mg allspice
	50. Like celery	2–5 µl commercial celery essence

*All standards were made up in approximately 20 g of a highly purified odorless paraffin wax. Once a compound was selected it was added to the paraffin wax in increasing amounts until the required effect was obtained. The concentrations quoted are therefore only approximate. SOURCE: Williams (1975).

The final assessment sheet, Figure 13–2, included overall and odor class intensity (no odor, very weak, moderate, strong, very strong) and complexity (uninteresting, very simple, simple, moderate, complex, very complex). The appropriateness of each of the descriptive adjectives to odor class was evaluated (no similarity to adjective, little similarity but most appropriate of adjectives listed, poorly represented, some similarity, fairly well represented, and well represented).

Williams noted particularly the difficulty of getting his trained panel to use the scorecard consistently. The judges varied from time to time, and the sensation reported varied with concentration. This

Profile assessment of cider/perry aroma

Cider/perry no. ———————   Name ————————————————————

General aroma comments   Date ————————————————————

	Control score when assessed	Sample score
Overall intensity (score 0–5)		
Complexity (score 0–5)		

Odor class				**Description**			
	Intensity score 0–5				Appropriateness score 0–5		
	Control when assessed	Sample before tasting	after tasting	Adjective	Control when assessed	Sample before tasting	after tasting
1. Cough provoking/ irritating				Choking like SO_2 (1)			
				Like high conc. of acetaldehyde (2)			
				Like high conc. of 1-pentanol (3)			
				Like high conc. of acetic acid (4)			
				Own description ———————			

The other classes and adjectives, with the additions listed below, are as given in Table 13-1, these being scored in a similar manner to the above.

Odor class	**Adjective**
2. Sharp	(5) Like fruit (specify fruit in Section 9)*
3. Dry/alcohol/fuselly	Green, subdivided into:
	(12) Like fruit (specify fruit in Section 9)*
	(13) Green grass/vegetablelike
8. Scented	(33) Floral
10. Sugary/cooked	(40) Like cooked fruit (specify fruit in Section 9)*

*Author's note. See Table 13-1, Section IX.

Figure 13-2 Profile assessment sheet for cider/perry aroma. (From Williams 1975.)

procedure is appealing because it was tested for validity by a qualified panel. Once the panel was trained and the vocabulary established, the panel was used for evaluating ciders and perrys.

Descriptive analysis was recently applied to Bordeaux wines by Noble et al. (1982). Aroma terms and reference standards were used. Multivariate analysis of variance was used on the aroma and flavor terms. Canonical variates analysis (CVA) was then performed.

They prepared the following standards for certain winelike odors (each added to 30 ml of Carignane red table wine): berry (blackberry/raspberry): 10 ml liquor from canned blackberries, 2–3 ml of thawed frozen raspberries, 5–6 g strawberry jam, and 5–6 g raspberry jam; blackcurrant (canned/Ribena): 7–10 ml liquor from canned blackcurrants, 2–4 ml Sainsbury's Blackcurrant Drink; synthetic fruit: 5 ml Cherryade (Corona Drinks), 1 peardrop; green bean/green olive: 4–5 ml liquor from canned green olives and 8–10 ml liquor from canned green beans; black pepper: 4 grains black pepper (ground); raisin: 10 raisins; soy/Marmite: 0.5 ml soya sauce and 0.5–1 g Marmite yeast extract; vanilla: 0.25 ml vanilla flavoring essence; phenolic/spicy: 5–10 ml 4-ethyl guaiacol; and ethanolic: 10 ml 95% ethanol. The authors noted that some judges used these descriptive terms inconsistently. Using only the consistent judges, there were significant differences between two wines for the descriptive terms for blackcurrant ($p < 0.05$), green bean/green olive ($p < 0.001$), and bitterness and astringency as used for two red Bordeaux wines. Furthermore, the judges used an intensity scale differently, which was a significant source of variation in their results.

Quantitative Procedures

Stone et al. (1974) introduced a quantitative descriptive sensory analysis method (QDA). The QDA technique depends on or uses: (1) introspection to develop perceived sensory attributes (with statistical testing for reliability); (2) development of a language (by training under guidance); (3) selection of subjects based on performance; (4) collection of up to 16 judgments per subject to monitor individual and group performance; (5) isolated booths; (6) an interval scale to measure perceived intensities of individual attributes; (7) analyses of variance (one- and two-way) applied to individual and group data; (8) correlation coefficients to determine relationships between various scales; and (9) principal component analysis, factor analysis, and so on to determine primary sensory values and to eliminate redundancy.

Computer programs are used to determine subject consistency and thus whether further training is needed. The scales used are also evaluated as to their ability to discriminate differences. The difference between products or specific attributes is also measured. They excuse inconsistent judges or give them more training.

Interaction (judge-by-product confusion in scoring) can also be measured. This is especially important when a judge scores a series of samples in the reverse order from the other judges. However, the perverse judge's response may reflect a real difference in perception of the product.

The various sensory attributes of the product are evaluated separately. For each attribute, a scale of 6 inches is provided, with two labeled anchor points ½ inch from the ends of the scale and one at the center. For example, the scale for sweetness would look like this:

Weak   Moderate   Strong

After tasting the product, the judge marks a cross at the point representing the magnitude of the sensation in question. The distance from the end of the scale to the cross is a measure of this magnitude. Stone et al. (1974, 1980) believe that the scale is linear; that is, that with several data points, a straight-line plot of measured distance versus true sweetness (or other sensory attribute) is obtained (i.e., an interval scale). Acree (1980) notes that it has also been described as a ratio scale and may in fact be a form of cross-modal matching and not involve any psychological scaling. (See page 161 for a discussion of various scales.)

The procedure requires extensive training with the product (about 20 hours) and individual testing. The individual and panel data are evaluated by analysis of variance. Correlation coefficients are calculated to determine the degree of correlation between the scales. Primary sensory values are measured by principal component analysis, factor analysis, and so on. Finally, a multidimensional model is developed and its relation to consumer response or other external factors established.

From the data, one should be able to identify inconsistent responses of panel members (indicating the need for more training) and the adequacy of the judges' discrimination between different levels of a given sensory attribute. One can also determine whether individual scales are producing consistent results and whether the scales are adequately discriminating between products. Finally, the extent to which products differ in the specific attributes can be measured, and the most accurate and consistent judges can be identified.

Computer programs for one-way and two-way analyses of variance are used to measure the agreement between a judge and the panel as a whole. The interaction sum of squares is estimated for each judge and the F-value is calculated. A high F-value for an individual judge indicates his or her disagreement with the panel; that is, there is interaction between the product and the judge.

Descriptive analysis should also prove useful in developing a more rational glossary of wines and in developing consistent descriptive differences between various types of varietal wines. It might also be used for determining whether consistent descriptive differences exist between generic types—for example, California burgundy and California claret or California chablis and California rhine. The present Wine Institute (1978) specifications for these types are not sufficiently precise for differentiating them.

Clapperton (1973) favored profile procedures for describing and, as far as possible, quantifying beer flavor, and Dhanaraj et al.

(1981), using apples, developed a quality profile for objective sensory evaluation.

Our conclusion is that descriptive sensory analysis, in the hands of highly trained personnel, will prove useful in solving certain industrial and research sensory evaluation problems. The problem remains, however, that the panelist's response in sensory analysis depends not only on perception of the meaning of the question but also on perception of the stimulus. Whether this problem can be eliminated by rigorous training is not clear, but possibly it can be minimized by recognition of the problem.

Meyers and Lamm (1975) found that verbal arguments were more polarizing than individual written briefs. Personal observation by the authors indicates that this is correct. They did not find that verbal group discussions produced more useful ideas. To the contrary, group brainstorming produced fewer ideas than individual efforts. Kalven and Ziesel (1966) concluded, "The (jury) deliberation process . . . is an interesting combination of rational persuasion, sheer social pressure, and the psychological mechanism by which individual perceptions undergo change when exposed to group discussion."

Multivariate Analysis

Multivariate analysis involves the treatment of data in which more than one characteristic of each sample is measured or scored. Many data collection processes yield multivariate data. The analysis of such data can be time consuming and tedious, but the development of modern computers and the availability of package programs have greatly increased the use of multivariate methods. Overall wine quality is often related to several attributes or characteristics, some of which are interrelated, and frequently investigators explore the nature of such relationships by applying multivariate methods, including multivariate analysis of variance. These procedures have been discussed by many authors—for example, Anderson (1958), Kendall

(1957), Levitt (1974), Press (1972), and Tukey (1977). Some common forms of multivariate analysis are *cluster, factor, principal component,* and *discriminant analyses.*

Cluster Analysis   The aim of this procedure is to group large numbers of attributes or characteristics into smaller clusters on the basis of similarities. This technique is usually used in conjunction with other multivariate methods. Usually geometrical configurations, when possible, are employed to provide visual displays. Similar attributes or products are represented by plotted points, which appear as clusters. The process can be extended even though geometrical representation may not be possible. The reduction of a mass of data forming clusters of similar attributes results in a corresponding simplification of the analysis. Godwin et al. (1978) used the procedure in evaluating sensory–objective relations of processed green beans.

Factor Analysis and Principal Component Analysis   These are collections of operations used in determining the existence of an underlying order or structure in a large amount of data that appear unrelated. Many investigators are critical of the procedure because of the lack of mathematical rigor. However, as a result of the reduction in data size, the procedures often make possible recognition of nonobvious relationships. Factor analysis has been widely used in the food industry and in many cases has furnished valuable information concerning data interrelationships. It is useful in the development of lists of discriminators (Wu et al. 1977). Once a set of discriminators has been established, other methods of multivariate analysis can be used to relate sensory evaluations to compositional differences. Harper (1956) used factor analysis in the examination of complex data on foodstuffs, and Frijters (1976) employed principal component analysis in the evaluation of a texture profile for chicken breasts. The use of principal component analysis in the selection of consistent judges was recommended by van Rooyen (1982). Multivariate analysis of variance was used by Palmer (1974) in the study of flavor terms applied to tea, and Vuataz et al. (1974) applied the procedure in the study of 18 different milk chocolates evaluated by panelists for 12 attributes.

Noble (1982), using principal component analysis of selected volatiles, was able to distinguish White Riesling from non–White Riesling wines. White Rieslings contained more ethyl-3-methyl butyrate, 2-phenethanol, vitispirane, trimethyldihydronapthalene, naptha-lene (and butyl hexanoate), and 3 unidentified peaks. The non–White Riesling wines contained more ethyl crotonate, 2-methyl-butyl acetate, and hexyl acetate.

Discriminant Analysis   Once a suitable set of discriminators has been selected, classification of wines or other products can proceed. Discriminant analysis is one of the most powerful procedures of multivariate analysis. It provides a mathematical combination of attributes that is most effective in distinguishing among similar wines or products. The use of several attributes of quality, examined singly, does not usually provide for sufficient discrimination among wines. The use of linear discriminant analysis in which characterization is no longer based on values of individual attributes but on a linear combi-nation of them minimizes the error of classification. The procedure is also used to look for correlations between a "dependent" value (such as the muscat aroma of a wine) and the "independent" variables (gas chromatographic peaks or their logarithms). The result is an equation relating the two, including any interactions that may be present. The method is discussed by many authors. Moret et al. (1980) used the method in the classification of three Venetian wines, and Scarponi et al. (1981) reported that the analysis of data from three wine sam-ples demonstrated the validity of the method in the differentiation of wines. Gas chromatograms combined with discriminant analysis are being used in the classification of products. Hoff et al. (1978) used the procedure in the flavor profiling of beer.

Stepwise discriminant analysis of some volatile components was used by Marsais et al. (1981a) to distinguish Colombar wines of two regions and Chenin blanc wines of three regions. The components with highest discriminatory value were isoamyl acetate, hexyl acetate, hexanol, phenethanol, and 1-butanol, varying with the cultivar. The authors note that subtle differences in fermentation condition could be important. Marsais et al. (1981b) reported similar results with red cultivars.

Multidimensional Scaling Techniques These procedures deal with the analysis of similarity or preference judgments. Judges express similarity or dissimilarity judgments in terms of some type of ordering or in terms of ratio or interval scales. This information is shown as points or distances in a multidimensional space. Products can be classified by their relative interproduct distances. Those of similar quality appear close together, and those that are dissimilar appear far apart. This representation provides a quick impression of qualitative variations among products by inspecting various clusters of points. Green and Rao (1972) employed multidimensional scaling to provide at a glance information about qualitative relations among odors and tastes and their linguistic descriptors. Vuataz (1977) outlined procedures in multidimensional data analysis as applied to sensory evaluation, and Stungis (1976) discussed this and other multivariate techniques and provided examples of their uses.

Magnitude Estimation

Magnitude estimation refers to a class of psychophysical scaling procedures. It is designed to measure the relationship between sensory and physical continua in a proportional manner. Although there are variations of the procedure, in its simplest form, the method permits judges (usually inexperienced) to start with any number and to generate, without restriction, their own numbers to represent sensory stimuli so that the ratios of the numerical scale reflect ratios of sensory perception levels. Two products assigned ratings of 10 and 40 respectively for sweetness indicate that the second is perceived to be four times as sweet as the first. Judges do not run out of numbers since the scale is infinite, and judgments represent proportions, allowing conversion to percentages so that any two ratio scales can be compared directly. Also it is possible to establish the physical concentration that results in proportional changes in sensation. From the procedure emerges a power function of the form

$$\text{Perceived sensory magnitude} = k(\text{physical stimulus})^m,$$

which in log–log coordinates is

$$\log(\text{perceived sensory magnitude}) = m \log(\text{physical stimulus}) + \log k \tag{43}$$

where m is the slope of the line and k is the intercept on the sensory axis. This is the psychophysical power law. The value of m is unaffected by the size of the magnitude estimate. The magnitude estimation procedure yields reproducible scale values. Moskowitz (1977a, 1977b) outlined the procedure and discussed certain biases involved. Correlating sensory and instrumental data is difficult because we do not know the "true" or operative stimulus for odor or texture perception. As Moskowitz (1981) writes, "The overwhelming evidence is that we do not know the adequate or appropriate stimulus for most perceptions involving food."

Magnitude estimation is primarily useful in the formulation of food products when components are at above-threshold amounts (Meilgaard and Reid 1979). Marks and Stevens (1968) discussed the effects when sensory intensity is evaluated in a region around threshold. In this region, the function generated by magnitude estimation is no longer linear in log–log coordinates but becomes steeper.

La constitution d'un vocabulaire caracteristique pour un produit alimentaire est une entreprise longue que consistera à faire un choix parmi une abondance de termes et à garder un nombre suffisant pour décrire l'arôme de la façon la plus complète possible.

J. ADDA AND P. JOUNELA-ERIKSSON

Glossary

Semantics is the study of the meaning of words. Most words are subject to multiple definition and have both referential and emotive functions. A referential word refers to a specific object or action, or points to something outside of itself (symbols are inherently referential). An emotional word expresses feelings and may aim at stirring those of the hearer—perhaps spurring the listener to action. *Nice, beautiful, wonderful, good,* and *bad* are emotive words. Referential words, such as *grape, berry, bottle,* or *vine,* refer to specific objects. Obviously, in accurately describing specific odors or tastes (referential) one does not use emotive words because these can be so differently interpreted by different people (depending on experience and cultural background).

Words also have descriptive and evaluative meaning. Lehrer (1975) found *sweet* and *dry* to have both meanings. *Bitter* and *sour* also are both descriptive and evaluative. Lehrer (1975) asked the question whether prolonged casual contact and conversation would produce some uniformity in applying words to wine, or whether uniformity would only result from formal tutoring. We favor the latter because it saves time.

In ordinary conversation we all use nonemotive words in an emotive sense. In "an apple is red," *apple* is referential, but it is emotive in "she is the apple of my eye." Emotive language has its place and we need it, but it is subject to much misinterpretation. Language (written or spoken) involves the speaker and the listener and how each views its sense, feeling, tone, and intention. Feeling and tone are important in poetry and also have their place in describing wines for emotional purposes. But one should be careful in using emotive words to describe nonemotional things. Avoid using anthropomorphic words (see pages 333–336).

Cey-Bert (1982) notes that the terminology of wine has emotive, symbolic, and social dimensions and constitutes a language of its own. In classical Greek and Roman thought, wine was associated with symbolism: its origin, labor of the grape grower, vintage, religious and health values, tradition, pleasure, and festive, poetical, and other symbolic attributes. In modern secular society, Cey-Bert believes, four of these still exist: the dietetic values, origin, sensory value, and the ritual of consummation.

Lehrer (1975) asks why people talk about wines when they are drinking them? Is it an opportunity to show off one's knowledge? To brag about the wines? Or to put down one or more of the group (i.e., to establish some sort of dominance in the group)? Lehrer thinks it is for the purpose of establishing contact between people and to establish links. Talk also interacts with information-sharing functions of language, provides an opportunity for reflection, and gives us assurance about our environment. Discussions about wine, Lehrer adds, are probably like other aesthetic conversations. Furthermore, by talking about the wine, one is more likely to remember the experience. If wine discussions are more for sharing experience than for conveying precise information, then some of this discussion is not important to the sensory evaluation of wine. However, professionals need a more scientific use of language.

With beer evaluation, Clapperton (1973) noted that "the derivation of a suitable and systematic vocabulary of descriptive terms and maintenance of people's interest and involvement are at least as important for attainment of a satisfactory level of performance as rigorous training of individuals to recognize specific aroma and flavor qualities."

Williams (1975) has emphasized the importance of a universally recognized vocabulary for evaluating cider quality. His list contains many indefinite terms. However, if his trained panel can differentiate "like mead" from "like honey," these terms appear to be valid. The value of his terms is that they are related to specific chemical compounds, mixtures of compounds, or reproducible artificial standards. Some of the words have subjective meanings that seem different in usage: fugitive, catty, like animals, like wet flannel, like peardrops, like mushrooms, old horse, and so on.

A glossary of terms for beers has been published by the American Society of Brewing Chemists (Meilgaard et al. 1979). The Society (1979) also suggested compounds to compare for recognition of specific odor, taste, and tactile sensations (i.e., alcoholic, spicy, and so on). The compounds (when distinct from the sensation) follow in parentheses: acetaldehyde,* acetic acid,* alcoholic* (ethanol), almond* (benzaldehyde), astringent* (quercitrin), bitter* (isohumulone), butyric acid,* caprylic* (octanoic acid), DMS* (dimethyl sulfide), earthy (gosmin), earthy (2-ethyl fenchol), ethyl acetate,* ethyl hexanoate, isoamyl acetate,* isovaleric acid,* melony (melonal), salty (sodium chloride), spicy (eugenol), sulfitic* (sodium metabisulfite), and sweet* (sucrose). Note that quercitrin also has some bitterness.

Interpretation of Words

Ribéreau-Gayon (1973), Vedel et al. (1972), and Peynaud (1980) have published lists of words expressing gradations in taste or odor characteristics. Vedel (1966) estimated that French judges used 600 to 700 different words to describe wines.

---

*Those terms marked with an asterisk would probably be equally useful for wines—with suitable adjustment of concentration.

Ribéreau-Gayon uses the series *plat* (flat), *lavé* (washed), and *aqueux* (watery) for the sweet taste in a series of wines of decreasing ethanol content. For the same ethanol content with decreasing sugar content, the sweet taste is expressed by the terms *moelleux* (mellow), *mou* (soft), and *alcalin* or *salé* (alkaline or salty). For decreasing acid content, he suggests *vert* (green), *acide* (acid), *dur* (hard), *mordant* (biting), *sec* (drying), *creux* (gaunt), and *maigre* (meager). For decreasing bitterness (*amertume*), he uses *astringent* (astringent), *âpre* (bitter), *ferme* (harsh), and *dur* (hard). Obviously he does not distinguish between bitterness and astringency, nor between the hardness due to sourness and that due to bitterness. For a balanced wine (sugar and acid), the terms he uses for decreasing ethanol content are *spiritueux* (spirituous), *chaud* (hot), *vineux* (vinous), *léger* (light), *faible* (feeble), and *petit* (slight). Obviously the translations are our responsibility and are probably to a certain extent inexact or inelegant.

If the terms are well understood by all the judges, they are appropriate. However, we know that even experienced judges (particularly from different regions) are apt to have very different concepts about the subjective sensory terms used above. In Vedel et al. (1972), the series *charpenté* (structured), *tannique* (tannic), *rude* (rough), *rêche* (harsh), and *astringent* (astringent) is used. In our experience, different judges have very different conceptions of the meanings of these terms and especially of their relations to each other. (See also the discussions of bitterness and astringency, pages 49–51.)

Ribéreau-Gayon (1973) made the useful observation that the meaning of terms may change with time. Wines that were formerly considered *souple* (supple or soft) would not be so graded today. Also, preferences change with time. There are many historical examples of such changes. Really dry wines predominated in Germany in the last century; until recently it was difficult to find a dry German white wine. Bordeaux wines of high volatile acidity were not damned at the turn of the century; today they are rare and justly condemned.

From 86 descriptive words, Wu et al. (1977) identified 33 that had the greatest meaning (using factor analysis, page 300). These were

aromatic (O); astringent (F) (puckery); balanced (round); biting; bitter (T); burnt-smokey* (O); coarse; delicate (soft, light); desirable
aftertaste; dry (T); fresh (O); fruity (O); grapey (O); hearty*; insipid
(flat)*; mature; medicinal (O); metallic (F?); musklike* (O); musty
(earthy, moldy) (O); salty* (T); sharp; smooth (F); spicy* (O?); sulfurous* (O); sweet (T); syrupy (F?); tart (T); vinegary (O); watery; winey
(O?); woody (O); and yeasty* (O). (O = odor, T = taste, F = feel.
Our guess.) Thus 14 are probably odors, 5 tastes, 4 tactile and 10
unidentified. Terms with an asterisk were later found to be nonsignificant for red or white wines or both. Thus only 25 descriptive words
remained. Of these 25, several (biting, coarse, round, etc.) are on our
less meaningful list (page 334). The rest are in the regular vocabulary,
including some, but not all, the nonsignificant words in the above
list. Their relatively naive panel failed to mark *sulfurous* in 12 American white wines (no analyses given, but several are normally sufficiently high in sulfur dioxide for it to be detectable). Also *astringent*
(puckery) and *woody* in white wines and *vinegary* and *watery* in both
red and white wines were marked, though one wonders what the
panelists meant. Some training of the panel in more consistent use of
the terms seems to be warranted.

This glossary includes both general descriptive terms used by
wine drinkers and some quantitative terms used by enologists. We
hope that enologists will develop more of the latter and that amateurs will use them. Amerine (1980) gives an American glossary of
words used to describe abnormal sensations from wines. He notes
that modern technology has reduced the number of these off-odors
to the extent that "the most serious off-odor is the wine with no
odor."

To us it is obvious that the development of a meaningful vocabulary for wines is even more difficult, partly because of the great
range of types and qualities of wines and partly because of the en-
trenchment of terms from several languages and a variety of commercial practices over the years. Ohara (1966) has published a list of over
350 terms (in English, French, German, and Japanese) used in the

sensory evaluation of wines. Although many of these terms are self-explanatory, some are too indefinite to be useful. Broadbent (1980) and Peynaud (1980) use large vocabularies of descriptive terms. Again, many words are useful, but some are too poetic. Primarily they would be useful to the experienced enophile. In principle, a glossary should be large enough to describe adequately the various sensory sensations but not be so large as to contain repetitions. Williams (1982) appeals for a rationalization of the vocabulary used for wine flavors.

In Lehrer's (1975) study, *dry* was used more than 30 times; *acidic, aromatic, clean, fruity, **light, refreshing,*** and *smooth* were applied less frequently (more than 20 times), and *astringent, balanced, bitter, **bland,** bouquet, **common, delicate,** developed, flowery, fragrant, full-bodied, **gentle, lively, ordinary, perfumed, pungent, scented, soft,** sour, sweet, **tangy, tart,*** and *young* (more than 10 times). Boldfaced terms seem less defensible and are in the Words to Avoid list on pages 334–336.

The definitions that follow will probably not satisfy all wine connoisseurs, nor are they intended to, since that is not possible. Experienced judges use many more terms and, justifiably, give varying meanings to those listed here. Whether experienced judges can communicate their "meanings" to others is not clear. These definitions are intended more for students, as they begin to learn how to evaluate wines critically. The symbols $(+)$ and $(-)$ refer to pleasantness and unpleasantness, respectively. We are aware of the subjective nature of such definitions and hope that future enologists will bring order out of the psychological and semantic chaos we find in this area.

To help standardize response to the sensory stimuli of wines, Noble (1982) asked experienced enologists to respond to their use of 102 specific odors and nine in-mouth sensations. The aroma classes were floral, fruity, herbaceous (fresh), herbaceous (cooked), spicy, and miscellaneous. The bouquet classes were fermentation-related, wood, cooperage-related (but not wood), age-related, oxidized, sulfur compounds, and miscellaneous. The flavor-by-mouth classes were taste and mouth feel/texture. From an industry survey, Noble hoped to develop a terminology that would be widely used and could be defined in terms of standards. This worthy project of the American Society of Enologists continues.

Words used to describe color have been omitted. We feel that all but the color-blind can develop their own vocabulary. The professional will probably use physical measurements to specify the parameters of color. However, the human eye is extraordinarily sensitive to small differences in colors, and the development of a rational color nomenclature would be desirable. (See page 28.) How does one distinguish scarlet, brilliant scarlet, flashing scarlet, bright ruby scarlet, limpid scarlet, ruby scarlet, and scarlet-toned?

Some terms have definite chemical meanings—for example, acetic, mercaptan, and sulfur dioxide. The amateur will be satisfied with semiquantitative sensory evaluations of such factors, whereas the professional will demand quantitative chemical data to verify the sensory impression.

Words to describe odors are a pain in the neck: first, there are too many, and second, they are poorly classified (and in fact may be unclassifiable).

Finally, we would make a plea for less fanciful terms than those so often found in the popular and trade press. Simplicity and clarity should be the initial goals, but above all the terms must have recognizable meanings with respect to the sensory evaluation of wines.

Unfortunately, existing wine terminology abounds in words and phrases that have little or no clearly definable meaning with respect to the sensory evaluation of wines. Some such terms are acceptable if used judiciously by experts when *they* know exactly what they mean. Many other terms cannot satisfy even this criterion, and quite a few are simply ridiculous. Some are anthropomorphic while others are burdened with too many (and even conflicting) meanings for use for describing wines.

Definitions

Acescence A fancy, but correct, word for vinegarlike. (−) See *acetic*.

Acetic The vinegarlike odor of acetic acid and ethyl acetate. (−) The acetic acid threshold in wine is below 0.07 g/100 ml, calculated as acetic acid. The legal limit in the United States is 0.14 g/100 ml in reds and 0.12 g/100 ml in other types. The California limits are 0.12 g/100 ml and 0.11 g/100 ml respectively. The ethyl acetate threshold is only about 0.007 g/100 ml. A limit of 0.015 g/100 ml has been suggested (Robertson and Rush 1979). A less precise word is *pricked*. A number of words for varying levels of acetic odor are used in Europe.

Acidic See *sour*.

Acidulous Unpleasantly *sour* (q.v.). (−) Usually used for wines of over 1% total acidity and a pH of 3.1 or less. More or less the same as the French *mordant*.

Aerated The aldehydelike odor of wines exposed to air as in racking, filtration, aging in the cask, or bottling. (−) More of a problem with white table wines than with other wines. For the incipient *oxidized* (q.v.) *odor*, see *faded*. Not all the ill effects of exposure to air can be blamed on the carbonyls. (Anon. 1974.)

Aftertaste The taste, odor, and tactile sensations that remain after the wine is swallowed or expectorated (mainly odor, i.e., *flavor* (q.v.). Probably due to the less volatile components that remain in or reach the olfactory region after the more volatile have disappeared. Fine red table wines should be high in this quality. (+) Wines with little of this quality are colloquially said to "finish short." (−) Chardonnay wines sometimes have plenty of this quality.

Alcoholic Wines with too high ethanol for the type. (−) See *heady* and *hot*.

Ample   A quantitative word for sensations. *Much* does as well (or as little).

Antiseptic   An off-odor from the reaction of chlorine-based sterilants and low-molecular-weight phenolic compounds (such as those in paints, pharmaceuticals, resins, and rubber products). (−) Williams (1975) used methyl salicylate as a standard for the pharmaceutical odor in ciders.

Apple   Used for wines as diverse as Chardonnay and White Riesling. Williams (1975) used hexyl acetate for "like apples." A natural apple essence and ethyl 2-methyl butyrate were also used as standards for the apple odor. With beer, ethyl hexanoate is recommended to compare to the apple odor. If *apple* refers to a supposed malic acid taste (as it apparently sometimes does), we find difficulty in justifying its use for odor.

Aroma   For typicality of odors in the wine that originate in the grape. Muscat is the classic example. To be distinguished from *bouquet* (q.v.).

Aromatic   The distinctive odor found in the wines of certain varieties. Is *spicy* (q.v.) a more general word, or are they the same thing? See *odor, spicy.*

Aromatized   See *sophisticated.*

Asbestos   The odor of wines filtered through asbestos pads. Rare or extinct since asbestos is not now used in filter pads, at least it certainly should not be.

Astringent   The puckery tactile sensation. (−) Most noticeable in young red table wines. *Harsh* (q.v.), *rough* (q.v.), and *tannic* are related words. The opposite is *smooth* (q.v.). Not to be confused with *bitter* (q.v.) or *sour* (q.v.). "Subtle astringency" and similar circumlocutions are to be avoided. Mildly astringent wines are reported to have a total phenol content of 1,300 mg/l (as gallic acid equivalent), whereas highly astringent wines contain 2,000 mg/l (Singleton and Noble 1976). "Bad" tannins are described as "those which give a wine an aggressive astringency" (Ribéreau-Gayon 1978). Some detergents (accidentally in wine) have an astringent sensation. Green bananas and unripe persimmons are astringent.

Bacon Used by some California enologists for an odor of unknown origin. More common with red table wines. (−?)

Bacterial An omnibus word for a number of off-odors originating with bacterial activity. Better to specify the responsible microorganism, if you can. (−) See also *odor: butyric, geraniumlike, mousy, propionic,* and *yeasty.* Yeasts (*Brettanomyces* sp. and *Dekkera* sp.) also produce off-odors (Phaff and Amerine 1979).

Baked The caramellike odor in sweet wines that have been heated at too high a temperature or for too long. Maillard and caramelization reactions are responsible (Webb and Noble 1976). (−) However, in California sherries and other types of baked wines (Madeira, etc.), it is normal (+) if not too accentuated. *Cooked* seems to refer to the same or a similar odor. *Burnt* (q.v.) may have pain qualities. See *raisin.*

Balanced Used for both odor and taste sensations that are present in optimum amounts. (+) Harmonious is similar with more pleasant connotations. *Unbalanced* is the opposite, but be prepared to define what it means. If *balanced,* explain in what.

Bitter A true taste sensation, usually persisting on the back of the tongue. (Usually −) It is not confined to red table wines. A trace of bitterness is noted in some dry white table wines, especially if fermented on the skins too long. In cases of high ethanol, is this the cause? Partially masked by the sweet taste. Many flavonol phenolics have a bitter taste (Singleton and Noble 1976). These tastes are probably additive. Acrolein is responsible for bitterness in bacterial-spoiled wines where glycerol is attacked.

Bitter almond The odor of hydrogen cyanide, resulting from poor filtration of wines treated with potassium ferrocyanide for removal of excess copper and iron. Rare and below the toxic level. (−)

Treated wines do not age well, and white wines may develop too low an oxidation-reduction potential.

Bittersweet   The meaning is clear enough, but it is not common. Is it significant that the Italians have a word for it—*ammandorlato?*

Black currant   How many people can recognize this odor in nature? Included because many cannot find anything else to describe Médoc wines. One of the varietal odors of Cabernet Sauvignon. See page 115.

Bland   Some wines are so innocuous in taste and odor that this word comes naturally, but use sparingly.

Body   The tactile sensation differentiating low-ethanol from high-ethanol wines, that is, *thin* (q.v.) from *full-bodied* (q.v.). The distinction is more difficult if the wine is sweet. Some wines are naturally low in body (Moselles), and we do not penalize them too much for it. Others are naturally high in body (many, but not all, Rhone red wines and some California Zinfandels). Whatever else is included in body, glycerol is of minimal importance. To equate body with richness of flavor is wrong, in our opinion.

Botrytised   The odor of sweet wines made from sound grapes shriveled by *Botrytis.* (+) When it is mixed with other molds and the odor is moldy, it is undesirable. (−) When the wine is dry, it is always (−).

Bouquet   The odors in wines from fermentation, processing, and aging, particularly those that develop after bottling. (+) Whatever else a supernacular red wine must have, bottle bouquet is essential. At times, European enologists use *bouquet* for *aroma* (q.v.).

Brilliant   The appearance of a wine that is free of suspended material. (+)

Burnt   An odor, originally of wines to which boiled-down must had been added. Now used for wines to which musts heated to extract color have been added, especially when heated too high or too long. One well-known Burgundy is incorrectly praised for this odor because it is unique. (+ in Marsala, − in red table wines.)

An acrid odor from poor fortifying spirits has also been suggested. See *odor, pomacy.*

Burny   A pain sensation in the nose or on the tongue. (−) Associated with *hot* (q.v.) wines, that is, *alcoholic* (q.v.). Ethanol and related compounds are suspect. Perhaps the same as the acrid odor of poor spirits?

Buttery   Used for an odor from the malolactic fermentation. (+ or −) Possibly *diacetyl* (q.v.) is meant? If so, use it.

Butyric   The distinctive and objectionable and, fortunately, rare, odor from butyric acid and perhaps related compounds produced by bacterial action, especially from attack on glycerol. (−) Goaty? A maximum of 3 mg/l has been suggested (Robertson and Rush 1979). The threshold in beer is 1 mg/l.

Caramel   The caramellike odor of heated sweet wines. Madeiras and California sweet sherries are the prototypes. (+ for them and − elsewhere) *Baked* (q.v.) may be similar, but *madeirized* (q.v.) is not. Grape concentrate produced in the usual low-vacuum pan has the odor. Caramel syrup is added (legally) to brandies and vermouth. (+) 5-Hydroxymethylfurfural is also produced. It has a camomilelike odor that may be desirable up to a limit.

Carboned (or charcoaled)   Develops when carbon or charcoal is used to remove undesirable colors or odors, or both. (−) See *odor, oxidized.*

Cedar or cedarwood   Used mainly by British enophiles for the *bouquet* (q.v.) of aged red Bordeaux wines. If the odor is specific we have not complained, although we do not know what it is.

Character or characteristic   One cannot improve on Broadbent (1977) for the latter (and by implication for the former): "often sweepingly used to avoid a detailed description." Avoid.

Chocolate   A bouquet of red Bordeaux wines, but what it refers to we do not know. (+ or −) Avoid or use sparingly and only if you know what it means.

Clean Overworked for absence of defects. It is not much of a compliment to a wine to say it is "clean." Avoid.

Clear The appearance of a wine that has a slight haze or a few suspended particles. (−)

Closed-up A poetic way of saying *undeveloped* (q.v.). (−) If used, best to explain what you mean.

Cloudy The appearance of a wine with a colloidal haze and particulate matter. (−)

Cloying An excessively sweet wine taste. Usually also lacking acidity. (−) May have tactile aspects as well. See *unctuous* for a similar, but less negative, meaning.

Coarse Probably intended to describe an imbalance of tactile and taste (and odor?) sensations. Now so weighted down with incompatible meanings that it is best avoided. The French *corsé* and Spanish *basta* have different and more favorable connotations.

Complex The juxtaposition of several odors. (+) If nonolfactory sensations are included, best explain lest the word be burdened with too many meanings.

Cooked See *odor: baked, burnt,* or *caramel.*

Cork borers Corked bottles stored in dry conditions with some light may be attacked by various insects. The wine then sometimes acquires a *corky* (q.v.) odor (Götz 1976).

Corked or corky The undesirable odor of a few bottled wines. Three types are distinguished by Lefebvre (1981): (1) a putrid odor from the cork is said to be rare and of unknown origin; (2) an oaky odor is believed due to cork tannins and is present soon after corking; (3) *mousy* (q.v.) or *moldy* (q.v.) *odors* are blamed on poorly stored (moldy) corks. The moldiness is extracted slowly during the aging of the wine due to its periodic expansion and contraction, hence more often found in wines from *ullaged* (q.v.) bottles. *Penicillium multicolor, P. frequentans,* and *P. velutina* are implicated (Schaeffer et al. 1978). Corks exposed to microbial agents, methyl thiopyrazine, or high sulfur dioxide may result in an *off* (q.v.)-odor (Tanner and Zanier 1978). We do not know whether corked and corky are the same, but we are not able to distinguish them consistently. We agree with Peynaud (1981) that the definitions are not precise, especially as to origin. See also pages 40–41.

Cresol See *phenol.*

Developed Essentially *mature* (q.v.).

Diacetyl An *off* (q.v.)-odor that is difficult to characterize. Due to bacterial action, primarily in red table wines. Possibly the *buttery* (q.v.) or *breadcrust* odor. Up to 1 to 3 mg/l, it may add complexity ($+$), but at higher concentrations surely undesirable ($-$). If appreciable acetaldehyde is present, it is difficult to establish a threshold for diacetyl (Amerine and Roessler 1971).

Disinfectant See *antiseptic.*

Dry Absence of the sweet taste—that is, of wines with less than about 1% sugar. ($+$ or $-$, depending on the type of wine) Consumers tend to prefer sweet to dry wines if they do not know they are sweet. Unwary experts have also been fooled. "Bone-dry," "chalk-dry," "dry-tannin," "medium-dry," "spicy-dry," and "stylishly dry" are to be avoided.

Dull The appearance of a wine with a colloidal haze. ($-$) Less than *cloudy* (q.v.) and more than *clear* (q.v.).

Earthy An unpleasant odor perceived in the mouth when the wine warms up there. It is difficult to recognize or describe. ($-$) Found in wines of certain regions. How much is soil, climate, time-of-harvest, processing, or microbial in origin is not known. Wines made with grapes that have been washed at Davis have been as *earthy* as those from unwashed grapes!

Esterified The common and objectionable ester in wine odor is ethyl acetate, which is vinegary. At 175 mg/l, the odor of the wine is definitely spoiled. Robertson and Rush (1979) suggested 150 mg/l as the upper limit in wines. What Webb and Berg (1955) called excessive esterification may have been ethyl acetate and other esters.

Ethyl acetate   Another source of the vinegary odor. (—) See *acetic* and *esterified*.

Faded   Incipient *oxidation* (q.v.) on the nose, thus noticeable in acetaldehyde. More or less the same as the French *éventé*. *Over-the-hill* is a poetic further stage. See *odor, aerated*.

Fermentation or fermenting   The yeasty odor of newly made wines, possibly includes sulfides. (Usually —) A trace in neutral-flavored wines may not be objectionable. See *fresh*.

Filter   See *aerated* and *asbestos*. Use of too much bentonite or kieselguhr as filter aids may give a slight *off* (q.v.)-*odor* to the first wine filtered.

Finish   See *aftertaste* for all that is necessary.

Flat   Lack of the sour taste. (—) Such wines are not only defective in taste but usually in color and odor as well. Due to use of low-acid grapes, excessive malo-lactic fermentation, overcorrection of high acidity, overchaptalization, and, in some cases, too generous a hand with the water hose. Consumers differ in their acceptance and rejection of flat-tasting wines. What does "flat middle taste" mean? Also used for sparkling wines that have lost most of their carbon dioxide. (—)

Flavor   The in-mouth odor and other sensations. Usually odor should be used. But it is appropriate for sensations that arise only after the wine is warmed in the mouth. Avoid "bunch of flavors" or "amply flavored."

Flinty   This odor has not come our way, but perhaps we do not know what to look for? Would *metallic* (q.v.) do as well? Laederer (in Duttweiler 1968) identified the flinty odor with wines from grapes grown on silicious soils at Dezaley, Switzerland. See *smoky*.

Flowery   Used for the floral odor of many young wines from White Riesling to Gamay. Is it 2-phenethanol with its roselike odor? Generally associated with young wines of high total acidity and low pH. The wines appear to be on the reduced side, hence may be high in free sulfur dioxide. Traces of the *fermentation* (q.v.) *odor* may be present.

Foxy A complex of odors found in grapes of *Vitis labrusca* and its hybrids and in wines made from them. Methyl and ethyl anthranilate and other compounds (page 98) are involved. European consumers profess to dislike the odor, but many Americans as well as Azorians, Brazilians, Sicilians, and others have cultivated a taste or tolerance for it. Some of the new hybrids are reported to have a raspberry or strawberry odor.

Freshness or fresh Believed to be the *flavor* (q.v.) of young wines, but probably also related to a desirable sour taste. A further stage of *fermentation* (q.v.). (+ in most young wines)

Frosted Very rare in California but reported from Germany. Could it be *oxidized* (q.v.)? Some are said to have a bananalike odor, possibly from amyl acetate or?

Fruitiness or fruity The grapelike flavor and taste, particularly of young wines of high acidity. (+) A refreshing wine. Lack of fruitiness is deplorable. (−)

Full-bodied See *body*. Avoid, use low-, medium-, or high-body as needed.

Fusel The highly characteristic and generally obnoxious odors of the so-called higher alcohols (butyl, propyl, amyl, isoamyl, etc.). Seldom noted in table wines. We recall one red table wine with 300 mg/l where it was noticeable but not unlikeable. Fusel oils may accumulate in the distillate from poor distillation practices. When used for fortifying dessert wines, the fusel odor will be found in the wine. However, a moderate amount is tolerated and seemingly appreciated in some Portuguese ports.

Gassy The taste and tactile (and often visual and even auditory) sensations of carbon dioxide escaping from a wine. (− in wines that are supposed to be still, but + in many wines from Switzerland and the Loire) The threshold for the taste and tactile sensations is about 100 mg/l. Some California wines have carbon dioxide added up to the legal limit for still wines (0.392 g/100 ml). There may be too low an amount in some young wines. Creaming is used when some foam is produced. Piquant we now believe is not an incipient state of gassiness. Avoid its use.

Geraniumlike The highly undesirable odor resulting from bacterial activity in wines containing sorbic acid. (−) The revealing compound is 2-ethoxy-hexa-3, 5-diene. See Crowell and Guymon (1975). Not garliclike.

Grapey or grapy The same or very similar odor discussed as *fruity* (q.v.). We prefer *fruity* but admit to using *grapey odor* when we nod.

Grassy The characteristic aroma of wines made from Sauvignon blanc grapes, particularly when made from grapes grown in climatic regions as cool as I and II. Much less noticeable in grapes grown in regions IV and V if fully ripe. (+ unless too pronounced, then −) Grassiness is the same? Chenin blanc and White Riesling have been described as grassy, but we do not know why.

Green The odor of wines made from unripe grapes. (Usually −) Associated with a high-acid sour taste, but it is not a taste unless so specified. Then *acidulous* (q.v.) does as well. Webb and Berg (1955) connected it with leaf alcohol and leaf aldehyde. Williams (1975) used hexanol or hex-3-enol as standards for a green odor in ciders. He also subdivided it into "like-fruit," "green grass," "floral," and "cooked fruit."

Green olive The typical aroma of wines made from Cabernet Sauvignon grapes (Amerine and Singleton 1976). It is due to a number of compounds. See page 115. Some enophilists use *odor, black currant* (q.v.) for this, or a similar aroma.

Green-tea A new word in California for the *bouquet* (q.v.) (or *aroma* [q.v.]) of Cabernet Sauvignon wines. Time will tell whether it helps or hinders our description of these wines.

Guava An odor reported in South African Chenin blanc and Colombard wines (Du Plessis and Augustyn 1982). Believed to be due to 4-methyl-4-mercapto-pentan-2-one.

Hard Is it taste or tactile? Avoid, especially for wines high in volatile acid.

Harmony Used in some scorecards. Roughly equal to the overall or general quality of the wine.

Harsh For high astringency? Avoid.

Hazy Undesirable appearance. We think *clear* (q.v.), *dull* (q.v.), and *cloudy* (q.v.) are enough. (Always −)

Heady High in alcohol. (−)

Heated See *odor: aerated, caramellike, cooked,* and *oxidized.*

Herbaceous An odor, particularly in wines made from certain varieties of grapes when grown under cool climatic conditions. (+ if not too pronounced, then −) Found in the wines of Cabernet Sauvignon and Sauvignon blanc wines from regions as diverse as the Loire, Bordeaux, and the cooler coastal areas of California, especially when picked late in a cool season. Also described as the *bell-pepper odor.* See page 116.

Hot An unpleasant pain sensation in the mouth or nose. (−) Variously attributed to high ethanol–low sweetness, higher alcohols, and to unknown compounds. *Baked* (q.v.) is not the same. *Burny* (q.v.) is similar.

Hydrogen sulfide See *odor, sulfide.*

Kerosene The Australian word for the aroma of White Riesling wines. Are they slightly *oxidized* (q.v.)? We think we know what they are talking about, but *kerosene* is too negative for the aroma of a pleasant wine.

Lactic See *odor, sauerkraut.*

Leafy An odor found in young wines. (−) Possibly due to leaf aldehyde and leaf alcohol? See *odor, green,* and *stemmy.*

Lees The odor of wines left too long on the fresh lees, particularly under warm conditions. (−) A most objectionable rotten odor, sometimes with an odor like *mercaptan* (q.v.).

Legs See page 156 for their origin. The expressions "very heavy legs," "heavy legs," "medium legs," and so on seem imprecise and should be avoided. The illustrations do not seem to indicate a difference based on ethanol content.

Light Methyl sulfide, methyl disulfide, carbon bisulfide, and ethyl and methyl thiolacetates have all been identified (Leppänen et al. 1980) in wines. (−) The thresholds of the thiolacetates are too high for any direct influence on odor but they can be hydrolized to give free thiols. This may explain the "light" odor found in some sparkling wines exposed to the light (Maujean et al. 1978). It is the *goût de lumière,* but it is not a taste. Same as *sunstruck* (q.v.).

Maceration carbonique (or carbonic maceration) The odor (−, +) produced in wines fermented uncrushed under anaerobic conditions. It is disagreeable to some, but others have acquired a taste for it. We haven't.

Madeirized See *odor: baked, burnt,* and *caramel.* Most such wines are also *oxidized* (q.v.) to a greater or lesser degree.

Mature The pleasing odor of wines, particularly red wines. (+) Neither too young nor too old. *Ripe* has the same meaning, to us, so why use it?

Medicinal See *odor: antiseptic, petroleum,* and *phenol.*

Mellow Another word that means different things to different people. If it refers to *sweetness,* why not say so? Sometimes it may mean *soft,* whatever that may be. Avoid. See page 335.

Mercaptan The objectionable onionlike or garliclike odor of methyl and ethyl mercaptans and sulfides. (−) The specific odor of dimethyl sulfide is reported as a desirable odor in aged white table wines (Anon. 1979; Marais 1979). (+) Its threshold is about 0.05 mg/l.

Metallic We included this here because it occurs in the literature often. Few modern wines have enough metals in them to affect the taste of a wine. More likely it is a tactile sensation of low-ethanol, dry, high-acid white wines or of the astringent feel of some high polyphenolic wines. (−) Nowadays it is unnecessary.

Mildewy See *odor, moldy*.

Minty Used for the aroma of some red wines.

Moldy *Aspergillis* sp., *Penicillium* sp., *Rhizopus* sp., and *Uncinula necator* will grow on grapes under varying conditions. Wines made from these infected grapes impart a moldy or mildewy odor to the wines. (−) These and other molds may grow in empty wine containers and, unless the molds are removed before placing wines in the containers, the wines will acquire a *moldy* odor. It is also present in wines made from grapes that were attacked by *Botrytis cinerea* and which already or subsequently were infected with one or several of the molds listed above. An ounce of prevention is worth a pound of cure. If you can distinguish *mildewy* from *moldy*, do so. See *phenolic*.

Mousy The highly objectionable odor of table and dessert wines, usually those made from late-harvested, low-acid, high-pH grapes. Acetamide and acrolein (pages 292 and 314) have been suggested as causes. Occurs when the malolactic fermentation attacks tartaric acid, producing lactic acid, acetic acid, carbon dioxide, and the undesirable *mousy* odor. Easy to control: watch the wines. Not as rare as we would like.

Musty Used by "connoisseurs" for something that is *off* (q.v.) in odor but is not moldy. (−) Avoid unless you can consistently identify it. See Amerine (1981).

Naive Originally used for wines of little merit, by persons who presume—but lack—knowledge. Another anthropomorphical horror. Avoid except in poetic situations. See page 335.

Naphthalene An *off* (q.v.)-*odor* from corks contaminated with this compound. (−) Reported in Australia. Surely rare.

Neutral A wine lacking distinctive or recognizable odor. (−) *Vinous* (q.v.) says the same thing and is preferred. *Clean* (q.v.) is equally meaningless.

Nose An upper-class and pretentious word for odor. Avoid.

Nutty Use *woody* (q.v.) or *oaky* (q.v.) even. Webb and Berg (1955) used it for *madeirized* (q.v.). In that case, *baked* (q.v.) seems adequate. *Nutty* is too ambiguous. Avoid.

Oaky There may be a difference between *oaky* and *woody* (q.v.), in California sherry, but we fail to find it. (Usually −) With rare exceptions, does not apply to California baked wines, which seldom see an oak cask or barrel for very long.

Off An undesirable odor, less often *flavor* (q.v.) and seldom taste. (−) Try to identify the origin of the off-sensation—for example, *moldy* (q.v.) off-odor. *Odd, odor, sophisticated* (q.v.), and *spoiled* have similar meanings but should be carefully used (see pages 39 and 308).

Overaged *Oxidized* (q.v.) usually serves as well, but *overaged* is a more general breakdown of the wine. (−) Should it be used specifically for white table wines kept too long in wooden cooperage with some darkening of the color? See *odor, faded*.

Overripe It may be possible, and it is certainly desirable, to distinguish an overripe odor (+) in wines made from fully-matured grapes from the *raisinlike* (q.v.) *odor* of wines made from grapes with a high percentage of raisined fruit. (−)

Oxidized and oxidation Mainly the odor of carbonyl compounds, primarily acetaldehyde. The threshold may be as low as 30 or 40 mg/l in white table wines, as low as 20 mg/l in sparkling wines. In dessert wines, particularly dry fino-type sherries, it is (+). *Madeirized* (q.v.) is heat-induced, often with *caramel* (q.v.) odor. *Overaged* is the same or similar (with woodiness). Not all the ill effects of exposure to oxygen are accounted for by the carbonyls (Anon. 1979). In a wine with 1 mg/l of *diacetyl* (q.v.) and 8 to 20 mg/l of acetaldehyde, an oxidized odor was reported (Pisarnitskii et al. 1969).

Palatable   Of uncertain meaning. The same as *pleasant* (q.v.)? If *palatable* must be used, it should be for tastes, reserving *pleasant* for odors.

Palate   Beloved by Australian enophiles. From the word, one would expect it to refer to taste or tactile sensations. But it seems more often to refer to odors or flavors. The use of *middle palate* is common, but who knows what that means? What do the following mean: "on the palate a distinctive spicy odor," "lots of fruit on the palate," "crisp on the palate," "sharp on the palate"?

Peppery   A sensation reported in white table wines from various areas, especially California. (−) The origin is not known. It may be related to sulfur dioxide. Qualified enologists have identified a peppery odor in red Rhone wines. Broadbent (1977) says "probably high[er] alcohols" but this seems doubtful. But what is it?

Petroleum   The odor is rare but we can think of circumstances when it might occur: shipping wine in petroleum-contaminated tanks, mixing wines with compressed air containing petroleum, petroleum-treated grape stakes, from smudge pots, and so on. (−)

Phenol or phenolic   Pentachlorphenol is used as a preservative for wooden vineyard stakes. Its own odor is not unpleasant, but, when methylated and dechlorinated by soil microorganisms, very obnoxious odors are formed and can contaminate grapes and their wines. Believed to be the source of the *Muffton* odor of some German wines (Haubs 1977). Boidron (1981) found a phenolic-like odor in red wines made from moldy grapes. Styrene and possible 1-ol-3 octene may be responsible.

Plastic   The *off* (q.v.)-odor of wines stored in certain kinds of plastic containers. (−) The revealing compound is free styrene.

Pleasant   The same as palatable? No. A favorable odor? How to define or to list the parameters for? (+) See pages 8–10.

Pomace or pomacy The objectionable odor of wines fermented on the skins at too high a temperature. (−) Possibly from yeast autolysis at high temperature.

Propionic The highly undesirable goaty odor of wines spoiled by bacteria. Fortunately it is now rare. (−)

Puckery See *astringent,* which is preferred.

Pungent Implying that the odor is strong and penetrating? Best avoided for most table wines. Muscatels and dessert wines may conceivably have a pungent odor. (+ or −) May be useful for highly flavored wines, such as those of *V. labrusca* and fruit wines.

Putrid A stinky awful odor of bacterially spoiled wines. It is found in wines where the bacteria have attacked glycerol. (−) Nowadays uncommon.

Raisin The odor of semidried or wholly dried grapes. In the former case, it may be just *overripe* (q.v.) (+), as for certain red wines (Burgundy, for example). But it is (−) in the latter case (except for Malaga and sweet oloroso sherries). *Sunburned* (−) is similar but less *caramellike.*

Rancid An *off* (q.v.)-odor not reported from California (Amerine 1980). It is found in spirits (Williams and Strauss 1978) due to unsaturated aldehydes. It is believed due to the oxidation of fatty acids from grape seeds. Williams (1975) used butyric acid as the standard for the rancid odor in ciders. (−) Where it came from in ciders is not known.

Rancio The special and distinctive odor of very old, *oxidized* (q.v.), high-ethanol, usually sweet red wines. (+ for the type wines) The only wines that uniformly have the odor are the Prioratos of northern Spain and some old red wines in the south of France. Some of these are produced by aging red wine in glass demijohns in the sun. We have not noted it in California. Some of the older red dessert wines in Australia may have it.

Raspberry See *foxy.* Also used for the aroma of Zinfandel wines. See page 125.

Reduced The odor of young wines, particularly dry white table wines. The wine is in a chemically reduced state. In such wines, traces of reduced compound may occur (*sulfides* [q.v.]). (−) The color of white wines in this state will be very light in color and may have a *yeasty* (q.v.) odor. Peynaud (1980) considers well-corked red table wines to be in a reduced state, at least the first few years of their aging.

Resin or resinous The turpentine odor of retsina wine. (+) For nonretsina wine contaminated by contact with containers, filter, or fillers that were previously in contact with retsina. (−) Obviously one must cultivate a taste for such a non*vinous* (q.v.) odor. We don't think it is worth the effort.

Ripe See *mature*.

Rough The *astringent* (q.v.) tactile sensation, *not* the *bitter* (q.v.) taste. The Italian *aspro* comes close to describing it. Amerine (1981) suggests increasing astringency for *hard* (q.v.), *rough*, and *harsh* (q.v.).

Rubbery The cooked-cabbage, rubber-boot, or old-rubber odor. It occurs in wines made from grapes grown in hot regions, often harvested late at low acidity and high pH. It has been called the Fresno odor from its occurrence in that region after Prohibition. (−) Earlier harvesting and faster crushing of the fruit has eliminated it (until someone makes a mistake). See Brown (1950).

Sharp Should be limited to the *acetic* (q.v.) vinegary odor, or some early stage of acetification. (−) If used otherwise, specify what you mean. See Brown (1950) and Webb and Berg (1955).

Salty A rare taste in wines. (−) May be tolerated in old, very dry, flor sherries. Improper operation of ion-exchange columns and leakage of refrigerant may be other sources. Argentinean wines made from grapes grown on soils with high sodium and magnesium chlorides are said to have the taste.

Sauerkraut The lactic (and of other compounds too) odor of bacterially spoiled wines. (−) Often due to a continuation of an active malolactic fermentation. See Amerine et al. (1959) and Laederer (in Duttweiler 1968). Found in some pressure-tank-fermented sparkling wines. (Always —)

Short-finish A favorite of some enophiles. Does it mean lack of odor or taste? (—?)

Smoky The aroma of Sauvignon wines. (+ or —) Should not be too pronounced. It is not the same as *flinty* (q.v.). Few, if any, smoked wines have been made since Roman times. *Grassy* (q.v.) is preferred to *smoky* in California.

Smooth The tactile sensation for lack of *astringency* (q.v.), *harshness* (q.v.) or *roughness* (q.v.). (+) Avoid *feminine, sensuous, soft,* and *velvety*. Possibly more than lack of astringency. Noted more often in wines of above-normal ethanol content. Do not use for lack of sourness.

Soapy We formerly frowned on its use. A lower acid stage from *flat* (q.v.) may justify its use.

Sophisticated A foreign odor from nongrape and unauthorized ingredients, intentionally or unintentionally added. (—) At the turn of the century, "wine" odors were for sale. This is now illegal. However, retsina, natural-flavored wines, and vermouths have special nongrape, but legal, ingredients that may be used in their production. The danger is that normal wines may come in contact with containers or equipment that formerly contained these flavored wines. They are then said to have a *sophisticated* (q.v.) *odor.*

Sour or sourness The acid taste of all the volatile and nonvolatile acids of wines (particularly the latter). Do not use for wines high in *acetic* (q.v.) acid. The opposite is *flat* (q.v.) or *soapy* (q.v.). Wines made from green (unripe) grapes will have the taste. A certain sourness is essential. Appreciation of this taste is probably acquired. Children generally abhor sour-tasting foods. See *tart*.

Sour–sweet A disagreeable taste. (—) Found in bacterially spoiled wines, especially from lactic acid bacteria in sweet wines, which produce mannitol or mannite. Rare.

Spicy A distinctive *aromatic* (q.v.) odor of wines made from certain varieties of grapes—for example, Gewürtztraminer. (+, or − if too pronounced or deficient) The permutations of meaning of *spicy* are a serious semantic problem. Should be used with care. Williams (1977) used 4-ethyl guaiacol as a standard for the spicy odor in ciders.

Stagnant Wines placed in containers that contained stagnant water acquire this disagreeable odor. (−) Now rare, at least in California and other regions where wooden fermentors have been abandoned.

Stalky or stemmy The odor reported from wines produced from musts containing fresh green stems. Similar to the *leafy* (q.v.) odor. (−) A *bitter* (q.v.) taste has been blamed on fermenting with the stems. Webb and Berg (1955) suggested that it is produced by too long a fermentation on the skins and is a "modified complex of bitter and green sensations."

Straw Few wines are now made from grapes that have been dried on straw before crushing. A strawlike odor in wines of high-pH grapes in California has not been verified. Possibly from bacterial activity. (−)

Structure or structured Probably means *balanced* (q.v.), which does as well or better.

Style A very complex and sometimes subjective concept. A wine may have style and not quality. Breed, aside from semantic problems, seems to be the same.

Sulfide The disagreeable (rotten-egg) odor due to hydrogen sulfide. (−) The identity of the sulfides and *mercaptans* (q.v.) is not known. The threshold in wines is about 1 to 5 parts per billion. Never forgotten or forgivable, as proper vineyard sulfuring and proper handling (aeration, racking, and proper use of sulfur dioxide, etc.) of the new wine should prevent objectionable amounts in wines.

Sulfur dioxide   A common *off* (q.v.)-odor, mainly of white wines. If detected, always to be criticized. (−) The threshold is about 100 mg/l, but this varies with the composition and age of the wine and with the sensitivity of the subject. Some experienced judges are either insensitive to or tolerant of higher levels than others. The threshold is difficult to establish because of rapid adaptation. A limit of 150 mg/l was suggested by Robertson and Rush (1979). No collaborative consumer tests have come to our attention. It is the free sulfur dioxide that is objectionable. See page 37.

Sunburned   Excessively high vineyard temperatures early in the maturation of the grape berry may result in shriveling of exposed fruit. Whether it produces an odor different from *overripe* (q.v.) or *raisin* (q.v.) we do not know. (−)

Sunstruck   The odor reported in Champagnes exposed to *light* (q.v.). Charpentier and Maujean (1981) suggested reactions between riboflavin and sulfur-containing amino acids. See also *odor, light* (q.v.).

Sweet   The taste. (+ or −, depending on the type of wine) A very sweet wine may be *cloying* (q.v.), a less sweet one still unpleasantly *sweetish* (q.v.). See also *dry.* Do not use for odors.

Sweetish   Unpleasantly *sweet* (q.v.), often found in low-acid wines. (−) *Cloying* (q.v.) and *unctuous* (q.v.) are less objectionable.

Sweet–sour   See *sour–sweet.*

Syrupy   The tactile sensation of a very *sweet* (q.v.) wine, particularly one that is low in ethanol. (−)

Tart   A pleasant, sour taste in young wines. (+) Webb and Berg (1955) give a range of 0.65 to 0.85 g/100 ml (as tartaric) and a pH of 3.1 to 3.4 for such wines. See *acidulous* and *sour.* Do not confuse with tactile sensations.

Tealike   Used for the aroma of Cabernet Sauvignon wines (aged?). The meaning is not clear to us, but many commentators use it.

Tired See *aerated, oxidized,* and *vapid.* Don't use.

Tobacco For some, an *off* (q.v.)-odor in Bordeaux wines (−), but the *cigar-box, tobacco-rich,* or *tobacco-leaf odor* (q.v.) seems to be appreciated by others. (+) Best to avoid unless you are sure.

Ullage When casks are not kept full or when bottles leak, they are said to be on *ullage.* The wines become *oxidized* (q.v.) and, in the case of ullaged bottles, may also become *corky* (q.v.), sometimes from *cork borers* (q.v.).

Unbalanced See *balanced.*

Undeveloped Wines that require further aging, hence primarily for red wines, both dessert and table. (−) Immature is so near the same thing that the additional word can be avoided. The opposite of *developed* (q.v.).

Unripe See *green* or *acidulous.*

Vanilla Vanilla beans are used in some vermouths. If detectable, use of level of vanilla odor is appropriate. Vanillin, which has a vanillalike odor, is found in wines that have been aged in new oak barrels, particularly of American white oak.

Vapid A mildly oxidized odor (−), from which the wine usually recovers. See Webb and Berg (1955).

Vegetal or vegetative A pronounced *grassy* (q.v.) or *herbaceous* (q.v.) *odor.* (−)

Vinegary The odor of acetic acid and ethyl acetate. (−) Always objectionable if detected unless you have a perverted sense of wine quality. Possibly better than nothing?

Vinosity Refers to the ethanol content. Possibly mainly measured by the tactile sensation?

Vinous Without a specific, distinguishable odor. *Clean* (q.v.) and *neutral* (q.v.) are related.

Watery Same as (or very similar to) *thin* (q.v.). (−)

Weedy An undesirable odor from weeds being harvested with the grapes. (−) Due to *Aristolochia* sp. (birth wort, etc.) or *Chenopo-*

dium sp. (lamb's quarters, etc.). Eucalyptus leaves may also get into the harvested fruit and communicate an undesirable odor to the wine.

Whiskey Used bourbon barrels have been used for wines in this country. If not recoopered and thoroughly cleaned, they may give a whiskey odor to wines stored in them. (−)

Woody The odor of wines stored too long in oak containers, particularly barrels. Oak containers that have not been properly treated before use will communicate the odor sooner than properly prepared containers. (−) A little (what is little?) is believed by some to benefit red table wines. But if it is recognizable as woody, it should be considered (−). See pages 78 and 96 for the compounds responsible. Singleton and Noble (1976) reported that several phenols contribute to the *woody odor* (q.v.).

Yeasty The odor of fermenting yeasts, possibly the same as *fermentation* or *fermenting* (q.v.). (−) Yeasts such as *Brettanomyces* sp. and *Dekkera* sp. produce specific *off* (q.v.)-*odors* in wines (Phaff and Amerine 1979). We do not understand the Australian usage that implies oxidation.

Young The fresh, fruity, unoxidized, and possibly very slightly *yeasty* (q.v.) *odor*. In some young white table wines, it is (+). In red or aged table wines, it is (−). *Fresh* (q.v.) is as good or a better word. Youthful seems to be the same as young. Avoid.

Words to Avoid

It is not our intent to condemn utterly the following terms (although some of them deserve it) for your wine vocabulary, but merely to warn you to use them with caution, if at all. If they *are* used, they should be defined carefully, and their meanings should be understood and agreed upon by all the judges on the panel or in the group.

acute
aggressive[†]
agreeable*[†]
allspice
ample
anise
apple
apricot
asparagus
austere*[†]
austere finish*
awkward[†]
backward*
bacon
banana
beefy (or lack of it)*
beery
beetlike (perhaps)
berry (which?)
big*
bite or biting
blackberry
bramble berry
bramble tannin
breed (or breeding)*
    See style, page 330.
briarwood berries
butterscotch
candy (flavor)
caraway
chalky* (earthy?)
character? (such as
    lots of Nebbiolo
    character)

charm or charming*[†]
chemical
cherry
cherry tartness
chewy
cinnamon
citrus
classic
clean-cut[†]
clean tartness
clovelike
clumsy[†]
coarse*
cold
common*
complete (some
    aspect of
    maturity?)
complicated (some
    aspect of
    complexity?)
concentrated
concrete (or wet-
    concrete odor)
cranberry
crisp
currant
decent[†]
definition (lack of)
deep (bouquet)
delicate* (and
    especially delicate
    tannins)
delicious*

depth (or lack of)
dirty
distinguished*[†]
drying out
dull (taste or odor?)
dumb*[†]
dusty
elegant*[†]
elusive*
empty
enormous
ethereal
evanescent nose
evolved
exciting[†]
fantastic
fat or fatty
feminine[†]
fiery (hot?)
fine*
finesse* (or worse,
    feminine finesse)
finish (or short-)
firm (young?)
flabby (flat?)
flaccid
flashy[†]
fleeting
fleshy
flinty (not even
    for Chablis)
floral
forceful[†]
foreign

---

*Avoid at all costs.
[†]Anthropomorphic, hence avoid.

forward[†]
fragrant or fragrance
full*
gentle*
glorious nose
glycerol
goaty
good (rather good
   is worse)
grace[†]
graceful[†]
grand*
grapefruity
great*
grip*[†]
gutsy[†]
hard* (if acidic, say
   so)
harmonious
harsh*
heady (high ethanol
   or CO_2)
hearty*[†]
heavy* (high
   ethanol?)
hollow*
honest[†]
honeyed
huge*
incomparable*
inelegant
ingratiating*[†]
insinuating*
insipid
integrated
intense*[†]
lackluster (color)

layered (multiple
   layers, layered
   wood, etc.)
lean
leeks
lemonlike
lemony tart
lengthy
licorice
licoricey fruit
light*
lingering*
lithe[†]
little*
lively*
long* (aftertaste?)
lovely[†]
luscious (bouquet?)
lush (lush taste, lush
   fruit, lush tail, etc.;
   reserve for
   alcoholics)
manly[†]
marrowy
masculine[†]
meager*
meaty
medium-dry
medium-sweet
mellow
melon (which?)
metallic
mild*[†]
multifaceted
multilayered
musk or musky
naive*[†]

natural[†]
nervous[†]
noble*[†] (rarely
   definable)
nuance (as of mint)
nutty
off-dry
oily
old (or too-)
orange-honey
orange-marmalade
   (sweetness)
oregano
ordinary*
overbearing[†]
palatable
parsley
passion fruit
peach
pear (unripe)
penetrating*
perfumed (or
   perfumy)
persistent
pine (O.K. in retsina)
pineapple
piquant*
pleasant*[†]
pluminess or
   plumlike
plump
poor*
porty (if oxidized or
   raisiny, say so)
potent
potential
powerful

precocious[†]
pretty[†]
profile
promising (why?)
pronounced
porportioned
pungent
pure*
race
raspberry
redolent
redwood
refreshing*
refined[†]
rich*
robust[†]
rotten (from what?)
round or rounded
rugged[†]
runny
sage
sap
savory
scent or scented
   (certainly not
   scented bouquet, a
   non sequitur?)
seductive[†]
sensuous*[†]
severe[†]
sharp (if vinegary,
   say so)
short-finish (bad?)

sick* (bacterial,
   yeasty, or
   nonbacterial?)
silky*
simple
small* (thin?)
smoky-vanilla
soda pop (flavor)
soft*
solid
sound*
spearmint
spiced
splendid*
steely*
stiff
strange
strong*
sturdy[†]
stylish[†]
suave*[†]
substantial
subtle
sugary finish
sunny
superficial*[†]
supple (and certainly,
   not very)
synthetic
tail (better for cats
   and dogs)
tame*
tang or tangy

tasty*
tender[†]
tenuous
thick
tired*[†]
tough[†]
triumphant
twiggy
unclean (which?)
unpleasant
unresolved (young?)
velvety*
Veronese nose!
vigorous*
vivacious[†]
voluptuous[†]
walnut
warm*
well-bred[†]
wet-straw
wildflower
winey
wintergreen
withered (oxidized?)
wood-berry
woodruff (except in
   May wine and
   vermouth)
wood violet
yucky
zestful[†]

WORDS TO AVOID

It is therefore essential to establish a vocabulary of organoleptic terms—a vocabulary sufficiently rich and precise that each word in the language of enology brings to mind a sensation, just as each word in the language of philosophy brings to mind an idea.

P. POUPON

Il y aurait encore cent outres images possibles suivant le lyrisme du dégustateur. . . .

E. PEYNAUD

APPENDIXES

APPENDIX A–1 Multipliers for estimating significance of difference by range. One-way classification, 5% level.

Number of judges	Number of wines								
	2	3	4	5	6	7	8	9	10
2	3.43	2.35	1.74	1.39	1.15	0.99	0.87	0.77	0.70
	3.43	1.76	1.18	0.88	0.70	0.58	0.50	0.44	0.39
3	1.90	1.44	1.14	0.94	0.80	0.70	0.62	0.56	0.51
	1.90	1.14	0.81	0.63	0.52	0.44	0.38	0.33	0.30
4	1.62	1.25	1.01	0.84	0.72	0.63	0.57	0.51	0.47
	1.62	1.02	0.74	0.58	0.48	0.40	0.35	0.31	0.28
5	1.53	1.19	0.96	0.81	0.70	0.61	0.55	0.50	0.45
	1.53	0.98	0.72	0.56	0.47	0.40	0.34	0.30	0.27
6	1.50	1.17	0.95	0.80	0.69	0.61	0.55	0.49	0.45
	1.50	0.96	0.71	0.56	0.46	0.40	0.34	0.30	0.27
7	1.49	1.17	0.95	0.80	0.69	0.61	0.55	0.50	0.45
	1.49	0.96	0.71	0.56	0.47	0.40	0.35	0.31	0.28
8	1.49	1.18	0.96	0.81	0.70	0.62	0.55	0.50	0.46
	1.49	0.97	0.72	0.57	0.47	0.41	0.35	0.31	0.28
9	1.50	1.19	0.97	0.82	0.71	0.62	0.56	0.51	0.47
	1.50	0.98	0.73	0.58	0.48	0.41	0.36	0.31	0.28
10	1.52	1.20	0.98	0.83	0.72	0.63	0.57	0.52	0.47
	1.52	0.99	0.74	0.59	0.49	0.42	0.37	0.32	0.29
11	1.54	1.22	0.99	0.84	0.73	0.64	0.58	0.52	0.48
	1.54	0.99	0.75	0.60	0.49	0.42	0.37	0.32	0.29
12	1.56	1.23	1.01	0.85	0.74	0.65	0.58	0.53	0.49
	1.56	1.00	0.75	0.60	0.50	0.43	0.38	0.32	0.30

The entries in this table are to be multiplied by the sum of ranges within wines. The upper value must be exceeded by the range in wine totals to indicate significance. If significance is indicated, the lower value must be exceeded by pairs of wine totals to indicate significance between individual wines.

SOURCE: Adapted from unpublished tables compiled by Thomas E. Kurtz, Richard F. Link, John W. Tukey, and David L. Wallace. By permission of John W. Tukey and David L. Wallace.

APPENDIX A-2 Multipliers for estimating significance of difference by range. One-way classification, 1% level.

Number of judges	Number of wines								
	2	3	4	5	6	7	8	9	10
2	7.92	4.32	2.84	2.10	1.66	1.38	1.17	1.02	0.91
	7.92	3.25	1.96	1.39	1.07	0.87	0.74	0.63	0.56
3	3.14	2.12	1.57	1.25	1.04	0.89	0.78	0.69	0.62
	3.14	1.73	1.19	0.91	0.73	0.61	0.53	0.46	0.41
4	2.48	1.74	1.33	1.08	0.91	0.78	0.69	0.62	0.56
	2.48	1.47	1.04	0.80	0.66	0.55	0.48	0.44	0.38
5	2.24	1.60	1.24	1.02	0.86	0.75	0.66	0.59	0.54
	2.24	1.37	0.98	0.77	0.63	0.54	0.47	0.43	0.37
6	2.14	1.55	1.21	0.99	0.85	0.74	0.65	0.59	0.53
	2.14	1.32	0.96	0.76	0.62	0.53	0.46	0.42	0.36
7	2.10	1.53	1.20	0.99	0.84	0.73	0.65	0.59	0.53
	2.10	1.33	0.96	0.76	0.63	0.53	0.46	0.42	0.37
8	2.09	1.53	1.20	0.99	0.85	0.74	0.66	0.59	0.54
	2.09	1.33	0.97	0.77	0.63	0.54	0.47	0.42	0.37
9	2.09	1.54	1.21	1.00	0.85	0.75	0.66	0.60	0.54
	2.09	1.34	0.98	0.77	0.64	0.55	0.48	0.43	0.38
10	2.10	1.55	1.22	1.01	0.86	0.76	0.67	0.61	0.55
	2.10	1.35	0.99	0.78	0.65	0.55	0.48	0.43	0.38
11	2.11	1.56	1.23	1.02	0.87	0.76	0.68	0.61	0.56
	2.11	1.35	0.99	0.78	0.65	0.56	0.49	0.44	0.39
12	2.13	1.58	1.25	1.04	0.89	0.78	0.69	0.62	0.57
	2.13	1.36	1.00	0.79	0.66	0.56	0.49	0.44	0.40

The entries in this table are to be multiplied by the sum of ranges within wines. The upper value must be exceeded by the range in wine totals to indicate significance. If significance is indicated, the lower value must be exceeded by pairs of wine totals to indicate significance between individual wines.

SOURCE: Adapted from unpublished tables compiled by Thomas E. Kurtz, Richard F. Link, John W. Tukey, and David L. Wallace. By permission of John Tukey and David L. Wallace.

APPENDIX B-1 Multipliers for estimating significance of difference by range. Two-way classification, 5% level.

Number of judges	Number of wines										
	2	3	4	5	6	7	8	9	10	11	12
2	6.35	2.19	1.52	1.16	0.94	0.79	0.69	0.60	0.54	0.49	0.45
	6.35	1.96	1.39	1.12	0.95	0.84	0.76	0.70	0.65	0.61	0.58
3	1.96	1.14	0.88	0.72	0.61	0.53	0.47	0.42	0.38	0.35	0.32
	2.19	1.14	0.90	0.76	0.67	0.61	0.56	0.52	0.49	0.46	0.44
4	1.43	0.96	0.76	0.63	0.54	0.47	0.42	0.38	0.34	0.31	0.29
	1.54	0.93	0.76	0.65	0.58	0.53	0.49	0.45	0.43	0.40	0.38
5	1.27	0.89	0.71	0.60	0.51	0.45	0.40	0.36	0.33	0.30	0.28
	1.28	0.84	0.69	0.60	0.53	0.49	0.45	0.42	0.40	0.38	0.36
6	1.19	0.87	0.70	0.58	0.50	0.44	0.39	0.36	0.33	0.30	0.28
	1.14	0.78	0.64	0.56	0.50	0.46	0.43	0.40	0.38	0.36	0.34
7	1.16	0.86	0.69	0.58	0.50	0.44	0.40	0.36	0.33	0.30	0.28
	1.06	0.74	0.62	0.54	0.48	0.44	0.41	0.38	0.36	0.34	0.33
8	1.15	0.86	0.69	0.58	0.50	0.44	0.40	0.36	0.33	0.30	0.28
	1.01	0.71	0.59	0.52	0.47	0.43	0.40	0.37	0.35	0.33	0.32
9	1.15	0.86	0.70	0.59	0.51	0.45	0.40	0.36	0.33	0.31	0.29
	0.97	0.69	0.58	0.51	0.46	0.42	0.39	0.36	0.34	0.33	0.31
10	1.15	0.87	0.71	0.60	0.51	0.45	0.41	0.37	0.34	0.31	0.29
	0.93	0.67	0.56	0.50	0.45	0.41	0.38	0.36	0.34	0.32	0.31
11	1.16	0.88	0.71	0.60	0.52	0.46	0.41	0.37	0.34	0.32	0.29
	0.91	0.66	0.55	0.49	0.44	0.40	0.38	0.35	0.33	0.32	0.30
12	1.16	0.89	0.72	0.61	0.53	0.47	0.42	0.38	0.35	0.32	0.30
	0.89	0.65	0.55	0.48	0.43	0.40	0.37	0.35	0.33	0.31	0.30

The entries in this table are to be multiplied by the sum of the ranges of differences between adjacent wine scores to obtain the difference required for significance for wine totals (use upper entry) and/or judge totals (use lower entry).

SOURCE: Adapted from unpublished tables compiled by Thomas E. Kurtz, Richard F. Link, John W. Tukey, and David L. Wallace. By permission of John W. Tukey and David L. Wallace.

APPENDIX B-2 Multipliers for estimating significance of difference by range. Two-way classification, 1% level.

Number of judges	Number of wines										
	2	3	4	5	6	7	8	9	10	11	12
2	31.83	5.00	2.91	2.00	1.51	1.20	1.00	0.86	0.75	0.66	0.60
	31.83	4.51	2.72	1.99	1.59	1.35	1.19	1.07	0.97	0.90	0.84
3	4.51	1.84	1.31	1.01	0.82	0.70	0.60	0.53	0.48	0.43	0.39
	5.00	1.84	1.35	1.10	0.94	0.83	0.76	0.69	0.65	0.61	0.57
4	2.63	1.40	1.04	0.83	0.69	0.59	0.52	0.46	0.42	0.38	0.35
	2.75	1.35	1.04	0.87	0.76	0.68	0.63	0.58	0.54	0.51	0.48
5	2.11	1.25	0.95	0.77	0.64	0.56	0.49	0.44	0.40	0.36	0.33
	2.05	1.14	0.90	0.77	0.68	0.61	0.56	0.52	0.49	0.46	0.44
6	1.88	1.18	0.91	0.74	0.63	0.54	0.48	0.43	0.39	0.36	0.33
	1.71	1.02	0.82	0.71	0.63	0.57	0.52	0.49	0.46	0.43	0.41
7	1.78	1.15	0.89	0.73	0.62	0.54	0.48	0.43	0.39	0.36	0.33
	1.52	0.95	0.77	0.66	0.59	0.54	0.50	0.46	0.44	0.41	0.39
8	1.72	1.14	0.89	0.73	0.62	0.54	0.48	0.43	0.39	0.36	0.33
	1.40	0.90	0.73	0.63	0.57	0.52	0.48	0.45	0.42	0.40	0.38
9	1.69	1.14	0.89	0.73	0.62	0.54	0.48	0.43	0.39	0.36	0.33
	1.31	0.86	0.71	0.61	0.55	0.50	0.46	0.43	0.41	0.39	0.37
10	1.67	1.14	0.89	0.74	0.63	0.55	0.48	0.44	0.40	0.36	0.34
	1.24	0.83	0.68	0.59	0.53	0.49	0.45	0.42	0.40	0.38	0.36
11	1.67	1.15	0.90	0.74	0.63	0.55	0.49	0.44	0.40	0.37	0.34
	1.19	0.80	0.67	0.58	0.52	0.48	0.44	0.41	0.39	0.37	0.35
12	1.67	1.15	0.91	0.75	0.64	0.56	0.50	0.45	0.41	0.37	0.35
	1.15	0.78	0.65	0.57	0.51	0.47	0.43	0.41	0.38	0.36	0.35

The entries in this table are to be multiplied by the sum of the ranges of differences between adjacent wine scores to obtain the difference required for significance for wine totals (use upper entry) and/or judge totals (use lower entry).

SOURCE: Adapted from unpublished tables compiled by Thomas E. Kurtz, Richard F. Link, John W. Tukey, and David L. Wallace. By permission of John W. Tukey and David L. Wallace.

APPENDIX C   Normal distribution.

The entries in this table are the areas under the normal
probability curve to the right of the marginal value of the normal
deviate z (or to the left of $-z$); that is, they are the probabilities
that a random value of z will equal or exceed the marginal value.

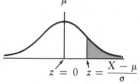

z	.00	.01	.02	.03	.04	.05	.06	.07	.08	.09
0.0	.5000	.4960	.4920	.4880	.4840	.4801	.4761	.4721	.4681	.4641
0.1	.4602	.4562	.4522	.4483	.4443	.4404	.4364	.4325	.4286	.4247
0.2	.4207	.4168	.4129	.4090	.4052	.4013	.3974	.3936	.3897	.3859
0.3	.3821	.3783	.3745	.3707	.3669	.3632	.3594	.3557	.3520	.3483
0.4	.3446	.3409	.3372	.3336	.3300	.3264	.3228	.3192	.3156	.3121
0.5	.3085	.3050	.3015	.2981	.2946	.2912	.2877	.2843	.2810	.2776
0.6	.2743	.2709	.2676	.2643	.2611	.2578	.2546	.2514	.2483	.2451
0.7	.2420	.2389	.2358	.2327	.2296	.2266	.2236	.2206	.2177	.2148
0.8	.2119	.2090	.2061	.2033	.2005	.1977	.1949	.1922	.1894	.1867
0.9	.1841	.1814	.1788	.1762	.1736	.1711	.1685	.1660	.1635	.1611
1.0	.1587	.1562	.1539	.1515	.1492	.1469	.1446	.1423	.1401	.1379
1.1	.1357	.1335	.1314	.1292	.1271	.1251	.1230	.1210	.1190	.1170
1.2	.1151	.1131	.1112	.1093	.1075	.1056	.1038	.1020	.1003	.0985
1.3	.0968	.0951	.0934	.0918	.0901	.0885	.0869	.0853	.0838	.0823
1.4	.0808	.0793	.0778	.0764	.0749	.0735	.0721	.0708	.0694	.0681
1.5	.0668	.0655	.0643	.0630	.0618	.0606	.0594	.0582	.0571	.0559
1.6	.0548	.0537	.0526	.0516	.0505	.0495	.0485	.0475	.0465	.0455
1.7	.0446	.0436	.0427	.0418	.0409	.0401	.0392	.0384	.0375	.0367
1.8	.0359	.0351	.0344	.0336	.0329	.0322	.0314	.0307	.0301	.0294
1.9	.0287	.0281	.0274	.0268	.0262	.0256	.0250	.0244	.0239	.0233
2.0	.0228	.0222	.0217	.0212	.0207	.0202	.0197	.0192	.0188	.0183
2.1	.0179	.0174	.0170	.0166	.0162	.0158	.0154	.0150	.0146	.0143
2.2	.0139	.0136	.0132	.0129	.0125	.0122	.0119	.0116	.0113	.0110
2.3	.0107	.0104	.0102	.0099	.0096	.0094	.0091	.0089	.0087	.0084
2.4	.0082	.0080	.0078	.0075	.0073	.0071	.0069	.0068	.0066	.0064
2.5	.0062	.0060	.0059	.0057	.0055	.0054	.0052	.0051	.0049	.0048
2.6	.0047	.0045	.0044	.0043	.0041	.0040	.0039	.0038	.0037	.0036
2.7	.0035	.0034	.0033	.0032	.0031	.0030	.0029	.0028	.0027	.0026
2.8	.0026	.0026	.0024	.0023	.0023	.0022	.0021	.0021	.0020	.0019
2.9	.0019	.0018	.0018	.0017	.0016	.0016	.0015	.0015	.0014	.0014
3.0	.0013	.0013	.0013	.0012	.0012	.0011	.0011	.0011	.0010	.0010
3.1	.0010	.0009	.0009	.0009	.0008	.0008	.0008	.0008	.0007	.0007
3.2	.0007	.0007	.0006	.0006	.0006	.0006	.0006	.0005	.0005	.0005
3.3	.0005	.0005	.0005	.0004	.0004	.0004	.0004	.0004	.0004	.0003
3.4	.0003	.0003	.0003	.0003	.0003	.0003	.0003	.0003	.0003	.0002
3.6	.0002	.0002	.0001	.0001	.0001	.0001	.0001	.0001	.0001	.0001
3.9	.0000									

APPENDIX D Chi-square distribution.

The entries in this table are the χ^2-values for distributions with from 1 to 30 degrees of freedom, at 10 values of the probability.

df	Probability of a larger value of χ^2									
	0.99	0.95	0.50	0.30	0.20	0.10	0.05	0.02	0.01	0.001
1	0.0002	0.004	0.46	1.07	1.64	2.71	3.84	5.41	6.64	10.83
2	0.020	0.103	1.39	2.41	3.22	4.60	5.99	7.82	9.21	13.82
3	0.115	0.35	2.37	3.66	4.64	6.25	7.82	9.84	11.34	16.27
4	0.30	0.71	3.36	4.88	5.99	7.78	9.49	11.67	13.28	18.46
5	0.55	1.14	4.35	6.06	7.29	9.24	11.07	13.39	15.09	20.52
6	0.87	1.64	5.35	7.23	8.56	10.64	12.59	15.03	16.81	22.46
7	1.24	2.17	6.35	8.38	9.80	12.02	14.07	16.62	18.48	24.32
8	1.65	2.73	7.34	9.52	11.03	13.36	15.51	18.17	20.09	26.12
9	2.09	3.32	8.34	10.66	12.24	14.68	16.92	19.68	21.67	27.88
10	2.56	3.94	9.34	11.78	13.44	15.99	18.31	21.16	23.21	29.59
11	3.05	4.58	10.34	12.90	14.63	17.28	19.68	22.62	24.72	31.26
12	3.57	5.23	11.34	14.01	15.81	18.55	21.03	24.05	26.22	32.91
13	4.11	5.89	12.34	15.12	16.98	19.81	22.36	25.47	27.69	34.53
14	4.66	6.57	13.34	16.22	18.15	21.06	23.68	26.87	29.14	36.12
15	5.23	7.26	14.34	17.32	19.31	22.31	25.00	28.26	30.58	37.70
16	5.81	7.96	15.34	18.42	20.46	23.54	26.30	29.63	32.00	39.25
17	6.41	8.67	16.34	19.51	21.62	24.77	27.59	31.00	33.41	40.79
18	7.02	9.39	17.34	20.60	22.76	25.99	28.87	32.35	34.80	42.31
19	7.63	10.12	18.34	21.69	23.90	27.20	30.14	33.69	36.19	43.82
20	8.26	10.85	19.34	22.78	25.04	28.41	31.41	35.02	37.57	45.32
21	8.90	11.59	20.34	23.86	26.17	29.62	32.67	36.34	38.93	46.80
22	9.54	12.34	21.34	24.94	27.30	30.81	33.92	37.66	40.29	48.27
23	10.20	13.09	22.34	26.02	28.43	32.01	35.17	38.97	41.64	49.73
24	10.86	13.85	23.34	27.10	29.55	33.20	36.42	40.27	42.98	51.18
25	11.52	14.61	24.34	28.17	30.68	34.38	37.65	41.57	44.31	52.62
26	12.20	15.38	25.34	29.25	31.80	35.56	38.88	42.86	45.64	54.05
27	12.88	16.15	26.34	30.32	32.91	36.74	40.11	44.14	46.96	55.48
28	13.56	16.93	27.34	31.39	34.03	37.92	41.34	45.42	48.28	56.89
29	14.26	17.71	28.34	32.46	35.14	39.09	42.56	46.69	49.59	58.30
30	14.95	18.49	29.34	33.53	36.25	40.26	43.77	47.96	50.89	59.70

SOURCE: Abridged from Table IV of R. A. Fisher and F. Yates, *Statistical Tables for Biological, Agricultural, and Medical Research*, 6th ed., 1974. Longman Group Ltd., London (previously published by Oliver and Boyd Ltd., Edinburgh). By permission of the authors and publisher.

APPENDIX E
Minimum numbers of correct judgments to establish significance at various probability levels for paired-difference and duo–trio tests (one-tailed, $p = \frac{1}{2}$)*.

No. of trials (n)	Probability levels						
	0.05	0.04	0.03	0.02	0.01	0.005	0.001
7	7	7	7	7	7		
8	7	7	8	8	8	8	
9	8	8	8	8	9	9	
10	9	9	9	9	10	10	10
11	9	9	10	10	10	11	11
12	10	10	10	10	11	11	12
13	10	11	11	11	12	12	13
14	11	11	11	12	12	13	13
15	12	12	12	12	13	13	14
16	12	12	13	13	14	14	15
17	13	13	13	14	14	15	16
18	13	14	14	14	15	15	16
19	14	14	15	15	15	16	17
20	15	15	15	16	16	17	18
21	15	15	16	16	17	17	18
22	16	16	16	17	17	18	19
23	16	17	17	17	18	19	20
24	17	17	18	18	19	19	20
25	18	18	18	19	19	20	21
26	18	18	19	19	20	20	22
27	19	19	19	20	20	21	22
28	19	20	20	20	21	22	23
29	20	20	21	21	22	22	24
30	20	21	21	22	22	23	24
31	21	21	22	22	23	24	25
32	22	22	22	23	24	24	26
33	22	23	23	23	24	25	26
34	23	23	23	24	25	25	27
35	23	24	24	25	25	26	27

*Values (X) not appearing in table may be derived from $X = (n + z\sqrt{n} + 1)/2$.

SOURCE: Abridged from tables compiled by E. B. Roessler, R. M. Pangborn, J. L. Sidel, and H. Stone, *J. Food Sci*. 43: 940–943 (1978).

No. of trials (n)	Probability levels						
	0.05	0.04	0.03	0.02	0.01	0.005	0.001
36	24	24	25	25	26	27	28
37	24	25	25	26	26	27	29
38	25	25	26	26	27	28	29
39	26	26	26	27	28	28	30
40	26	27	27	27	28	29	30
41	27	27	27	28	29	30	31
42	27	28	28	29	29	30	32
43	28	28	29	29	30	31	32
44	28	29	29	30	31	31	33
45	29	29	30	30	31	32	34
46	30	30	30	31	32	33	34
47	30	30	31	31	32	33	35
48	31	31	31	32	33	34	36
49	31	32	32	33	34	34	36
50	32	32	33	33	34	35	37
60	37	38	38	39	40	41	43
70	43	43	44	45	46	47	49
80	48	49	49	50	51	52	55
90	54	54	55	56	57	58	61
100	59	60	60	61	63	64	66

APPENDIX F Minimum numbers of agreeing judgments necessary to establish significance at various probability levels for the paired-preference test (two-tailed, $p = \frac{1}{2}$)*.

No. of trials (n)	Probability levels						
	0.05	0.04	0.03	0.02	0.01	0.005	0.001
7	7	7	7	7			
8	8	8	8	8	8		
9	8	8	9	9	9	9	
10	9	9	9	10	10	10	
11	10	10	10	10	11	11	11
12	10	10	11	11	11	12	12
13	11	11	11	12	12	12	13
14	12	12	12	12	13	13	14
15	12	12	13	13	13	14	14
16	13	13	13	14	14	14	15
17	13	14	14	14	15	15	16
18	14	14	15	15	15	16	17
19	15	15	15	15	16	16	17
20	15	16	16	16	17	17	18
21	16	16	16	17	17	18	19
22	17	17	17	17	18	18	19
23	17	17	18	18	19	19	20
24	18	18	18	19	19	20	21
25	18	19	19	19	20	20	21
26	19	19	19	20	20	21	22
27	20	20	20	20	21	22	23
28	20	20	21	21	22	22	23
29	21	21	21	22	22	23	24
30	21	22	22	22	23	24	25
31	22	22	22	23	24	24	25
32	23	23	23	23	24	25	26
33	23	23	24	24	25	25	27
34	24	24	24	25	25	26	27
35	24	25	25	25	26	27	28

*Values (X) not appearing in table may be derived from $X = (n + z\sqrt{n} + 1)/2$.

Source: Abridged from tables compiled by E. B. Roessler, R. M. Pangborn, J. L. Sidel, and H. Stone, *J. Food Sci.* 43: 940–943 (1978).

No. of trials (n)	Probability levels						
	0.05	0.04	0.03	0.02	0.01	0.005	0.001
36	25	25	25	26	27	27	29
37	25	26	26	26	27	28	29
38	26	26	27	27	28	29	30
39	27	27	27	28	28	29	31
40	27	27	28	28	29	30	31
41	28	28	28	29	30	30	32
42	28	29	29	29	30	31	32
43	29	29	30	30	31	32	33
44	29	30	30	30	31	32	34
45	30	30	31	31	32	33	34
46	31	31	31	32	33	33	35
47	31	31	32	32	33	34	36
48	32	32	32	33	34	35	36
49	32	33	33	34	34	35	37
50	33	33	34	34	35	36	37
60	39	39	39	40	41	42	44
70	44	45	45	46	47	48	50
80	50	50	51	51	52	53	56
90	55	56	56	57	58	59	61
100	61	61	62	63	64	65	67

APPENDIX G Minimum numbers of correct judgments to establish significance at various probability levels for the triangle test (one-tailed, $p = \frac{1}{3}$)*.

No. of trials (n)	Probability levels						
	0.05	0.04	0.03	0.02	0.01	0.005	0.001
5	4	5	5	5	5	5	
6	5	5	5	5	6	6	
7	5	6	6	6	6	7	7
8	6	6	6	6	7	7	8
9	6	7	7	7	7	8	8
10	7	7	7	7	8	8	9
11	7	7	8	8	8	9	10
12	8	8	8	8	9	9	10
13	8	8	9	9	9	10	11
14	9	9	9	9	10	10	11
15	9	9	10	10	10	11	12
16	9	10	10	10	11	11	12
17	10	10	10	11	11	12	13
18	10	11	11	11	12	12	13
19	11	11	11	12	12	13	14
20	11	11	12	12	13	13	14
21	12	12	12	13	13	14	15
22	12	12	13	13	14	14	15
23	12	13	13	13	14	15	16
24	13	13	13	14	15	15	16
25	13	14	14	14	15	16	17
26	14	14	14	15	15	16	17
27	14	14	15	15	16	17	18
28	15	15	15	16	16	17	18
29	15	15	16	16	17	17	19
30	15	16	16	16	17	18	19

*Values (X) not appearing in table may be derived from $X = (2n + 2.83\ z\sqrt{n} + 3)/6$.

SOURCE: Abridged from tables compiled by E. B. Roessler, R. M. Pangborn, J. L. Sidel, and H. Stone, *J. Food Sci.* 43: 940–943 (1978).

No. of trials (n)	Probability levels						
	0.05	0.04	0.03	0.02	0.01	0.005	0.001
31	16	16	16	17	18	18	20
32	16	16	17	17	18	19	20
33	17	17	17	18	18	19	21
34	17	17	18	18	19	20	21
35	17	18	18	19	19	20	22
36	18	18	18	19	20	20	22
37	18	18	19	19	20	21	22
38	19	19	19	20	21	21	23
39	19	19	20	20	21	22	23
40	19	20	20	21	21	22	24
41	20	20	20	21	22	23	24
42	20	20	21	21	22	23	25
43	20	21	21	22	23	24	25
44	21	21	22	22	23	24	26
45	21	22	22	23	24	24	26
46	22	22	22	23	24	25	27
47	22	22	23	23	24	25	27
48	22	23	23	24	25	26	27
49	23	23	24	24	25	26	28
50	23	24	24	25	26	26	28
60	27	27	28	29	30	31	33
70	31	31	32	33	34	35	37
80	35	35	36	36	38	39	41
90	38	39	40	40	42	43	45
100	42	43	43	44	45	47	49

APPENDIX H Probability of X or more correct judgments in n trials (one-tailed, $p = q = \frac{1}{2}$).

n \ X	0	1	2	3	4	5	6	7	8	9	10	11	12	13	14	15
5		969	812	500	188	031										
6		984	891	656	344	109	016									
7		992	938	773	500	227	062	008								
8		996	965	855	637	363	145	035	004							
9		998	980	910	746	500	254	090	020	002						
10		999	989	945	828	623	377	172	055	011	001					
11			994	967	887	726	500	274	113	033	006	003				
12			997	981	927	806	613	387	194	073	019	011	002			
13			998	989	954	867	709	500	291	133	046	011	006	001		
14			999	994	971	910	788	605	395	212	090	029	018	004	002	
15				996	982	941	849	696	500	304	151	059	038	011	006	001
16				998	989	962	895	773	598	402	227	105	072	025	015	004
17				999	994	975	928	834	685	500	315	166	119	048	032	010
18				999	996	985	952	881	760	593	407	240	180	084	058	021
19					998	990	968	916	820	676	500	324	252	132	095	039
20					999	994	979	942	868	748	588	412	332	192	143	067
21					999	996	987	961	905	808	668	500	416	262	202	105
22						998	992	974	933	857	738	584	500	339	262	154
23						999	995	983	953	895	798	661	581	419	271	154
24						999	997	989	968	924	846	729	581	419	271	154
25							998	993	978	946	885	788	655	500	345	212

26	279	423	577	721	837	916	962	986	995	999
27	351	500	649	779	876	939	974	990	997	999
28	425	575	714	828	908	956	982	994	998	
29	500	644	771	868	932	969	988	996	999	
30	572	708	819	900	951	979	992	997	999	
31	640	763	859	925	965	985	995	998		
32	702	811	892	945	975	990	997	999		
33	757	852	919	960	982	993	998	999		
34	804	885	939	971	988	995	999			
35	845	912	955	980	992	997	999			
36	879	934	967	986	994	998	999			
37	906	951	976	990	996	999				
38	928	964	983	993	997	999				
39	946	973	988	995	998	999				
40	960	981	992	997	999					
41	970	986	994	998	999					
42	978	990	996	999						
43	984	993	997	999						
44	989	995	998	999						
45	992	997	999							
46	994	998	999							
47	996	998	999							
48	996	999								
49	998	999								
50	999									

NOTE: Initial decimal points have been omitted.

SOURCE: Abridged from tables compiled by E. B. Roessler, R. M. Pangborn, J. L. Sidel, and H. Stone, J. Food Sci. 43: 940–943 (1978).

APPENDIX I Probability of X or more correct judgments in n trials (one-tailed, $p = \frac{1}{3}$).

n \ X	0	1	2	3	4	5	6	7	8	9	10	11	12	13	14	15
5		868	539	210	045	004										
6		912	649	320	100	018	001									
7		941	737	429	173	045	007									
8		961	805	532	259	088	020	003								
9		974	857	623	350	145	042	008	001							
10		983	896	701	441	213	077	020	003							
11		988	925	766	527	289	122	039	009	001						
12		992	946	819	607	368	178	066	019	004						
13		995	961	861	678	448	241	104	035	009	002					
14		997	973	895	739	524	310	149	058	017	004	001				
15		998	981	921	791	596	382	203	088	031	008	002				
16		998	986	941	834	661	453	263	126	050	016	004	001			
17		999	990	956	870	719	522	326	172	075	027	008	002			
18		999	993	967	898	769	588	391	223	108	043	014	004	001		
19		999	995	976	921	812	648	457	279	146	065	024	007	002		
20			997	982	940	848	703	521	339	191	092	038	013	004	001	
21			998	987	954	879	751	581	399	240	125	056	021	007	002	
22			998	991	965	904	794	638	460	293	163	079	033	012	003	001
23			999	993	974	924	831	690	519	349	206	107	048	019	006	002
24			999	995	980	941	862	737	576	406	254	140	068	028	010	003
25			999	996	985	954	888	778	630	462	304	178	092	042	016	006

26	009	025	058	121	220	357	518	679	815	910	964	989	997
27	014	036	079	154	266	411	572	725	847	928	972	992	998
28	022	050	104	191	314	464	623	765	874	943	979	994	999
29	031	068	133	232	364	517	670	801	897	955	984	996	999
30	043	090	166	276	415	568	714	833	916	965	988	997	999
31	059	115	203	322	466	617	754	861	932	972	991	998	
32	078	144	243	370	516	662	789	885	946	978	993	998	
33	100	177	285	419	565	705	821	905	957	983	995	999	
34	126	213	330	468	612	744	849	922	965	987	996	999	
35	155	252	376	516	656	779	873	937	973	990	997	999	
36	187	293	422	562	697	810	895	949	978	992	998		
37	223	336	469	607	735	838	913	959	983	994	998		
38	261	381	515	650	769	863	928	967	987	996	999		
39	301	425	560	689	800	885	941	973	990	997	999		
40	342	470	603	726	829	903	952	979	992	997	999		
41	385	515	644	761	854	920	961	983	994	998			
42	428	558	683	791	876	933	968	987	995	999			
43	471	600	719	820	895	945	974	990	996	999			
44	514	639	753	845	912	955	980	992	997	999			
45	556	677	783	867	926	963	984	994	998	999			
46	596	713	811	887	938	970	987	995	998				
47	635	745	836	904	949	976	990	996	998				
48	672	776	859	919	958	980	992	997	999				
49	706	803	879	932	965	984	994	998	999				
50	739	829	896	943	972	987	995	998	999				

NOTE: Initial decimal points have been omitted.

SOURCE: Abridged from tables compiled by E. B. Roessler, R. M. Pangborn, J. L. Sidel, and H. Stone, *J. Food Sci.* 43: 940–943 (1978).

APPENDIX J   Probability of X or more agreeing judgments in n trials (two-tailed, $p = q = \frac{1}{2}$).

n \ X	3	4	5	6	7	8	9	10	11	12	13	14	15	16	17	18	19
5	625	312	062														
6		688	219	031													
7			453	125	016												
8			727	289	070	008											
9				508	180	039	004										
10				754	344	109	021	002									
11					549	227	065	011	001								
12					774	388	146	039	006								
13						581	267	092	022	003							
14						791	424	180	057	013	002						
15							607	302	118	035	007	001					
16							804	454	210	077	021	004	001				
17								629	332	143	049	013	002				
18								815	481	238	096	031	008	001			
19									648	359	167	064	019	004	001		
20									824	503	263	115	041	012	003		
21										664	383	189	078	027	007	001	
22										832	523	286	134	052	017	004	001
23											678	405	210	093	035	011	003

n\X	13	14	15	16	17	18	19	20	21	22	23	24	25	26	27	28	29
24	839	541	307	152	064	023	007	002									
25		690	424	230	108	043	015	004	001								
26		845	557	327	169	076	029	009	002	001							
27			701	442	248	122	052	019	006	002							
28			851	572	345	185	087	036	013	004	001						
29				711	458	265	136	061	024	008	002						
30				856	585	362	200	099	043	016	005	001					
31					720	473	281	150	071	030	011	003	001				
32					860	597	377	215	100	050	020	007	002	001			
33						728	487	296	163	080	035	014	005	001			
34						864	608	392	229	121	058	024	009	003	001		
35							736	500	310	175	090	041	017	006	002		
36							868	618	405	243	132	065	029	011	004	001	
37								743	511	324	188	099	047	020	008	003	001
38								871	627	418	256	143	073	034	014	005	002

NOTE: Initial decimal points have been omitted.

SOURCE: Abridged from tables compiled by E. B. Roessler, R. M. Pangborn, J. L. Sidel, and H. Stone. *J. Food Sci.* 43: 940–943 (1978).

APPENDIX K t-distribution.

The entries in this table are the t-values for distributions with from 1 to ∞ degrees of freedom, at 10 values of the two-tailed probability (sum of the two tail areas) and the 10 corresponding values of the one-tailed probability (one tail area).

df	Probability of a larger value of t, sign ignored (two-tailed test)									
	0.5	0.4	0.3	0.2	0.1	0.05	0.02	0.01	0.002	0.001
1	1.000	1.376	1.963	3.078	6.314	12.706	31.821	63.657	318.31	636.619
2	0.816	1.061	1.386	1.886	2.920	4.303	6.965	9.925	22.327	31.598
3	0.765	0.978	1.250	1.638	2.353	3.182	4.541	5.841	10.214	12.941
4	0.741	0.941	1.190	1.533	2.132	2.776	3.747	4.604	7.173	8.610
5	0.727	0.920	1.156	1.476	2.015	2.571	3.365	4.032	5.893	6.859
6	0.718	0.906	1.134	1.440	1.943	2.447	3.143	3.707	5.208	5.959
7	0.711	0.896	1.119	1.415	1.895	2.365	2.998	3.499	4.785	5.405
8	0.706	0.889	1.108	1.397	1.860	2.306	2.896	3.355	4.501	5.041
9	0.703	0.883	1.100	1.383	1.833	2.262	2.821	3.250	4.297	4.781
10	0.700	0.879	1.093	1.372	1.812	2.228	2.764	3.169	4.144	4.587
11	0.697	0.876	1.088	1.363	1.796	2.201	2.718	3.106	4.025	4.437
12	0.695	0.873	1.083	1.356	1.782	2.179	2.681	3.055	3.930	4.318
13	0.694	0.870	1.079	1.350	1.771	2.160	2.650	3.012	3.852	4.221
14	0.692	0.868	1.076	1.345	1.761	2.145	2.624	2.977	3.787	4.140
15	0.691	0.866	1.074	1.341	1.753	2.131	2.602	2.947	3.733	4.073
16	0.690	0.865	1.071	1.337	1.746	2.120	2.583	2.921	3.686	4.015
17	0.689	0.863	1.069	1.333	1.740	2.110	2.567	2.898	3.646	3.965
18	0.688	0.862	1.067	1.330	1.734	2.101	2.552	2.878	3.610	3.922
19	0.688	0.861	1.066	1.328	1.729	2.093	2.539	2.861	3.579	3.883
20	0.687	0.860	1.064	1.325	1.725	2.086	2.528	2.845	3.552	3.850

df	0.25	0.2	0.15	0.1	0.05	0.025	0.01	0.005	0.001	0.0005
21	0.686	0.859	1.063	1.323	1.721	2.030	2.518	2.831	3.527	3.819
22	0.686	0.858	1.061	1.321	1.717	2.074	2.508	2.819	3.505	3.792
23	0.685	0.858	1.060	1.319	1.714	2.059	2.500	2.807	3.485	3.767
24	0.685	0.857	1.059	1.318	1.711	2.064	2.492	2.797	3.467	3.745
25	0.684	0.856	1.058	1.316	1.708	2.060	2.485	2.787	3.450	3.725
26	0.684	0.856	1.058	1.315	1.706	2.056	2.479	2.779	3.435	3.707
27	0.684	0.855	1.057	1.314	1.703	2.052	2.473	2.771	3.421	3.690
28	0.683	0.855	1.056	1.313	1.701	2.048	2.467	2.763	3.408	3.674
29	0.683	0.854	1.055	1.311	1.699	2.045	2.462	2.756	3.396	3.659
30	0.683	0.854	1.055	1.310	1.697	2.042	2.457	2.750	3.385	3.646
40	0.681	0.851	1.050	1.303	1.684	2.021	2.423	2.704	3.307	3.551
60	0.679	0.848	1.046	1.296	1.671	2.000	2.390	2.660	3.232	3.460
120	0.677	0.845	1.041	1.289	1.658	1.980	2.358	2.617	3.160	3.373
∞	0.674	0.842	1.036	1.282	1.645	1.960	2.326	2.576	3.090	3.291

Probability of a larger value of t, sign considered (one-tailed test)

SOURCE: Abridged from Table III of R. A. Fisher and F. Yates, *Statistical Tables for Biological, Agricultural, and Medical Research*, 6th ed., 1974. Longman Group Ltd., London (previously published by Oliver and Boyd Ltd., Edinburgh). By permission of the authors and publisher.

APPENDIX L-1 F-distribution, 5% level.

The entries in this table are the F-values for which the tail area equals 0.05.

0.05

	df for numerator									
df for denominator	1	2	3	4	5	6	8	12	24	∞
1	161.4	199.5	215.7	224.6	230.2	234.0	238.9	243.9	249.0	254.3
2	18.51	19.00	19.16	19.25	19.30	19.33	19.37	19.41	19.45	19.50
3	10.13	9.55	9.28	9.12	9.01	8.94	8.84	8.74	8.64	8.53
4	7.71	6.94	6.59	6.39	6.26	6.16	6.04	5.91	5.77	5.63
5	6.61	5.79	5.41	5.19	5.05	4.95	4.82	4.68	4.53	4.36
6	5.99	5.14	4.76	4.53	4.39	4.28	4.15	4.00	3.84	3.67
7	5.59	4.74	4.35	4.12	3.97	3.87	3.73	3.57	3.41	3.23
8	5.32	4.46	4.07	3.84	3.69	3.58	3.44	3.28	3.12	2.93
9	5.12	4.26	3.86	3.63	3.48	3.37	3.23	3.07	2.90	2.71
10	4.96	4.10	3.71	3.48	3.33	3.22	3.07	2.91	2.74	2.54
11	4.84	3.98	3.59	3.36	3.20	3.09	2.95	2.79	2.61	2.40
12	4.75	3.88	3.49	3.26	3.11	3.00	2.85	2.69	2.50	2.30
13	4.67	3.80	3.41	3.18	3.02	2.92	2.77	2.60	2.42	2.21
14	4.60	3.74	3.34	3.11	2.96	2.85	2.70	2.53	2.35	2.13
15	4.54	3.68	3.29	3.06	2.90	2.79	2.64	2.48	2.29	2.07
16	4.49	3.63	3.24	3.01	2.85	2.74	2.59	2.42	2.24	2.01
17	4.45	3.59	3.20	2.96	2.81	2.70	2.55	2.38	2.19	1.96
18	4.41	3.55	3.16	2.93	2.77	2.66	2.51	2.34	2.15	1.92
19	4.38	3.52	3.13	2.90	2.74	2.63	2.48	2.31	2.11	1.88
20	4.35	3.49	3.10	2.87	2.71	2.60	2.45	2.28	2.08	1.84

21	4.32	3.47	3.07	2.84	2.63	2.57	2.42	2.25	2.05	1.81
22	4.30	3.44	3.05	2.82	2.65	2.55	2.40	2.23	2.03	1.78
23	4.28	3.42	3.03	2.80	2.64	2.53	2.38	2.20	2.00	1.76
24	4.26	3.40	3.01	2.78	2.62	2.51	2.36	2.18	1.98	1.73
25	4.24	3.38	2.99	2.76	2.60	2.49	2.34	2.16	1.96	1.71
26	4.22	3.37	2.98	2.74	2.59	2.47	2.32	2.15	1.95	1.69
27	4.21	3.35	2.96	2.73	2.57	2.46	2.30	2.13	1.93	1.67
28	4.20	3.34	2.95	2.71	2.56	2.44	2.29	2.12	1.91	1.65
29	4.18	3.33	2.93	2.70	2.54	2.43	2.28	2.10	1.90	1.64
30	4.17	3.32	2.92	2.69	2.53	2.42	2.27	2.09	1.89	1.62
40	4.08	3.23	2.84	2.61	2.45	2.34	2.18	2.00	1.79	1.51
60	4.00	3.15	2.76	2.52	2.37	2.25	2.10	1.92	1.70	1.39
120	3.92	3.07	2.68	2.45	2.29	2.17	2.02	1.83	1.61	1.25
∞	3.84	2.99	2.60	2.37	2.21	2.10	1.94	1.75	1.52	1.00

SOURCE: Abridged from Table V of R. A. Fisher and F. Yates, *Statistical Tables for Biological, Agricultural, and Medical Research*, 6th ed., 1974. Longman Group Ltd., London (previously published by Oliver and Boyd Ltd., Edinburgh). By permission of the authors and publisher.

APPENDIX L–2   *F*-distribution, 1% level.

The entries in this table are the *F*-values for which the tail area equals 0.01.

0.01

df for denominator	df for numerator									
	1	2	3	4	5	6	8	12	24	∞
1	4052	4999	5403	5625	5764	5859	5982	6106	6234	6366
2	98.50	99.00	99.17	99.25	99.30	99.33	99.37	99.42	99.46	99.50
3	34.12	30.82	29.46	28.71	28.24	27.91	27.49	27.05	26.60	26.12
4	21.20	18.00	16.69	15.98	15.52	15.21	14.80	14.37	13.93	13.46
5	16.26	13.27	12.06	11.39	10.97	10.67	10.29	9.89	9.47	9.02
6	13.74	10.92	9.78	9.15	8.75	8.47	8.10	7.72	7.31	6.88
7	12.25	9.55	8.45	7.85	7.46	7.19	6.84	6.47	6.07	5.65
8	11.26	8.65	7.59	7.01	6.63	6.37	6.03	5.67	5.28	4.86
9	10.56	8.02	6.99	6.42	6.06	5.80	5.47	5.11	4.73	4.31
10	10.04	7.56	6.55	5.99	5.64	5.39	5.06	4.71	4.33	3.91
11	9.65	7.20	6.22	5.67	5.32	5.07	4.74	4.40	4.02	3.60
12	9.33	6.93	5.95	5.41	5.06	4.82	4.50	4.16	3.78	3.36
13	9.07	6.70	5.74	5.20	4.86	4.62	4.30	3.96	3.59	3.16
14	8.86	6.51	5.56	5.03	4.69	4.46	4.14	3.80	3.43	3.00
15	8.68	6.36	5.42	4.89	4.56	4.32	4.00	3.67	3.29	2.87
16	8.53	6.23	5.29	4.77	4.44	4.20	3.89	3.55	3.18	2.75
17	8.40	6.11	5.18	4.67	4.34	4.10	3.79	3.45	3.08	2.65
18	8.28	6.01	5.09	4.58	4.25	4.01	3.71	3.37	3.00	2.57
19	8.18	5.93	5.01	4.50	4.17	3.94	3.63	3.30	2.92	2.49
20	8.10	5.85	4.94	4.43	4.10	3.87	3.56	3.23	2.86	2.42

21	8.02	5.78	4.87	4.37	4.04	3.81	3.51	3.17	2.80	2.36
22	7.94	5.72	4.82	4.31	3.99	3.76	3.45	3.12	2.75	2.31
23	7.88	5.66	4.76	4.26	3.94	3.71	3.41	3.07	2.70	2.26
24	7.82	5.61	4.72	4.22	3.90	3.67	3.36	3.03	2.66	2.21
25	7.77	5.57	4.68	4.18	3.86	3.63	3.32	2.99	2.62	2.17
26	7.72	5.53	4.46	4.14	3.82	3.59	3.29	2.96	2.58	2.13
27	7.68	5.49	4.60	4.11	3.78	3.56	3.26	2.93	2.55	2.10
28	7.64	5.45	4.57	4.07	3.75	3.53	3.23	2.90	2.52	2.06
29	7.60	5.42	4.54	4.04	3.73	3.50	3.20	2.87	2.49	2.03
30	7.56	5.39	4.51	4.02	3.70	3.47	3.17	2.84	2.47	2.01
40	7.31	5.18	4.31	3.83	3.51	3.29	2.99	2.66	2.29	1.80
60	7.08	4.98	4.13	3.65	3.34	3.12	2.82	2.50	2.12	1.60
120	6.85	4.79	3.95	3.48	3.17	2.96	2.66	2.34	1.95	1.38
∞	6.64	4.60	3.78	3.32	3.02	2.80	2.51	2.18	1.79	1.00

SOURCE: Abridged from Table V of R. A. Fisher and F. Yates, *Statistical Tables for Biological, Agricultural, and Medical Research*, 6th ed., 1974. Longman Group Ltd., London (previously published by Oliver and Boyd Ltd., Edinburgh). By permission of the authors and publisher.

APPENDIX L-3   F-distribution, 0.1% level.

The entries in this table are the F-values for which the tail area equals 0.001.

0.001

| df for denominator | \multicolumn{10}{c}{df for numerator} |
	1	2	3	4	5	6	8	12	24	∞
1	405284	500000	540379	562500	576405	585937	598144	610667	623497	636619
2	998.5	999.0	999.2	999.2	999.3	999.3	999.4	999.4	999.5	999.5
3	167.0	148.5	141.1	137.1	134.6	132.8	130.6	128.3	125.9	123.5
4	74.14	61.25	56.18	53.44	51.71	50.53	49.00	47.41	45.77	44.05
5	47.18	37.12	33.20	31.09	29.75	28.84	27.64	26.42	25.14	23.78
6	35.51	27.00	23.70	21.92	20.81	20.03	19.03	17.99	16.89	15.75
7	29.25	21.69	18.77	17.19	16.21	15.52	14.63	13.71	12.73	11.69
8	25.42	18.49	15.83	14.39	13.49	12.86	12.04	11.19	10.30	9.34
9	22.86	16.39	13.90	12.56	11.71	11.13	10.37	9.57	8.72	7.81
10	21.04	14.91	12.55	11.28	10.48	9.92	9.20	8.45	7.64	6.76
11	19.69	13.81	11.56	10.35	9.58	9.05	8.35	7.63	6.85	6.00
12	18.64	12.97	10.80	9.63	8.89	8.38	7.71	7.00	6.25	5.42
13	17.81	12.31	10.21	9.07	8.35	7.86	7.21	6.52	5.78	4.97
14	17.14	11.78	9.73	8.62	7.92	7.43	6.80	6.13	5.41	4.60
15	16.59	11.34	9.34	8.25	7.57	7.09	6.47	5.81	5.10	4.31
16	16.12	10.97	9.00	7.94	7.27	6.81	6.19	5.55	4.85	4.06
17	15.72	10.66	8.73	7.68	7.02	6.56	5.96	5.32	4.63	3.85
18	15.38	10.39	8.49	7.46	6.81	6.35	5.76	5.13	4.45	3.67
19	15.08	10.16	8.28	7.26	6.62	6.18	5.59	4.97	4.29	3.52
20	14.82	9.95	8.10	7.10	6.46	6.02	5.44	4.82	4.15	3.38

21	14.59	9.77	7.94	6.95	6.32	5.88	5.31	4.70	4.03	3.26
22	14.38	9.61	7.80	6.81	6.19	5.76	5.19	4.58	3.92	3.15
23	14.19	9.47	7.67	6.69	6.08	5.65	5.09	4.48	3.82	3.05
24	14.03	9.34	7.55	6.59	5.98	5.55	4.99	4.39	3.74	2.97
25	13.88	9.22	7.45	6.49	5.88	5.46	4.91	4.31	3.66	2.89
26	13.74	9.12	7.36	6.41	5.80	5.38	4.83	4.24	3.59	2.82
27	13.61	9.02	7.27	6.33	5.73	5.31	4.76	4.17	3.52	2.75
28	13.50	8.93	7.19	6.25	5.66	5.24	4.69	4.11	3.46	2.70
29	13.39	8.85	7.12	6.19	5.59	5.18	4.64	4.05	3.41	2.64
30	13.29	8.77	7.05	6.12	5.53	5.12	4.58	4.00	3.36	2.59
40	12.61	8.25	6.50	5.70	5.13	4.73	4.21	3.64	3.01	2.23
60	11.97	7.76	6.17	5.31	4.76	4.37	3.87	3.31	2.69	1.90
120	11.38	7.32	5.79	4.95	4.42	4.04	3.55	3.02	2.40	1.54
∞	10.83	6.91	5.42	4.62	4.10	3.74	3.27	2.74	2.13	1.00

SOURCE: Abridged from Table V of R. A. Fisher and F. Yates, *Statistical Tables for Biological, Agricultural, and Medical Research*, 6th ed., 1974. Longman Group Ltd., London (previously published by Oliver and Boyd Ltd., Edinburgh). By permission of the authors and publisher.

APPENDIX M-1   Duncan's new multiple ranges, 5% level.

The entries in this table are the Q_p-values used to find R_p, the shortest significant range, at the 5% level.

df	\multicolumn{9}{c}{Number of means p within range being tested}
	2	3	4	5	6	7	8	9	10
2	6.085								
3	4.501	4.516							
4	3.927	4.013	4.033						
5	3.635	3.749	3.797	3.814					
6	3.461	3.587	3.649	3.680	3.694				
7	3.344	3.477	3.548	3.588	3.611	3.622			
8	3.261	3.399	3.475	3.521	3.549	3.566	3.575		
9	3.199	3.339	3.420	3.470	3.502	3.523	3.536	3.544	
10	3.151	3.293	3.376	3.430	3.465	3.489	3.505	3.516	3.522
11	3.113	3.256	3.342	3.397	3.435	3.462	3.480	3.493	3.501
12	3.082	3.225	3.313	3.370	3.410	3.439	3.459	3.474	3.484
13	3.055	3.200	3.289	3.348	3.389	3.419	3.442	3.458	3.470
14	3.033	3.178	3.268	3.329	3.372	3.403	3.426	3.444	3.457
15	3.014	3.160	3.250	3.312	3.356	3.389	3.413	3.432	3.446
16	2.998	3.144	3.235	3.298	3.343	3.376	3.402	3.422	3.437
17	2.984	3.130	3.222	3.285	3.331	3.366	3.392	3.412	3.429
18	2.971	3.118	3.210	3.274	3.321	3.356	3.383	3.405	3.421
19	2.960	3.107	3.199	3.264	3.311	3.347	3.375	3.397	3.415
20	2.950	3.097	3.190	3.255	3.303	3.339	3.368	3.391	3.409
24	2.919	3.066	3.160	3.226	3.276	3.315	3.345	3.370	3.390
30	2.888	3.035	3.131	3.199	3.250	3.290	3.322	3.349	3.371
40	2.858	3.006	3.102	3.171	3.224	3.266	3.300	3.328	3.352
60	2.829	2.976	3.073	3.143	3.198	3.241	3.277	3.307	3.333
120	2.800	2.947	3.045	3.116	3.172	3.217	3.254	3.287	3.314
∞	2.772	2.918	3.017	3.089	3.146	3.193	3.232	3.265	3.294

SOURCE: Adapted from tables compiled by D. B. Duncan, *Biometrics* 11: 1–42 (1955) and modified by H. L. Harter, *ibid.* 16: 671–685 (1960) and 17: 321–324 (1961).

Number of means p within range being tested								
11	12	13	14	15	16	17	18	19

(The last entry in each row remains the same for all succeeding values of p.)

3.506								
3.491	3.496							
3.478	3.484	3.488						
3.467	3.474	3.479	3.482					
3.457	3.465	3.471	3.476	3.478				
3.449	3.458	3.465	3.470	3.473	3.477			
3.441	3.451	3.459	3.465	3.469	3.473	3.475		
3.435	3.445	3.454	3.460	3.465	3.470	3.472	3.474	
3.429	3.440	3.449	3.456	3.462	3.467	3.470	3.472	3.473
3.424	3.436	3.445	3.453	3.459	3.464	3.467	3.470	3.472
3.406	3.420	3.432	3.441	3.449	3.456	3.461	3.465	3.469
3.389	3.405	3.418	3.430	3.439	3.447	3.454	3.460	3.466
3.373	3.390	3.405	3.418	3.429	3.439	3.448	3.456	3.463
3.355	3.374	3.391	3.406	3.419	3.431	3.442	3.451	3.460
3.337	3.359	3.377	3.394	3.409	3.423	3.435	3.446	3.457
3.320	3.343	3.363	3.382	3.399	3.414	3.428	3.442	3.454

APPENDIX M-2 Duncan's new multiple ranges, 1% level.

The entries in this table are the Q_p-values used to find R_p, the shortest significant range, at the 1% level.

df	\multicolumn{9}{c}{Number of means p within range being tested}
	2	3	4	5	6	7	8	9	10
2	14.04								
3	8.261	8.321							
4	6.512	6.677	6.740						
5	5.702	5.893	5.989	6.040					
6	5.243	5.439	5.549	5.614	5.655				
7	4.949	5.145	5.260	5.334	5.383	5.416			
8	4.746	4.939	5.057	5.135	5.189	5.227	5.256		
9	4.596	4.787	4.906	4.986	5.043	5.086	5.118	5.142	
10	4.482	4.671	4.790	4.871	4.931	4.975	5.010	5.037	5.058
11	4.392	4.579	4.697	4.780	4.841	4.887	4.924	4.952	4.975
12	4.320	4.504	4.622	4.706	4.767	4.815	4.852	4.883	4.907
13	4.260	4.442	4.560	4.644	4.706	4.755	4.793	4.824	4.850
14	4.210	4.391	4.508	4.591	4.654	4.704	4.743	4.775	4.802
15	4.168	4.347	4.463	4.547	4.610	4.660	4.700	4.733	4.760
16	4.131	4.309	4.425	4.509	4.572	4.622	4.663	4.696	4.724
17	4.099	4.275	4.391	4.475	4.539	4.589	4.630	4.664	4.693
18	4.071	4.246	4.362	4.445	4.509	4.560	4.601	4.635	4.664
19	4.046	4.220	4.335	4.419	4.483	4.534	4.575	4.610	4.639
20	4.024	4.197	4.312	4.395	4.459	4.510	4.552	4.587	4.617
24	3.956	4.126	4.239	4.322	4.386	4.437	4.480	4.516	4.546
30	3.889	4.056	4.168	4.250	4.314	4.366	4.409	4.445	4.477
40	3.825	3.988	4.098	4.180	4.244	4.296	4.339	4.376	4.408
60	3.762	3.922	4.031	4.111	4.174	4.226	4.270	4.307	4.340
120	3.702	3.858	3.965	4.044	4.107	4.158	4.202	4.239	4.272
∞	3.643	3.796	3.900	3.978	4.040	4.091	4.135	4.172	4.205

SOURCE: Adapted from tables compiled by D. B. Duncan, *Biometrics* 11: 1–42 (1955) and modified by H. L. Harter, *ibid*. 16: 671–685 (1960) and 17: 321–324 (1961).

Number of means p within range being tested								
11	12	13	14	15	16	17	18	19

(The last entry in each row remains the same for all succeeding values of p.)

4.994								
4.927	4.944							
4.872	4.889	4.904						
4.824	4.843	4.859	4.872					
4.783	4.803	4.820	4.834	4.846				
4.748	4.768	4.786	4.800	4.813	4.825			
4.717	4.738	4.756	4.771	4.785	4.797	4.807		
4.689	4.711	4.729	4.745	4.759	4.772	4.783	4.792	
4.665	4.686	4.705	4.722	4.736	4.749	4.761	4.771	4.780
4.642	4.664	4.684	4.701	4.716	4.729	4.741	4.751	4.761
4.573	4.596	4.616	4.634	4.651	4.665	4.678	4.690	4.700
4.504	4.528	4.550	4.569	4.586	4.601	4.615	4.628	4.640
4.436	4.461	4.483	4.503	4.521	4.537	4.553	4.566	4.579
4.368	4.394	4.417	4.438	4.456	4.474	4.490	4.504	4.518
4.301	4.327	4.351	4.372	4.392	4.410	4.426	4.442	4.456
4.235	4.261	4.285	4.307	4.327	4.345	4.363	4.379	4.394

APPENDIX M-3 Duncan's new multiple ranges, 0.1% level.

The entries in this table are the Q_p-values used to find R_p, the shortest significant range, at the 0.1% level.

df	Number of means p within range being tested								
	2	3	4	5	6	7	8	9	10
2	44.69								
3	18.28	18.45							
4	12.81	12.52	12.67						
5	9.714	10.05	10.24	10.35					
6	8.427	8.743	8.932	9.055	9.139				
7	7.648	7.943	8.127	8.252	8.342	8.409			
8	7.130	7.407	7.584	7.708	7.799	7.869	7.924		
9	6.762	7.024	7.195	7.316	7.407	7.478	7.535	7.582	
10	6.487	6.738	6.902	7.021	7.111	7.182	7.240	7.287	7.327
11	6.275	6.516	6.676	6.791	6.880	6.950	7.008	7.056	7.097
12	6.106	6.340	6.494	6.607	6.695	6.765	6.822	6.870	6.911
13	5.970	6.195	6.346	6.457	6.543	6.612	6.670	6.718	6.759
14	5.856	6.075	6.223	6.332	6.416	6.485	6.542	6.590	6.631
15	5.760	5.974	6.119	6.225	6.309	6.377	6.433	6.481	6.522
16	5.678	5.888	6.030	6.135	6.217	6.284	6.340	6.388	6.429
17	5.608	5.813	5.953	6.056	6.138	6.204	6.260	6.307	6.348
18	5.546	5.748	5.886	5.988	6.068	6.134	6.189	6.236	6.277
19	5.492	5.691	5.826	5.927	6.007	6.072	6.127	6.174	6.214
20	5.444	5.640	5.774	5.873	5.952	6.017	6.071	6.117	6.158
24	5.297	5.484	5.612	5.708	5.784	5.846	5.899	5.945	5.984
30	5.156	5.335	5.457	5.549	5.622	5.682	5.734	5.778	5.817
40	5.022	5.191	5.308	5.396	5.466	5.524	5.574	5.617	5.654
60	4.894	5.055	5.166	5.249	5.317	5.372	5.420	5.461	5.498
120	4.771	4.924	5.029	5.109	5.173	5.226	5.271	5.311	5.346
∞	4.654	4.798	4.898	4.974	5.034	5.085	5.128	5.166	5.199

SOURCE: Adapted from tables compiled by D. B. Duncan, *Biometrics* 11: 1–42 (1955) and modified by H. L. Harter, *ibid.* 16: 671–685 (1960) and 17: 321–324 (1961).

Number of means p within range being tested								
11	12	13	14	15	16	17	18	19

(The last entry in each row remains the same for all succeeding values of p.)

7.132								
6.947	6.978							
6.795	6.826	6.854						
6.667	6.699	6.727	6.752					
6.558	6.590	6.619	6.644	6.666				
6.465	6.497	6.525	6.551	6.574	6.595			
6.384	6.416	6.444	6.470	6.493	6.514	6.533		
6.313	6.345	6.373	6.399	6.422	6.443	6.462	6.480	
6.250	6.281	6.310	6.336	6.359	6.380	6.400	6.418	6.434
6.193	6.225	6.254	6.279	6.303	6.324	6.344	6.362	6.379
6.020	6.051	6.079	6.105	6.129	6.150	6.170	6.188	6.205
5.851	5.882	5.910	5.935	5.958	5.980	6.000	6.018	6.036
5.688	5.718	5.745	5.770	5.793	5.814	5.834	5.852	5.869
5.530	5.559	5.586	5.610	5.632	5.653	5.672	5.690	5.707
5.377	5.405	5.431	5.454	5.476	5.496	5.515	5.532	5.549
5.229	5.256	5.280	5.303	5.324	5.343	5.361	5.378	5.394

APPENDIX N   Correlation coefficients.

The entries in this table are the R-values for distributions with from 1 to 100 degrees of freedom, at 5 values of the probability.

df $(k - 2)$	Probability of a larger value of R				
	0.10	0.05	0.02	0.01	0.001
1	.98769	.99692	.999507	.999877	.9999988
2	.90000	.95000	.98000	.990000	.99900
3	.8054	.8783	.93433	.95873	.99116
4	.7293	.8114	.8822	.91720	.97406
5	.6694	.7545	.8329	.8745	.95074
6	.6215	.7067	.7887	.8343	.92493
7	.5822	.6664	.7498	.7977	.8982
8	.5494	.6319	.7155	.7646	.8721
9	.5214	.6021	.6851	.7348	.8471
10	.4973	.5760	.6581	.7079	.8233
11	.4762	.5529	.6339	.6835	.8010
12	.4575	.5324	.6120	.6614	.7800
13	.4409	.5139	.5923	.6411	.7603
14	.4259	.4973	.5742	.6226	.7420
15	.4124	.4821	.5577	.6055	.7246

SOURCE: Abridged from Table VII of R. A. Fisher and F. Yates, *Statistical Tables for Biological, Agricultural, and Medical Research*, 6th ed., 1974. Longman Group Ltd., London (previously published by Oliver and Boyd Ltd., Edinburgh). By permission of the authors and publisher.

df	Probability of a larger value of R				
$(k - 2)$	0.10	0.05	0.02	0.01	0.001
16	.4000	.4683	.5425	.5897	.7084
17	.3887	.4555	.5285	.5751	.6932
18	.3783	.4438	.5155	.5614	.6787
19	.3687	.4329	.5034	.5487	.6652
20	.3598	.4227	.4921	.5368	.6524
25	.3233	.3809	.4451	.4869	.5974
30	.2960	.3494	.4093	.4487	.5541
35	.2746	.3246	.3810	.4182	.5189
40	.2573	.3044	.3578	.3932	.4896
45	.2428	.2875	.3384	.3721	.4648
50	.2306	.2732	.3218	.3541	.4433
60	.2108	.2500	.2948	.3248	.4078
70	.1954	.2319	.2737	.3017	.3799
80	.1829	.2172	.2565	.2830	.3568
90	.1726	.2050	.2422	.2673	.3375
100	.1638	.1946	.2301	.2540	.3211

APPENDIX O-1 Rank totals excluded for significant differences, 5% level.
Any rank total outside the given range is significant.

Number of judges	Number of wines										
	2	3	4	5	6	7	8	9	10	11	12
3				4–14	4–17	4–20	4–23	5–25	5–28	5–31	5–34
4		5–11	5–15	6–18	6–22	7–25	7–29	8–32	8–36	8–39	9–43
5		6–14	7–18	8–22	9–26	9–31	10–35	11–39	12–43	12–48	13–52
6	7–11	8–16	9–21	10–26	11–31	12–36	13–41	14–46	15–51	17–55	18–60
7	8–13	10–18	11–24	12–30	14–35	15–41	17–46	18–52	19–58	21–63	22–69
8	9–15	11–21	13–27	15–33	17–39	18–46	20–52	22–58	24–64	25–71	27–77
9	11–16	13–23	15–30	17–37	19–44	22–50	24–57	26–64	28–71	30–78	32–85
10	12–18	14–26	17–33	19–41	22–48	25–55	27–63	30–70	32–78	35–85	37–93
11	13–20	16–28	19–36	22–44	25–52	28–60	31–68	34–76	36–85	39–93	42–101
12	15–21	18–30	21–39	25–47	28–56	31–65	34–74	38–82	41–91	44–100	47–109
13	16–23	20–32	24–41	27–51	31–60	35–69	38–79	42–88	45–98	49–107	52–117
14	17–25	22–34	26–44	30–54	34–64	38–74	42–84	46–94	50–104	54–114	57–125
15	19–26	23–37	28–47	32–58	37–68	41–79	46–89	50–100	54–111	58–122	63–132
16	20–28	25–39	30–50	35–61	40–72	45–83	49–95	54–106	59–117	63–129	68–140
17	22–29	27–41	32–53	38–64	43–76	48–88	53–100	58–112	63–124	68–136	73–148
18	23–31	29–43	34–56	40–68	46–80	52–92	57–105	61–118	68–130	73–143	79–155
19	24–33	30–46	37–58	43–71	49–84	55–97	61–110	67–123	73–136	78–150	84–163
20	26–34	32–48	39–61	45–75	52–88	58–102	65–115	71–129	77–143	83–157	90–170

Source: Adapted from tables compiled by A. Kramer, *Food Technol.* 17(12): 124–125 (1963).

APPENDIX O-2 Rank totals excluded for significant differences, 1% level.

Any rank total outside the given range is significant.

Number of judges	\multicolumn{11}{c}{Number of wines}										
	2	3	4	5	6	7	8	9	10	11	12
3									4–29	4–32	4–35
4				5–19	5–23	5–27	6–30	6–34	6–38	6–42	7–45
5			6–19	7–23	7–28	8–32	8–37	9–41	9–46	10–50	10–55
6		7–17	8–22	9–27	9–33	10–38	11–43	12–48	13–53	13–59	14–64
7		8–20	10–25	11–31	12–37	13–43	14–49	15–55	16–61	17–67	18–73
8	9–15	10–22	11–29	13–35	14–42	16–48	17–55	19–61	20–68	21–75	23–81
9	10–17	12–24	13–32	15–39	17–46	19–53	21–60	22–68	24–75	26–82	27–90
10	11–19	13–27	15–35	18–42	20–50	22–58	24–66	26–74	28–82	30–90	32–98
11	12–21	15–29	17–38	20–46	22–55	25–63	27–72	30–80	32–89	34–98	37–106
12	14–22	17–31	19–41	22–50	25–59	28–68	31–77	33–87	36–96	39–105	42–114
13	15–24	18–34	21–44	25–53	28–63	31–73	34–83	37–93	40–103	43–113	46–123
14	16–26	20–36	24–46	27–57	31–67	34–78	38–88	41–98	45–109	48–120	51–131
15	18–27	22–38	26–49	30–60	34–71	37–83	41–94	45–105	49–116	53–127	56–139
16	19–29	23–41	28–52	32–64	36–76	41–87	45–99	49–111	53–123	57–135	62–146
17	20–31	25–43	30–55	35–67	39–80	44–92	49–104	53–117	58–129	62–142	67–154
18	22–32	27–45	32–58	37–71	42–84	47–97	52–110	57–123	62–136	67–149	72–162
19	23–34	29–47	34–61	40–74	45–88	50–102	56–115	61–129	67–142	72–156	77–170
20	24–36	30–50	36–64	42–78	48–92	54–106	60–120	65–135	71–149	77–163	82–178

SOURCE: Adapted from tables compiled by A. Kramer, *Food Technol.* 17(12): 124–125 (1963).

APPENDIX P Normal scores.

The entries in this table show the conversion of rankings to normal scores. Negative values are omitted for samples larger than 10.

Number of samples

Rank order	2	3	4	5	6	7	8	9	10
1	0.564	0.864	1.029	1.163	1.267	1.352	1.424	1.485	1.539
2	-0.564	0.000	0.297	0.495	0.642	0.757	0.852	0.932	1.001
3		-0.864	-0.297	0.000	0.202	0.353	0.473	0.572	0.656
4			-1.029	-0.495	-0.202	0.000	0.153	0.275	0.376
5				-1.163	-0.642	-0.353	-0.153	0.000	0.123
6					-1.267	-0.757	-0.473	-0.275	-0.123
7						-1.352	-0.852	-0.572	-0.376
8							-1.424	-0.932	-0.656
9								-1.485	-1.001
10									-1.539

Rank order	11	12	13	14	15	16	17	18	19	20
1	1.586	1.629	1.668	1.703	1.736	1.766	1.794	1.820	1.844	1.867
2	1.062	1.116	1.164	1.208	1.248	1.285	1.319	1.350	1.380	1.408
3	0.729	0.793	0.850	0.901	0.948	0.990	1.029	1.066	1.099	1.131
4	0.462	0.537	0.603	0.662	0.715	0.763	0.807	0.848	0.886	0.921
5	0.225	0.312	0.388	0.456	0.516	0.570	0.619	0.665	0.707	0.745
6	0.000	0.103	0.191	0.267	0.335	0.396	0.451	0.502	0.548	0.590
7			0.000	0.088	0.165	0.234	0.295	0.351	0.402	0.448
8					0.000	0.077	0.146	0.208	0.264	0.315
9							0.000	0.069	0.131	0.187
10									0.000	0.062

	21	22	23	24	25	26	27	28	29	30
1	1.889	1.910	1.929	1.948	1.965	1.982	1.998	2.014	2.029	2.043
2	1.434	1.458	1.481	1.503	1.524	1.544	1.563	1.581	1.599	1.616
3	1.160	1.188	1.214	1.239	1.263	1.285	1.306	1.327	1.346	1.365
4	0.954	0.985	1.014	1.041	1.067	1.091	1.115	1.137	1.158	1.179
5	0.782	0.815	0.847	0.877	0.905	0.932	0.957	0.981	1.004	1.026
6	0.630	0.667	0.701	0.734	0.764	0.793	0.820	0.846	0.871	0.894
7	0.491	0.532	0.569	0.604	0.637	0.668	0.697	0.725	0.752	0.777
8	0.362	0.406	0.446	0.484	0.519	0.553	0.584	0.614	0.642	0.669
9	0.238	0.286	0.330	0.370	0.409	0.444	0.478	0.510	0.540	0.568
10	0.118	0.170	0.218	0.262	0.303	0.341	0.377	0.411	0.443	0.473
11	0.000	0.056	0.108	0.156	0.200	0.241	0.280	0.316	0.350	0.382
12			0.000	0.052	0.100	0.144	0.185	0.224	0.260	0.294
13					0.000	0.048	0.092	0.134	0.172	0.209
14							0.000	0.044	0.086	0.125
15									0.000	0.041

SOURCE: Abridged from tables compiled by H. L. Harter, *Biometrika* **48**: 151–165 (1961).

APPENDIX Q Hand-calculator program:
Texas Instruments Programmable 59 or 58.

Applied Statistics Module
Two-way analysis of variance (wines + tasters ≤ 16)

(For example, with seven tasters, the procedure is limited
to not more than nine wines.)

Tasters
(n)

Wines (k)

Step	Procedure	Enter	Press	Display
1	Select program		[2nd] [Pgm] 06	0
2			[E]	0
3	Enter no. of tasters	n	[B]	
4	Enter no. of wines	k	[C]	
5	Repartition if $nk > 28$	nk	[2nd] [Op] 17	
6	Enter data for Taster 1 (Repeat for each taster)	X_{ij}	[A]	j (Be sure to wait for j to appear.)
7	Calculate $\overline{X}$ (mean)		[2nd] [B']	$\overline{X}$ (Record if wanted.)
8	Calculate s^2 (variance)		[2nd] [C']	s^2 (Record if wanted.)
9	Select program		[2nd] [Pgm] 16	No change s^2
10	Calculate SS (total)		[A]	SS (Record)
11	Calculate SSW (wines)		[B]	SSW (Record)
12	Calculate SST (tasters)		[2nd] [B']	SST (Record)
13	Calculate F for wines		[C]	F_w
14	df for numerator		[D]	df_1
15	df for denominator		[R/S]	df_2
16	Calculate F for tasters		[2nd] [C']	F_t
17	df for numerator		[D]	df_3
18	df for denominator		[R/S]	df_2

Rows 10–12: } Not necessary to record if printer used.

Row 14: From table find $F_{.05}$. If $F_w > F_{.05}$, sig. diff. among wines is indicated.

Row 16–18: From table find $F_{.05}$. If $F_t > F_{.05}$, sig. diff. among tasters is indicated.

If significant differences among wines are indicated proceed as follows:
(1) Find SSE (sum of squares for error) $= SS - SSW - SST$
(2) Find LSD (least significant difference among wine *totals* at 5% level) $=$

$$t_{.05} \sqrt{\frac{2n(SSE)}{df_2}}$$

APPENDIX Q

To find SSE and LSD, press the following in sequence:

(1) $SS - SSW = -SST = SSE$ (Print) or record

(2) $2 \times n = \times SSE = \div df_2 = \sqrt{} \times t_{.05} = LSD$ for wines (Print) or record

$2 \times k = \times SSE = \div df_2 = \sqrt{} \times t_{.05} = LSD$ for tasters (if $F_t > F_{.05}$)

$t_{.05}$ from t-table with df_2 (Appendix K)

Apply the Texas Instruments program to analyze the following set of data.

		Wines			
		1	2	3	4
	1	7	6	8	7
Tasters	2	2	4	4	4
	3	4	6	5	3

	Keystrokes	Display
	2nd Pgm 06	0
	E	0
3 tasters	3 B	
4 wines	4 C	
	7 A 6 A 8 A 7 A 2 A 4 A 4 A 4 A 4 A 6 A 5 A 3 A	
	2nd B′	Mean = 5
	2nd C′	Variance = 3
	2nd Pgm 16	No change
	A	$SS = 36.00$
	B	$SSW = 3.33$
	2nd B′	$SST = 26.00$
	C	$F_w = 1.00$
	D	$df_1 = 3$
	R/S	$df_2 = 6$
	2nd C′	$F_t = 11.70$
	D	$df_3 = 2$
	R/S	$df_4 = 6$

APPENDIX R Hand-calculator program: Hewlett Packard HP-41C or HP-41CV

HP-41C/CV Statistical Package
Two-way analysis of variance

Tasters (R) Wines (C) [   ] Size: 018

Step	Procedure	Enter	Press	Display
1	Initialize the program		XEO	ΣAOVTWO
	Row-Wise (Tasters)			
2	Repeat step 2–5 for $i = 1, 2, \ldots, r$			
3	Repeat step 3–4 for $j = 1, 2, \ldots, c$ Input x_{ij}	x_{ij}	A	(j)
4	If you made a mistake in inputting x_{im}, then correct by	x_{im}	C	$(m - 1)$
5	Calculate row sum and initialize the program for the next row		R/S	SUM $= (RS_i)$
6	After completion of the last row (row r), initialize the program for column-wise data entry		R/S	COLUMN-WISE
	Column-Wise (Wines)			
7	Repeat step 7–10 for $j = 1, 2, \ldots, c$			
8	Repeat step 8–9 for $i = 1, 2, \ldots, r$ Input x_{ij}	x_{ij}	A	(i)
9	If you made a mistake in inputting x_{nj}, then correct by	x_{nj}	C	$(h - 1)$
10	Calculate column sum and initialize the program for the next column		R/S	SUM $= (CS_j)$
11	Calculate ANOVA Table:			
	RSS (Tasters)		E	RSS $= (RSS)$
	CSS (Wines)		R/S	CSS $= (CSS)$
	TSS (Total)		R/S	TSS $= (TSS)$
	ESS (Error)		R/S	ESS $= (ESS)$
	df_1 (Tasters)		R/S	DF1 $= (df_1)$
	df_2 (Wines)		R/S	DF2 $= (df_2)$
	df_3 (Error)		R/S	DF3 $= (df_3)$
	F_1 (Tasters)		R/S	F1 $= (F_1)$
	F_1 (Wines)		R/S	F2 $= (F_2)$
12	Repeat step 11 if you want the results again			
13	For another set of data, initialize the program by $\rightarrow$ then go to step 2		A	ΣAOVTWO

Apply the Hewlett Packard program to analyze the following set of data.

		j	Column (wines)			
	i		1	2	3	4
		1	7	6	8	7
Row		2	2	4	4	4
(Tasters)		3	4	6	5	3

Keystrokes	Display
XEO ALPHA SIZE ALPHA 018	
XEO ALPHA ΣAOVTWO ALPHA	ΣAOVTWO
7 A 6 A 8 A 7 A	4.00
R/S	SUM = 28.00
2 A 4 A 4 A 4 A	4.00
R/S	SUM = 14.00
4 A 6 A 5 A 3 A	4.00
R/S	SUM = 18.00
R/S	COLUMN-WISE
7 A 2 A 4 A	3.00
R/S	SUM = 13.00
6 A 4 A 6 A	3.00
R/S	SUM = 16.00
8 A 4 A 5 A	3.00
R/S	SUM = 17.00
7 A 4 A 3 A	3.00
R/S	SUM = 14.00
E	RSS = 26.00
R/S	CSS = 3.33
R/S	TSS = 36.00
R/S	ESS = 6.67
R/S	DF1 = 2.00
R/S	DF2 = 3.00
R/S	DF3 = 6.00
R/S	F1 = 11.70
R/S	F2 = 1.00

Annotated Bibliography

Acree, T. E., 1980. Flavor characterization. *Kirk–Othmer Encycl. Chem. Technol.* 3rd ed. 10: 444–455.
Problems in studying flavor description.

Acree, T. E., 1981. The odor quality of labrusca grapes. *ACS Symp. Ser.* 170: 11–19.

Adda, J., and P. Jounela-Eriksson, 1979. L'étude des arômes: méthodes physicochimiques et méthodes sensorielles. *Cah. Nutr. Diet.* 14: 115–129.
A comparison of physical–chemical and sensory methods for studying odor of foods.

American Society of Brewing Chemists, 1979. Sensory analyses. Report of the subcommittee on sensory analysis. *J. Amer. Soc. Brew. Chem.* 37: 130–131.
Use of sensory evaluation in the brewing industry.

Amerine, M. A., 1954. Composition of wines. I. Organic constituents. *Adv. Food Res.* 5: 353–510.
Fairly complete for its time.

Amerine, M. A., 1964. The anatomy of a superb wine. *San Francisco* 6(13): 28–29.
California Cabernet Sauvignon wines considered.

Amerine, M. A., 1966. Flavor as a value. In *Food and civilization,* ed. S. M. Farber, N. L. Wilson, and R. H. L. Wilson. Springfield, Ill.: Charles C Thomas. 308 pp. (See pp. 22–38.)

Amerine, M. A., 1969. There really is quality in wines. *San Francisco* 11(10): 38–39.
Depends on who is looking for it. Satire.

Amerine, M. A., 1980. The words used to describe abnormal appearance, odor, taste and tactile sensations of wines. In *The analysis and control of less desirable flavors in foods and beverages,* ed. G. Charalambous. New York: Academic Press. 358 pp. (See pp. 319–351.)
A listing of the words and some analysis of their origin.

Amerine, M. A., 1981. Describing wines in meaningful words. *Proc. Training Conf. Fundamentals of Table Wine Processing* 7: 58–62. Davis, Calif., March 31–April 2, 1981.
A plea for consistent use of words describing wines.

Amerine, M. A., H. W. Berg, R. E. Kunkee, C. S. Ough, V. L. Singleton, and A. D. Webb, 1980. *The technology of winemaking.* 4th ed. Westport, Conn.: Avi. 794 pp.
Contains chapter on sensory evaluation for wineries.

Amerine, M. A., and M. A. Josyln, 1970. *Table wines: The technology of their production.* 2nd ed. Berkeley and Los Angeles: University of California Press. 997 pp.
Reactions of sulfur dioxide. Brief notes on sensory evaluation.

Amerine, M. A., and C. S. Ough, 1964. The sensory evaluation of California wines. *Lab. Pract.* 13(8): 712–716, 738.
How wines were judged at Davis and at the California State Fair.

Amerine, M. A., and C. S. Ough, 1980. *Methods for analysis of musts and wines.* New York: Wiley. 341 pp.

Amerine, M. A., R. M. Pangborn, and E. B. Roessler, 1965a. *Principles of sensory evaluation of food*. New York: Academic Press. 602 pp.
The state of the art and technology as of 1965; still applicable to many food-evaluation problems.

Amerine, M. A., and E. B. Roessler, 1969–70. The age and acidity of wines aged in wood. *Wine and Food,* No. 146, p. 120.
A skeptical look at claims of 100-year-old wines.

Amerine, M. A., and E. B. Roessler, 1971. Pleasantness and unpleasantness of odors added to white wine. *Amer. J. Enol. Vitic.* 22: 199–202.
Experienced judges were more sensitive and consistent than inexperienced. Sulfur dioxide gave increasingly unpleasant reactions as the concentration was increased with both experienced and inexperienced groups.

Amerine, M. A., E. B. Roessler, and F. Filipello, 1959. Modern sensory methods of evaluating wine. *Hilgardia* 28: 477–567.
The modern approach: useful methodology and vocabulary.

Amerine, M. A., E. B. Roessler, and C. S. Ough, 1965b. Acids and the acid taste. I. The effect of pH and titratable acidity. *Amer. J. Enol. Vitic.* 16: 29–37.
Shows how sensitive we can be to the acid taste.

Amerine, M. A., and V. L. Singleton, 1976. *Wine: An introduction for Americans.* 2nd ed. Berkeley and Los Angeles: University of California Press. 373 pp.

Anderson, T. W., 1958. *An introduction to multivariate statistical analysis.* New York: Wiley. 374 pp.

Anon., 1973. The ideal wine glass. *Search: Sci. Technol. Soc.* 4(½): 4.

Anon., 1979. *25th annual report.* Adelaide: The Australian Wine Research Institute. 36 pp. (See pp. 13, 15.)
Research on the cause of the aerated odor.

Antcliff, A. J., 1976. Variety identification in Australia. *Austral. Grapegrower Winemaker,* No. 153, pp. 10–11.

Arnold, R. A., and A. C. Noble, 1978. Bitterness and astringency of grape seed phenolics in a model wine solution. *Amer. J. Enol. Vitic.* 29: 150–152.
Astringency increased with increasing grape seed tannin content but bitterness did not.

Arnold, R. A., and A. C. Noble, 1979. Effect of pomace contact on the flavor of Chardonnay wine. *Amer. J. Enol. Vitic.* 30: 179–181.

Arnold, R. A., A. C. Noble, and V. L. Singleton, 1980. Bitterness and astringency of phenolic fractions of wine. *J. Agric. Food Chem.* 28: 675–678.
All grape-seed phenolics are astringent and bitter.

Associazione Enotecnici Italiani, 1975. Il primo congresso nazionale dell' O.N.A.U. *L'Enotecnico* 11(10): 21, 23.
A new scorecard.

Augustyn, O. P. H., and J. Marais, 1982. Aroma components in freon extracts of wine. *S. Afr. J. Enol. Vitic.* 3: 37–39.

Augustyn, O. P. H., and A. Rapp, 1982. Aroma components of *Vitis vinifera* L. cv. Chenin blanc grapes and their changes during maturation. *S. Afr. J. Enol. Vitic.* 3:47–51.

Augustyn, O. P. H., A. Rapp, and C. J. Van Wyk, 1982. Some volatile aroma components of *Vitis vinifera* L. cv. Sauvignon blanc. *S. Afr. J. Enol. Vitic.* 3:53–60.

Avakyants, S. P., E. G. Rastyannikov, B. S. Chernyaga, and V. I. Navrotskii, 1981. Khromato-mass-spektrometricheskoe issledovanie letuchikh veshchesto vina [Chromato-mass spectroscopic study of volatile substances in wine.] *Vinodel. Vinograd. SSSR* 41(5): 50–53.
The revealing odorous constituents of wines.

Baranowski, J. D., and C. W. Nagel, 1981. Isolation and identification of the hydroxy-cinnamic acid derivatives in White Riesling wine. *Amer. J. Enol. Vitic.* 32: 5–13.

Bartoshuk, L. M., 1975. Taste quality. *Life Sciences Research Report* 1: 229–242. Berlin: Dahlem Workshop on Appetite and Food Intake. *The meaning of the basic tastes.*

Basker, D., 1981. The number of assessors required for nonparametric taste difference tests. *J. Food Qual.* 4: 101–105.

Bassin, B., 1981. The fallacies of wine judgings. *Friends of Wine* 18(6): 132–133. *Perhaps true for many (most?) such judgings.*

Bayonove, C., R. Cordonnier, and P. Dubois, 1975. Étude d'une fraction caractéristique de l'arôme du raisin de la variété Cabernet-Sauvignon: mise en évidence de la 2-méthoxy-3-isobutylpyrazine. *Compt. rend.* 281: 75–78. *Identifies a revealing compound.*

Berg, H. W., F. Filipello, E. Hinreiner, and A. D. Webb, 1955a. Evaluation of thresholds and minimum difference concentrations for various constituents of wines. I. Water solutions of pure substances. *Food Technol.* 9: 29–37. *Basic data on taste and odor sensitivity.*

Berg, H. W., F. Filipello, E. Hinreiner, and A. D. Webb, 1955b. Ibid., II. Sweetness: the effect of ethyl alcohol, organic acids, and tannin. Ibid., 138–140. *Factors affecting the sweetness sensation.*

Boidron, J. N., 1981. Les dérivés terpéniques et l'arôme des raisins et des vins. In *Actualités oenologiques et viticoles*, ed. P. Ribéreau-Gayon and P. Sudraud. Paris: Dunod. 397 pp. (See pp. 253–262.) *The role of the terpenes in grape and wine aroma.*

Boidron, J. N., and P. Torres, 1979. Les arômes des muscats. Étude analytique et dégustative. *Bull. Tech. Pyr. Orient.*, No. 93, pp. 157–161.

Boulton, R., 1980. The relationships between total acidity, titratable acidity and pH in grape tissue. *Vitis* 19: 113–120.

Bradley, J. V., 1968. *Distribution-free statistical tests.* Englewood Cliffs, N.J.: Prentice-Hall. 388 pp.

Bradley, R. A., 1953. Some statistical methods in taste testing and quality evaluation. *Biometrics* 9(1): 22–38.

Brady, R., 1978. Secrets of wine tasting exposed! *New West* 3: 47–49. *Guessing the origin of wines is a parlor trick. Few specialize enough to do it.*

Broadbent, J. M., 1977. *Wine tasting: Enjoying, understanding.* 5th rev. ed. London: Christie Wine Publications. 119 pp. (There is a German edition.)
For experienced wine buyers and for amateurs.

Broadbent, J. M., 1980. *The great vintage wine book.* New York: Knopf. 119 pp.
Generally kind descriptions of hundreds of wines, old to recent.

Brown, E. M., 1950. A new off-odor in sweet wines. *Proc. Amer. Soc. Enol.* 1950: 110–112.
Observations on the possible cause of a new off-odor.

Bureau, G., M. Charpentier-Massonat, and M. Pansu, 1974. Étude des goûts anormaux apportés par le bouchon sur le vin de Champagne. *Rev. Franç. Oenol.* 56: 22–24.
Two yeasts as a possible cause of an off-odor.

Buser, H. R., and C. Zanier, 1982. Identification of 2,4,6-trichloro-anisole as a potent compound causing cork taint in wine. *J. Agric. Food Chem.* 30: 359–362.

Buxbaum, W., 1951. Weinbereitung nach Punkten; ein Mittel zur Qualitätssteigerung und Absatzförderung. *Deut. Weinbau* 5: 596–597.
Early use in Europe of a score card for evaluating wines.

Carroll, D. E., M. W. Hoover, and W. E. Nebitt, 1975. Characteristics of red wines of six cultivars of *Vitis rotundifolia. Mich. J. Food Sci.* 40: 919–921.

Castino, M., and R. Di Stefano, 1981. Effet della temperatura di conservazione sulle caratteristiche dell'Asti Spumante. *Rev. Vitic. Enol.* 34: 106–119.
Once more, low-temperature storage is best.

Cey-Bert, G. R., 1982. Evolution du language du vin en tant que moyen de communication. *Bull. Office Intern. Vigne Vin* 55(615): 408–425.

Charpentier, M., 1977. Apparition des goûts de bouchon en relation avec le developpement des levures dans le liège. *Rev. Franç. Oenol.*, No. 66, pp. 60–62.
Keep corks dry before use.

Charpentier, M., and A. Maujean, 1981. Sunlight flavors in Champagne wines. *Flavour 81, Weurman Symp.* 3: 609–615.

Clapperton, J. F., 1973. Derivation of a profile method for sensory analysis of beer. *J. Inst. Brew.* 79: 495–508.

Clapperton, J. F., and J. R. Piggott, 1978. Flavour characterization by trained and untrained assessors. *J. Inst. Brew.* 85: 275–277.

Cloquet, J., 1906. *L'art de la dégustation des vins.* Brussels: Lébeque. 70 pp.
Includes a vocabulary of what he considered to be appropriate terms.

Cobb, C. S., M. Bursey, and A. Rice, 1978. Major volatile components of Aurore wine: A gas chromatographic spectrographic analyses combining chemical ionization and electron impact ionization. *J. Food Sci.* 43: 1822–1825.
Identifies 26 compounds, 6 new.

Cochran, W. G., and G. M. Cox, 1957. *Experimental designs.* 2nd ed. New York: Wiley. 611 pp.

Conover, W. J., 1980. *Practical nonparametric statistics.* 2nd ed. New York: Wiley. 493 pp.

Corison, C. A., C. S. Berg, H. W. Nelson, and K. E. Nelson, 1979. Must acetic acid and ethyl acetate as mold and rot indicators in grapes. *Amer. J. Enol. Vitic.* 30: 130–134.

Cornell, J. A., and F. W. Knapp, 1972. Sensory evaluation using composite complete–incomplete block designs. *J. Food Sci.* 37: 876–882.

Cornell, J. A., and J. F. Schreckengost, 1975. Measuring panelists' consistency using composite complete–incomplete block designs. *J. Food Sci.* 40: 1130–1133.

Crowell, E. A., and J. F. Guymon, 1975. Wine constituents arising from sorbic acid addition, and identification of 2-ethoxyhexa-3,5-diene as source of geranium-like off odor. *Amer. J. Enol. Vitic.* 26: 97–102.

Daepp, H. U., 1968. Zur Weinbeurteilung mittels Sinnenprüfung-Beeinflussungsmöglichkeiten und Methoden. *Deut. Weinbau Jrb.* 1968: 197–213.
Practical advice on modern procedures for sensory evaluation of wines. Generally follows U.S. practices.

Davis, C., G. Fleet, and T. Lee, 1981. The microflora of wine corks. *Austral. Grapegrower Winemaker* 18(208): 42–44.
Molds and yeasts found in corks.

Davis, C. R., G. H. Fleet, and T. H. Lee, 1982. Inactivation of wine cork microflora by a commercial sulfur dioxide treatment. *Amer. J. Enol. Vitic.* 33: 124–127.

Dhanaraj, S., S. M. Ananthakrishna, and V. S. Govindarajan, 1981. Apple quality: development of descriptive quality profile for objective sensory evaluation. *J. Food Qual.* 4: 83–100.

Di Stefano, R., 1981. Terpene compounds of white muscat from Piemonte. *Vini Ital.* 20(130): 29–43. In English and Italian.
Terpenes in Muscat blanc grapes.

Dittrich, H. H., and E. Kerner, 1964. Diacetyl als Weinfehler; Ursache und Beseitigung des "Milchsäuretones." *Wein-Wissen.* 19: 528–538.

Don, R., 1977. *Wine.* 2nd ed. London: Hodder and Stoughton. 197 pp.
Sound advice on various types of wines.

Drawert, F., 1974. Winemaking as a biotechnological sequence. *Adv. Chem. Ser.* 137: 1–10.
Factors influencing the odorous constituents of grapes and wines.

Dubois, P., J. Regaud, and J. Dekimpe, 1976. Identification de la diméthyl-4,5 tétrahydrofuranedione-2,3 dans le vin jaune du Jura. *Lebensm.-Wissen.-Technol.* 9: 366–368.

Dubois, P., and J. Rigaud, 1981. A propos de goût de bouchon. *Vignes Vins,* No. 301, pp. 48–49.

Duncan, D. B., 1955. Multiple range and multiple F tests. *Biometrics* 11: 1–42.

Du Plessis, C. S., and O. P. H. Augustyn, 1982. Initial study on the guava aroma of Chenin blanc and Colombard wines. *South Afr. J. Enol. Vitic.* 2: 101–103.

Durac, J., 1974. *Wines and the art of tasting.* New York: Dutton. 241 pp.
Includes practical tests, but terms used are poorly defined.

Durbin, J., 1951. Incomplete blocks in ranking experiments. *Brit. J. Psychol. (Stat. Sec.)* 4: 85–90.

Duttweiler, G., ed., 1968. *Les vins Suisses.* Génève: Éditions Générales, S. A. 311 pp.
Detailed flavor distinctions by B. Laederer.

Engen, T., 1980. Why the aroma lingers on. *Psychol. Today* 13(5): 138.
Why odor memory lasts longer than taste memory.

Engen, T., R. A. Kilduff, and N. J. Rummo, 1975. The influence of alcohol on odor perception. *Chem. Senses Flavor* 1: 323–329.

Fagan, G. L., R. E. Kepner, and A. D. Webb, 1981. Production of linalool, *cis-* and *trans-*nerolidol, and *trans,trans-*farnesol by *Saccharomyces fermentati* growing as a film on simulated wine. *Vitis* 20: 36–42.

Fagan, G. L., R. E. Kepner, and A. D. Webb, 1982. Additional volatile components of Palomino film sherry. *Amer. J. Enol. Vitic.* 33: 47–50.
Identifies 14 new compounds in film-yeast sherry.

Feuillat, M., 1980. Vieillissement du vin de Champagne sur levures: phénomènes d'autolyse. Relations avec l'enrichissement et le développement des arômes du vin. *Rev. Franç. Oenol.* 16: 35–46.

Fisher, R. A., and F. Yates, 1974. *Statistical tables for biological, agricultural, and medical research.* 6th ed. London: Longman Group Ltd. (Previously published by Oliver and Boyd Ltd., Edinburgh.) 146 pp.

Foss, D. A., 1981. Sensory characterization. In *Flavor research: Recent advances,* ed. R. Teranishi, R. A. Flath, and H. Sugisawa. New York and Basel: M. Dekker. 381 pp. (See pp. 125–174.)

Foster, D., C. Pratt, and N. Schwartz, 1955. Variations in flavor judgments in a group situation. *Food Res.* 20: 539–544.

Friedman, M., 1937. The use of ranks to avoid the assumption of normality implicit in the analysis of variance. *J. Amer. Stat. Assn.* 32: 675–701.

Frijters, J. E. R., 1976. Evaluation of a texture profile for cooked chicken breast meat by principal component analysis. *Poultry Sci.* 55: 229–233.

Frijters, J. E. R., 1982. Expanded tables for conversion of a proportion of correct responses (P_c) to the measure of sensory difference (d') for the triangular method and the 3-alternative forced choice procedure. *J. Food Sci.* 47: 139–143.

Fuleki, T., 1975. A new objective index for the early screening of grape seedlings based on flavor character. *Rept. Comm. Hort. Res., Can. Hort. Council 1976,* pp. 182–183. See also *Vitis* 21: 111–120, 1982.
Methyl anthranilate (mg/l) $\times$ *100 + total volatile esters (mg/l)* = *Vineland Grape Flavor Index. An index of 14 or over is foxy.*

Gacula, M. C., Jr., 1978. Analysis of incomplete block designs with reference samples in every block. *J. Food Sci.* 43(5): 1461–1466.

Gale, G., 1975. Are some aesthetic judgments empirically true? *Amer. Phil. Quart.* 12: 341–348.
They are, if one accepts his premises.

Glories, Y., 1981. Nature et propriétés des anthocyanes et des tannins. In *Actualités oenologiques et viticoles,* ed. P. Ribéreau-Gayon

and P. Sudraud. Paris: Bordas. 397 pp. (See pp. 292–298.)
Their influence on sensory responses.

Godwin, D. R., R. E. Bargmann, and J. J. Powers, 1978. Use of cluster analysis to evaluate sensory–objective relations of processed green beans. *J. Food Sci.* 43: 1229–1234.
Advanced statistical procedure for relating sensory and chemical data.

Gorman, R., 1975. *Gorman on California premium wines.* Berkeley: Ten Speed Press. 306 pp.
A philosophical and practical essay on wine appreciation with notes on some California wines.

Got, N., 1955. *La dégustation des vins: classification et présentation; l'art de déguster et de présenter les vins.* Perpignan. 236 pp.
A general and gentle discussion of procedures for the sensory evaluation of wines. Useful terminology, but how does one measure the significance of the results?

Götz, B., 1976. Ueber 'Korkwürmer' und ihre Bekämpfung. *Deut. Wein-Ztg.* 102: 1222–1226.
Cork "worms," their control, and effect on wine odor.

Green, P. E., and V. R. Rao, 1972. *Applied multidimensional scaling.* New York: Holt, Rinehart & Winston. 292 pp.

Grosser, H. U., 1965. Fachliche Weinberteilung und Blutalkohol. *Wein-Wissenschaft* 20: 216–220.

Gyllensköld, H. [pseud. of Haqvin Carlheim-Gyllensköld], 1967. *Att Temperera Vin. Chambera, Värma, Kyla, Frappera Vin.* Stockholm: Wahlström et Widstrand. 34 pp.
How to bring the temperature of bottled wine to the optimum temperature.

Hagenow, G., 1969. Color-Odor-Sapor: zur Geschichte der Weinbereitung und der Weinkultur. *Deut. Weinbau Jrb., 1969,* pp. 195–200.
How sensory evaluation of wines has evolved in Europe.

Hannack, H., 1973. Schwellenwerte als Kriterium für Qualitätesbiere. *Brauwelt* 113: 699–702, 704.
Threshold values in beer evaluation.

Hanson, A., 1982. *Burgundy*. London: Faber and Faber. 378 pp.

Harper, R., 1956. Factor analysis as a technique for examining complex data on foodstuffs. *Appl. Stat.* 5: 32–48.

Harries, J. M., 1973. Complex sensory assessment. *J. Sci. Food Agric.* 24: 1571–1581.
Advanced statistical procedures for analyzing sensory data.

Harter, H. L., 1960. Critical values of Duncan's new multiple range test. *Biometrics* 16: 671–685.

Harter, H. L., 1961. Expected values of normal order statistics. *Biometrika* 48: 151–165.

Haubs, H., 1977. Untersuchungen über die Ursachen des "Mufftones." *Jahresbericht Forschungsanstalt Weinbau, Gartenbau ... Geisenheim amd Rhein, 1977*, pp. 51–52.
Cause of an off-odor from decomposition of a disinfectant.

Haushofer, H., and W. Meier, 1981. Rôle du dioxyde de carbone dans les vins autrichiens. *Bull. Office Intern. Vigne Vin* 54(610): 983–992.
The beneficial effects of carbon dioxide.

Henning, K., 1950. Ein neues Verfahren zur Punktwertung von Wein und Schaumwein. *Deut. Wein-Ztg.* 87: 171–172.
An early example of scoring wines in Germany.

Hinreiner, E., F. Filipello, H. W. Berg, and A. D. Webb, 1955a. Evaluation of thresholds and minimum difference concentrations for various constituents of wine. IV. Detectable differences in wines. *Food Technol.* 9: 489–490.

Hinreiner, E., F. Filipello, A. D. Webb, and H. W. Berg, 1955b. Ibid., III. Ethyl alcohol, glycerol, and acidity in aqueous solution. Ibid., 351–353.
Further studies on sensitivity to wine constituents.

Hoff, J. T., E. Chicoye, W. C. Herwig, and J. R. Helbert, 1978. Flavor profiling of beer using statistical treatments of GLC headspace data. In *Analysis of foods and beverages: Headspace techniques,* ed. G. Charalambous. New York: Academic Press. 394 pp.

Holzgang, D., 1981. *California wine list: A consumers guide to 144 Cabernet Sauvignons.* Los Angeles: Cheshire Booksellers. 56 pp.

Iman, R. L. and J. M. Davenport, 1980. Approximations of the critical region of the Friedman statistics. *Communications in Statistics, Theor. Meth.* A9(6): 571–595.
Tests of significance for ranked data.

Jackisch, P. F., 1979. Sensory identification of wine constituents. *Amer. Wine Soc. Manual* 6: 1–12.
An introduction.

Jackson, M. G., C. F. Timberlake, P. Bridle, and L. Vallis, 1978. Red wine quality: Correlations between colour, aroma and flavour and pigment and other parameters of young Beaujolais. *J. Sci. Food Agric.* 29: 715–727.

Jakob, L., and H. Matheir, 1982. Schulung und Auswahl von Prüfern. *Weinwirtschaft* 118: 10–14.

Jones, F. N., 1958. Prerequisites for test environment. In *Flavor research and food acceptance,* ed. A. D. Little. New York: Reinhold. 391 pp. (See pp. 107–111.)

Jounela-Eriksson, P., 1981. Panel experience and responses to the flavour of alcoholic beverages. In *Criteria of food acceptance,* ed. J. Solms and R. L. Hall. Küsnacht (Zürich): Forster Verlag, AG. 461 pp. (See pp. 253–258.)
Experience does help performance.

Kalven, H. J., Jr., and H. Ziesel, 1966. *The American jury.* Boston: Little, Brown. 559 pp.
Effect of jury discussion on the verdict.

Kare, M. R., 1975. Changes in taste with age: infancy to senescence. *Food Technol.* 29: 77.

Kendall, M. G., 1957. *A Course in Multivariate Analysis.* London: Griffin; New York: Hafner. 210 pp.
Minor corrections were made in the second printing in 1961.

Kendall, M. G., 1975. *Multivariate analysis.* London: Griffin. 210 pp.

Kepner, R. E., A. D. Webb, and L. Maggiora, 1969. Some volatile components of wines of *Vitis vinifera* varieties Cabernet Sauvignon and Ruby Cabernet. II. Acidic components. *Amer. J. Enol. Vitic.* 20: 25–31.

Kepner, R. E., A. D. Webb, and C. J. Muller, 1972. Identification of 4-hydroxy-3-methyl-octanoic acid/gamma-lactone (5-butyl-4-methyldihydro-2-(3H)-furanone) as a volatile component of oak-wood-aged wines of *Vitis vinifera* var. "Cabernet Sauvignon." *Amer. J. Enol. Vitic.* 23: 103–105.

Kiermeir, F., and U. Haevecker, 1972. *Sensorische Beurteilung von Lebensmitteln.* München: J. F. Bergmann. 101 pp. (See pp. 30–32.) *Over 1,000 references on all aspects of the sensory examination of foods.*

Kim, K., and C. S. Setser, 1980. Presentation order bias in consumer preference studies on sponge cakes. *J. Food Sci.* 45: 1073–1074.

Klenk, E., 1972. *Die Weinbereitung nach Farbe, Klarheit, Geruch, und Geschmack.* 3rd ed. Stuttgart: Verlag Eugen Ulmer. 172 pp. *Factors affecting the quality of German wines.*

Kramer, A., 1973. Tables for determining significance. *Food Technol.* 27(5): 64–69.
Significance for ranked data.

Kurtz, T. E., R. F. Link, J. W. Tukey, and D. L. Wallace, 1965. Short-cut multiple comparisons for balanced single and double classifications: Part 1, Results. *Technometrics* 7(2): 95–161.

Lake, M. E., 1969. *The flavour of wine: A qualitative approach for the serious wine taster.* Milton, Queensland: Jacaranda. 60 pp. *Instructive philosophical essay on wine appreciation. Subjective terminology.*

Lake, M. E., 1977. *Cabernet: notes of an Australian wineman.* Adelaide: Rigby Ltd. 64 pp.
About all we need to know about the appreciation of Cabernet wines.

Leavis, F. R., 1948. *The great tradition: George Eliot, Henry James, Joseph Conrad.* New York: G. W. Stewart. 266 pp.

Lefebvre, A., 1981. Le bouchage liège des vins. In *Actualités oenologiques et viticoles,* ed. P. Ribéreau-Gayon and P. Sudraud. Paris: Bordas. 397 pp. (See pp. 335–349.)
Effect of the cork on odor.

Léglise, M., 1976. *Initiation à la dégustation des grands vins: Défense et illustration des vins d'origine.* Lausanne. 167 pp.
More for reading than for practice. The romantic descriptive point of view.

Lehrer, A., 1974. *The semantics of wine tasting or in vino veritas.* Palo Alto, Calif.: Center for Advanced Study in the Behavioral Sciences. 61 leaves.
The meaning of words used to describe wines and the lack of agreement among individuals regarding their interpretations.

Lehrer, A., 1975. Talking about wine. *Language* 51: 901–923.
The difficulty of communicating sensory responses. How important is it to be precise?

Leppänen, O. A., J. Denslow, and P. O. Ronkainen, 1980. Determination of thioacetates and some other volatile sulfur compounds in alcoholic beverages. *Agric. Food Chem.* 28: 359–362.

Levitt, D. J., 1974. The use of sensory and instrumental assessment of organoleptic characteristics via multivariate statistical methods. *J. Texture Studies* 5: 183–200.

Long, Z., 1982. A methodical approach to sensory evaluation. *Wines & Vines* 63(3): 54, 56.

Loyaux, D., S. Roger, and J. Adda, 1981. The evolution of Champagne volatiles during aging. *J. Sci. Food Agric.* 32: 1254–1258.

Lyle, J., 1977. Visual assessment of meat products. In *Inst. Food Sci. Technol., Sensory Quality Control.* London: Society Chemical Indus-

try. 138 pp. (See pp. 49–53.)
The superiority of the human eye to distinguish differences in color.

McBurney, D. H., 1974. Are there primary tastes for man? *Chem. Senses Flavor* 1: 17–28.
There are.

McBurney, D. H., and L. J. Moskat, 1975. Taste thresholds in college-age smokers and nonsmokers. *Percept. Psychophysics* 18: 71–73.
No differences found.

Maga, J. A., 1974. Influence of color on taste thresholds. *Chem. Senses Flavor* 1: 115–119.
Color does have an effect on taste thresholds and flavor recognition.

Marais, J., 1979. Effect of storage time and temperature on the formation of dimethyl sulphide and on white wine quality. *Vitis* 18: 254–260.

Marcus, I. H., 1974. *How to test and improve your wine judging ability.* Berkeley: Wine Publications. 96 pp. Out of print.
A number of simple and useful tests that can easily be done at home and that will provide fun and profit for the serious student.

Mareschalchi, A., 1974. *La degustazione e l'apprezzamento dei vini.* 5th ed. Casale Monferrato: Casa Editrice S.A., Fratelli Mareschalchi. 200 pp.
Mainly the subjective concepts of 50 years ago, but with some modern ideas.

Marie, R., D. Boubals, and P. Flanzy, 1962. Sur la dégustation rationnelle des boissons. *Bull. Office Intern. Vigne Vin* 35: 756–787.
Use of analysis of variance and block designs for sensory problems.

Marks, L. E., and J. C. Stevens, 1968. The form of the psychophysical function near threshold. *Perception Psychophysics* 4: 315–318.

Marsais, J., P. C. Van Rooyen, and C. S. Du Plessis, 1981a. Differentiation between wines originating from different red wine cultivars and wine regions by discriminant analysis to gas chromatographic data. *S. Afr. J. Enol. Vitic.* 2: 19–23.

Marsais, J., P. C. Van Rooyen, and C. S. Du Plessis, 1981b. Classification of white cultivar wines by origin using volatile aroma components. *S. Afr. J. Enol. Vitic.* 2: 45–49.

Marteau, G., 1953. Récherche de la qualité par l'examen des vins. *Prog. Agric. Vitic.* 140: 281–289, 310–314.
Encourages attention and memory and deplores suggestion.

Maujean, A., M. Haye, and M. Feuillat, 1978. Contribution à l'étude de "goûts de lumière" dans le vin Champagne. II. Influence de la lumière sur le potential d'oxydoreduction. Corrélation avec la teneur en thiols du vin. *Connaiss. Vigne Vin* 12: 277–290.
The thiol origin of an off-odor of Champagne.

Meilgaard, M. C., C. E. Dagliesh, and J. F. Clapperton, 1979. Beer flavor terminology. *J. Amer. Soc. Brew. Chem.* 37: 47–52. See also *J. Amer. Soc. Brew. Chem.* 38: 99–107, 1980.

Meilgaard, M. C., and D. S. Reid, 1979. Determination of personal and group thresholds and use of magnitude estimation in flavour chemistry. In *Progress in flavour research,* ed. D. G. Land and H. E. Nursten. London: Applied Science Publishers Ltd. 371 pp. (See pp. 67–77.)
Uses ascending method of limits for thresholds. Use of magnitude estimation in formulation of new food products.

Mesnier, J., 1981. Avant-propos. In *La dégustation des vins: méthode pedagogique et excercices pratiques,* ed. C. Sarfati. Château de Suze-la-Rousse: Université du Vin. 155 pp. (See p. 1.)

Meyers, D. G., and H. Lamm, 1975. The polarizing effect of group discussion. *Amer. Scientist* 63: 297–303.

Moore, M. E., E. Linker, and M. Purcell, 1964. Taste-sensitivity after eating: a signal-detection approach. *Amer. J. Psychol.* 78: 107–111.

Moret, E., G. Scarponi, G. Capodaglio, S. Zanin, G. Camaiani, and A. Toniolo, 1980. Analytical parameters in the characterization of

three Venetian wines, application of statistical linear discriminant analysis. *Amer. J. Enol. Vitic.* 31: 245–249.
Use of analytical data to distinguish three wines.

Moskowitz, H. R., 1974. Sourness of acid mixtures. *J. Exper. Psychol.* 102: 640–647.

Moskowitz, H. R., 1977a. Magnitude estimation: Notes on what, how, when, and why to use it. *J. Food Quality* 3: 195–227.

Moskowitz, H. R., 1977b. Psychophysical and psychometric approaches to sensory evaluation. *CRC Crit. Rev. Food Sci. Nutr.* 9(1): 41–79.

Moskowitz, H. R., 1981. Relating subjective and instrumental measures: A psychophysical overview. *J. Food Qual.* 4: 15–33.

Moskowitz, H. R., and J. W. Chandler. 1977. New uses of magnitude estimation. In *Sensory properties of food,* ed. G. G. Birch, J. G. Brennan, and K. J. Parker. London: Applied Science Publishers. 326 pp. (See pp. 169–211.)

Mowbray, G. H., 1981. Elements of wine tasting. *Amer. Wine Soc. Manual* 11: 1–17.
An introduction to sensory evaluation of wines; includes taste and odor tests.

Muller, C. J., R. E. Kepner, and A. D. Webb, 1971. Identification of 3-(methylthio)propanol as an aroma constituent in Cabernet Sauvignon and Ruby Cabernet wines. *Amer. J. Enol. Vitic.* 22: 156–160.

Muller, C. J., R. E. Kepner, and A. D. Webb, 1972. Identification of 4-ethoxy-4-hydroxybutyric acid γ-lactone (5 ethoxydihydro-2-(3H)-furanone) as an aroma component of wine from *Vitis vinifera* var. Ruby Cabernet. *J. Agric. Food Chem.* 20: 193–195.

Nelson, R. R., 1980. Pleasure, enjoyment and quality. *Amer. Wine Soc. Essay* 1: 1–11.
A philosophical and psychological essay. Defines three levels of response to wine quality—a useful concept.

Newell, G. J., 1982. Use of linear logistic model for the analysis of sensory evaluation data. *J. Food Sci.* 47: 818–820.

Noble, A. C., 1978. Sensory and instrumental evaluation of wine aroma. In *Analyses of foods and beverages: headspace techniques,* ed. G. Charalambous. New York: Academic Press. 394 pp. (See pp. 202–203.)

Noble, A. C., 1979. Evaluation of Chardonnay wines obtained from sites with different soil compositions. *Amer. J. Enol. Vitic.* 30: 214–217.

Noble, A. C., 1982. Use of principal component analysis of wine headspace volatiles in varietal classification. *Vini Ital.* 23(135): 325–331.

Noble, A. C., R. A. Flath, and R. R. Forrey, 1980. Wine headspace analysis. Reproducibility and application to varietal classification. *J. Agric. Food Chem.* 28: 346–353.

Noble, A. C., A. A. Williams, and S. P. Langron, 1982. Descriptive analysis and quality of Bordeaux wines. Proc. Inter. Symp. Sensory Quality Food Bever., Bristol. In press.

Office International de la Vigne et du Vin, 1963. *Lexique de la vigne et du vin.* Paris: Office International de la Vigne et du Vin. 674 pp. *A multilingual dictionary, partially based on translation of the French terms.*

Ohara, Y., 1966. A guide to terms used in the sensory evaluation of wines. *Bull. Res. Inst. Ferment.* (Yamanashi Pref.) 13: 63–94. *From several languages, including Japanese.*

Okamura, S., and M. Watanabe, 1981. Determination of phenolic cinnamates in white wine and their effect on wine quality. *Agric. Biol. Chem.* 45: 2063–2070.

O'Mahoney, M., M. Goldenberg, J. Stedmon, and J. Alford, 1979. Confusion in use of taste adjectives "sour" and "bitter." *Chem. Senses Flavour* 4: 301–318.

Ooghe, W., H. Kastelijn, and A. de Waele, 1981. Détermination de l'origine d'un vin rouge à l'aide du spectre des acides amines. *Ann. Falsif. Exper. Chem. Toxicol.* 74: 381–408.

Osterwalder, A., 1948. Von Mäuselgeschmack der Weine, Obst- und Beerenweine. Ein Erwiderung. *Z. Obst- Weinbau* 57: 397–399, 420–421.
The classic work on the microbial origin of the mousy odor in wines.

Otsuka, K., I. Iki, S. Nozu, Y. Iimura, and A. Totsuka, 1980. Relationship between type and composition of sherry. *J. Ferment. Technol.* 58: 353–361.

Otsuka, K., Y. Zenibayashi, M. Itoh, and A. Totsuka, 1974. Presence and significance of two diastereomes of β-methyl-γ-octalactone in aged distilled spirits. *Agric. Biol. Chem.* 38: 485–490.

Ough, C. S., and G. A. Baker, 1961. Small panel sensory evaluations of wines by scoring. *Hilgardia* 30: 587–619.
The uncertainty of scorecards with more than 9 points.

Ough, C. S., and C. E. Daudt, 1981. Quantitative determination of volatile amines in grapes and wines. I. Effect of fermentation and storage temperature on amine concentrations. *Amer. J. Enol. Vitic.* 32: 185–188.

Ough, C. S., C. E. Daudt, and E. A. Crowell, 1981. Identification of new volatile amines in grapes and wines. *J. Agric. Food Chem.* 29: 938–941.

Ough, C. S., and W. A. Winton, 1976. An evaluation of the Davis scorecard and individual expert panel members. *Amer. J. Enol. Vitic.* 27: 136–144.

Owen, D. H., and P. K. Machamer, 1979. Bias-free improvement in wine discrimination. *Perception* 8: 199–209.

Palmer, D. H., 1974. Multivariate analysis of flavor terms used by experts and non-experts for describing teas. *J. Sci. Food Agric.* 25: 153–164.
The uninitiated had more problems describing teas than the initiated.

Pangborn, R. M., 1980. Sensory science today. *Cereal Foods World* 25: 637–640.

Parker, G. H., 1922. *Smell, taste, and allied senses in the vertebrates.* Philadelphia: Lippincott. 192 pp.
An early discussion of sensory thresholds.

Paul, F., 1964. Die technische Durchführung der organoleptischen Beurteilung von Weinen. *Mitt. Rebe Wein, Ser. A* (Klosterneuburg) 14: 197–209.
Modern procedures for sensory evaluation for wines. Considers 15 the minimum number of tests on a given wine for determining significance. Uses a 20-point scorecard.

Paul, F., 1967. Die "Rangziffernmethode," eine einfache Möglichkeit für den organoleptischen Vergleich zweier oder mehrer Proben. Ibid. 17: 280–288.
Use of ranking in wine evaluation.

Peterson, R. G., 1981. *[Relative value] Winemaker Notes.* Gonzales, Calif.: The Monterey Vineyard, March–April. 2 pp.

Peynaud, E., 1980. *Le goût du vin.* Paris: Dunod. 239 pp.
How we see, smell, and so on, and what the sensations tell us of the quality of the wine. Includes various procedures and how to analyze for the significance of the results! Recommended.

Peynaud, E., 1981. *Connaissance et travail du vin.* Nouv. ed. Paris: Dunod. 337 pp.
How treatment of grapes and wines influence the quality of the wine.

Phaff, H. J., and M. A. Amerine, 1979. Wine. *Microbial Technol.* 2: 131–153.
Possible effects of yeasts on wine quality.

Philbrick, K., A. C. Noble, and R. B. Boulton, 1982. The contribution of anionic species to perceived sourness. In preparation.
Factors influencing relative sourness of acids.

Pirsig, R. M., 1974. *Zen and the art of motorcycle maintenance: an inquiry into values.* New York: Morrow. 412 pp.
Philosophy of making quality judgments.

Pisarnitskii, A. F., A. K. Rodopulo, A. A. Bezzubov, and I. A. Gregorov, 1969. *Voprosu ob okislenii vina. [Oxidation of wine.] Vinodel. Vinograd. SSSR* 29(1): 12–14.

Pittaro, P., 1975. *Note teoriche sulla degustazione dei vini.* Milano: L'Enotecnico. 45 pp.
Italian recommendations for scoring, but no measures of central tendency or the significance of the results. Includes glossary.

Press, S. J., 1972. *Applied multivariate analysis.* New York: Holt, Rinehart & Winston. 521 pp.

Powers, J. J., C. B. Warren, and T. Masurat, 1981. Collaborative trials involving three methods of normalizing magnitude estimations. *Lebensm. Wissen.-Technol.* 14: 86–93.

Puisais, J., 1978. Le contrôle organoleptique de la qualité: techniques de dégustation. *Ann. Technol. Agric.* 27: 351–356.
General directions. Tests for qualifying judges.

Puisais, J., 1982. Appréciation analytique et sensorielle de la qualité des vins. *Bull. Office Intern. Vigne Vin* 65(614): 286–321.
Recommends chemical and sensory analysis of wines. No tests of sensory results, but tests of judges are recommended.

Puisais, J., R. L. Chabanon, A. Guiller, and J. Lacoste, 1969. *Précis d'initiation à la dégustation.* Paris: Institut Technique Vin. 90 pp.

Puisais, J., R. L. Chabanon, A. Guiller, and J. Lacoste, 1974. *Initiation into the art of wine tasting.* Madison, Wisc.: Interpublish. 95 pp.
The 1974 edition is a translation from the French edition, with some additions. There is also an Italian edition. Useful on the physiology of the senses.

Rankine, B. C., 1967. Formation of higher alcohols by wine yeasts, and relationship to taste thresholds. *J. Sci. Food Agric.* 18: 583–589.
Only isoamyl alcohol is present in high enough amounts to affect odor.

Rankine, B. C., 1971. Panel evaluation by tasting tests. *Austral. Wine, Brew. Spirit Rev.* 89(4): 34, 36.
How to make up solutions in wine for threshold tests.

Rankine, B. C., 1974. Wine tasting and judging. *Food Technol. Austral.* 26: 443–453.
Describes the "expert" wine judgings that are a feature of the Australian wine industry and gives suggested general specifications for wine types.

Rankine, B. C., J. C. M. Fornachon, and D. A. Bridson, 1969a. Diacetyl in Australian dry red wines and its significance in wine quality. *Vitis* 9: 129–134.
The difference threshold in wines was 1 to 1.3 mg/l.

Rankine, B. C., and K. F. Pocock, 1969b. Phenethanol and *n*-hexanol in wines: influence of yeast strain, grape variety, and other factors; and taste thresholds. Ibid., 23–37.
Thresholds varied from 30–200 and 4–30 mg/l, respectively.

Rapp, A., and H. Hastrich, 1976. Gaschromatographische Untersuchungen über die Aromastoffe von Weinbeeren. II. Möglichkeiten der Sortencharakterisierung. *Vitis* 15: 183–192.

Rapp, A., and H. Hastrich, 1978. Ibid. Die Bedeutung des Standortes für die Aromastoffzusammensetzung der Rebsorte Riesling. Ibid. 17: 288–298.

Rapp, A., and W. Knipser, 1979. 3,7-Dimethyl-okta-1,5-dien,3,7-diol: eine neue terpenoide Verbindung des Trauben- und Weinaromas. *Vitis* 18: 229–233.

Rapp, A., W. Knipser, and L. Engel, 1980a. Identifizierung von 3,7-Dimethyl-okta-1,7-dien-3, 6-diol im Trauben und Weinaromas von Muskatsorten. *Vitis* 19: 226–229.

Rapp, A., W. Knipser, L. Engel, H. Ullemeyer, and W. Heimann, 1980b. Fremdkomponenten im Aroma von Trauben und Weinen interspezifischer Rebsorten. I. Die Erdbeernote. *Vitis* 19: 13–23.

Ratti, R., 1981. *Come degustare i vini; manuale dell'assaggiatore.* Brescia: Edizioni AEB. 115 pp.
A popular treatise on the sensory evaluation of Italian wines; several scorecards are given. Some have 100 steps. The duo-trio test is mentioned and used for determining the significance of the results. There

is a glossary. The "tears" of wine are thought to be due to glycerol and ethanol!

Reynolds, A. G., T. Fuleki, and W. D. Evans, 1982. Inheritance of methyl anthranilate and total volatile esters in *Vitis* spp. *Amer. J. Enol. Vitic.* 33: 14–19.
Proposes an index of flavor intensity in breeding out foxiness.

Ribéreau-Gayon, J., 1973. Recherche des relations entre les caractères sensoriels des vins rouges et leur composition. *Connaiss. Vigne Vin* 7: 79–92.

Ribéreau-Gayon, J., E. Peynaud, P. Ribéreau-Gayon, and P. Sudraud, 1975. *Traité d'oenologie. Tome II. Charactères des vins. Maturation du raisin. Levures et bacteries.* Paris: Dunod. 556 pp.

Ribéreau-Gayon, P., 1978. Wine flavor. In *Flavor of food and beverages: Chemistry and technology,* ed. G. Charalambous and G. E. Inglett. New York: Academic Press. 422 pp. (See pp. 355–380.)

Robertson, J. M., B. L. Kirk, and A. C. Crum, 1976. The chemical comparison of some New Zealand red and rosé wines. *N.Z. Dept. Sci. Ind. Res., Chem. Div. Rept.* 2247: 1–43.
Suggests some maximum levels for certain constituents.

Robertson, J. M., and G. M. Rush, 1979. Chemical criteria for the detection of winemaking faults in red wines. *Food Technol. N.Z.* 14(1): 3–11.

Robinson, J., 1979. *The wine book.* London: Fontana Paperbacks. 256 pp.

Robinson, J. O., 1970. The misuse of taste names by untrained observers. *Brit. J. Psychol.* 61: 375–378.
Confusion of sour-bitters tastes due to lack of experience with bitterness.

Roessler, E. B., and M. A. Amerine, 1973. The "age" of Madeiras. *Amer. J. Enol. Vitic.* 24: 176–177.
The law of compound interest has not been repealed!

Roessler, E. B., R. M. Pangborn, J. L. Sidel, and H. Stone, 1978. Expanded statistical tables for estimating significance in paired-

preference, paired-difference, duo–trio and triangle tests. *J. Food Sci.* 43: 940–944.
Corrected tables.

Salo, P., L. Nybänen, and H. Suomalainen, 1972. Odor thresholds and relative intensities of volatile aromatic compounds in an artificial beverage resembling whiskey. *J. Food Sci.* 37: 394–398.

Sarfati, C., 1981. *La dégustation des vins. Méthode pédagogique et exercices pratiques.* Château de Suze-la-Rousse: Université du Vin. 155 pp.
How to train degustateurs in classes. Includes glossary.

Sauvageot, F., 1982. *L'évaluation sensorielle des denrées alimentaires.* Paris: Technique et Documentation. 196 pp.

Scarponi, G., I. Moret, and G. Capodaglio, 1981. Application of multiple discriminant analysis in the chemoanalytical differentiation of wines according to origin. Part II. *Rev. Vitic. Enol.* 34(6): 254–266.

Schaeffer, A., J. P. Meyer, and A. Guillerm, 1978. Étude sur l'origine du 'goût de bouchon.' *Rev. Franç. Oenol.* 16: 25–29.

Schlotter, H. A., 1982. Modifications défavorables de vins consécutives à l'introduction de certaines technologies modernes. *Bull. Office Intern. Vigne Vin* 55(616): 484–493.

Schneyder, J. 1982. Appréciation analytique et sensorielle de la qualité des vins. *Bull. Office Intern. Vigne Vin* 55(612): 108–128.
Suggests international standard wine samples to qualify judges.

Schöffling, H., R. Ley, and W. Faber, 1980. Statistical analysis of a wine evaluation test with new varieties in the upper Moselle wine-growing district. *Harpers Wine Spirit Gaz.* 4987: 80 ff.
A comparison of trained and untrained judges, various areas and winemakers.

Schöffling, H., and F. Weiling, 1973. Ueber eine Testweinprobe zur Selekton geeigneter Rebsorten für den Anbau unter den extremen Bedingungen des Weinbaugebietes "Obermosel." *Weinwissenschaft*

28: 203–209.
Why use consumers and experts in variety trials. Not clear to us.

Schreier, P., 1979. Flavor composition of wines: a review. *CRC Crit. Rev. Food Sci. Nutr.* 12: 59–111.
The definitive listing for its date.

Schreier, P., 1980. Wine aroma composition: identification of additional volatile compounds. *J. Agric. Food Chem.* 28: 926–928.

Schreier, P., F. Drawert, and A. Junker, 1977. Gaschromatographische Bestimmung der Inhaltsstoffe von Gärungsgetränken. X. Quantitative Bestimmung von Weinaromastoffen im $\mu g/l$-Bereich. *Chem. Mikrobiol. Technol. Lebensm.* 5: 45–52.

Schreier, P., F. Drawert, A. Junker, and L. Reiner, 1976. Anwendung der multiplen Diskriminanzanalyse zur Differenzierung von Rebsorten anhand der quantitativen Verteilung flüchtiger Weininhaltsstoffe. *Mitt. Hoeheren Bunderlehr-Versuchs-anst. Wein- Obstbau* (Klosterneuburg) 26: 225–234.

Schreier, P., and J. H. Paroschy, 1981. Volatile constituents from Concord, Niagara (*Vitis labrusca*) and Elvira (*V. labrusca* $\times$ *V. riparia*) grapes. *Can. Inst. Food Sci. Technol. J.* 14: 112–118.
Confirms the variety of compounds found.

Schrodt, W., and L. Jacob, 1966. Die statistisch erfassbaren Wechselwirkung bei der technischen Weinprobe mit Wiederholungen. *Mitt. Rebe Wein, Ser. A* (Klosterneuburg) 16: 357–369.
Use of appropriate statistical procedures for determining significance in sensory evaluation of wines.

Schwacke, 1935. Warum schmeckt warmer Wein saurer als kalter? *Wein Rebe* 17: 123–124.
Warm wine tastes more acid than cold wine because it is more ionized; so he says.

Scriven, L. E., and C. V. Sternling, 1960. The Marangoni effects. *Nature* 187: 186–188.
A historical review.

Seldon, P., 1979. A simple way to test your palate. *Vintage* 8(8): 44–50.
Not so simple to us.

Sernagiotto, E., 1969. Metodo attuale di degustazione dei vini. *Quaderno Tecnici Assoc. Enotecnici Italiani* 1: 1–7.
An introduction to their score card.

Sidel, J. L., and H. Stone, 1976. Experimental design and analyses of sensory tests. *Food Technol.* 30(11): 32–38.

Simpson, R. F., 1980. Volatile aroma components of Australian port wines. *J. Sci. Food Agric.* 31: 214–222.

Singleton, V. L., 1981. Using wooden cooperage in the winery today. *Proc. Training Conf. Fundamentals of Table Wine Processing* 7: 38–47.

Singleton, V. L., and A. C. Noble, 1976. Wine flavor and phenolic substances. *Amer. Chem. Soc. Symp. Ser.* 26: 47–70.

Singleton, V. L., H. A. Sieberhagen, P. de Wet, and C. J. Van Wyk, 1975. Composition and sensory quality of wines prepared from white grapes by fermentation with and without grape solids. *Amer. J. Enol. Vitic.* 26: 62–69.
Bitterness is distinguished from astringency.

Slingsby, R. W., R. E. Kepner, C. J. Muller, and A. D. Webb, 1980. Some volatile components of *Vitis vinifera* variety Cabernet Sauvignon wine. *Amer. J. Enol. Vitic.* 31: 360–363.

Somers, T. C., and M. E. Evans, 1974. Wine quality correlations with colour density and anthocyanin equilibria in a group of young wines. *J. Sci. Food Agric.* 25: 1369–1379.

Sponholz, W.-R., H. H. Dittrich, F. Haas, and B. Wunsch, 1981. Die Bildung von flüchtigen Fettsäuren durch *Saccaromyces*-Hefen während der Vergärung von Traubenmosten. *Z. Lebensm. Unter.-Forsch.* 173: 297–300.
The volatile acids in new wines from sound grapes and fermentation are mainly formic and acetic.

Stern, D. J., A. Lee, W. H. McFadden, and K. L. Stevens, 1967. Volatiles from grapes: identification of volatiles from Concord essence. *J. Agric. Food Chem.* 15: 1100–1103.

Stevens, K. L., A. Lee, W. H. McFadden, and R. Teranishi, 1965. Volatiles from grapes. I. Some volatiles from Concord essence. *J. Food Sci.* 30: 1106–1107.

Stone, H., J. L. Sidel, and J. Bloomquist, 1980. Quantitative descriptive analysis. *Cereal Foods World* 25: 642–644.

Stone, H., K. Sidel, S. Oliver, A. Woolsey, and R. C. Singleton, 1974. *A scoring method for sensory evaluation of materials.* Menlo Park, Calif.: Stanford Research Institute. 31 pp. (See also *Food Technol.* 28(11): 24, 26, 28–29, 32, 34, 1974.)
Application of computer programming for analyzing sensory data.

Stungis, G. E., 1976. Overview of applied multivariate analysis. In *Correlating sensory objective measurements: New methods for answering old problems,* ed. J. J. Powers and H. R. Moskowitz. Philadelphia: Amer. Soc. Testing Materials. (*Its* STP 594: 1–134.)

Sudraud, P., 1977. Évolution des taux d'acidité volatile dépuis le debut du siècle. *Ann. Technol. Agric.* 27: 349–350.
Wines considered spoiled today were accepted in 1900.

Tanner, H., and C. Zanier, 1978. Erfahrung mit Flaschenverschlussen aus Naturkorken. *Weinwirtschaft* 22: 608–613.

Tanner, H., and C. Zanier, 1982. Zur analytischen Differenzirung von Muffton and Korkgeschmack. *Weinwirtschaft* 118: 15–16.

Tanner, H., C. Zanier, and H. R. Buser. 1981. 2,4,6-Trichloranisol: eine dominierende Komponente der Korkgeschmacks. *Schweiz. Z. Obst. Weinbau* 117: 97–103. See also pp. 752–757.

Thumfart, W., K.-H. Plattig, and N. Schlicht, 1980. Geruchs- und Geschmacksschwellen älterer Menschen. *Z. Gerontol.* 13: 158–188.
Taste and odor thresholds decrease with age.

Timberlake, C. F., 1981. Parameters of red wine quality. *Food Technol. Austral.* 33(3): 139–140, 142, 144.

Tomassone, R., and C. Flanzy, 1977. Présentation synthétique de diverses méthodes d'analyse de données fournies par un jury de dégustateurs. *Ann. Technol. Agr.* 26: 373–418.
A review of appropriate statistical procedures for ranked data.

Tromp, A., and W. J. Conradie, 1979. An effective scoring system for sensory evaluation of experimental wines. *Amer. J. Enol. Vitic.* 30: 278–283.

Tromp, A., and C. J. Van Wyk, 1977. The influence of colour on the assessment of red wine quality. *Proc. S. Afr. Soc. Enol. Vitic.* 1977, pp. 107–118.

Troost, G., 1972. *Technologie des Weines.* 4th ed. Stuttgart: Verlag Eugen Ulmer. 931 pp. (See pp. 594–627.)
A general review of the best methods for sensory examination of German wines.

Troost, G., and E. Wanner, 1962. *Weinprobe. Weinansprache.* Frankfurt-am-Main: Verlag Sigurd Horn. 63 pp.
A general summary of the sensory evaluation of wines in Germany.

Tukey, J. W., 1953. Some selected quick and easy methods of statistical analysis. *Trans. N.Y. Acad. Sci.* 16: 88–97.

Tukey, J. W., 1977. *Exploratory data analysis.* Reading, Mass.: Addison-Wesley. 688 pp.
Multivariate methods of analysis.

Usseglio-Tomasset, L., 1981. Caratteristiche ed evoluzione del quadro aromatico del Moscato Bianco del Piemonte e dell'Asti Spumante. *L'Enotecnico* 17(8): 9–13.

Van der Merwe, C. A., and C. J. Van Wyk, 1981. The contribution of some fermentation products to the odor of dry white wines. *Amer. J. Enol. Vitic.* 32: 41–46.
How fatty acid esters and higher alcohols affect the odor quality of wines.

van Rooyen, P. C., 1982. Evaluation of the Nietvoorij wine score card and experimental wine panelists utilizing pattern recognition techniques. Stellenbosch, South Africa: Oenological and Viticultural Research Institute. Personal communication.

Van Wyk, C. J., A. D. Webb, and R. E. Kepner, 1967. Some volatile components of *Vitis vinifera* variety White Riesling: 1, 2, 3. *J. Food Sci.* 32: 660–664, 664–668, 669–674.
The aromatic constituents of the variety identified.

Vedel, A., 1966. Terminologie gustative oenologique. *Vignes Vins*, No. 149, p. 15.

Vedel, A., G. Charle, P. Charnay, and J. Tourneau, 1972. *Essai sur la dégustation des vins.* Mâcon: Soc. Edit. Inform. Viti-Vinicoles.
Some suggestive ideas regarding the relation between words and the influence of odor persistence on quality.

Von Sydow, E., H. Moskowitz, H. Jacobs, and H. Meiselman, 1974. Taste–odor interaction in fruit juices. *Lebensm. Wissen.-Technol.* 7: 18–24.
Shows that there is an interaction.

Vuataz, L., 1977. Some points of methodology in multidimensional data analysis as applied to sensory evaluation. *Nestle Research News, 1976/1977,* pp. 57–71.

Vuataz, L., J. Sotek, and H. M. Rahim, 1974. Profile analysis and classification. *Proc. IV Intern. Congr. Food Sci. Technol.* (Madrid) 1: 68–78.
Good discussion of several multivariate methods.

Wald, A., 1947. *Sequential analysis.* New York: Wiley. 212 pp.

Walk, R. D., 1966. Perceptual learning and the discrimination of wines. *Psychom. Sci.* 5: 57–58.

Webb, A. D., and H. W. Berg, 1955. Terms used for tasting. *Wines & Vines* 36(7): 25–28. (Also Wine Institute, San Francisco, 1962. 20 pp.)

Webb, A. D., R. E. Kepner, and W. E. Galetto. 1964. Comparison of aromas of flor sherry, baked sherry, and submerged-culture sherry. *Amer. J. Enol. Vitic.* 15: 1–10.

Webb, A. D., and C. J. Muller, 1972. Volatile aroma components of wines and other fermented beverages. *Adv. Appl. Microbiol.* 15: 75–146.

Webb, A. D., and A. C. Noble, 1976. Aroma of sherry wine. *Biotechnol. Bioengin.* 18: 939–952.

Weiss, J. J., 1980. Selection of sensory judges. *J. Food Quality* 4: 55–63.

Williams, A. A., 1975. The development of a vocabulary and profile assessment method for evaluating the flavour contribution of cider and perry aroma constituents. *J. Sci. Food Agric.* 26: 567–582. *Useful vocabulary, some of it applicable to wines.*

Williams, A. A., 1977. Flavor research: a return to sensory evaluation. *Proc. Intern. Symp. Olfaction Taste* 6: 401–408.

Williams, A. A., 1978. Interpretation of sensory significance of chemical data in flavor research. 3. Sensory analysis. *Intern. Flavours Food Addit.* 9(4). 171–175.

Williams, A. A., 1982. Recent developments in the field of wine flavour. *J. Inst. Brewing* 88: 45–53. *An up-to-date evaluation of the flavor components of wines.*

Williams, A. A., and C. S. Carter, 1977. A language and procedure for the sensory assessment of Cox's Orange Pippin apples. *J. Sci. Food Agric.* 28: 1090–1104.

Williams, A. A., A. G. Lea, and C. F. Timberlake, 1977. Measurement of flavor quality in apples, apple juices, and fermented ciders. *ACS Symp. Ser.* 51: 71–88.

Williams, A. A., and M. J. Lewis, 1978. Aroma analysis of fruits and fruit products: Pitfalls and current problems. *Ber.-Intern. Fruchsaft-Union, Wiss.-Tech. Komm.* 15: 183–211.

Williams, A. A., and P. R. Rosser, 1981. Aroma enhancing effects of ethanol. *Chem. Senses Flavor* 6: 149–153.

Williams, P. J., and C. R. Strauss, 1978. Spirit recovered from heap-fermented grape marc: nature, origin, and removal of off-odor. *J. Sci. Food Agric.* 29: 527–533.

Williams, P. J., C. R. Strauss, and B. Wilson, 1980. New linalool derivatives of Muscat of Alexandria grapes and wines. *Phytochem.* 19: 1137–1139.

Williams, P. J., C. R. Strauss, and B. Wilson, 1981. Classification of the monoterpenoid composition of muscat grapes. *Amer. J. Enol. Vitic.* 32: 230–235.

Williams, P. J., C. R. Strauss, B. Wilson, and R. A. Massy-Westropp, 1982. Use of C_{18} reversed-phase liquid chromatography for the isolation of monoterpene glycosides and norisoprenoid precursors from grape juice and wines. *J. Chromatogr.* 235: 471–480.

Wilson, C. W. M., 1972. The pharmacological actions of alcohol in relation to nutrition. *Proc. Nutr. Soc.* 31: 91–98.
Use of statistics in analyzing results.

Wine Institute, 1978. California Wine Type Specifications. Rev. ed. San Francisco: Wine Institute. 8 pp.
Very general definitions of California wine types.

Wu, L. S., R. E. Bargmann, and J. J. Powers, 1977. Factor analysis applied to wine descriptions. *J. Food Sci.* 42: 944–952.
Identifies 33 descriptive words for describing wines (of 86 tested) that had the greatest meaning for their panel (which they claim was not naive).

Yates, F., 1936. Incomplete randomized blocks. *Ann. Eugenics* 7: 121–140.

Yoneyama, C., and T. Kushida, 1980. [Quality characteristics of Koshu white wine tested by chromatographic profile analysis.] *J. Inst. Enol. Vitic., Yamanashi Univ.* 15: 9–13.
Lower nucleic-acid related compounds and higher cinnamate compounds in Koshu white wines compared to European and American wines.

Yoxall, H. W., 1972. *The enjoyment of wine.* London: Michael Joseph. 200 pp.
Sensible advice on wine appreciation and evaluation.

Zeeman, W., J. P. Snyman, and C. J. Van Wyk. 1980. The influence of yeast strain and malolactic fermentation on some volatile bouquet substances and on quality of table wines. Proc. Grape Wine Centennial Symp., University of California, Davis, pp. 79–90. (publ. 1982.)

Index

For specific odors *see* odors; for specific tastes *see* tastes. For some regional names see California, France, and Germany. A variety of grape is signified by (v).

Abel, Niels, 223
absolute value, 193
acceptance, 143
acescence, 10, 30, 101, 214, 312.
  See also acetic acid; ethyl acetate;
  volatile acidity
acetal, 33, 76–77, 130
acetaldehyde, 43, 75, 81, 92, 127, 128,
  129, 130, 146, 160, 163, 165, 292,
  295, 307, 318, 319, 325, 326
acetamides, 33, 292, 324
acetic acid, 39, 49, 83–84, 146, 163,
  292, 295, 307, 312, 319, 324, 328,
  329, 332; legal limits, 39, 312.
  See also ethyl acetate; vinegary;
  volatile acidity
acetoin, 76
acetone, 76
acetovanillin, 77
acetylamine, 79
acetylfuran, 75
acidity, 22, 25, 27, 48, 49, 62, 70, 71,
  82–84, 91, 92, 93, 96, 100, 101, 103,
  104, 111, 114, 122, 123, 124, 126,
  132, 135, 136, 147, 212, 214, 216,
  312, 317, 328, 329, 331; high, 50,
  53, 320, 324; sensitivity to, 147. *See
  also* flatness; pH; names of various
  acids; taste (sourness)
acidulous, 49, 71, 107, 312, 321, 332
aconitic acid, 83
acrolein, 50, 314, 324
active amyl alcohol. *See*
  2-methyl-1-butanol
adaptation, 31, 35, 45, 59, 60, 140,
  143, 153, 154, 195, 249, 259, 331
additive effect, 33, 80
adipic acid, 83
aesthetics, 3, 5, 7, 9, 10, 12–13, 19,
  142, 306
aftertaste, 35, 309, 312, 319
age, effect on individuals, 144
aging, 15, 20–21, 27, 34–35, 37, 43,
  50, 51, 58, 73, 80, 89, 101, 107,
  109, 111, 112, 114, 120, 121, 122,
  125, 130, 132, 134, 135, 217, 310,

312, 317, 327, 328, 331. *See also*
  bouquet
alcoholic. *See* hot
alcohols, 33, 38, 71–74, 147. *See also*
  ethanol; fusel oils; individual
  alcohols
aldehydes, 33, 34, 37, 38, 43, 53,
  74–76, 130, 312, 327. *See also*
  acetaldehyde; individual aldehydes;
  odor, oxidized
Aleatico (v), 113, 131
Algeria, 113
Alicante Bouschet (v), 27, 113
Aligoté (v), 101–102
alkylthio ester, 98
allergenic, 32, 37
allspice, 294
allyl disulfide, 293
alternative hypothesis. *See* hypothesis,
  alternative
amines, 79
amino acids, 42, 79, 82, 331
amontillado, 124, 130
ample, 313
amyl alcohol, active. *See also*
  2-methyl-1-butanol; *n*-, 1-pentanol
amyl, acetate, 320; α-, amine, 79
analysis of variance, 146, 161, 186,
  222, 232–256, 259–273, 279–287,
  298; distribution-free, 221; multiple,
  296; multivariant, 299–302; one-way,
  233–239, 297, 298; tables, 235, 236,
  237, 242, 243, 246, 248, 255, 256,
  264, 267, 268, 282, 285; two-way,
  240–256, 297, 298
angelica, 133
anosmic, 33
anthocyanins, 30
appearance, 6, 10, 25, 26, 30–31, 54,
  93, 155, 157, 214, 216, 218, 290,
  291, 315, 317, 322
appendixes, 339–381
apple, essence, 293; wines, 74, 81, 135,
  136. *See also* cider
arabitol, 74
Aramon (v), 126